WHEN VICTIMIZATION OF POLAND WAS NEVER IN DOUBT

Fostering Knowledge of and Sympathy for Poland in the Early American Republic: 1811-1849, as Reported in the Niles' Register

Compiled, Edited and Annotated
by
Anthony Joseph Bajdek

Dedicated to the loving memory of my parents,
Agnes H. and Joseph M. Bajdek
Who instilled the flame of *polskość* in me.

Cover image by Aleksander Orłowski
Compiled, edited and annotated by Anthony Joseph Bajdek
Winged Hussar Publishing, LLC, 1525 Hulse Road, Unit 1, Point Pleasant, NJ 08742

This edition published in 2021 Copyright ©Winged Hussar Publishing, LLC

ISBN 978-1-950423-43-9
LOC 2021934054

Bibliographical references and index
1.Poland. 2. History. 3. Reference

A 19TH CENTURY POLISH POET'S PERSPECTIVE ON THE PAINFUL CONDITION OF THE POLISH PEOPLE

Bo choć w pokoju zakwitnie świat cały,
Choć się sprzymierzą rządy, ludy, zdania
Syn twój wyzwany do boju bez chwały
I do męczeństwa, bez zmartwychpowstania...

Bo on nie pójdzie, jak dawni rycerze,
Utkwić zwycięski krzyż w Jeruzalemie,
Albo jak świata nowego żołnierze
Na wolność orać... krwią polewać ziemię....

For even though the whole world flourishes in peace,
Though governments, peoples and opinions will ally
Your son is called to battle without glory
And to martyrdom, without resurrection...

For he will not go as the knights of old,
To plant the victorious Cross in Jerusalem,
Or as the soldiers of the New World,
To plow Freedom's soil... to water it with blood....

(Excerpted from the poem, "To A Polish Mother" [*Do Matki Polki*] that had been composed in 1830 by Adam Mickiewicz, 1798-1855, Poland's and Europe's great, if not greatest, 19th century Romantic poet, and presented in free translation by the author of this book.)

Adam Mickiewicz (sketched by Joachim Lelewel, 1786-1861)

On this book's cover, and on this page as well, prominently displayed for good reason are two artistic renderings of the Rzeź Pragi ("Massacre in Praga") in the history of Poland. The cover illustrates the related work of the Polish painter and lithographer Aleksander Orłowski (1777-1832), in which he depicted Imperial Russia's supposedly-disciplined regular infantry soldiers, in action on November 4, 1794, inside the home of a Polish family in Praga, which still remains a vital suburb on the opposite shore of the Wisła (Vistula) River, across from Warszawa (Warsaw), Poland's capital. In the scene on the front cover, the head of the family household is about to be hacked to death by a sword and bayoneted by Russian soldiers, whereas the mistress of the house appears already dead. Common Russian soldiers of those days seldom, if at all, honored international conventions about respecting the sanctity of noncombatant enemy civilians.

Apart from the book's cover, the illustration on this page depicts Imperial Russia's irregular and much less disciplined Cossack cavalrymen in action on the same fateful day in Praga. Now in the collection of the National Library of Poland, it was the 19th century woodcut of an unknown Polish artist based on the work of the highly-renowned Polish painter, Juliusz Kossak (1824-1899).

The Cossack cavalry, operating as the fully-integrated component of the Imperial Russian Army commanded by Field Marshal Alexander Vasilyevich Suvorov (1730-1800), was allowed by Suvarov to sack Praga which resulted in the planned massacre of the 20,000 Polish residents as a means to frighten the population of Warsaw into surrendering. When the day ended, Suvorov excitedly wrote to Her Imperial Majesty, Czarina Catherine II (1762-1796) of Russia, that "the whole of Praga is strewn with dead bodies...blood was flowing in streams," ending with "Huzzah! Warsaw is ours." In 1795, acting in concert with Prussia and Austria, Russia proceeded to complete the final stage to partition Poland out of existence as a free and independent nation. Earlier stages of partition had occurred in 1772 and 1793. Poland finally regained its freedom and independence 123 years later when World War I ended in 1918 .

The back cover illustrates the Battle of Ostrołęka that was fought on May 26, 1831.

As Reported in the "Niles' Register"

INTRODUCTION TO THE TASK AT HAND

At this point of the 21st century, with the looming 200th anniversary of Poland's November Uprising of 1830 against Imperial Russia some ten years away, Americans as well as others who are well-informed about the long history of Poland's painful epic struggles to exist as a free and independent nation, have been taken aback by sources in some otherwise friendly sister states of the European Union, elsewhere as well, and unsurprisingly, principally by the Russian Federation, who propose that Poland's claim of having been victimized for 249 years, beginning when Poland initially was partitioned in 1772 by its contiguous neighbors, Russia, Prussia and Austria, has been, and remains, an exaggeration, pure and simple. Russia has continued along that same path of disinformation well into the 21st century as exemplified by its further claim that Poland also was responsible for having started World War II.

This is the reason I have dedicated myself to document and illuminate Poland's rightful claim of victimization, initially by way of presentations I made under the title, "Fostering Knowledge of and Sympathy for Poland in the Early American Republic, *Niles' Register*, 1811-1849" at academic conferences and other meetings such as, for example, at Columbia University, the United States Military Academy, and to the venerable Kościuszko Mound Committee (Komitet Kopca Kościuszki) of Kraków, Poland, wherein I described what Americans had been reading about Poland by virtue of an exemplar of the free press in the United States during the period, 1811 to 1849. Concomitantly, as I identified and compiled the evidence, I also decided to seek its broader publication as a book in its own right, principally for the edification of 21st century American readers who generally have no idea about the specific factual particulars documenting the story that I have compiled and now relate. This book, however, should not be viewed as a history of Poland per se, but rather, as the history of American press coverage of events in Poland during the period 1811 – 1849.

To the question, "what did American readers of *Niles' Register* learn about Poland and how did they react to what they read in the

4

first half of the 19th century?" -- I propose to illustrate: (1) what on one hand had been the extent of news coverage that Americans had read about Poland, and its adversarial contiguous neighbors, the Russian Empire, the Kingdom of Prussia, and the Austrian Empire; (2) as well as the related diplomatic affairs of Great Britain and France; and (3) the extent of the sympathetic response to help Poland and its exiles in America that had been manifested by ordinary informed citizens of the United States, by members of their state legislatures, by some of their state governors and by some members of the United States Congress, along with President Andrew Jackson, during the period.

In the United States from 1811 to 1849, a very small number of works, contrasting in length, written by Polish exiles related to what Americans variously termed to be either the Polish Revolution of 1830 or the Polish Insurrection of 1830 (e.g., *A History of the Polish Revolution of 1830*, by Joseph Hordynski, published by Scribners, Boston, 1833; *The Remembrances of a Polish Exile*, by August Antoni Jakubowski, printed by Adam Waldie, Philadelphia, 1835; *The Poles in the United States of America, Preceded by the Earlier History of the Slavonians and by the History of Poland* by Karol Kraitsir, Philadelphia, 1837; and *Poland, Russia, and the Policy of the Latter Towards the United States*, by Gaspar Tochman, printed in Baltimore by John D. Toy, 1844). They described the sources both personal and impersonal, along with the extent and details of the Revolution that began in November 1830 in Warsaw, approached its zenith during 1831, and extended agonizingly by way of pockets of resistance into 1833 and beyond, illuminated by way of the aforementioned respective points of publication in 1833, 1835, and 1837, and in the case of Tochman's relatively short opus in 1844, which included the list of his addresses, upon invitation, on the matter of Poland's struggles for the right to exist free and independent, to the upper and lower chambers of the state legislatures of "New York, Massachusetts, New Hampshire, Vermont, Connecticut, Virginia, Ohio, Indiana and Kentucky, and before the members of the New Jersey State Convention." He also traveled tirelessly to address public meetings on the subject of Poland throughout much of, but not all, the United States, which during the final year (1849) of publication for *Niles' National Register* -- as it had been known at that stage of its history -- consisted of thirty states, with the 30th state, Wisconsin, having been admitted to the Union in 1848.

During the same period, in contrast, there were reportedly at least 500 to 700 or more newspapers in the United States. In 1833, however, there was only one free public library supported by taxation. It was located in Peterborough, New Hampshire. However, the thrust to create free public libraries accelerated subsequently to the extent that in the United States Census of 1840, it was reported by the Niles' National Register, in its issue of March 24, 1849, page 192, which is included in this book as numbered Article 292 of 302, that 234 more public libraries had been added since 1833, with a total national collection of 1,209,800 volumes serving some 16,756,972 Americans across the twenty-five states constituting the Republic of the United States of America. At that time of the Census of 1840, however, the venerable Boston Public Library, the "first large free municipal library in the United States," was not to be established until 1848, some eight years later.

Case in point, most Americans learned about what was going on in the world, Poland included, by way of newspapers issued regularly on a weekly basis for the most part. Thus, they could read about history as it was being made in yearly, monthly and weekly chronological succession which had been an advantage over books that average working-class Americans neither could afford to purchase nor visit public libraries to read, simply because, in the case of the latter option, they worked during the week well beyond the hours of libraries being opened to the public. What readers of Niles' Register had been exposed to had been truly remarkable, insofar as it included news from all over the known world that, viewed from my perspective, provided me with a unique opportunity waiting to be seized.

No one, as far as I know, has ever comprehensively researched American press coverage of Poland's existential struggles during the period 1811 to 1849, in the manner that I have chosen, and the extent to which American public opinion responded to Poland's nightmarish existential threat, that stated forthrightly, had been its resistance to what today can be best described as clear and flagrant, nearly always brutish rather than subtle, examples of Russia's "ethnic cleansing" of Poland. Essentially, as one 19th century observer of the related events summarized that idea at the time, as being, that Russia wanted Poland but did not want Polish people. Whereas the term "ethnic cleansing" hadn't been known during the first half of the 19th century, its progressively-developing attributes practiced by Russia in Poland, for purposes of "Russifying" ethnic Poles, clearly had been those usually associated with our modern understanding of ethnic cleansing in extremis. Just as importantly, albeit that Americans had been familiar with nouns describing murder (i.e., homicide, infanticide, matricide and parricide) as included in Noah Webster's Dictionary of 1828 (now available online free of charge), the related term "genocide" also hadn't been known during the first half of the 19th century. However, as the 19th century attributes associated with the origin of the 20th century understanding of ethnic cleansing in extremis became progressively manifest to me by inference of Russia's first-half-of-the-19th-century's unnamed "ethnic cleansing" of Poland, the full impact of which served as a stunning model, and proceeded both uninterrupted and largely avoided meaningful condemnation by the West, all of which had been characterized by the unknown observer's comment about having lived during, and perhaps through, the post-1830 period in Poland as having been, to repeat, that *Russia wanted Poland, but did not want Polish people.*

It will be seen via the news reports contained in this book, that what Russia sought to achieve during the reign of Czar Nicholas I (1825-1855), and was open about the matter, had been the "annihilation" of Poland, the Polish nationality and the Roman Catholic Church in Poland. *Annihilation had been the word used by European news correspondents of the period to describe Russia's intent following the November Uprising.* In short, annihilation of people for having chosen to sustain their Polishness (polskość) as a nation and nationality post-November 29, 1830 -- the day on which the fateful November Uprising began -- logically relates, as I see it, symbiotically with our 21st century understanding of the word *genocide* (a word that also didn't exist for Noah Webster in 1828). Thus, for the period 1831 to 1849, Russia's application of a policy of annihilation to Poland and the Polish nationality, very likely shared the same imperceptible location on the continuum separating *ethnic cleansing* from the second yet-to-be-conceived word, *genocide,* with that of the latter destined to being further defined *over time* conceptually by the 19th century synonym-of-the-day, annihilation. Noah Webster's Dictionary of 1828 identified *annihilation* by the terms, "to reduce to nothing" and "to destroy the existence of" -- both of which aptly described Russia's plans for once-free and independent Poland and the Polish nationality.

In addition to employing the word annihilation to best describe Russia's policy toward Poland, the Polish people and the Roman Catholic Church in Poland, as it related to the reign of Czar Nicholas I (1825-1855), some European news correspondents also employed the word extinction.

Indeed, one correspondent of the period had categorized Russia's military involvement against Poland in 1830-1832 as having been waged as "a war of extermination." (See *Article 107.*)

And here, I might add, *Niles' Register* reported that Russia also practiced ethnic cleansing in extremis of the Armenians of Crimea (see *Article 6*) on one reported occasion, when in September 1778, after defeating the Nogai Tartars and driving them out of the land on the west side of the Sea of Azov, Russia decided to re-locate some 75,000 Armenians from Crimea to replace the Nogai Tartars. However, while in transit and upon reaching their destination, likely on foot for the most part, the weather reportedly became progressively wintry. Thus, the Armenians -- under Russian, and likely, Cossack military escort as well -- despairingly found themselves in the open, without promised shelters being ready to receive them, and so they had to dig holes in the ground and cover themselves as best as they could from the harsh seasonal elements. Only some 7,000 Armenians reportedly survived, an episode which Russia likely blamed on the re-location project administrator. Point of the story? Having cleaned out the Nogai Tartars from the west side of the Sea of Azov, and removing the Armenians from the Crimea to replace the Nogai Tartars there, Russia also derived a third benefit by way of the "accidental" deaths of 68,000 (90.7%) of the relatively-less undesirable, yet nonetheless expendable, in its eyes, Armenians that had been forced to abandon their homes in the Crimea. Where on the above-mentioned continuum would the calamity of the Armenians of Crimea being forced to replace the Nogai Tartars in 1778 be located? Could that horrible episode have been a deliberate act rather than an accident? An answer depends on 21st research, provided that the 1778 archives of Imperial Russia were to be available for inspection. The likelihood, however, of that ever occurring is highly improbable, if not impossible.

The sad and painful fate of said Armenians of Crimea in 1778, and the equally-sad and painful fate of Poland and the Poles on a much larger scale from 1795 through 1849 had been connected with Russia's growth as an uncontrollable European and Eurasian power, where its cleansing proclivities attracted condemnation -- largely of the "toothless" variety -- by other nations of the western parts of the continent, including Great Britain, which never forgot the sobering fact that in 1814, for example, the combined central and eastern European allied armies of Russia, Prussia and Austria, led by Czar Alexander I (1801-1825) of Russia, entered Paris in hot pursuit of Napoleon Bonaparte and his loyal forces that led to his abdication as Emperor of France, and the ensuing startling occupation of France by the victorious allies until 1817 when they (Russia, Prussia, Austria and Great Britain) met at Aix-la-Chapelle and agreed to terminate their occupation.

Conceptually, unlike a 21st understanding of genocide, in contrast, annihilation is not dependent on the volume of whoever or whatever is to be or had been annihilated, even though, in practical terms, the victims of genocide and the victims of annihilation suffer the same fate, that being a violently-imposed and painful transition to perpetual oblivion, or, in terms of Christian belief, depending on how a person

8

conducted his or her life, either the conscious state of eternal Heavenly bliss or the perpetual fires and horrors of hell.

Conceptually as well, the Armenians of the Crimea in 1778 and the Poles of 1831-1849 had been annihilated because of their ethnicities, which had been an inescapable fact at those points of their respective histories. Although the Russians tried repeatedly to Russify the Poles, the term genocide is too strong a word to apply because the Kingdom Poland did remain, but it was not free and independent. Thus, a methodical and incremental annihilation of the Polish nation and nationality, along with the Roman Catholic Church of Poland, is more appropriately used to describe the situation.

As such, the use of the term annihilation is wholly appropriate to their separate stories in 1778 and 1831-1849 respectively, albeit relatively very briefly but nonetheless painfully in the case of the Armenians of Crimea; but at great length for the Poles of what had once been the Commonwealth of Poland and Lithuania prior to the Partitions of 1772, 1793 and 1795 by Russia, Prussia and Austria.

Therefore, today, for the vast majority of Americans, those of Polish descent included, Poland's painful history of battling against being *ethnically-cleansed and annihilated* as a nation and nationality by Imperial Russia, as viewed by the American press from 1811 to 1849, can also be best described as constituting a long-standing void, until now.

My initiative seeks to end that void by recounting what Americans actually had read about Poland by way of *Niles' Register* in words exactly as they had been written principally by contemporary European news correspondents and shared with their American counterparts, largely by way of American editors, with Hezekiah Niles (1777-1839) being the sole exemplar for the purposes of this book. It also seeks to demonstrate the extent to which he had been successful in fulfilling his objective for having created his publication, as he stated on page 1, volume 1, number 1, known as *The Weekly Register* at that time, on September 7, 1811:

"Some have feared that we should 'dabble too much in politics' -- i.e., party politics, and others have apprehended 'the work will not stand.' It is in our power to remove the first case of apprehension -- but the latter depends on the public as well as ourselves. The first shall be removed, as the Register proposes -- it is not intended for electioneering purposes, of course party politics will be avoided; yet, by the insertion of original and selected essays, as both sides of great national questions, we shall hold it our duty to preserve a history of the feelings of the times on men and things."

Consequently, my particular American-based recounting in 2021 of Poland's struggles to exist as a free and independent European nation, and of great importance, *nationality as well*, during the first half of the 19th century, rests mainly on the career of the American journalist and editor, Hezekiah Niles (1777-1839) of Baltimore, Maryland. As a well-read, well-informed, erudite man, he viewed the world based on the internal and external conduct of its nations, kingdoms and empires, and on the corresponding quality of their leaders. During the life-span (1811-1849) of his weekly newspaper, known generally as the *Niles' Register* (it began by him in 1811 as *The Weekly Register*, in 1814 it became *Niles' Weekly Register*, and from 1837 until 1849, ended as *Niles' National Register*), Hezekiah Niles opened the eyes of Americans to news about Poland being reported by always-resourceful and brave European (of course, with the British importantly included) correspondents, all of whom generally submitted reports on Poland's brutal mis-treatment by Imperial Russia in particular, precisely during most of the reign of Czar Nicholas I (1825-1855), and into 1849 when *Niles' Weekly Register* ended its distinguished lifespan.

European-based surnames are typically, but not exclusively, synonymous with any nationality that depends on the existence of a specific nation. In many respects, this particular book documents the painful existence which post-Partition Poles experienced for having become a nationality without its own free and independent Polish nation, during which time they simply had been expected by their conquerors to accept the harsh fact of having been compelled to become the loyal subjects of Russia, Prussia or Austria by the fact of conquest, and if not, destined to wandering about in Europe as stateless pilgrims for refusing to become Russians, Prussians or Austrians, rather than remaining Poles. Inspired in 1832 by their great national poet, Adam Mickiewicz (1798-1855), who in his opening lines of the "Litany of the Pilgrimage" (*Litanja Pielgrzymstwa*), wrote: "God our Father, who led your people from Egyptian bondage and returned them to the Holy Land, Return us to our Homeland...." (Boże Ojcze, któryś wywiódł lud Twój z niewoli egipskiej, i wrócił do Ziemi Świętej, wróc nas do Ojczyzny naszej...."). As such, this book is a tribute to, and reminder of, the undeserved suffering of the people of Poland largely by way of ethnic cleansing of every variety, attribute and degree, and also having been subjected to persistent acts of *annihilation*, imposed on them near-exclusively by Imperial Russia, because they simply had chosen to remain faithful to the memory of their Polish ancestors in language, culture, religion and governance.

As Reported in the "Niles' Register"

My objective, therefore, is to provide for 21st century Americans generally, and for Polish Americans and friends of Poland in particular, a rare view of what was being reported about the state of affairs in Poland principally by European, and secondarily but importantly, by American journalists, *exactly as the news of the day was being written verbatim in those times*, rather than summarizing what they had written. Selecting to present the actual *Niles' Register* news articles about Poland from 1811 to 1849, as opposed, for example, to simply commenting about selected and isolated passages of news reports, I believe, does justice to the British, French, German and Polish correspondents, both those formally so by profession and those informally so by inclination, all of whom had committed themselves to record and report the *truth*, and who more often than not risked their lives to report -- in the face of the reality of Poland's borders having often been closed by Russia, Prussia and Austria -- what they had seen and heard in partitioned and down-trodden Poland which struggled ever relentlessly for free and independent political and cultural survival, against all odds.

In general I have refrained from interpreting what was reported. When I do offer pertinent comments, however, they will serve principally to further illuminate the text and will be contained within clearly-identified rectangular borders (i.e., boxes). Moreover, when I comment about Polish surnames and places, for example, they will be spelled in proper Polish usage, diacritics included, despite the fact that this book's 302 operative authentic news articles (i.e., *Articles*) themselves, written largely by non-Poles, who more often than not misspelled Polish surnames and places (e.g., Kosciusko rather than Kościuszko, in the case of Polish surnames; Galicia rather than Galicja, in the case of Polish provinces; and Dantzic or Danzig rather than Gdańsk, and Cracow rather than Kraków, in the case of Polish cities). Please consider that, even in the period of 1811-1849 among most western Europeans, and certainly among Americans, the Polish language had been near-universally unknown and exotic, a point for which non-Polish correspondents of that era should not bear our modern-day criticism. In short, I propose that they did the best they could do under the circumstances.

Interestingly, as I had compiled and transcribed the final 302 operative *Articles*, each being identified as a numbered *Article* of news, I discovered that American usage of the English language, particularly in the spelling of words from 1811 to 1849, differed somewhat from standards of English usage of the 21st century in the United States, a process, insofar I had committed myself to *use the written English language as it had been reported in those days*, involved a daily struggle to pre-

11

vail against my desktop computer's spell-check and grammar-check software.

Finally, I must point out that none of the final 302 *Articles* that I had read online (out of an array of 785 examined which will be explained as this Introduction comes to an end), could be scanned and saved. That being so, whereas I could print them onto an 8-by-11 sheet of paper, I then had to transcribe everything, in the manner of a medieval monk, stroke by stroke, word for word, sentence by sentence, paragraph by paragraph, and page by page, so as to create the basis of a manuscript that would lead to becoming the integral major portion of the factual substance of this book's news content as written from 1811 to 1849, in a process that, on and off, took some three years, during which time I very often found myself relying on a magnifying glass to decipher a faded printed page, paragraph, sentence or word discolored by age and at times with blurred print as well, spanning in time anywhere from 210 years ago for the year 1811 and 172 years ago for the year 1849, using the year 2021 as the basis of comparison.

Throughout, I served as my own research assistant, during which *aged, faded and/or blurred newsprint* often rendered identifying the difference between, for example, a 2, 3, 5, 6, 8 and 9 impossible (as it relates to the top and/or bottom *curl* of all but two of those six numbers), so that columns of aggregated numbers did not always precisely match the totals. In such cases, I could only do my best in estimating and transcribing said numbers that appeared on the original printed pages of *Niles' Register*, of necessity with my magnifying glass in hand, which to say the least, had been a tediously slow and frustrating process, and not necessarily fully accurate in itself, if casually transcribed, yet something that the typical book-copying medieval monk hadn't necessarily been forced to contend with. Given that I committed myself to a high standard of precision, in transcribing with accuracy, all that I had read during the process of identifying and compiling the final 302 news articles (i.e., *Articles*), the lingering problem of the precise identification of aggregated numbers had been vexing, to say the least. Especially so, when clearly-identified numbers that I was able to read without any difficulty, simply failed to be substantiated in the totals reported by *Niles' Register* which in itself had constituted yet another unanticipated challenge. It added to the amount of time, in some instances a relatively great amount of time, that I would have to dedicate to a particular numerical table, but in the end, I had been able to resolve each problem for the most part to my satisfaction, at least, without or with an appropriate related comment, as the case may have been.

Nevertheless, my commitment to transcribe the news exactly

as it had been written, I humbly propose, has been in its own right throughout, as strong as Hezekiah Niles' commitment, and that of his three successors (William Ogden Niles, Jeremiah Hughes and George Beatty, whose names and dates of service as Editor appear in the Appendix as well), to gather and print the news about Poland appearing in *Niles' Register* from 1811 to 1849.

Overall, for the entire period of the existence of *Niles' Register*, the frequency distribution of this book's 302 *Articles* (or "documents" if you will, as I considered them to be, composed of news-briefs and news articles of varying lengths), that I had examined and transcribed in my research, when considered by decades, had been: 1811-1819 = 16%; 1820-1829 = 16%; 1830-1839 = 48%; and 1840-1849 = 20%.

In many respects, the 302 *Articles* also constitute *documents* of the era in the true sense of the word, insofar as they establish the factual basis of this book's compelling story of Poland's epic struggles for the right to exist as a free and independent nation against daunting and impossible odds. For the most part, I also have proposed to allow the Articles to speak for themselves in the matter of standards of English usage in the United States from 1811 to 1849 when, for example, a word such as "show" was more often than not spelled as shew, "aide" as in "aide-de-camp" was spelled as *aid de camp* without hyphens, "frenzy" was spelled as *phrenzy*, and a human "skull" was spelled as *scull*; and "everybody," "everything" and "everywhere" were spelled as *every body, every thing* and *every where* without hyphens; and the word "notwithstanding" was spelled as not withstanding; and where 21st century hyphenated expressions such as "well-organized" were rendered as well organized, without a hyphen; the word "connection" was spelled as connexion; and finally, where a 21st century phrase such as "who had done this" was written as *"who done this"* and with yet another such example having been expressed as "14 millions of dollars" in 1811-1849, as opposed to "14 million dollars" in our modern 21st century era.

Since virtually all the news relating to Poland arriving in America at Boston, New York City, Philadelphia, Baltimore and Charleston originated in Europe largely by way of British, French, German and Polish correspondents, who sent their reports principally by way of European newspapers and to a lesser extent by personal letters, I must repeat that in their original texts, the spelling of Polish surnames accurately, along with the related spelling of preponderantly Polish cities, towns, villages and geographical locations by them (except for the Poles), understandably left much to be desired for the most part during 1811 to 1849. As time went by, however, non-Polish European and American correspondents and editors (e.g., those of *Niles' Register* in the case of the latter), had improved their mastery of spelling Polish surnames and places accurately, the only major exception having been the Kościuszko surname that all Americans persistently spelled as Kosciusko during the first half of the 19th century, except on one occasion (as will be seen in *Article 216* by way of a letter from Prince Adam Jerzy Czartoryski in Paris to Polish exiles in the United States), but without the diacritic. Yet in the 21st century, we should be more vigilant about the matter, not surrendering to the practice of allowing others to misspell and/or routinely mispronounce -- sometimes disparagingly -- Polish surnames, for which our 19th and 20th century ancestors struggled to prevent from becoming Russianized or Germanized, or worse. By copying all of the original "documents" constituting the basis of my research, and then going on to personally transcribe (i.e., word-process) each of them in the original English usage as written during the period of history in question, though tedious and time-consuming for the reasons noted, enabled me to become thoroughly familiar with what American subscribers and other readers of *Niles' Register* had been informing themselves of with regard to Poland. As my research and study progressed, I had been amazed by the depth and breadth of knowledge (better identified as intelligence) about Poland to which Americans had been exposed, and also, most importantly, how they reacted to it.

Importantly as well, at least in the initial task of compiling and then selecting the final 302 operative numbered Articles that constitute the documented substance of this book, the index system established by Hezekiah Niles generally utilized multiple references to a particular article of news, as he himself had stated at the completion of the Index of Volume 13, for example, on page viii of the January 24, 1818 issue of the *Niles' Weekly Register*:

"In general, there are two or more references to every important article contained in this volume. But persons, places and things situated or happening in countries or states, if not found under their own alphabetical arrangement, will be found under the country or state that they belong to. As, for instance, for "Prince regent" see British; for "Moscow" see Russia, etc."

Fortunately for me, after having retired in 2004 as an Associate Dean, on the administrative side, and a Senior Lecturer in History, on the faculty side, after some four decades of service at Northeastern University in Boston, I became a subscriber, largely but not exclusively, for the purpose of this book, for having on-line access to what was known on the internet as the *Niles' Register Cumulative Index*, which had been the private collection of owner and editor William H. "Bill" Earle of Baltimore, Maryland, until he donated his entire collection to the Maryland State Archives in 2018. It indeed had been my good fortune as a paid subscriber to have been able to search for and collect and transcribe all of my pre-operative documents for this book before he finally had relinquished ownership and control of his personal collection. In my opinion, Earle's great service, and I might add, a superior service, to historians had been to significantly reduce, if not eliminate, the "poking-around" as he had termed the process to be, for searching through the maze of Hezekiah Niles' et al many original indexes, by Earle's having coalesced and modernized them, so that as a subscriber, I could identify, access and print the original pages of *Niles' Register* with relative, but not fully total, ease. In contrast, there was no ease whatsoever in transcribing them for purposes of this book as I noted above.

That being said, in closing this Introduction, about the matter of the index-related "two or more references" principle originally established by Hezekiah Niles, and much later modernized by William H. "Bill" Earle, for establishing my final 302 *Articles*, I had to search through at least twice the amount, and considerably more for that matter (i.e., 785), from which I derived the final 302 *Articles* that constitute and document my research for the content of this book.

Insofar as *Niles' Register* covered world news as well as news of the United States, it is appropriate that I mention this book's 785 references, of which 745 specifically apply to Poland, and related matters, in the wider context of its worldwide news coverage, with that having been the number of news references concerning other nations or states, those having been: the United States (85,552); France (11,384); Spain (6,501); England (4,754); Mexico (5,945); Russia (3,575); Columbia (3,165); Canada (2,992); Ireland (2,822); Portugal (2,258); Greece (2,103); Austria (1,621); Venezuela (1,521); Brazil (1,336); Cuba (1,324); China (1,275); Prussia (1,219); Peru (1,197); Egypt (1,196); India (1,103); Argentina (1,092); Liberia (1,066); and Belgium (1,025).

Nations or states receiving less than 1,000 references, but at least 100, had been: Ecuador (834); Poland (745); Haiti (735); Panama (610); Algeria (608); Sweden (571); Chile (554); Denmark (481); Uruguay (387); the Ottoman Empire (383); Holland (369); Scotland (361); Switzerland (334); Norway (245); Bolivia (203); Morocco (179); Afghanistan (169); Santo Domingo (169); Australia (167); Guatemala (159); and Tunisia (113).

Finally, nations or states receiving less than 100 references had been: Paraguay (88); Nicaragua (77); Honduras (61); Japan (33); Romania (23); Bulgaria (20); Lithuania (18); Finland (17); Abyssinia (14); Bosnia (12); Libya (5); and Serbia (1).

With regard to Lithuania, please note that some of its 18 news references had been included with those of Poland, as one in those days would expect, given that the Russian, Prussian and Austrian Partitions of 1772, 1793 and 1795 specifically addressed the permanent destruction of the Commonwealth of Poland and Lithuania, an entity known to Europeans generally, as well as among Americans, as Poland, for short.

For readers who might be disappointed that news coverage about Poland by *Niles' Register* as it relates to the subject of this book hadn't been far greater in volume and content, one must consider that Poland's contiguous partitioners (Russia, Prussia and Austria), as will be seen in *Article 1*, pledged with great specificity in 1797 to permanently eradicate the memory of Poland's very existence and never mention its name, forever. In short, had the Partitions never occurred, perhaps news coverage about the Commonwealth of Poland and Lithuania would likely have been somewhat more-to-far-greater in extent. On the other hand, rather than bemoan and decry the comparatively modest volume of news coverage about Poland in this opus, readers should focus instead on the substance and quality of that coverage to the extent that it illuminates and achieves this book's stated objective.

All told, therefore, news coverage relating to Poland both directly for the most part, and indirectly for the balance, by Niles' Register during the period, 1811-1849 is presented on the following pages. Rather than employing footnotes, my commentary on the articles is presented in the rectangular "boxes" accompanying the stories.

As Reported in the "Niles' Register"

Hezekiah Niles (1777-1839) by John Wesley Jarvis, 1827

Part One: 1811 - 1819

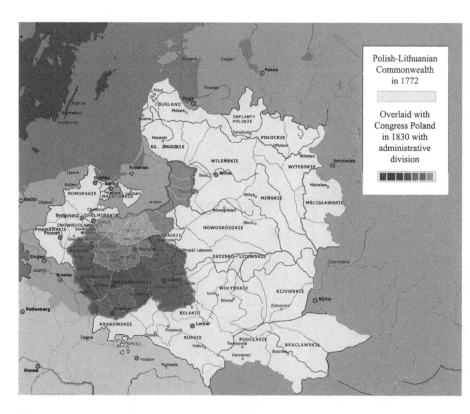

The extent, in a light color, of the Polish-Lithuanian Commonwealth before its First Partition in 1772 by Russia, Prussia and Austria, and subsequently what remained of it in darker colors in 1830 as the Kingdom of Poland (also known as Congress Poland insofar it had been established in 1814 by the Congress of Vienna) whose Russian King was also the Czar (Emperor) of Russia.

Article 1. (November 9, 1811, pages 163 and 164):

Appropriately, the story at hand begins with the article titled, "Statistical Notices of Russia," which appeared in this issue of *The Weekly Register* that introduced Russia to American readers by its founder, Hezekiah Niles. Although Russia absorbed the greatest extent of territory constituting the former Commonwealth of Poland and Lithuania following the Russian, Prussian and Austrian engineered Partitions of 1772, 1793 and 1795, the word "Poland" wasn't mentioned in the "Statistical Notices of Russia," as planned by Poland's partitioners, by way of their closing Treaty of Partition of January 1797 wherein it was agreed that: "in view of the necessity to abolish everything that could revive the memory of the existence of the Kingdom of Poland, now that the annulment of this body politic has been effected... that the high contracting parties are agreed and undertake never to include in their titles... the name or designation of the Kingdom of Poland, which shall remain suppressed as from the present and *forever....*" (See Norman Davies, "God's Playground: A History of Poland," © 1982, Volume I, page 542.)

All of this, both in theory and in practice, had been perpetrated, with Russia being the leader to eliminate the memory of Poland in the history of Europe and the world forever. What transgression, one may ask, had the Poles committed to have had the memory of their existence suppressed, past, present and forever at the time?

An answer to that question had been published in 1839 by the book written by the Marquis de Custine (1790-1857), a French aristocrat, who had traveled through Russia extensively, and had titled his opus, La Russe en 1839, and which 150 years later in 1989 was re-published in the United States as: "EMPIRE OF THE CZAR: A Journey through Eternal Russia." On page 614 of the latter book's 619 pages, Custine succinctly offered the following statement of fact to his European contemporaries, and by extension, to Americans as well, that:

"Russia sees in Europe a prey which our dissensions will sooner or later yield to it: she foments anarchy among us in the hope of profiting by a corruption which she favors because it is favorable to her views: it is the history of Poland recommencing on a larger scale. For many years past Paris has read revolutionary journals paid by Russia. 'Europe,' they say at Petersburg, 'is following the road that Poland took; she is enervating herself by a vain liberalism, whilst we continue powerful precisely because we are not free: let us be patient under the yoke; others shall some day pay for our shame'."

In short, Poland's transgression, at least in the eyes of its Russian adversaries at the time, it appears, had been its "vain liberalism" as judged by clearly the most repressive authoritarian-totalitarian regime in the world whose people were not free, and still so remain in that state, to this point in the 21st century.

As fate would have it, however, only some eighteen years following the Treaty of Partition of 1797, and under changed political considerations, Czar Alexander I (1801-1825), who led the allied coalition of Russia, Prussia and Austria, in concert with England, in the defeat of Imperial France under Napoleon Bonaparte, and took the title of *King of Poland* which he held until his death in 1825. While he lived, he was known as the "Emperor of All the Russias and King of Poland." His successor, Czar Nicholas I (1825-1855), also held the same titles. And here, please note that in that Imperial title, the use of the word "Russias" rather than "Russians" had not been a mistake, as will be explained as this book progresses.

What happened, one may ask, to the solemn pledge of 1797 made by the monarchs of Russia, Prussia and Austria "never to include in their titles…the name or designation of the Kingdom of Poland"? Political expediency, and a personal concern on the part of Czar Alexander of Russia who believed that, as a child brought up and educated in the ideals of the European Enlightenment, his superior intelligence, inherent liberal tendencies, and including a rarely-expressed understanding of Poland's existential dilemma from his perspective, of course, all of which were to be based, as he planned, on a mutually-respected constitutional monarchy and society that he personally would establish and protect for Poland, in an Imperial Russia *devoid* of its own equivalent constitution, the totality of which would work to bridge the gap between Poles and Russians, and secure lasting national peace and prosperity for Poland and Poles alike under his personal guidance and leadership, as an integral part of the Russian Empire. A tall order, indeed, as the expression goes.

The post-1795 aspiration of the Poles, in contrast, had always focused on the restoration of a free and independent Kingdom of Poland, with a constitution of their own making as in 1791, and a king, for example, of their *own unanimous or near-unanimous* choosing as it had been for Jan Sobieski in 1674, among the nations of Europe and the world; to the Russians, Alexander included, the Kingdom of Poland could only exist as an unquestioning and loyal integral part of the Russian Empire whose Czar also served as the King of Poland. Coalescing the visions of the Poles with that of the Czar were doomed to fail, as in the case of a failed marriage, but during his life, Alexander had aspired to make the marriage work by granting Poland a constitution and its own army, sustaining some Napoleonic innovations, and having been a friend influenced to some degree by the life-long Polish patriot, Adam Czartoryski (1770-1861), whom he had appointed to serve, during his formative years as Czar, both as Imperial Russia's Foreign Minister and Chairman of the Council of Ministers of Imperial Russia (1804-1806).

His successor, Nicholas I, however, neither had the patience nor the inclinations and vision of his predecessor in the matter of Poland. Indeed, it is safe to say that knowledge of the true character of Russia continued to be viewed by Americans generally *via the manner* in which Russia, under the leadership of Nicholas (1825-1855), conducted a repressive, largely confrontational, bloody and vindictive authoritarian relationship with Poland and its people.

For the reader's consideration, therefore, I propose that the Treaty of Partition of 1797 had served as the preface to the opening chapter of the documented history and justification, pursued largely by Imperial Russia, for the *ethnic cleansing and annihilation* of Poland, the Polish nationality and the Roman Catholic Church in Poland during the reign of Nicholas I, generally using Poland's alleged "vain liberalism" as his convenient justification, on one hand, and inflicting said incrementally-harsh punishment on the Poles for the November Uprising of 1830 and during its prolonged aftermath, on the other hand. With that being said, the first *Niles' Register* news Article of November 9, 1811 – where Poland is not identified except by inference in the benign phrase, "New acquisitions since 1782" – next follows:

STATISTICAL NOTICES OF RUSSIA

The Russian Empire contains a greater extent of country than ever before was governed by an individual.* [*The Persian and Roman empires, at their utmost height, contained about 1,700,000 square miles.] It reaches from the gulf of Bothnia, on the west, to the sea of Kamschatska, in the east; and, in some places, from the 45th to the 72nd deg. of north latitude; computed to have a surface of 4,900,000 square miles, and to contain between 45 and 50 millions of people.

The greatest extent of territory is in Asia. Russia, in Europe, has about 1,400,000 square miles, and 41,500,000 inhabitants, or 35 to a square mile, the empire averages between nine and ten.

The enumeration of 1783 was taken with great accuracy; it appeared there were then, in the 41 governments of Russia, 12,838,529 male persons. Supposing an equal number of females, the amount will be: 5,677,800
Add for the Cossacks and other unnumbered tribes, 1,720,000
Whole population in 1783:   27,397,000
New acquisitions since 1782, including Finland,
likely wrested from Sweden: 6,355,000

22

As Reported in the "Niles' Register"

Natural increase since 1783, say one half of the original number in that year, allowing the population to double itself in 56 years without regarding the geometrical proportion on which population advances:

	13,698,500
Whole population in 1811:	47,440,000

Please note, that I actually had no problem with identifying the original separate aggregated numbers appearing in the foregoing nine lines immediately above. Note as well, however, that the type-setter likely forgot to carry the 800 appearing at the end of the first line into the first sub-total appearing in the third line that should have produced 27,397,800 rather than 27,397,000, a point, when considered along with the 500 appearing at the end of the aggregated numbers appearing on the eighth line, should alone have produced, on the ninth line, a grand total of 47,451,300 rather than 47,440,000. This serves as an example of what I had to contend with in the matter. Was it the error of the typesetter? Or perhaps the 25,677,800 should have been 25,667,000 and the 13,698,500 should have been 13,698,000 instead? Or had it been the responsibility of Hezekiah Niles to correct the error of his typesetter? Maybe the error hadn't been with the typesetter, but rather, with the European or other sources (i.e., "geographical treatises") that Hezekiah Niles had consulted for the basis of his article. In such a situation, Niles would not have corrected the source of the error, but printed it as it was, with a related notation. However, searching for an erratum posting by him, amidst the characteristic very dense text of *The Weekly Register*, devoid of illustrations and advertisements, as a procedural operative principle on my part, would have brought my research to a near-standstill, if in fact there were to be other such considerations (and there had been as I learned progressively) throughout the original texts that I examined and transcribed, thereby unnecessarily defeating my purpose, by becoming mired in validation of aggregated numbers appearing in some of the tables. Being assured by Hezekiah Niles himself (see below) of the "pretty correct principles" as he phrased it, associated with what he introduced, in this article, to fellow Americans of his times, I proceeded as such throughout.

Of which we allow, only five millions and a half to Russia, in Asia. This estimate raises the population nearly 10 millions more than is generally admitted in our geographical treatises; but is founded, we apprehend, upon pretty correct principles. In 1803 there were married in the empire, 302,467 couples. Died, 791,979. Born, 1,279,321 -- multiply the latter by 33 years, which is sometimes considered as a generation, and we have a grand total of 42,217,593. In this statement nothing is exaggerated, but much must have been omitted, for from the wild nations inhabiting Russian Asia, the receipt of correct returns could not be expected. Besides, when we call to mind the immense improvements that have latterly been made in this country; examine its roads and canals, and the various excitements held out to industry, in the general amelioration of the condition of the people (though yet extremely wretched) and view the exertions made to encourage agriculture and commerce, we are inclined to believe we are still below the real amount of the population of the empire, which is certainly increasing.

Though the population of Russia is greater than that of France, the physical force of the empire is much less; owing to the scattered situation of the people, and the moral impossibility of concentrating their force at any given point.

France, it is said, can spare a million of men for her armies, and sometimes has sent 600,000 troops out of her territory, to carry war into the countries of her neighbors. Russia, by the most powerful and arbitrary exertions, more cruel perhaps than the French conscription itself, has never been able to muster half of this force for that purpose. Her army is said to consist of about 600,000 men of whom 500,000 are effectives.

The last return we have seen of the Russian navy, rendezvousing chiefly at Cronstadt, Revel and Archangel, gave 8 ships of 110 guns; 42 of 74 and 66; 27 frigates of 38, 32 and 28; 50 galleys; 300 gun boats, and about 30 smaller armed vessels. Besides these, the fleet in the Black Sea was said to consist of 18 ships of the line, and about 30 frigates, corvettes, etc.; 20,000 sailors were then kept in the pay of the government.

The revenues of Russia, arising from capitation taxes, customs, monopolies, etc. amount to about $60,000,000 per annum -- a very modest sum considering the population and resources of the country, but a mighty amount when the high value of money, or cheapness of labor, is duly estimated. It is sufficient for all the expenses of government, though the court is among the most luxurious and profligate in the world.

Gold and silver mines have been worked in Russia for many years. The whole produce, for about 100 years past, is estimated at

42,675 lbs. of the former, and 1,564,750 lbs. of the latter.

The whole annual produce of the copper mines is computed to be 7,350,000 lbs. The greatest exportation of iron was 3,303,249 poods, valued at $5,204,125 -- of this value there was exported from Petersburg more than four millions and a half.

The timber and boards exported have been valued at $1,500,000 per annum.

Hemp, exported, (1793) 2,771,728 poods, worth $6,066,615. Flax, 1,146,125 poods, valued at $1,104,100, with great quantities of hemp seed and flax seed, and nearly two millions of gallons of hemp seed oil. The value of the flax exported amounted (in 1802) to nearly six millions of dollars.

Russia manufactures an immense quantity of sail cloth and linen. In 1802, the export was estimated at $3,537,853.

In 1803 there was exported from the ports on the Baltic and Archangel, 34,500 tons of tallow, worth more than nine millions and a half dollars. The further produce of neat cattle, (exported) the same year was estimated at $3,118,571.

The above reference to "neat cattle" hadn't been an error. Now considered archaic in use, the word neat is, among its several definitions, defined in modern American dictionaries as "a cow or other domestic bovine animal." In 1828, the *Noah Webster Dictionary* defined, for one definition, it being: "of the bovine genus, as bulls, oxen and cows. In America, the word is used in composition, as in neats tongue, neats foot oil, and tautologically in neat cattle.

Wheat, rye, barley and oats, the same year, worth $11,496,215. The balance of trade in favor of Russia is said to amount to $5,000,000 *per ann.*

Accounts in Russia are kept in Rubles and Copecs -- 100 of the latter make one of the former, worth an American dollar. When we hear of *rubles* and *copecs* we understand precisely so many dollars and cents, for the value is exactly the same.

WEIGHTS -- 96 *solotnicks* make a Russian lb., 40 lbs. which make a *pood* are equal to 35¾ American lbs.; 10 poods make a *berquet*; 6 *berquets* a *[illegible word]*. A *berquet* of 10 *poods* is equal to 356 ½ lbs., American.

MEASURES -- Liquid, 3 *Krushkas* are equal to 1 American gallon - 8 *krushkas* make 1 *Vedros*. Dry, a *Chetwerik* is equal to 5¼ American bushels.

LENGTH -- The *Arsheen* contains 28 American inches. The *Sashen* is 3 Arsheens. The *verst* or Russian mile is equal to 1,500 *Arsheens*, or 1,166 $^{2/3}$ yards, a little more than $^{5}/_{8}$ of the English or American mile. 12 feet Russian are equal to 11 English.

(to be continued).

Please note that it had been Hezekiah Niles who completed the above article with the statement -- "to be continued" -- which he placed in parentheses.

Article 2. (September 12, 1812, page 32):

THE CHRONICLE. We have three bulletins of the French Army. The first is dated at Gumbinnon in Prussian Lithuania, June 20, the second at Wilkowiski, on the 22nd and the third at Kowna, June 26. They detail no event of importance.

On its way from Paris to Moscow in the fateful year 1812, Napoleon's Grande Armée entered territory that through the year 1771 had once been an integral part of the Commonwealth of Poland and Lithuania.

Article 3. (September 26, 1812, pages 50 and 51):

This article pertained to the June 22, 1812 opening in Warsaw of the Diet of the Grand Duchy of Warsaw that had been the creation in 1807 of Emperor Napoleon Bonaparte of France, to the joy of Poles who sought Poland's restoration as a free and independent nation. With the failure of Napoleon's invasion of Russia where he was defeated in 1812, and in 1814, his defeat in France by the allied armies of Russia, Prussia and Austria, along with his abdication, ended the Grand Duchy of Warsaw, and also ended its concurrent re-establishment on June 28, 1812 as the Kingdom of Poland, under Imperial French protection. Please note again, that from the outset I have deliberately misspelled Polish surnames and locations throughout this study, as will be seen here, just as they had been misspelled in the original pages of The Weekly Register as it was known until 1814 when it became known as Niles' Weekly Register. Do not hold that against the English-speaking American journalists, or their European counterparts, for that matter, of the period for whom, except for the Poles, Slavic surnames had been largely unknown and relatively exotic. What, above all, was remarkable is that the American readers of Niles' Register (as it had been known generally) had access to otherwise-unknown information and intelligence about Poland, as they did about Russia relating to Poland. My transcription of this September 12, 1812 news article, wherein the Wolonicz, and Czartoryski and Wybicki surnames were presented as Woloniez and Czartorinski, and Wibycki illustrate this point of the misspelling of Polish surnames, despite the fact that three other Polish surnames included in this news-brief had been spelled correctly.

Warsaw, June 22. – The following are some of the details respecting the opening of the Diet : On the 26th, the Senators, the Ministers, the Council of State, the Nuncios, the Deputies, his excellency or the archbishop of Malines, Ambassador of his majesty the emperor Napoleon, assembled at the palace in the halls appropriated for this purpose, and thence proceeded along the corridors to the collegiate church of St. John, in order to pray to the God of Armies for his assistance in the grand work which was to be the object of the deliberations of the Diet. His excellency the president of the council of ministers, M. Potocki, was stationed near the throne, surrounded by the ministers; the senators placed themselves in the stalls of the canons, the Nuncios and the Deputies on the benches of the Church. His excellency the archbishop of Malines, accompanied by the secretary and the auditors of the legation, was introduced by his excellency the prefect of Warsaw, and took his place between the throne and the senators, on the right side of the altar. A crowd of spectators filled the church, in the midst of which the veterans and the cadets of the school of artillery and engineers, were ranged in line. His excellency the senator Gawronski, bishop of Crakow, celebrated Mass. The counsellor of state Woloniez, distinguished for his talents as an orator, pronounced from the pulpit a discourse, which made a most lively impression on the whole assembly. After Divine Service, the senators and nuncios, with the deputies, returned to their respective chambers. His excellency the French ambassador, was conducted, with the whole of his suite, to the principal room of the senators' chamber.

The Marshal of the Diet invited the chamber of Nuncios to follow him, with a view to assemble in the senators' chamber. As soon as they arrived, there his excellency M. Potocki, called prince Czartorinski to administer the oath to him near the throne, and to present to him a marshal's staff. Whence the forms were gone through, prince Potocki proclaimed – "in the name of the King, Duke of Warsaw, I give to prince Czartorinski permission to speak." The speech of this respectable prince was heard with all the interest which it deserved. Many of the principal members then spoke in succession. After the harangue

27

of his excellency the minister of the treasury, the marshal of the Diet announced to the assembly, that he had received in his capacity of marshal of the Diet, a requisition, signed by a certain member of that part of Poland which had passed under the dominion of Russia. His excellency the Secretary of the senate, read the address, the substance of which was, that in the happy circumstances in which Poland found itself at present placed, they besought the Diet in the name of their countrymen who were groaning under the yoke of Russia, to use its mediation with Napoleon the Great, who had already delivered one part of Poland, to condescend to release them also from this odious yoke.

Several senators delivered their sentiments upon this address. His excellency the senator Wibycki proposed to appoint a deputation, for the purpose of deliberating and presenting a project upon this subject. The president of the council of ministers declared, that the government entertained the same sentiments as the senate, respecting this address, had nominated in the king's name, the members of this deputation, whom he chose from the senate, the council of state, that of the members of the chamber of nuncios. In order to give these ministers time enough to accomplish the business with which they were charged, the president of the council of ministers adjourned the sitting until the 28th of June, and that it was in that sitting that the re-establishment of the kingdom of Poland was decreed.

Article 4. (October 24, 1812, pages 121 and 122):

In this issue, Hezekiah Niles continued to provide his subscribers of *The Weekly Register* the basis of establishing a worldview beyond the confines of the United States so that they would have a frame of reference for what he would expose them to by way of his innovative weekly news magazine to serve as a source of knowledge in a format that was totally devoid of advertisements and illustrations other than statistical tables in the case of the latter. As a matter of fact, the entire subsequent publication history of *Niles' Weekly Register* that it had changed its masthead to in 1814, and which became known in 1837 as *Niles' National Register*, never included advertisements or illustrations other than statistical tables. As such, he titled this particular referenced article, "General Statistical Table."

As Reported in the "Niles' Register"

GENERAL STATISTICAL TABLE

The following table has been formed, after much labour, expressly for this work, for the purpose of general reference. We are aware that it is incorrect in many particulars, but on the whole it may be accepted as approaching pretty nearly to truth, so far as facts can be discerned in the varied statements of the learned and scientific. And it may serve the ordinary purposes of our readers.

The whole globe is estimated to have a surface of 148,510,627 square miles, of which the habitable portion is said to have 38,990,569 square miles, and supposed to contain 760 millions of inhabitants.

Asia, is computed to have 10,768,823 square miles, and 500 millions of people

Europe,	2,749,349	160 millions
America,	14,000,000	50 millions
Africa,	9,576,208	50 millions

These estimates are very arbitrary. As to the contents and population of Asia and Europe, the various authors consulted are nearly agreed, but while some of them swell the population of America and Africa to 150 millions each, there are others who depress them, as low, respectively, as 20 or 30 millions. The 'unknown parts,' added to the last given calculations, is supposed to make general content of the habitable world, as stated.

The Chinese empire is the most populous, but the Russian the most extensive. The United States have the second rank as to the nominal contents of their territory.

Pekin, Nankin and Jedo, rivals in population, are the greatest cities of Asia, and are said to have 3 millions of inhabitants, each.

London is the most populous city in Europe, by the census of 1810, it contained 1,099,104 inhabitants, of whom 483,781 were males and 615,323 females.

Mexico is the largest city in America; by the census of 1794 it had 112,929 inhabitants, and its population has since considerably increased. Philadelphia and New York are the next in rank in the new world.

Grand Caira is the best peopled African city of which we are informed, it is computed to have more than 300,000 inhabitants, but there are some reasons to believe that, in the interior, are several cities far more populous, of which we know little at present but from vague rumor.

When Victimization of Poland Was Never in Doubt

Empires, Kingdoms	Sq. miles	Whole pop.	Capital	Pop.	Per sq. mile	Rev.$ mill'ns	Head tax in $
China	1,749,000	383,000,000	Pekin	3,000,000	212	300	79
Russia	4,900,000	47,440,000	St. Petersburg	180,000	9	60	1.05
France	236,840	43,423,000	Paris	547,756	184	160	3.06
Japan	118,000	30,000,000	Jedo	3,000,000	254	----	----
Austria	131,740	15,519,623	Vienna	250,000	118	32	2.07
Turkey	960,000	22,000,000	Constantinople	500,000	21	50	2.27
Persia	800,000	10,000,000	Ispahan	100,000	13	----	---
Birman	250,000	17,000,000	Ummarapoota	----	68	----	----
British (king.)	104,656	16,552,144	London	1,099,104	160	355	21.50
Spain	150,000	10,327,800	Madrid	150,000	67	----	----
Portugal	27,280	1,838,879	Lisbon	230,000	69	----	----
Naples	22,000	4,000,000	Naples	380,000	181	----	----
Denmark	163,041	2,148,438	Copenhagen	100,000	13	7	3.21
Sweden	169,000	2,353,355	Stockholm	72,000	15	64	2.70
Prussia	44,464	4,559,556	Konigsburg	50,000	103	----	----
Westphalia	----	2,912,303	Cassel	25,000	----	54	----
Bavaria	26,176	3,231,570	Munich	40,000	124	8	2.78
Wirtemburg	----	1,183,000	Stutgard	20,000	----	3	----
Saxony	----	2,085,476	Dresden	60,000	----	54	----
Sicily (island)	10,000	1,500,000	Palermo	180,000	150	14	1.00
Sardinia (isle)	6,600	456,990	Cagliari	25,000	69	4	1.00
Warsaw*	27,312	2,277,000	Warsaw	60,000	84	3	1.40
USA	2,000,000	7,239,902	Washington	8,208	4	14	2.00
C. of Rhine**	113,424	15,577,344	----	----	138	384	2.49

*Warsaw = The Grand Duchy of Warsaw; **C. of Rhine = The Confederation of the Rhine*

Upon completing the above portion of his "General Statistical Table," Hezekiah Niles proceeded to include brief comments about all the empires, kingdoms and states that he had referenced in it. For self-evident purposes, I have extrapolated only those empires, kingdoms and states having applicability to Europe and the United States, as this Article continued.

Russia, in Europe, contains 1,400,000 square miles, inhabited by about 41 millions of people, or 33 to a square mile, their Asiatic possessions are very thinly populated, vast regions being hideous deserts, destitute of fixed inhabitants. For Particulars, see *WEEKLY REGISTER*, vol. 1, p. 163.

France proper, 148,840 sq. miles, Holland, the Netherlands, and the former possessions of several petty German princes, 20,000 sq. miles; the kingdom of Italy, with Istria, Dalmatia, etc. about 50,000 square miles: all which, with Piedmont, Savoy, the former country of Nice, now forming *departments of France*, make up the aggregate. See *WEEKLY REGISTER*, vol. 1, p.39.

Before her late wars with France, Austria possessed 226,876 sq. miles, 26,970,030 inhabitants, and a revenue of 48,244,000 dollars. See

30

As Reported in the "Niles' Register"

WEEKLY REGISTER, vol. 1, p. 118.

Turkey, in Europe, in 9 millions, in 10 millions (respectively).

England and Wales, 49,460 square miles, Scotland 27,749 do., Ireland 27,457. By the census of 1810, England contained 9,499,408 inhabitants; Wales, 607,380; and Scotland, 1,804,864; to which they add for the army and navy 640,500, making a grand total of 12,552,144. We have not seen an enumeration of the people of Ireland, from the accounts laid before Parliament, there are probably about 500,000 dwelling houses; averaging them at 8 inhabitants each, we have a gross aggregate of four millions: which is probably about the true amount. The revenue, as here stated, is required for the *present year, independent of loans*. It may emphatically be called the *land of taxation*.

Such was Spain before the invasion by Bonaparte. Its population, has, doubtless, greatly decreased, of the present revenue no estimate can be made; under the old monarchy it was said to amount to 25 millions, or $2 for each head.

The preceding remarks on Spain also apply to Portugal. The revenue of the crown, the chief of which, however, was derived immediately from Brazil, was estimated at twelve millions per annum.

The revenue derived by the 'king of the two Sicilies,' from Naples, before his expulsion from the continent, was about 5 millions.

A very considerable part of the dominions of Denmark, is contained in the mountains of Norway and the frozen regions of Lapland. The provinces of Denmark proper are well populated; and the whole amount of Danish subjects at this time, probably exceeds two millions and a half, great improvements in the condition of the peasantry being latterly made.

See *WEEKLY REGISTER*, vol. 1, p. 109, for many interesting particulars (on Sweden).

Prussia, before the late war with France, possessed 88,980 sq. miles, with a population of 9,015,150 inhabitants; and the revenue was about 15 millions of dollars. Its present resources are unknown.

Westphalia, Bavaria, Wirtemburg and Saxony, are kingdoms lately erected by the emperor of France. They form a part of the 'confederation of the Rhine' noticed below.

The Grand Duchy of Warsaw, is a power created by France, at the expense of Prussia and Austria, who aggrandized themselves at the expense of the Poles. It has lately been said that this country will be honored with a king.

(The United States, Including Louisiana), a vague estimate. The population of the eighteen states is equal to about 12 persons to a square mile. Our revenue, derived from duties on imports, is constantly fluctuating, we have put it at 14 millions, being about what it would at this time amount to in a regular course of things. See the WEEKLY REGISTER passim.

'The Confederation of the Rhine' is an association of many petty kingdoms and states, brought about by France, with the chief view (it appears to us) of acting as a barrier to Austria, Russia, etc. and of otherwise aiding the emperor in his wars. See the general table, vol. 1, p. 24. Blanks are left in those places we could not fill up with satisfaction, at present. *When better information is afforded, we shall convey it to our readers, and they may complete the table with a pen.*

The phrase ("may complete the table with a pen") in the final paragraph above suggests that some, if not all, *Niles' Register* subscribers, did not discard their copies after reading them, but maintained them in their homes as personal libraries of sorts. Inconsistency of spelling, in those times, also has "Württemberg" as "Wirtemburg".

Article 5. (April 23, 1814, page 136):

Intoxicated with victory, the allies took the proffered bribe and entered *France*. Already were some of its beautiful provinces subjected to the barbarisms of the *Cossacks*, and humanity bled at every pore, ravishment and robbery, and all the horrors of savage warfare, desolated their country. Parties of them had approached nigh into Paris, and that great city was destined to incalculable woes, and utter destruction! In the mean time, Napoleon collected in himself and assured of the fidelity of the people, was calmly adopting his measures to collect and furnish an army to punish the *invaders*. When the fulness of time had come, he put himself at the head of his people, who with 'patriotic' enthusiasm rushed to his standard, victory perched upon it, and the spoilers are discomfited in every quarter!

On the 22nd there arrived in Paris 4,000 prisoners, Bavarian and Wirtembergers, these with other bodies of prisoners, not particularly mentioned, makes the whole amount of prisoners sent to Paris, 14,000 Russians, and 4,000 others, within a few days. Many smaller affairs had taken place very destructive to the allies, who have sustained immense losses. The French peasantry, roused to desperation by the conduct of the Cossacks, have made their nation's business their own individual concern, and fallen on and destroyed the small parties of the allies on all occasions.

With Napoleon Bonaparte's retreat from Moscow and finally to Paris with Russian forces in hot pursuit, ordinary French men and women had experienced the terror of having Cossacks attacking their towns and villages as here depicted by Peter von Hess, a soldier in the Prussian forces allied with Russia, in what he described as Cossacks of the Don River taking a French village by surprise. The Cossacks were hated in France. Please remember Niles' Register never used illustrations, but this book does.

Article 6. (April 30, 1814, pages 141-146):

In this issue of *Niles' Weekly Register*, Hezekiah Niles departed from the near-universal adulation of Czar Alexander I (1801-1825), whom Russians termed to be "Alexander the Blessed," the God-fearing Russian Orthodox Christian savior of Europe for defeating a godless Napoleon Bonaparte, and who then had ordered Russian troops to occupy Paris, had been greeted personally in London by Britain's monarch, and had received an honorary degree from Oxford University for his service to humanity! As such, Niles wrote a lengthy, critical anti-Russian rebuttal, essentially what we deem in the 21st century to be an op-ed, titled, "The Russians and the Cossacks," appearing in the pages of the April 30, 1814 issue of the *Niles' Weekly Register* that began the process which provided some three decades of his personal campaign to provide his American readers, as my research for this study and book substantiates, with a more informed view of Russia in all its aspects and, to his lasting credit, of Russia's decades-long sustained victimization of Poland in particular.

Of special note for this particular article, I have placed in my transcription, all footnotes included in the original lengthy article, using the method introduced in *Article 1*, where they appear just prior to and in brackets* [* etc.], rather than parentheses, in the body of the text immediately after the sign (i.e., asterisk sign: *), used for the footnote -- rather than at the bottom of the page which the structure of my book precludes. Finally, words appearing in the original text, spelled in the manner of the times (e.g., *wizzard* rather than wizard), serve as a reminder throughout my transcriptions of words to illustrate the manner in which the English-speaking world of the United States spelled them during the period 1811-1849.

The Russians and the Cossacks.

If Ovid were living in these our days, he might relate to future ages transformations more strange than any that he so fancifully described: and the new metamorphoses would have this advantage over the old, and hosts of contemporary writers would support the wondrous stories he might sing in sweet hexameter. He would relate how the 'Anti-Christ' and 'whore of Babylon,' (The reader will please to observe that these are the petty names that the *English* priests call the *Pope*, against whom or whose religion I prefer no censure, further that it is, like that of England, connected with the state.), for whose downfall *forty* or *fifty thousand* pensioned *English* priests prayed most mightily, from generation to generation, Sundays and Holidays, 'years in and years out,' and to which the people said 'Amen,' was, by the mere force of his opposition to the great wizard Napoleon, suddenly converted into a venerable and excellent old gentleman, 'the bulwark of religion, liberty and law!' And how that George Guelph, whose coronation oath and bigotry, refused and *refuses to his own subjects* the free exercise of the *Roman Catholic religion*, was, by the same wizard, metamorphosed into the great champion for *that* religion at *Rome*, where his guards done duty to protect the person and powers of the Supreme Pontiff, late the 'Anti-Christ,' for whose destruction the priests *yet* called as lustily as ever!

He might elegantly describe how the force of the same opposition to Napoleon, transformed the *'French sergeant and revolutionary cut-throat,'* Bernadotte, into a great, magnanimous and high-minded prince, the honor and pride of the north, and *prop of order* and *morality in Europe!*

He would then tell of the changes of the people of *Spain** [*The Editor believes that the condition of the people of Spain has been ma-

34

terially altered for the better, in *consequence* of the recent events, and hopes that they have shaken off many of the despotisms of the *church* and state. To *Spain*, as to all other countries, he wishes freedom, not from *France* to be under *England*, or *vice versa*, but real *independence*.]; and shew how the inquisition became the stav of 'liberalism' and relate that the weak-minded *Ferdinand* was turned into the most wise and enlightened prince: and what is more strange, he would, perhaps, have to say, that he was turned back again to his original state by the said wizzard *Napoleon*.

But time would fail to recapitulate all the transformations that he might record: suffice it to say, that angels would be turned into devils, and devils into angels, in the exact proportion, and from the circumstance alone, of their adherence with or opposition to, the mighty necromancer! Nay, that so powerful was the influence of his charms, that even those who took no part for or against him, were made into satyrs, hydras and furies! But we wish to be serious and invite attention to the facts and remarks below. *Let us look truth in the face and see things as they are.*

The sight might be displeasing to some, and they may rage and foam at it, but their froth is like the rain and the wind that assailed the good man's house, who had laid his foundation on a rock; and all I have to desire is, that, instead of *scolding*, they would *refute*; 'make a book,' as *Job* said. 'O, that mine enemy would write a book!'

Except at those *particular* times when *Russia* has been allied with *Great Britain*, she has been universally regarded as but one step removed from barbarism. This character, as it respects the mass of her population, is the testimony of all travelers whose works I have seen, and of the English especially: and of the *Cossacks*, every one speaks of as hordes of robbers; brave, it is true, but savage and unjust; and, in their general manners, but little milder than some of the Indians of North America. These may be unpleasant expressions to some who, by splendid processions, long speeches, and great feasts have celebrated the victories of this people, as tending to *civilize* the world and to re-establish *order and law*, but that they are not the less just on that account. I gladly admit that *Russia* has produced a few splendid characters, and that she has many subjects that would do honor to any country; as also that at *St. Petersburg*, and, perhaps, in some other places, society may be considered as enlightened and humane; but the fact is indisputable, that the world cannot furnish a body of people more ignorant, more brutal, more slavish -- I do not except even the inhabitants of *Africa*, the despised negro of the burning zone. The people of *Russia* are slaves -- miserable slaves, subject to the caprice of a master in all cases of persons or property; even the females, married or single, being liable to the lusts of their lords! It is with pleasure I remark, that the condition of the *Russian peasant* is apparently ameliorating; *still he is a slave, and sold and transferred with the soil he inhabits, like the blacks of the West Indies or of the southern states.** [*With these people, a separate race of men, fastened upon us by the 'religion' and 'humanity' of *Great Britain, our republican institutions are certainly disgraced: we are so situated that, as we cannot easily incorporate them into our society, we must bear with and hope for a gradual diminution of the evil, in which considerable progress is made.* But they are far better off than the peasantry of *Russia* and have as much intelligence.]

> With his remarks about the source of slavery in the United States, Hezekiah Niles revealed his own life-long adherence to, and support for, abolitionism in the early American Republic.

The spirit of government is savage, as may be seen in the manner of punishing criminals. Take the following example. Let no one object to it, because it was written by a *Frenchman*, for, notwithstanding, it is true; and I, at least, may be excused for using it, since Dr. Morse has accepted it. (See *Morse's Universal Geography*, II, p. 75.)

A particular account of the manner in which the knout was inflicted on a Russian is given in Mons. L'Abbe Chappe D'Auteroche's journey into Siberia. Madame Lapouchin was one of the finest women belonging to the court of the empress Elizabeth, and was intimately connected with a foreign ambassador then engaged in a conspiracy; this lady, therefore, being suspected of being concerned in it, was condemned by the empress Elizabeth, to undergo the punishment of the knout. She appeared at the place of execution in a genteel undress, which contributed still to heighten her beauty. The sweetness of her countenance and vivacity were such as might indicate indiscretion, but not even the shadow of guilt; although I have been assured by every person of whom I have made inquiry, that she was really guilty. Young, lovely, admired, and sought for at the court, of which she was the life and spirit, instead of the number of admirers her beauty usually drew after her, she saw herself surrounded only by executioners. She looked on them with astonishment, seeming to doubt whether such preparations were intended for her. One of the executioners then pulled off the kind of cloak which covered her bosom; her modesty taking the alarm, made her start back a few steps, she also turned pale, and burst into tears. Her clothes were soon stripped off, and in a few moments she was naked to the waist, exposed to the eager looks of a vast concourse of people profoundly silent. One of the executioners then seized her by both hands, and turning half round, threw her on his back, bending forwards, so as to raise her a few inches from the ground: the other executioner then laid hold of her delicate limbs, with his rough hands hardened at the plough, and without any remorse, adjusted her on the back of his companion, in the properest posture for receiving the punishment. Sometimes he laid his large hand brutally upon her head, in order to make her keep it down; sometimes like a butcher going to slay a lamb, he seemed to soothe her, as soon as he had fixed her in the most favorable attitude. This executioner then took a kind of whip, called knout, made of a long strap of leather prepared for this purpose; he then retreated a few steps measuring the requisite distance with a steady eye: and leaping backwards, gave a stroke with the end of the

whip so as to carry away a strip of skin from the neck to the bottom of the back; then striking his feet against the ground, he took his aim for applying a second blow parallel to the former; so that in a few moments all the skin of her back was cut away in small slips, most of which remained hanging to the shift. Her tongue was cut out immediately after, and she was directly banished into Siberia. In 1762 she was recalled from banishment by Peter III.'

Matvei Ivanovich Platov, Hetman of the Cossacks (painting by George Dawe)

The history of *Russia* is the history of murders and outlawry. '*Catherine the Great*' murdered her husband, assassinated prince *Ivan*, the 'legitimate heir' of the throne, and 'usurped' the government. The infamous strumpet took to her bed the villains who done the first deed of horror, and lived her reign in open whoredom; and she had, as it were, a regiment of male prostitutes* [*whom she made princes and generals] to satisfy her lusts; but to these degraded wretches, the *nobility of Russia* (the Corinthian 'capitals' of society), as *Edmund Burke* called that class of imposters, humbly paid their court. The manner in which these prostitutes were selected shews the niceties of the empress on such occasions, and is deserving a place in this sketch. It is It is furnished by a gentleman of acknowledged worth, Mr. Tooke:

'When her majesty had fixed her choice on a new favorite, she created him her grand general aid-de-camp, in order that he may accompany her everywhere without reproach or observation. Thenceforward the favorite occupied, in the palace, an apartment beneath that of the empress, to which it communicated by a private staircase. The first day of his installation he received 100,000 rubles, and every month he found 12,000 on his dressing table. The marshal of the court was commissioned to provide him a table of 24 covers, and to defray all the expenses of the household. The favorite attended the empress on all parties of amusement: at the opera, at balls, promenades, excursions of pleasure and the like, and was not allowed to leave the palace without permission. He was given to understand that it would not be taken well if he conversed familiarly with other women; and if he went to dine with any of his friends, the mistress of the house was always absent.

Whenever the empress cast her eyes on one of her subjects, in the design of raising him to the post of favorite, she caused him to be invited to dinner by some lady of her confidence, on whom she dropped in as if by chance. There she would enter into discourse with the newcomer, with a view to discover whether or not he was worthy of the favor she designed to grant him. When the judgement she formed was favorable, the confidant was informed of it by a significant look, and took care to notify it to him who had the honor to please. The day following he received a visit from the physician of the court, who came to inquire into the state of his health: and the same evening he accompanied the empress at the hermitage, and took possession of the apartment that had been prepared for him.

It was on the selection of Potemkin that these formalities began: and since that time, they have been constantly observed.

When a favorite had lost the power of making himself agreeable, there was also a particular manner of giving him his dismission. He received orders to travel; and from that moment he was debarred all access to her majesty. But he was sure of finding, at the place of destination, recompences worthy of the munificent Catherine.'* [*Plato Zuboff, an officer of the horse guards, supplied his place as the 'favorite' of the empress.] This aspiring young man, not content with wealth and honors, affected public employments: and *it is asserted that the idea of the second division of Poland originated with him.* In a short time, he became omnipotent at Petersburg. He was decorated with the title of Prince; received the post of grand master of the artillery; all the admirals, generals, and ministers of the empire were to be seen at his levee bending lowly before him; and, if we are to believe the author of a work of some reputation, paying their compliments at the same time, in great form, to his favorite monkey.]

These prostitutes cost the people of Russia, in the space of thirty-four years, the enormous sum of 88,820,000 rubles; a greater amount, perhaps, than the abominable hag spent on the public works which have rendered her *'immortal!'* It is admitted, that during her government, from various causes, the arts were cultivated, and some considerable improvement made in the situation of the peasantry; but still she was a *Jezebel* that should have been cast to the dogs. To the five brothers of the name of *Orloff*, who done the double service of murdering her husband and gratifying her lust, she gave, among other things, *forty-five thousand peasants*: that is, forty-five thousand *men, women and children, Russians*, for SLAVES! Thus she gave to the rest; and from 120 to 150,000 Russians became the property (more so than our negro slaves are) of the vile creatures that had submitted to her embraces, several of whom were as mere brutes with the human form.* [*Suppose that the *duke of York* could have bestowed on *Mary Ann Clark*, eight or ten thousand Englishmen, with their wives and children, and confer them as absolute property in the said hussey, what would we think of it? Of one of *Catharine's* prostitutes the following story is told, and I know no reason why it may not be believed. Like other great men, he thought he should have a library -- his direction to the bookseller was in this manner -- 'as to the books I am not particular (he could not read), but put them up as the empress has them, big books at the bottom, *little* books at the top!'] She possessed considerable talents, but was regardless of every law of God or man that stood in the way of her ambition or lechery, both which were insatiable. She was succeeded by her son *Paul*, a savage or a madman; or, perhaps, both. He, however, did one good thing: he had the bones of his father, Peter, taken up, and buried in great state; causing those who had slain him (yet great personages at court!) to attend as chief mourners! Paul, by turns, was for and against France; and the allies becoming very weary of his freaks, he also was murdered, as was anticipated in London. The 'amiable Alexander' succeeded; and because little or no enquiry was made into the assassination of his father, and from the circumstances that those who were supposed to have been the assassins frequented the court, he has not escaped the suspicion of moral parricide.

Such is the religion, the morality and order of the Russian government. Nor is the political history of Russia less disgusting. That mighty empire is immediately composed of conquered countries, usurped provinces, and ravaged territories. Of Poland it is hardly necessary to speak; everyone knows that the kingdom was, while at peace with them, partitioned by the 'magnanimous' Russians, Austrians and Prussians; they who are fighting for the 'integrity of kingdoms' and the 'liberties of Europe!' (See the note at the end.) Catherine also seized Cortland, drove out the reigning prince, and conferred the dukedom on one of her prostitutes. She quarreled with the Turks, and with every neighbor she had, that she might get more territory, and avowed and gloried in the design of extending her scepter to the Bosphorus, though she had a country under her control equal in extent to all Europe. All the conquered countries Alexander still holds in slavery; yet he is the preserver of the 'freedom of mankind!'

The government of Russia is a government of horror. Everything is made to bend to the will of the emperor, or the caprice of those in whom he confides. Read the following, furnished by a distinguished Englishman, William Eaton, Esq. Many like incidents occurred:

'While I was in the quarantine on the Russian frontier, in September, 1778, there passed 75,000 Christians, obliged by the Russians to emigrate from the Crimea, of whom 35,767 were males. The Armenian women, who came from Kaffa, were more beautiful, and I think approached nearer that perfect form, which the Grecians have left us in their statues, than the women of Tino. These people were sent to inhabit the country abandoned by the Nogai Tartars, (on its being conquered by the Russians), near the west coast of the sea of Azof; but the winter coming on before the houses for them were ready, a great part of them had no other shelter from the cold than what was afforded them by holes dug in the ground, covered with what they could procure: they were people who all came from comfortable homes, and the greatest part of them perished; seven thousand only were alive a few days ago! Other colonies had no better fate, owing to the bad management of those who were commissioned to provide for them, and not the climate.

The villain-king of Prussia, by forcing the Polanders to receive an adulterated coin, which he had made for the purpose, gained at the lowest calculation, seven millions of dollars by the maneuver. 'Having, (says Guthrie) stripped the country of money and provisions, his next attempt was to thin it still more of its inhabitants. To people his own dominions at the expense of Poland had been his great aim: for this purpose he devised a new contribution: every town and village was obliged to furnish a certain number of marriageable girls; the parents to give, as a portion, a feather bed, four pillows, a cow, two hogs, and three ducats in gold. Some were bound hand and foot, and carried off as criminals. His exactions from the abbeys, convents, cathedrals, and nobles, were so heavy, and exceeded at last their abilities so much, that the priests abandoned their churches, and the nobles their lands. These exactions continued with unabated rigor, from the year 1771 to the time the treaty of partition was declared, and possession taken of the provinces usurped. From these proceedings it would appear that his Prussian majesty knew of no rights but his own; no pretensions but those of the house of Brandenburg; no other rules of justice but his own pride and ambition.' Russians were even more severe on the Poles than the Prussians, terror preceded and followed their movements. Austria behaved the best; yet she must be regarded as a principal in the whole iniquity.]

These are the Russians and their government. The Cossacks are even worse: their business is robbery, their trade destruction. Nothing is sacred, nothing is inviolable, that is within their power. With more freedom than the Russians, they are more blood thirsty and cruel. Platoff, a great man among them, offered his daughter, with a large dowry, to anyone that would assassinate (mind, the word is ASSASSINATE) Bonaparte. There is nothing to surprise us in these notions of Platoff: but that he should be applauded for them at a public feast at Edinburg,* [*See Weekly Register, vol. IV, page 144] the capital of the enlightened kingdom of Scotland, (where the people are so religious that they say grace by the hour, and will hardly brew beer on Saturday lest it should work on the Sabbath) merely shews us that.

To these brief outlines of the character of the Russian nations, we add the following testimonies of the people of France to establish the pretensions of the people to the reformation of society, and the re-establishment of order and law! They are from Paris papers, and chiefly extracted from 'official representations.'

Parties of Austrians and Cossacks reached Fontainbleu. The great business of the former was to check the barbarisms of the latter; yet they plundered everything. Many of these Tartars that were killed by the peasants were found to have eight or ten watches.

The municipal council of Sezanne say, 'We had the misfortune to be invaded by 2,000 Cossacks, no more safety for citizens, no more respect for women, robbery, rapes, horrid treatments, was the order of the day.'

The deputation of the city of Nogens represent, that the excesses there 'were not the work of a few stragglers,' the generals themselves personally plundered, they talked much of giving up Paris to pillage, and of sending the women to people the Russian deserts.

Apart from "giving up Paris to pillage," the fact that Cossack generals reportedly "talked much of sending the (French) women to people the Russian deserts" had been a readily well-known characteristic of the Cossack attitude toward women of Europe's far west (i.e., France) and near west (i.e., Poland), for whose bodies they both lusted and evidently needed simply to produce more children for perpetuating, what had been viewed by civilized Europeans, as the thoroughly unappealing and savage Cossack life-style at that time of history. Suwarrow, refers to Marshal Alexander Suvarov.

The deputation from Provine, after stating the exactions made, say, 'they assassinated peaceful inhabitants: quartered a mayor: put a child in the fire to obtain from its mother what they wanted; to satisfy their brutal passion, they violated in many places, girls and married women, one of whom was sixty years old, one who was pregnant, and who was brought to bed some moments after. They even entered on horseback and armed into the hospital, where they robbed and mangled all they found, they spread everywhere death and destruction.' They exulted in the hope of the glorious mischief that they would do at Paris!

The deputation from Chateau Thierry say, 'we come, our hearts overwhelmed with grief, to deposit in your bosom a faint sketch of the excesses committed in our unfortunate city during the short stay of our barbarous enemies'; then follows a long detail of horrors like the preceding.

The Cossack general Sacken, 'being wounded, was brought into a house, he there received the most assiduous attentions, some days afterwards this house was pillaged. The owner went to implore the protection of the general, but he refused it with sternness, and his only reply was this, To pillage, to burn, to violate, is the law of man.'

It is needless to continue the harrowing detail, such, with the burning of houses, etc. were the terrible incidents that everywhere occurred. But the peasantry, driven to desperation by their signal atrocities, exacted a special vengeance. They chased and pursued them in all directions, like mad dogs, and shot them down whenever opportunity offered. In the village of Yenne, it is said, they threw eighty of them, alive, into the flames of the houses, that they themselves had kindled!

What would have been the fate of Paris, may be imagined by what occurred at Praga and Ismail, where the brutal Suwarrow commanded; the wretch that was toasted in Philadelphia, and many other places in the United States some years ago, by baccanalian assemblages of persons assuming the pompous appellation of the 'friends of religion, liberty and law.' The following is a brief account of what the Russians did at these places:

On the 4th of November 1791[sic], the Russians, 50,000 strong, attacked Praga, the suburb of Warsaw.

'After a severe conflict of eight hours, the resistance on the part of the Poles ceased; but the massacre of the sanguinary Suwarrow continued for two hours longer; and the pillage lasted till noon on the following day. Five thousand Poles were computed to have been slain in the assault; the remainder were either imprisoned or dispersed.

The citizens were compelled to lay down their arms; and their houses were plundered by the merciless Russians, who, after the battle had ceased nearly ten hours, about nine o'clock at night set fire to the town, and again began to massacre the inhabitants. Nine thousand persons, unarmed men, defenceless women, and harmless infants, perished either in the flames or by the sword, and nearly the whole of the suburb was reduced to ashes. In the whole of this surge it is computed that not less than 30,000 Poles lost their lives.'

Alexander Suvorov (artist unknown)

Ismail was taken by Suwarrow by storm, December 22, 1790, after a gallant defence. The whole garrison, stated at thirty thousand men, and indeed all the inhabitants, were abandoned to the fury of the brutal soldiery, and the whole were massacred in cold blood.

'Such are thy Gods, O Israel,' Such the idols that perverted heads and weak minds have raised up to reform mankind, and rescue society from barbarism.

Suppose, some Frenchman were vile enough to offer the body of his daughter, with a large dowry, as reward to anyone that would ASSASSINATE the Prince Regent of England, and that at a public table in Baltimore, the mayor of the city presiding, the health of that young lady should be given as a toast, with a wish that she might soon have a husband on the condition specified; and that the toast should be received with 'rapturous applause' by the company. What would those who have held 'Cossack' festivals in the United States say and think of the mayor of Baltimore?

The fact that Hezekiah Niles referenced "Cossack festivals" having been held in the United States at the time was a stunning piece of information that I would never have known occurred, if I hadn't undertaken to work on this book. Those festivals assuredly caught the attention of the Russian Legation in Washington City -- now Washington, DC -- whose Minister (i.e., Ambassador) Andrei Yakovlevich Dashkov, who had served in that capacity from 1808 to 1817, must have happily informed Czar Alexander, via a special courier, of that unprecedented Russian public relations coup in the United States.

This question has been asked in the Register but is repeated for the special use of the concerned, and I pray them to attend to it. *Platoff, the Russian Cossack*, offered his daughter to an assassin of Napoleon, the young lady's 'speedy marriage' was toasted by the Provost and *Scotch Cossacks* at Edinburgh, and he, old *Platoff*, who offered this bribe of *assassination*, has been enthusiastically toasted by the *Cossacks of the United States*, in their late festivals."

Suppose that *Tecumseh* had offered his darling daughter, with a thousand human scalps for her dowry, to anyone who would steal into Mr. *Madison's* chamber and tomahawk him in his sleep, and a body of Christian people should toast the early nuptials of that lady, would we believe them to be *'bulwarks of religion?'*

The Madison referenced in the final paragraph above was James Madison, the fourth President of the United States, who had served in that capacity from 1809 to 1817.

As the great political parties of the United States affect to view the successes of France and England (i.e., the allies) in reverse lights, as leading to the peace and prosperity of this republic, and as one party, by splendid processions and speeches and orations (nineteen newspaper columns long) and luxurious feasts, have celebrated the freezing to death of tens of thousands of Frenchmen in Russia if the other party were, in like manner, to rejoice at the burning to death of eighty Russians in France, caught in the act of conflagrating the dwellings of the peaceable inhabitants, what would we say to it? Yet the latter might be done with at least as much propriety as the former.

44

As Reported in the "Niles' Register"

Suppose some horrid Winnebagoe, a veteran in the work of death, were to proceed to Paris, and there, in his proper costume, with the dreadful tomahawk in his belt that had been sunken into the sculls of fifteen Americans were paraded round the city seated by the mayor, that he were feasted at the great hotel, and greeted with huzzahs wherever he went, and that the ladies, as well as the gentlemen, should admire the savage, and particularly admire his tomahawk, what would we say of the civilization of the good people of Paris? Yet, gentle reader, thus was a Cossack received, caressed and treated in London, armed with a spear with which he said he had put fifteen Frenchmen to death.

From the French countryside to the "City of Lights," the fact of Napoleonic forces, in the final analysis, having been defeated principally by the forces of Russia is depicted here as its Czar Alexander I (1811-1825) entered Paris by way of the Arch of Triumph, preceded by his deadly Cossack cavalry regiments. The fact of Russian forces having occupied Paris as well as France in 1814 had been a sobering reality for the nations of Western Europe throughout the first half of the 19th century when Poland had hoped that Great Britain and/or France would send their armies to fight alongside Poland's freedom fighters against Imperial Russia.

This article has extended a great length, and yet much more might be profitably said on the subject. I will only add, God help the world when religion, order, and law are to be supported by Russians. Yet, there are many traits of character in the Russians that I admire; and I esteem Alexander as the best man that wears a crown in Europe. But, bad is the best.

45

I have spoken plainly. I have no enmity to Russia or love for France. I wish them to be and remain, great, powerful and prosperous empires; yet do I rejoice most heartily that the British scheme for the partition of France has failed, and that the invaders have paid the forfeit of their crimes. To my countrymen, who hate France so unmercifully or love England so heartily, as to have forgotten their moral and American character in the celebrations of the premature death of tens of thousands of Frenchmen and in applauding the Cossacks, I recommend a calm and dispassionate perusal of this article, that they may be blessed in knowing themselves.

'O would kind heaven the giftie gie us,
To see ourselves as others see us.'

Note: In 1764, the empress of Russia transmitted to the court of Warsaw an act of renunciation, signed with her own hand, and sealed with the seal of the empire, in which she declares, 'that she did by no means arrogate to herself, her heirs or successors, or to the empire any right or claim in the districts or territories which are actually in possession, or subject to the authority of the kingdom of Poland, or great duchy of Lithuania; but that on the contrary, her said majesty would guarantee to the said kingdom of Poland and duchy of Lithuania all the immunities, lands, territories, and districts, which the kingdom and duchy ought by right to possess, or did now actually possess; and would at all times, and forever maintain them in full and free enjoyment thereof, against the attempts of all and every one who should, at any time, or, on any pretext, endeavor to dispossess them of the same.' In the same year did the king of Prussia, sign, with his own hand, an act, wherein he declared, 'that he had no claims, formed no pretensions on Poland, or any part thereof; that he renounced all claims on that kingdom, either as a king of Prussia, elector of Brandenburg or duke of Pomerania.' In the same instrument he guarantees in the most solemn manner, the territories and rights of Poland against every power whatever. The empress queen of Hungary so late as the month of January 1771, wrote a letter with her own hand to the king of Poland, in which she gave him the strongest assurances, 'that her friendship for him and the republic was firm and unalterable; that the motions of her troops ought not to alarm him; that she had never entertained a thought of seizing part of his dominions, nor would even suffer any other power to do it.' From which, according, to the political creed of princes, we may infer, that to guarantee the rights, liberties, and revenues of a state, means to annihilate those liberties, seize upon those rights, and appropriate those revenues to their own use. Such is the faith of princes.

[Guthrie.]

As noted, 'Guthrie' was none other than Hezekiah Niles. Interestingly, after having described, in the foregoing article of April 30, 1814, the November 4, 1794 Russian and Cossack massacre of Poles in Praga, as having occurred on November 4, 1791, which I speculate had been an example of a proverbial 'typo' of his typesetter where the final digit was set in error as 1 rather than 4, Hezekiah Niles continued to relate the theme of that episode of Russian barbarity and depravity, with the year corrected from 1791 to 1794, by describing the Suvarov-led Russian slaughter of Poles in Warsaw, as was to be reported below nearly twelve years later in the Niles' Weekly Register of December 2, 1826, pages 223-224 as follows:

"The barbarities of the Turks and the prospect still held out that Russia, coveting more territory would assault them, has brought the recollection of the doings of the Russians in Poland. Warsaw was gallantly defended, but 10,000 men could not hold out against 50,000, the city was taken and the people laid down their arms. In the following night, ten hours after all resistance had ceased, orders were given to fire the town and massacre all men, women and children, who attempted to flee the flames. It was done, nine thousand persons were burnt or butchered, and the 'holy men' of Russia sung te Deums because of the slaughter, of which the hell-bound Suwarrow was the agent of his barbarian government. The Turks have never went beyond this, and it was Christians murdering Christians."

Clearly, by way of his op-ed article, "The Russians and the Cossacks." Hezekiah Niles, a well-read and informed, erudite man, let it be known where he stood in the matter of the role of Russia in the affairs of Europe, and as well, given the "Cossack festivals" held in the United States marking the fall of Napoleon Bonaparte, driven by the careless, uninformed minds of other Americans who had been influenced by British propaganda against Napoleon about which Niles cautioned his fellow Americans, merits repetition in closing for 21st century American admirers of Vladimir Putin of the Russian Federation:

"To my countrymen, who hate France so unmercifully or love England so heartily, as to have forgotten their moral and American character in the celebrations of the premature death of tens of thousands of Frenchmen and in applauding the Cossacks, I recommend a calm and dispassionate perusal of this article, that they may be blessed in knowing themselves."

That statement alone, in many respects, as it related to Russians and the Cossacks, could be held to have represented one of Hezekiah Niles' major purposes, among a good many others, for his having created and directed the purposeful course for the Niles' Register throughout his service as its Editor (1811-1839), and indeed for his three successors until 1849 as well.

"Some horrid Winnebagoe" refers to the Winnebago Indian tribe.

Finally, as it pertains to Hezekiah Niles' closing inclusion of the ostensibly odd quotation: "O would kind heaven the giftie gie us…," had been taken from a poem written in 1786 in the Scottish dialect by Robert Burns (1759-1796), the national poet of Scotland, that had been titled, "To a Louse, On Seeing One on a Lady's Bonnet at Church," wherein the Scottish expression, giftie gie us, in English translation meant "give us the gift."

Article 7. (December 10, 1814, page 220):

With respect to Poland, no person can be sanguine enough to expect, that it will be restored to independence during the present order of things. The partitioning of Poland will form an important part of the discussions to take place at the approaching congress. A report has been circulated, that the emperor Alexander has some intentions of erecting it into an independent kingdom, under a Russian prince; and were this accomplished, Poland would be but a vassal state of Russia; but the court of Vienna, it is said, will oppose this arrangement, and insist on the dismemberment of the territory. It is thus the allies give liberty to Europe; and when we reflect, that in Spain despotism in churches and state is restored in all its horrors, while continued inroads upon liberty are made in France, and the most ridiculous attempts are made to restore priest craft, and the exploded notion of divine right of kings, we cannot help saying that, *the liberties of Europe never appeared in a less thriving way.*

Here, the reference to "the approaching congress" concerned the Congress of Vienna (1814-1815), and the role that Russian Czar Alexander (1801-1825) was to play in the affairs of Europe as reflected in the disposition of once free and independent Poland prior to 1768.

Article 8. (January 14, 1815, page 320):

It is said that Poland is to be added to the dominion of Russia.

As the result of his personal interest in Poland's struggle to exist as a free and independent nation, and despite the improbabilities of that aspiration of the Poles succeeding, Hezekiah Niles employed every opportunity to keep Poland in the minds of his American readers of the *Niles' Weekly Register*, even though it may have been by way of a short phrase or simply in one free-standing sentence or paragraph, as was the case illustrated above in his January 14, 1815 issue wherein he stated an inescapable fact of realpolitik in Europe at that time.

Article 9. (March 25, 1815, pages 63 and 64):

Of the proceedings of the congress of Vienna, nothing is known. It is said, however, that it had reached its crisis. The grasping of Russia at Poland, and Prussia at Saxony is displeasing to the other powers, especially Austria, France and England, and it is stated that coolness existed among them.... London, Jan. 10. The Times, has today, attacked the emperor Alexander in the most violent terms. 'Occupied with the acquisition of Poland, the emperor does not find a moment's leisure to correct his tariff of duties; a tariff so contrary to the interest of English commerce....' The same paper gives a letter from Vienna, containing some very curious observations relative to the negotiation. 'France and Austria have both pressed the English ambassador to take steps of a violent nature against the plans of Russia relative to Poland: the result was an extreme coldness between Russia and England. France left us alone, opposed to the whole northern powers already irritated, and she may perhaps, now stipulate with Russia, for her own private views relative to Belgium'.

In the post-Napoleonic world, Austria -- the Empire that had colluded with Russia and Prussia for the final Partition of Poland in 1795 -- appealed, in concert with France, to the "English" ambassador to "take steps of a violent nature against the plans of Russia relative to Poland," clearly had been an eye-opener for Americans on matter of the perfidy and self-serving objectives of the uncontrolled autocratic divine right monarchs of Europe. Note as well that Austria had been one of the partitioning powers of Poland in two (1772 and 1795) of the three Partitions, the second one that it hadn't participated in having occurred in 1793, with Russia and Prussia participating in all three Partitions, of which Russia had been the driving force.

Article 10. (May 6, 1815, page 176):

The Russian army in Poland is ordered into Germany.

Articles 11 and 12. (June 24, 1815, pages 294 and 295):

Who does not recollect with how great an outcry Bonaparte was charged with ambition, for assuming the title of the king of *Italy*? But the emperor of Russia takes that of king of Poland without the latest hint of anything of the kind! Let the 'Cossacks' reconcile their conspiracy if they can. *I* always said that *all* the 'legitimates' were influenced by the *same* spirit, and the fact will soon appear that I was right. (page 294)

The emperor of Russia has erected into a kingdom that part of Poland which he occupied, re-united to the former duchy of Warsaw, and taken the title of king of Poland. (page 295)

Hezekiah Niles had expressed his opinion of Czar Alexander I of Russia in this issue.

Article 13. (July 1, 1815, page 318):

In this issue, *Niles' Weekly Register* reported on a plan to partition post-Napoleonic France at the Congress of Vienna that met from November 1814 to June 1815. This should come as no surprise insofar as Russia, Prussia and Austria, who as allies had fought successfully against Napoleon, also colluded earlier in 1772, 1793 and 1795 to partition Poland out of a free and independent national existence. France and Austria had always been dynastic adversaries for leadership in Europe, and as such, it also came as no great surprise that the idea of France being partitioned had been considered by the victorious powers that defeated Napoleon Bonaparte when they met in the Congress of Vienna. Imagine that, partitioning France. Clearly, France had no choice than to object to such an audacious and dangerous proposal.

Partition of France. We have seen many hints in the German papers of a new design to partition France, to serve her as the 'high allies' have done with Poland, Saxony, etc. The London Courier extraordinary of May 5, says, 'Prince Talleyrand, has, they say, endeavored to obtain from the congress, a declaration that the integrity of the French territory should be guaranteed; but no regard was paid to his representations'.

Article 14. (July 15, 1815, page 349):

It is understood that Alexander has not ordered a single soldier out of Poland. [I hope that the Poles will drive them out.]

As the terse news-brief above illustrates, Hezekiah Niles always expressed his support for the Polish cause and his disgust with Russia's treatment of Poland as he did in this issue of *Niles' Weekly Register*, and again in its issue of July 22, 1815, and did so again seven days later on July 29, 1815.

Article 15. (July 22, 1815, page 364):

During the zenith of Napoleon's mastery of Europe, he placed on the thrones of European nations rulers favorable to his plans for the Continent. Following his demise, all of his appointees were replaced by the "legitimate" monarchs that he had dispossessed. Poland's pre-Partition monarchy, however, had not been restored, not only because its last king, Stanisław August Poniatowski (who reigned from 1764 to 1795), died without legitimate issue, but largely because it was not in the interest of Russia, Prussia and Austria to restore a unified free and independent Poland.

A spirit of independence is up in Poland. May God grant her gallant people strength to expel their Russian, Prussian, and Austrian oppressors, a trio of knaves, that have parceled them out and treated them like cattle. 'Down with the tyrants' -- 'let the republic be *restored*, and the 'long agony' be over, in the annihilation of the 'legitimates'.

Article 16. (July 29, 1815, page 381):

"The emperor Alexander, in a letter to the president of the Polish Diet, announces his assumption of the title of the king of Poland, and that the kingdom would be united to his dominions by the bond of *its own constitution*. H. M. adds, that he has particular pleasure in making it known, that it is the unanimous decision of the powers assembled in Congress."

Please note that the reference to the initials "H. M" simply meant His Majesty.

Article 17. (October 21, 1815, page 132):

"Poland has cordially submitted to Russia, agreeably to the provisions of the great treaty of Vienna. Prince Sulkowski has laid the homage and oaths of the army of Poland at the feet of *Alexander,* as emperor of all the Russias and king of Poland."

The phrase, "all the Russias," implied the existence of the Great Russia, Little Russia and White Russia component parts of the Empire as conceived by Russia's rulers over the ages. The referenced Prince Antoni Paweł Sułkowski (1785 – 1836) had been a Napoleonic general and Polish Patriot.

Article 18. (December 9, 1815, page 260):

The essential facts-of-life reality of Poland's having been restored as the "Kingdom of Poland" where its King was also the Emperor of Russia, were described sarcastically.

Prince Antoni Paweł Sułkowski

The kingdom of Poland, it appears, is to have no diplomatic corps, nor ministers of foreign relations, and will have no ministry near courts of foreign powers. (This is the boasted independence which the magnanimous Alexander has been promising that unfortunate country. It is now nothing more than a province of Russia.)

Being the moving story of Polish soldiers, largely forced to serve after 1795 in the Russian army, which had defeated Napoleon and pursued him into France, where he abdicated in 1814. The Polish soldiers had been part of the Russian army of occupation in France, when they accidentally came across Tadeusz Kościuszko, where after 1796, he ventured to live in exile, among other places, that had been caused when in 1796 Czar Paul I (1796-1801) released Kościuszko from captivity in St. Petersburg, Russia's capital, and exiled him from Poland, forever. The episode of Polish soldiers coming across Kościuszko in France had been reported by Hezekiah Niles to Americans as follows:

Article 19. (February 3, 1816, page 403):

From M. H. M. Williams' *Narrative of Events in France*: A Polish regiment, forming part of the advanced guard of the Russian army, after expelling the French from Troyes, marched upon Fontainebleau. The troops were foraging in a neighboring village, and were about to commit disorders, which would have considerable loss to the proprietors, without benefit to themselves; such as piercing the banks, or forcing the sluices of some fish ponds. While they were thus employed, and their officers looking on, they were astonished to hear the word of command, bidding them to cease, pronounced in their own language, by a person in the dress of the upper class of peasants; they ceased their attempt at further spoliation and drew near the stranger. He represented to the troops the useless mischief they were about to commit and ordered them to withdraw. The officers coming up, were lectured in their turn, and heard with the same astonishment the laws of predatory warfare explained to them: 'When I had command of the army of which your regiment is a part, I punished very severely such acts as you seem to authorize by your presence; and it is not on those soldiers, but on *you* that punishment would have fallen.' To be thus tutored by a French farmer, in their own language, in such circumstances, and in such terms, was almost past endurance. They beheld the peasant at the same time taking off their hats and surrounding the speaker, as if to protect him, in case of violence; whilst the oldest among their own

53

soldiers, anxiously gazing on the features of the stranger, were seized with a kind of involuntary trembling. Conjured more peremptorily, though respectfully, to disclose his quality and his nature, the peasant, drawing his hand across his eyes to wipe off a starting tear, exclaimed, with a half stifled voice, 'I am Kosciusko!' The movement was electric. The soldiers threw down their arms, and, according to the custom of their country, covered their heads with sand. It was the prostration of the heart. On Kosciusko's return to his house in the neighborhood of this scene, he found a Russian military post established to protect it. The emperor Alexander, having learnt from M. de la Harpe, that Kosciusko resided in the country, ordered for him a guard of honor, and the country around his dwelling escaped all plunder and contributions. Kosciusko had withdrawn some years hence from the guilty world of Bonaparte, to cultivate a little farm, rejecting every offer made him by Napoleon, who had learnt to appreciate his worth. Kosciusko knew him well. I called him one day to bid him farewell, having read in the official paper of the drafting his address to the Poles on the subject of recovering his freedom, being named to the command of the Polish army by Bonaparte. Kosciusko heard me with a smile at my credulity; but on my shewing him the address with his signature, he exclaimed, 'This is all a forgery! Bonaparte knew me too well to insult me with any offer in this predatory expedition; he adopted this mode which I

General Tadeusz Kościuszko,
1746 - 1817 (Schweikert)

can neither answer nor recant, and which he attempted to color with the pretext of liberty. His notions and mine, respecting Poland, are as at great a distance, as are our sentiments on every other subject'.

Conspicuous in the story above, and revelatory of his guarded personality and ethical-moral inclinations, is Czar Alexander's alleged, but very likely, order that a Russian military guard of honor be detached so as to protect Kościuszko (most likely from Russian and Cossack forces than from any of the Poles) and the vulnerable French countryside surrounding his modest residence.

Article 20. (February 17, 1816, page 431)

It is stated that the emperor of Russia has ordered all the Russian troops out of Poland. This is really a 'deliverance'.

Article 21. (June 1, 1816, page 229)

Conformably to the wishes of the Polish army, the emperor of Russia has ordered a monument erected to the memory of prince Poniatowski, in Poland.

Article 22. (August 17, 1816, page 409)

The *monopoly of tobacco* in Poland, for 6 years, has been sold by the emperor of Russia for the sum of 800,000 Polish florins a year, something more than 200,000 dollars. As some may not exactly understand the nature of these contracts, we simply state, that the persons purchasing the monopoly of an article, have the exclusive right of dealing in that article, within the territory and for the time agreed upon. It is the most iniquitous and oppressive mode of raising a revenue ever yet adopted; and never can be permitted where the people are other than slaves.

Congress Poland in 1815 known also as the Kingdom of Poland (Królewstwo Polskie).

Article 23. (December 14, 1816, page 254):

The emperor of Russia reviewed 25,000 Polish troops at Warsaw on the 5th Oct..., and the resolution of the diet for a military conscription ['A HORRIBLE FRENCH CONSCRIPTION!'] is confirmed. The Polish regular army is to consist of 50,000 men, to be made up by drawing lots. It is, substantially, by *conscription* that the majority of all Europe is organized, but there is no sympathy if it be *legitimately* done. (German paper).

Moscow, Aug. 11 (O. S.), They say that the pious intention of the Emperor, to build at Moscow a magnificent temple to Christ the Redeemer has been already considered, and that it is resolved to put it into execution."

56

As reported above in the final paragraph, demonstrations of piety had characterized the life of Czar Alexander, likely having been caused, as some observers speculate, because while he had clear foreknowledge of his father's assassination in 1801, he did nothing to prevent it. His complicity in the act of parricide likely haunted his life, so much so, that following his own death in 1825, a legend manifested itself, in which he, as a penitent, became known as Fyodor Kuzmich, a wandering Russian Orthodox holy man, who performed many acts of Christian charity and personal contrition in Siberia, among Russia's native peasants and involuntary exiles, large numbers of whom had to have been of Polish lineage, and who lived in wretched poverty, disease and ignorance, the latter because of the deliberate absence of news of any sort, rather than intellectual ability. In the early 20th century, during the chaos of the Russian Revolution that occurred in World War I, at which time Czar Nicholas II (1896-1918) abdicated and was assassinated, along with his wife and children in July 1918 by the Bolshevik Communists, unruly Russian mobs allegedly broke into the Peter and Paul Cathedral of St. Petersburg that contained Alexander's sarcophagus, and upon opening it, they reportedly found it empty, a point that added credibility to the legend of Fyodor Kuzmich -- along with an episode that had occurred in 1921 under changed circumstances -- continues to engage the attention of some scholars and other researchers to this day.

Finally, pertaining to the date of the original source of the news-brief, "Moscow, Aug. 11 (O.S.)" implied that, whereas in 1582, Europe's Roman Catholic and Protestant countries replaced use of the "Julian calendar" with the "Gregorian calendar," the Russian Orthodox Church (and Eastern Orthodoxy in general) sustained adherence to the Julian Calendar which became known popularly as the "Old Style" (O.S.) calendar, which was some 13 days behind the Gregorian calendar.

Article 24. (March 8, 1817, page 30):

Every man, without distinction of rank, origin, or religion, is to perform military service as required by his master, the emperor of Russia, for the space of ten years, beginning at the age of 20 and ending with that of 30.

Article 25. (March 15, 1817, page 34)

> Hezekiah Niles again expressed his contempt for Czarina Catherine II of Russia.

The history of *Catherine* is too well known to require a detail here. Of an obscure beginning and a stranger in Russia, and placed near to the throne of her marriage to the 'Lord's anointed' -- she snatched, with blood-stained hands, the scepter from her *husband*, and 'lawful master,' and marched over his dead body to 'usurp' the 'legitimate authorities' of Russia, having also put out of the way all his relatives and adherents! We may admire the talents of this woman; yet a more ambitious, more wicked, more profligate creature, never lived. But *she*, of all persons in the world, ought to have been the last to hint at the killing of a king, or speak of the usurpation of a government, she had no claim whatever to the throne of Russia, except that built upon the true principle by which all thrones are supported: the bayonets of the soldiery, that she prostituted herself to debauch.

Article 26. (May 24, 1817, pages 206 and 207)

> Remembering the often-heard expression, "lost in translation," note that in this highly interesting news article, the referenced "archbishop of Gnesh" had been the archbishop of Gniezno, Poland.

THE POPE'S BRIEF.

To the editor of the *London Morning Chronicle*.

Sir -- Having observed in the morning paper of this day (April 10th), a loose translation of an important papal document, which will probably be quoted for generations to come, I send you a more literal version, together with the Latin itself, that you may compare them, and print the English for your readers. I am, etc., etc.

Translation of the bull against bible societies, issued June 20th, 1816, by Pope Pius VII, to the archbishop of Gnesh, primate of Poland.

As Reported in the "Niles' Register"

PIUS P. P. VII.

Venerable brother -- Health and apostolic benediction. In our last letter to you we promised, very soon, to return an answer to yours; in which you have appealed to this holy see, in the name of the other bishops of Poland, respecting what are called *bible societies,* and have earnestly inquired of us what you ought to do in this affair. We long since, indeed, wished to comply with your request, but an incredible variety of weighty concerns have so pressed upon us on every side, that, to this day, we could not yield to your solicitation.

We have been truly shocked at this crafty device, by which the very foundations of religion are undermined; and having, because of the great importance of the subject, conferred in council with our venerable brethren, the cardinals of the holy Roman church, we have, with the utmost care and attention, deliberated upon the measures proper to be adopted by our pontifical authority, *in order to remedy and abolish this pestilence as far as possible.* In the mean time we heartily congratulate you, venerable brother, and we commend you again and again in the name of the Lord, as it is fit we should, upon the singular zeal you have displayed under circumstances so dangerous to Christianity, in having denounced to the apostolic see, *this defilement of the faith so imminently dangerous to souls.* And although we perceive that it is not at all necessary to excite him to activity who is making haste, since of your own accord you have already shown an ardent desire to detect and overthrow the impious machinations of these innovators: *yet, in conformity with our office, we again and again exhort you, that whatever you can achieve by power, provide for by counsel, or effect by authority, you will daily execute with the utmost earnestness,* placing yourself as a wall for the house of Israel.

With this view we issue the present Brief, viz. that we may convey to you *a signal testimony of your approbation of the excellent conduct* and also may endeavor, therein still more and more to excite your pastoral solicitude and diligence. For the general good imperiously requires you to combine all your means and energies to *frustrate the plans, which are prepared by its enemies for the destruction of our most holy religion:* whence it becomes an episcopal duty, *that you first of all expose the wickedness of this nefarious scheme,* as you have already done so admirably, to the view of the faithful and openly publish the same, according to the rules prescribed by the Church, with all the erudition and wisdom which you possess; namely *'that the Bible printed by heretics, is to be numbered among other prohibited books, conformably to the rules of the Index* (Sec. No. 2 and 3), *for it is evident from experience, that the holy Scriptures, when circulated in the vulgar tongue, have through the temerity of men, produced more harm than benefit.* (Rule IV.) And this is the more to be dreaded in times so depraved, when our holy religion is assailed from every quarter with great cunning and effort, and the most grievous wounds are inflicted on the church. It is, therefore, *necessary to adhere to the salutary decree of the Congregation of the Index* (June 13th, 1757), *that no versions of the bible in the vulgar tongue be permitted, except such as are approved by the apostolic see, or published with annotations extracted from the writings of the holy fathers of the church.*

We confidently hope that, in these turbulent circumstances, the Poles will give the clearest proofs of their attachment to the religion of their ancestors; and by your care, as well as that of the other prelates of this kingdom *whom, on account of the faith we congratulate in the Lord,* trusting that they all may very abundantly justify the opinion we have entertained of them.

It is moreover necessary that you should transmit to us, as soon as possible, the bible that Jacob Wuick published in the Polish language with a commentary, as well as a copy of the edition of it lately put forth without those annotations, taken from the writings of the holy fathers of our church, or other learned Catholics, with your opinion upon it; that thus, from collating them together, it may be ascertained after mature investigation, that certain errors lie insidiously concealed therein, and that we may pronounce our judgment on this affair for the preservation of the true faith.

Continue, therefore venerable brother, to pursue this truly pious course upon which you have entered, viz. diligently to fight the battle of the Lord for the sound doctrine, and warn the people intrusted to your care, that they fall not into the snares which are prepared for their everlasting ruin. The church demands this from you as well as from the other bishops, *whom our rescript equally concerns;* and we most anxiously expect it, that the deep sorrow that we feel on account of *this new species of tares which an adversary has so abundantly sown,* may, by this cheering hope, be somewhat alleviated; and we always most heartily invoke the choicest blessings upon yourself and your fellow-bishops, for the good of the Lord's flock, which we impart to you and them by our apostolic benediction.

Given at Rome, at St. Mary the Greater, June 29, 1816, the 17th year of our Pontificate.

PIUS P. P. VII.

At first glance, what is remarkable about the Pope's letter (i.e., brief) is that neither did he ask about the condition of partitioned Poland and the suffering of its people, especially in the Russian-controlled Kingdom of Poland, nor did he offer prayers on their behalf, as well as for those under Prussian and Austrian rule. His sole concern had been the need to suppress the "Bible societies" among Poles. In short, he seemed to exhibit a purely "all business" approach to the task at hand, as one is initially surprised by, rather than engage in extending the slightest social niceties to the leader of the downtrodden Catholic faithful, whose ranks of parish priests were also being gradually decimated by Russian authorities, a process that would reach its zenith in 1833 when Russian Orthodox Church authorities introduced a Russian Orthodox state catechism for implementation in the Kingdom of Poland, as will appear in Article 196 later on in this book. The Pope could not have been uninformed about Russia's long-range plans to end the Roman Catholic faith in Poland. Yet to me, there seemed to be more than meets the eye in all of this.

Could the source of the bible societies have originated in St. Petersburg? Perhaps. An answer to that question, as Pius VII implies in the second opening paragraph, in the phrase, "excite him to activity who is making haste," raises yet another question. In short, was the hastener, the Russian Czar, the Austrian Kaizer, the Prussian Köenig, or Satan? Or all of them? (Please note that the word Czar in Russian and the word Kaizer in German were their linguistic versions of the Latin word, Caesar, which meant "Emperor." Unlike Russia and Austria which at the time had been Empires, Prussia in contrast had been only a Kingdom ruled by a King which in German translation had been Köenig.)

It clearly hadn't been the Roman Catholic priest Jakub Wujek (1541-1597) per se, referenced by the Pope as Wuick, who had been a Jesuit theologian and doctor of divinity, and in fact translated the Bible into Polish during his lifetime, but never advocated creation of "bible societies" which apparently were rising in the time of the pontificate of Pius VII (1800-1823). The spread of the bible societies most likely seem to have been, among other related initiatives, the opening stage of a thinly-veiled partial work of Imperial Czarist counter-intelligence activity designed to create havoc and weaken the authority of the Roman Catholic Church in Poland. Indeed, as my book progresses, it becomes readily documented that the objective of Imperial Russia under Czar Nicholas I (1825-1855), for example, had been, ultimately, the total "annihilation" of the Roman Catholic Church and Faith in Poland, along with Poland and its nationality. The process may have been set in motion years earlier, i.e., 1812. In that year, Czar Alexander actively supported creation of the "Russian Bible Society," the objective of which had been to establish one great European Christian family, "on a one shepherd, one flock basis," as the author, Svetoslav Manoilov of Sofia University in Bulgaria, states in his article, "Emperor Alexander I's Project for a United Christian Europe" (available online under the title as written, or by accessing www.ehlee.humnet.unipi.it/books5/3/02.pdf). The coincidence, in short, of the "bible societies" that appeared in Poland in 1816 or so, and Czar Alexander's earlier support in 1812 for the creation of the "Russian Bible Society," seem to have been more than a mere coincidence, at least in my opinion. Thus, the Pope's written concern about the problem of the bible societies in Poland, I propose, did in fact constitute "more than meets the eye," as the expression goes. Clearly, the Pope seems to have had access to credible intelligence about the objective of the "Russian Bible Society" as it may have been designed for implementation in Poland, an objective that had far greater implications than simply translating the Bible into the "so-called "vulgar tongues" of Europe, Poland included. The original readers of the article published at the time by Niles' Weekly Register, however, would not have known anything about the Russian Bible Society per se, but simply viewed the "bible societies" as having been an exclusively internal Polish Roman Catholic Church problem, and a benign one at that for Americans, when one considers that a Bible existed in virtually every Protestant Christian home in the United States.

Article 27. (July 26, 1817, page 345)

Was the Enlightenment-influenced, somewhat liberal-leaning Czar Alexander I (1801-1825) of Russia, the lesser or greater of three evils, with the other two being the repressive monarchs of Prussia and Austria?

An opinion begins to prevail in England that *Alexander* is not quite so 'magnanimous and disinterested' as they supposed he was. His movements are viewed with jealousy, but they dare not quarrel with him. He is silently marching to the mastery of continental Europe, if he does not already possess it. Turkey has quietly ceded to him the rich provinces of Moldavia and Wallachia, and it is understood that he wants a slice from Austria, which she will hardly refuse; *Poland* is his own, *Prussia* is a vassal state, and the *Bourbons* are his slaves. But we feel very little interest in these affairs, if *holy alliances* and *legitimate* kings are to prevail, we had rather that Alexander should be at the top of the wheel than any of the rest of them. He has more sense and virtue in his own person, perhaps, than the whole stock of all the rest of the legitimates, (not excepting the *learned* and *accomplished* Guelphs) would amount to, collected.

FRENCH IN RUSSIA: Mr. James, in his travels in Russia, gives the official return of the losses of the French army up to June, 1813, which amounted to: Killed and Wounded: 10 Generals; 144 Officers; 128,411 Privates. Prisoners: 52 Generals; 2,891 Officers; 186,250 Privates.

It is unlikely that Hezekiah Niles, never an admirer of Czar Alexander of Russia, had written the first news-brief. Perhaps he did, but we will never know for a fact, except for the sarcastic reference to the "learned and accomplished Guelphs" -- being the Hanoverian Germans of the royal line of Great Britain -- whom he also never held in high esteem. Of course, It may have been written in London beforehand by some anti-Hanoverian subject of the realm, but very unlikely, because the article concerned Czar Alexander of Russia, about whom Hezekiah Niles occasionally assigned positive credit where credit was due.

Article 28. (August 16, 1817, page 397)

The number of persons who have emigrated from Baden this year, is said to be 20,000, of whom about 2,000 have gone to Poland, and the remainder to North America. (They have not yet arrived.)

Article 29. (August 30, 1817, page 12):

Some Scotch families have emigrated to Poland....

Article 30. (September 6, 1817, page 26):

In this next news-brief, Hezekiah Niles correctly referenced the Scots as such, rather than referencing them as being the "Scotch" as he had referenced earlier on August 30, 1817.

A number of Scots have emigrated to Poland. By a decree of Alexander, they are exempt from military conscription.

Article 31. (September 13, 1817, pages 45 and 46):

The patent of the emperor of Austria has been published in Gallicia, for the establishment of a representative constitution in Gallicia, Lodomeria, and the Bukowine. This constitution is said to be the result of an agreement between the powers interested in the affairs of Poland, and under which also, all the states and provinces, heretofore forming part of that kingdom, are to have representative constitutions.

Article 32. (October 25, 1817, page 142)

> Progressively alarming specifics, in the milieu of what 21st century persons would deem to be a police-state, about the duties of the citizens of Breslau (known among pre-Partition Polish residents as Wrocław, that exists today as one of modern Poland's major cities), had been reported by Niles' Weekly Register.

Breslau, August 23. In consequence of a riot which took place on account of the arrest of some citizens, whom it was attempted to set at liberty, and respecting which the particular details are not known, the government issues a proclamation, as follows:

1. Every house-keeper must keep his door shut, nor suffer any of the inmates to go out without urgent necessity; and also to keep the windows shut.
2. Parents, teachers, masters, etc., take care that all persons under their care remain at home.
3. All public houses of every description to remain shut, and the sale of strong liquors not allowed on any pretext.
4. No more than three persons may stand together in the streets, nor, may single individuals stand still there. Whoever transgresses this order will be driven away by force of arms, and no regard paid to his life.
5. Every large collection of people will be dispersed by the unreserved employment of artillery.

Article 33. (November 1, 1817, page 157)

Russia. The emperor, with more than 100 distinguished guests of his Court, dined on the quarter deck of vice admiral Crown's ship at Cronstadt. Crown is a Scotchman, and second in command of the Russian navy. British writers, in many ways, manifest great jealousy at the power of Russia....

Prince Radzivil who sometimes unites the elegance of southern taste with the barbarous pomp of Sarmatia, once entered Warsaw in his carriage, *drawn by six white bears*, taken in his own Lithuanian forests, and completely broken and richly harnessed for the purpose. (London paper).

They write from Poland, that a forester, having heard that a reward of 500 florins was offered to any person who would kill a wolf which was the terror of the neighborhood, resolved to obtain it. This furious animal, accustomed during the late campaign, to live upon the dead bodies of soldiers, would not attack the flocks, but used to fly upon the shepherds and devour them. The forester took his child, only about two years old, and fastened it to a tree near his cottage, with a view to attract the animal, while he remained upon the watch with a musket. The wolf came, and was instantly killed; the infant sustained no injury, and the man claimed the reward. – *ib.*

Article 34. (November 11, 1817, page 331)

A London paper of Nov. 7, observes. -- It is said that the emperor Alexander means to revisit the Polish capital in the month of June next, when it is expected the promised constitution will be completed and a diet called together. What degree of liberty will be secured to the Poles under the forthcoming charter, remains to be ascertained, but let us hope for the credit of Alexander 'the Deliverer' -- that it will at least equal that guaranteed them by the institutions granted them by Bonaparte. The latter did more, during the short course of his rule, for the mass of the Polish people,

Prince Antoni Henryk Radziwiłł.

than all their *former* kings, with the exception of the unfortunate Poniatowski, had done. By one dash of his pen, he crumbled the whole superstructure of the feudal law. He broke the chain which for several centuries, had bound the leg of the peasant to the soil, and the humblest Pole, we mean of course the inhabitant of the Duchy of Warsaw, was equal, in the eyes of the law, to the proudest noble.

Article 35. (January 24, 1818, page 357)

Hezekiah Niles included this initial very brief report that United States Congressman William Henry Harrison (1773-1841) of Ohio had offered a resolution for consideration by his fellow House members to honor the memory of Tadeusz Kościuszko, the American and Polish hero and patriot, altruist and champion of freedom, independence, democracy and equality, and as well, as the patron saint of West Point, who had passed away in exile in Soleure, Switzerland on October 15, 1817.

On Tuesday, January 20..., Mr. Harrison offered the following resolution for consideration: 'Resolved, That a committee be appointed jointly with such committee as may be appointed by the senate, to consider and report what measures it be proper to adopt, to manifest the public respect for the memory of general Thaddeus Kosciusko, formerly an officer in the service of the United States, and the uniform and distinguished friend of liberty and the rights of man.' [Mr. Harrison introduced this motion by some feeling remarks on the subject of it, and by a review of the principal events of gen. Kosciusko's life.]

Article 36. (February 7, 1818, pages 383 to 385):

What follows below is the remarkable, and much larger, full-blown tribute to the memory of Tadeusz Kościuszko (1746-1817) that reveals the high esteem in which he was held by Americans at the time of his passing. The fact that Ohio's United States Congressman William Henry Harrison, a former United States Army Major General, member of the United States House of Representatives, future United States Senator, United States

As Reported in the "Niles' Register"

Ambassador to Colombia, and eventually the ninth President of the United States, wrote and spoke to the matter of what Hezekiah Niles, on February 7, 1818, termed to be a "very handsome tribute to the memory" of Kościuszko, is worthy of special note. On the other hand, the referenced, highly moving letter from Kościuszko to John Dickinson is held not to be universally authentic (whereas at the time it had been held to be fully authentic) by contemporary historians of our modern era, despite the fact that it had been written in a manner and content similar to others that Kościuszko had written during his lifetime. Although the matter of authenticity hadn't been known in 1818, 'his' views on life, freedom and government had been reflected in the letter. The article, did, moreover, importantly keep Poland's having been victimized by Russia, Prussia and Austria at the forefront of American public opinion at the time.

General Kosciusko.

We seem to owe an apology to our readers for having so long delayed the insertion of *Gen. Harrison's* very handsome tribute of respect to the memory of Kosciusko, a man that possessed in himself more great and estimable qualities than belong to the herd of *Bourbons* and *Guelphs*.

> 'It is a very easy thing
> To make a man a king
> But since the race of kings began,
> How hard to make a king a man! -- Pet. Pindar.'

During the ascendancy of the Holy Roman Empire (800 – 1806), the faction known as the Guelphs supported the Pope versus the faction known as the Ghibellines that supported the Holy Roman Emperor against the Pope in the internal politics of the Empire .

The following extracts of a letter from Kosciusko to the late John Dickinson, will be read with great satisfaction by those who have admired his character:

'November 1783

I have been constantly on the wing since I left you, my mind occupied by objects, and my body tired by the fatigues of travelling. I congratulate you on the *British* troops having evacuated *New York*.

But now, that you are perfectly quiet, and masters of your own abodes, what will you do? what will be your political views? what will be your domestic conduct? how far will your reciprocal jealousies extend? who will have powers to stop them? That public spirit, which distinguished you during the course of the revolution, will it last long against the prosperity of commerce, and the luxury that ever attends it, and against the insinuations of enemies that would *divide* you? I declare now to you, I think that there does not exist a country that can vie with you in flourishing prospects, know there is not one where man is more free, or where fortunes are more equal. In travelling thro' remote parts of your continent, I learn how to compare the lives of your farmers to those of the patriarchs. It is there that misery discovers the golden age. And a poor *European* finds means in settling there to change his slavery for liberty, his wants for ease. Scarcely he lives for two years, but his ideas *enlarge*, he becomes man, and *almost* citizen, he is forced to quit his habitudes, his prejudices, *and even his vices*, and to *take the sentiments* and *virtues of his neighbors*. Yes, I have there seen the subjects formerly of a bishop think freely on religion, and heard the natives of reason.

These are the notions that I have formed of your continent, if you have the goodness to relieve me in my doubts, you will add new favors to your former kindness. *As I have always my country in sight*, I go begging every where instructions, not for my satisfaction, *but to be able to fill honorably* one day *my task of citizen*.

When I think, dear sir, that with three millions of people, without money, you have shaken off the yoke of a people like *England*, and have acquired much extensive territory, and that *Poland* has suffered herself to be robbed of five millions of souls, and a vast country, I ask, what can be the reason of this difference?

But whilst we wait to recover our rights, have a care to preserve yours, and remember always the maxim of Cicero, *'respublica res est populi, cum autem injustus ipse populus, non jam vitiosa, sed omnino nulla respublica est.'*

Cicero's statement, possibly meaning, in free translation: "a commonwealth is the property of the people, but when its people themselves are unjust persons, who no longer see that, there is no commonwealth at all."

If the state of my country remains always the same, I will say to my *countrymen*, come, pass overs the seas, and insure to your children liberty and prosperity. If my countrymen do not listen to me, I will say to my *family*, come. If my family refuse, I will *go by myself and die free* with you.

Yet, though I shall be happy to see you, as that supposition is founded only on the bad fortune of my country, *may you never see again* your friend.'

The following were the observations of Mr. *Harrison*, on introducing the motion for honoring the memory of Kosciusko, on the 20th ult.

'The public papers have announced an event which is well calculated to excite the sympathy of every American bosom. Kosciusko, the martyr of liberty, is no more! We are informed that he died at Soleure, in France, some time in October last.

In tracing the events of this great man's life, we find in him that *consistency of conduct* which is the more to be admired as it is so rarely to be met with. He was not at the time the friend of mankind, and at another the instrument of their oppression; but he preserved throughout his career those noble principles which distinguished him in its commencement, which influenced him at an early period of his life to leave his country and his friends, and in another hemisphere to fight for the rights of humanity.

Kosciusko was born and educated in Poland, of a noble and distinguished family, a country where the distinctions in society are perhaps carried to greater lengths than in any other. His Creator had, however, endowed him with a soul capable of rising above the narrow prejudices of a caste, and of breaking the shackles which a vicious education had imposed on his mind.

When very young, he was informed by the voice of fame, that the standard of liberty had been erected in America, that an insulted and oppressed people had determined to be free, or perish in the attempt. His ardent and generous mind caught, with enthusiasm, the holy flame, and from that moment he became the devoted soldier of liberty.

His rank in the American army afforded him an opportunity greatly to distinguish himself. But he was remarked throughout his service, for all the qualities which adorn the human character. His heroic conduct in the field, could only be equaled by his moderation and affability in the walks of private life. He was idolized by his soldiers for his bravery, and beloved and respected by the officers for the goodness of his heart, and the great qualities of his mind.

Contributing greatly, by his exertions, to the establishment to the independence of America, he might have remained, and shared the blessings so dispensed, under the protection of a chief who loved and admired him, and in the bosom of a grateful and affectionate people.

Kosciusko, had, however, other views. It is not known that, until the period that I am speaking of, he had formed any distinct idea of what could, or indeed what ought, to be done for his own. But in the revolutionary war he drank deeply of the principles which produced it. In his conversation with the intelligent men of our country, he acquired new views of the science of government and the rights of man. He had seen too that to be free it was only necessary that a nation should will it, and to be happy it was only necessary that a nation should be free. And was it not possible to procure these blessings for Poland? For Poland, the country of his birth, which had a claim to all his efforts, to all his services? That unhappy nation groaned under a complication of evils which had scarcely a parallel in history. The mass of the people were the abject slaves of the nobles -- the nobles, torn into factions, were alternately the instruments and victims of their powerful and ambitious neighbors. By corruption, intrigue, and force, some of the fairest provinces had been separated from the republic, and the people, like beasts, transferred to foreign despots, who were again watching for a second dismemberment. To regenerate a people thus debased, to obtain for a country thus circumstanced, the blessings of liberty and independence, was a work as much difficulty as danger. But to a mind like Kosciusko's the difficulty and danger of an enterprise served as stimulants to undertake.

The annals of these times give us no detailed account of the progress of Kosciusko in accomplishing his great work, from the period of his return from America to the adoption of the *new* constitution of Poland, in 1791. This interval, however, of apparent inaction, was most usefully employed to illumine the mental darkness which enveloped his countrymen. To stimulate the ignorant and bigoted peasantry with the hope of future emancipation, to teach a proud but gallant nobility that true glory is only to be found in the path of duty and patriotism, interests the most opposed, prejudices the most stubborn, and habits the most inveterate, were reconciled, dissipated, and broken, by the ascendancy of his virtues and example. The storm which he had foreseen, and for which he had been preparing, at length burst upon Poland. A feeble and unpopular government bent before its fury and submitted itself to the Russian yoke of the invader. But the nation disdained to follow its example; in their extremity every eye was turned on the hero who had already fought their battles, the sage who had enlightened them, and the patriot who has set the example of personal sacrifices to accomplish the emancipation of the people.

Kosciusko was unanimously appointed generalissimo of Poland, with unlimited powers, until the enemy should be driven from the country. On *his* virtue the nation reposed with the utmost confidence, and it is some consolation to reflect, amidst the general depravity of mankind, the two instances, in the same age, have occurred, where powers of this kind were employed solely for the purposes for which they were given.

It is not my intention, sir, to follow the Polish chief throughout the career of victory, which, for a considerable time crowned his efforts. Guided by his talents, and led by his valor, his undisciplined, illy armed militia charged with effect the veteran Russian and Prussian: the mailed cuirassiers of the great Frederic, for the first time, broke and fled before lighter and appropriate cavalry of Poland. But to the discerning eye of Kosciusko, the light which it shed was that of a sickly and portentous appearance, indicating a storm more dreadful than that which he had resisted.

He prepared to meet it with firmness, but with means entirely inadequate. To the advantages of numbers, of tactics, of discipline, and inexhaustible resources, the combined despots had secured a faction in the heart of Poland. And if that country can boast of having produced its Washington, it is disgraced also by giving birth to a second Arnold. The day at length came which was to decide the fate of a nation and a hero. Heaven, for wise purposes, determined that it should be the last of Polish liberty. It was decided, indeed, before the battle commenced. The traitor Poninski, who covered with a detachment the advance of the Polish army, abandoned his position to the enemy, and retreated.

Kosciusko was astonished, but not dismayed. The disposition of his army would have done honor to Hannibal. The succeeding conflict was terrible. When the talents of the general could no longer direct the mingled mass of combatants, the arm of the warrior was brought to the aid of his soldiers. He performed prodigies of valor. The fabled power of Ajax, in defending the Grecian ships, was realized by the Polish hero. Nor was he badly seconded by his troops. As long as his voice could guide, or his example fire their valor, they were irresistible. In this unequal contest, Kosciusko was long seen, and finally lost to their view.

'Hope for season bade the world farewell,
And freedom shriek'd when Kosciusko fell.'

He fell covered with wounds, but still survived. A Cossack would have pierced his breast, when an officer interposed. 'Suffer him to execute his purpose,' said the bleeding hero, 'I am a devoted soldier of my country, and will not survive its liberties.' The name of Kosciusko struck to the heart of the Tartar, like that of Marius upon the Cimbrian warrior. The uplifted weapon dropped from his hand.

Kosciusko was conveyed to the dungeons of Petersburgh and, to the eternal disgrace of the empress Catharine, she made him the object of her vengeance, when he could be no longer the object of her fears. Her more generous son restored him to liberty. The remainder of his life has been spent in virtuous retirement. Whilst in this situation in France, an anecdote is related of him which strongly illustrates the command which his virtues and his services had obtained over the minds of his countrymen.

In the late invasion of France, some Polish regiments, in the service of Russia, passed through the village in which he lived. Some pillaging of the inhabitants brought Kosciusko from his cottage. 'When I was a Polish soldier,' said he, addressing the pillagers, 'the property of the peaceful citizen was respected.' 'And who art thou,' said an officer, 'who addresses us with this tone of authority?' 'I am Kosciusko.' There was magic in that word. It ran from corps to corps. The march was suspended. They gathered around, and gazed, with astonishment and awe, upon the mighty ruin he presented. 'Could it indeed be their hero,' whose fame was identified with that of their country! A thousand interesting reflections burst upon their minds; they remembered his patriotism, his devotion to liberty, his triumphs, and his glorious fall. Their iron hearts were softened, and the tear of sensibility trickled down their weather-beaten faces. We can easily conceive, sir, what would be the feelings of the hero himself in such a scene. His great heart must have heaved with emotion, to find himself once more surrounded by the companions of his glory; and that he would have been upon the point of saying to them:

'Behold your general, come once more
To lead you on to laurel'd victory,
To fame, to freedom.'

The delusion could have lasted but for a moment. He was himself, alas! A miserable cripple, and, for them, they were no longer the soldiers of liberty, but the instruments of ambition and tyranny. Overwhelmed with grief at the reflection, he would retire to his cottage, to mourn afresh over the miseries of his country.

Such was the man, sir, for whose memory I ask from an American congress, a slight tribute of respect. Not, sir, to perpetuate his fame, but our gratitude. His fame will last as long as liberty remains upon the earth; as long as the votary offers incense upon her altar, the name of Kosciusko will be invoked. And if, by the common consent of the world, a temple shall be erected to those who have rendered most service to mankind, if the statue of our great countryman shall occupy the place of the *most worthy*, that of Kosciusko will be found by his side, and the wreath of laurel will be entwined with the palm of virtue to adorn his brow.

> Immediately following upon completion of his address, Harrison offered a resolution which, in turn, precipitated a rebuttal, the basis of which focused on William Washington (1752-1810), a distant cousin and Revolutionary War comrade-in-arms, of George Washington.

In the House of Representatives, Jan. 22:

Mr. Harrison, of Ohio, offered the following resolution, *Resolved*, That this house, entertaining the highest respect for the memory of general Kosciusko, his service, etc., the members thereof will testify the same by wearing crape on the left arm for one month. After some debate, Mr. Harrison withdrew his resolution altogether.'

[The short debate on this question is reserved, but shall certainly be given at a future day, in justice to the subject. It is enough now to state, that the merits of *Kosciusko*, the advocate of freedom, and the friend of man, were fully admitted; but it was shewn, that no such respect as was now proposed had been paid to any of the departed worthies native or foreign, who had aided in the achievement of our independence, except in the single case of general Washington, which was admitted to be an exception to all general rules. Having as recently as 1810, refused a like tribute to the memory of col. *William Washington*, on his decease, was too late now, it was deemed, to commence a new system in this respect.]

Article 37. (February 7, 1818, page 404)

Cracow, Nov. 4, The labors of the commissioners of the three allied courts, for marking the boundaries of our new republic (what *republic?*) have been completed, that the territory of Cracow is marked out by posts, on which are placed the areas of the republic and the neighboring frontier powers.

In the brief article above, it appears that the correspondent either hadn't realized that the Free City of Kraków, also known as the Republic of Kraków, had been created by the Congress of Vienna, which is unlikely, or the news-brief which he had written was done so sarcastically, because the Republic of Kraków's existence had depended principally on Russia's willingness to allow its existence, which served as a reminder of the once free, independent and intact Commonwealth of Poland and Lithuania. Russia, of course, would not allow memory Poland's free and independent history.

Article 38. (June 13, 1818, Page 280)

In this news-brief, and the one of June 27, 1818 that follows, Niles' Weekly Register reported on the disposition of the earthly remains of Tadeusz Kościuszko (1746-1817), wherein "prince Tablonowsky" had been referenced initially, as it related to Czar Alexander's alleged offer to pay for "a monument" to be erected to Kościuszko's memory. It also drew attention to the disagreement over whether Kościuszko's remains should be left in Switzerland or removed to Poland for final interment. Subsequently, Article 39 of June 27 corrected Jablonowsky (actually Jabłonowski in Polish) from Tablonowsky, and admittedly introduced me to a new word -- "manes" -- that appears in the final sentence. Today, the word means "the revered spirit of one who has died." In Noah Webster's Dictionary of 1828, it meant principally and to the point, "the remains of the dead," but also as "the ghost, shade or soul of a deceased person." Please note as well that surnames are

74

spelled exactly as they had been in Niles' Weekly Register. When I comment about Kościuszko, however, I do so in its proper Polish spelling.

Kosciusko. – The *London Courier* says, a curious dispute has arisen respecting the possession of the remains of the venerated patriot general *Kosciusko.* The prince Tablonowsky arrived at Soleure on the 16th ult. in order to claim the body, for the purpose of its receiving funeral honors in Poland, when the general's executor unexpectedly protested against the removal, alleging that *Kosciusko* had expressly desired to be buried with simplicity, and had chosen Switzerland for the interment of his remains. Thus, the affair appears to rest for the present.

Article 39. (June 27, 1818, page 307)

Kosciusko. *Paris, April 20.* Several of the Parisian papers have intimated that the delivery of the remains of Kosciusko, at Soleure, to prince Jablonowsky, has been refused; but the Gazette de Lausanne of the 14th inst. announces that these precious relicts departed thence the 24th March, accompanied by the prince and M. Veltner, the intimate friend of the deceased. 'The emperor of Russia,' continues the Journal, 'has named the city of Cracow for the reception of this deposit; and that the monarch himself has made a proposition to the Polish government for the erection of a monument to the manes of Kosciusko!!!'

Article 40. (July 4, 1818, page 325)

The grand duke Constantine, the brother of emperor Alexander, and viceroy of Poland, has been elected to the diet of Poland by the citizens of the Prague suburb of Warsaw. The grand duke had 103 votes, the next highest had three.

Article 41. (November 7, 1818, page 166)

Since the year 1814, the small-pox has not been seen at Stettin.

> Poles knew Stettin as Szczecin.

Article 42. (April 3, 1819, page 111)

A statistical survey of Poland has been published at Warsaw. That kingdom, in its present state, remains 2,121 square miles (15 to a degree), 481 towns, 22,694 villages, and a population of 732,324 souls, of which 212,944 are Jews.

Article 43. (April 17, 1819, page 144)

> In its issue of April 17, 1819, Niles' Weekly Register reported on the suicide rates in some of Germany's principal cities on the year 1817, Breslau included. Poles knew Breslau as Wrocław.

A London paper publishes the following to shew that people *kill themselves* as frequently in other countries as they do in England:

'A very general notion is entertained, that more suicides are committed in England than in other countries; and day after day the newspapers are filled with communications, in which this is always assumed as an undoubted fact. The late publication of Mr. Kamptz, of Berlin, founded on official returns proves that, in the towns of Prussia, the suicides are more numerous than they are in England. For instance:

	Population.	Suicides in 1817.
Berlin	160,584	57
Potsdam, not including the military	15,426	77
Frankfort on Oder	12,500	41
Breslau	63,020	58
Leignitz	10,000	37
Reichanbach	3,500	56
Magdeburgh	27,869	50
Mersburg	6,000	30
Dusseldorf	15,050	24

We do not believe that in any one town of the British dominions, the capital not excepted, amount to one tenth of the rate of Reichanbach, which is no less than 1 to 62.

Article 44. (June 19, 1819, page 292)

In introducing his editorial series, "Mitigation of Slavery," Hezekiah Niles reported in #5 of that series that his contempt for Russia and its Czarina Catherine II hadn't lessened over the years.

Every body knows that the greatest advances which Russia has made in intelligence and power, is the result of the ameliorated condition of the common people, all of whom were, and many millions of them are yet, more degraded slaves than any to be found in the West Indies. It is not twenty-two years since the empress Catherine II died, this woman gave about 150,000 men, women, and children, in absolute property, to her male-prostitutes, in consideration of *her* favors!

What would we think, if a lady in the United States, who had acquired her *property* by the murder of her husband, were to give a *man* or *woman* to a fellow for coming to bed to her!

Article 45. (September 4, 1819, page 15)

There is a freedom of the press at Warsaw that is very pleasing. The editors of a liberal journal for opposing certain police regulations, have been much cherished by the people.

That may either have been true, but only briefly, or had originated from a source of poor intelligence about the actual state of affairs in Warsaw concerning the press, where many rumors of all sorts likely abounded.

Article 46. (November 13, 1819, page 173)

> Hopes had risen about the imminent arrival of a somewhat liberal Alexander:

The emperor of Russia, it is said, was to be crowned king of Poland in the month of October. The ceremony was to take place in the city of Warsaw.

Article 47. (November 27, 1819, page 206)

> But soon followed a touch of sobering reality, expressed sarcastically:

Magnanimous Alexander has abolished the liberty of the press in Poland, and so in another way became a *'deliverer'!*

Article 48. (December 11, 1819, page 252)

> Two new-briefs in this issue of *Niles' Weekly Register* alerted Americans that, in the absence of the Monroe Doctrine that would not occur until December 1823, Russia laid claim to California, and also that Russia maintained a considerable army of occupation in Warsaw.

RUSSIA: "By an arrival from China, it is said that a Russian frigate arrived at Canton, and reported that the territory on the coast of California, which is about 800 miles in length, has been ceded by Spain to Russia, in payment for the assistance by the emperor Alexander to his Catholic majesty, in fitting out the expedition for Buenos Ayres and Lima."

POLAND: "Thirty-five thousand troops were reviewed at Warsaw on the 15th of October by the King of Wurtemberg."

Piotr Wysocki (1797 – 1875) by Jan Nepomucen Żyliński (1790 – 1838).
Wysocki helped initiate the November uprising against the Russians

Grand Duke Constantine, brother of Tsars Alexander and Nicholas, who was ap-
pointed Viceroy of Poland. (painting by George Dawe, 1834). Indeed, a man with
a troubled and troubling personality for those around him, Viceroy and Grand
Duke Constantine (1779-1831) had renounced his right of succession to succeed
his older brother Alexander (reigned 1801-1825) as Czar of Russia, in favor of his
younger brother, Grand Duke Nicholas, who went on to reign as Czar of Russia
from 1825 to 1855.

Part Two: 1820 - 1829

Article 49. (June 17, 1820, page 286)

A beautiful monument has been erected at Janow, in memory of Kosciusko.

Article 50. (October 28, 1820, front-page)

There is a report that the emperor of Russia will re-establish the kingdom of *Poland,* but we cannot place any faith in it.

The foregoing was reported by *Niles' Weekly Register* on its front-page (actually page 129 insofar as all issues were organized by Volume number, with extensive consecutive pages within each volume). See APPENDIX at the end of this book for the inclusive dates of all 75 Volumes.

Article 51. (November 4, 1820, page 152)

The diet was opened on the 13th September, by the emperor *Alexander.* He spoke of the recent changes in Spain, Naples, and Portugal in an *unfriendly* manner.

Article 52. (November 11, 1820, page 169)

In this editorial Hezekiah Niles summarized the essential points of Czar Alexander's important address to the Diet (known as the Sejm in Polish) of the Kingdom of Poland in Warsaw on September 13, 1820. By way of the Congress of Vienna, the allies that defeated Napoleon had restored the so-called "legitimate" monarchs, or their successors, that Napoleon had removed from their thrones. Poland had been excluded insofar as its King was Alexander, the Czar of Russia.

The speech of Alexander to the Polish Diet, see page 172, is well called a 'most remarkable one.' It clearly manifests his notions about legitimacy, and shows that he is resolved to maintain his subjects in the most abject obedience. An English paper mentions this speech in the following terms: 'The Dutch mail supplies us with the speech delivered by the emperor Alexander to the Polish Diet, on the 13th Sept. which, instead of affording any hope, that his majesty mediates the general purpose which report had recently ascribed to him, of re-establishing Poland in its integrity, as an independent state, distinctly states, as the basis of any benefits which are to be conferred on its inhabitants, the perpetuity of their union with Russia.

He talks, indeed, to the Poles of Christian morality, and truth and error, with all the mystical obscurity of Madame Krudener. *But he finishes with displaying the cloven foot.* He roundly tells them of his determination to root out the seeds of destruction as soon as they appear, and that he will never negotiate about his principles, nor submit to consent to any thing that may oppose them; which being interpreted, means that the slightest effort to recover their independence, will be visited with sudden vengeance; and that having, by outwitting the Congress of Vienna, once got them within his grasp, he is firmly resolved that no future negotiation shall ever tear them from it'.

Worthy of note in Article 52 had been the influential circumstances of Juliana von Krüdener (1764-1824), the socially well-placed Russian Christian mystic of German origin who had convinced Czar Alexander and his court at St. Petersburg, that Alexander had been chosen by God to defeat Napoleon Bonaparte, thus preserving Christianity in European civilization, and thereby making of him, Alexander "the Blessed" among his fellow Russian Orthodox Christian believers. Nonetheless, by referencing Alexander's "cloven foot" (as is held to be one of the many imagined physical characteristics of Satan), Hezekiah Niles clearly expressed his opinion, rightly or wrongly, that the word of the Czar had been deceptive and untrustworthy, as it pertained to Poland.

Article 53. (November 11, 1820, pages 172 and 173)

In the same issue on pages 172 and 173, Hezekiah Niles went on to print, as he had promised to do on page 169, Alexander's entire speech to Poland's Diet in which the Czar proposed to protect Poland against "the spirit of *evil.*"

The emperor Alexander to the Polish Diet. Warsaw, September 16. His majesty, the emperor of Russia, king of Poland, opened, on the 13th, the diet of the kingdom of Poland, with the following most remarkable speech: *'Representatives of the kingdom of Poland!* It is with great satisfaction that I find myself a second time among you, and with pleasure renew to you the assurance that I follow the impulse of my heart and carry into execution one of my most dearest wishes, when I assemble you here to co-operate in the maintenance and developments of your social institutions.

My confidence in you has been the origin of these institutions; your confidence in me will consolidate them.

My object, when I gave them to you, was to combine the power of the sovereign with the intermediate power, with the rights and legal wants of society.

I consider these bonds as indispensable; but to be durable, they require a support, in want of which every thing earthly decays and degenerates.

Let us not forget that institutions of this kind are only human work. Like man himself, they want a support for their weakness, a guide against error; and like him, they can only find such a support and guide in Christian morality, and its divine doctrines.

You have remained Poles; you bear that honorable name; but I have told you once before, that only the application of the principles of beneficent morality, can restore to you so honorable a right. Follow, therefore, on your part those wholesome doctrines; draw from their source that sense of probity which they command you, both towards yourselves and others; draw from them the love of truth which aims at truth alone, which hears and speaks only her language; then you will powerfully support me in consolidating the work of your regeneration.

I have spoken to you in words of truth; for it is truth that I ask from you. I wish to hear it from your mouths; let me hear it with frankness, but also with composure and cordiality.

It will appear to you in full light as soon as you seek it in reality, and not in vain abstractions, as soon as you judge of your situation according to the testimony of events, and not according to theories, which, in our days, fallen or rising ambition endeavors to bring forward.

Lastly, truth will mark your opinions as soon as you regard only the voice of the great interests that are confided to you, as soon as you banish from your recollections all acrimony, every partial object, and thus show yourselves worthy of your honorable mission.

Then, and not before, you will have fulfilled your obligations. I will now fulfill mine.

My ministers will lay before you a view of all the measures of organization and administration which have been adopted within these two years. You will, doubtless, recognize with joy the good which they have effected, when you compare it with all *evils*, the deception of which were to be effaced. The wish to attain this object has, perhaps, not always followed the way which the form of administration, that I readily gave, and you prescribed. Perhaps, too urgent and simultaneous wants have caused, by their occurrence an increase in the necessary expenditure.

My views, however, have not changed; and it is my firm will that, in future, the regulations once laid down will be directly adhered to, and the most scrupulous care be taken to economize the resources of the payers of the contributions.

The wishes that you have laid before me have been most seriously considered. You will hear how they have been partly satisfied already, and shall in part be fulfilled in future. You will hear why it has been necessary to delay the accomplishment of some, to renounce that of others. Among those that the government has willingly granted, are the project of the law, which will be laid before you.

[His majesty then enumerates some of the proposed laws, which he desires they will thoroughly examine when submitted to their consideration and concludes as follows:]

There are countries where use and abuse are placed in one and the same line, where the spirit of *evil* excites the vain want of slavish habitation, and again attempts to recover its dreadful sway. Already it predominates in one part of Europe, already it heaps those crimes and convulsions on each other.

Notwithstanding these unhappy events, my system of government will remain always the same. I have drawn its principles from the most profound sense of my duties.

I shall always fulfill those duties scrupulously. But this would not be perfectly done, if I were blind to the great truths that experience teaches.

Doubtless the age in which we live requires protecting the laws, as the basis and guarantee of social order. But the age also imposes upon princes the duty of preserving those laws from the mischievous influence of ever restless, ever blind passion.

In this respect, a heavy responsibility lies on you, as well as on me. It commands you faithfully to follow the path which your judgement, your upright sense of duty prescribes to you. It commands me to warn you frankly of the dangers that might surround you, in order to defend your constitution against them; it obliges me to judge of the measures on which I am called to decide, according to their real consequences, not according to appellations with which party spirit endeavors sometime to blacken, sometimes to adorn them. *Lastly, it obliges me, in order to prevent the production of evil, of the necessity of violent remedies, to root out the seeds of destruction as soon as they appear.*

This is my unalterable resolution. I will never negotiate about my principles, nor ever submit to consent to anything that may oppose them.

Poles! The more firmly the paternal bond is consolidated, which unites you forever with Russia, the more you are penetrated with the considerations which they awake in you, the more will the career which I have opened to you be extended and facilitated. A few steps more under the guidance of wisdom and moderation, marked by confidence and probity, and you will be at the goal of your hopes and choice. The experience that the calm operation of your liberty, consolidates your national existence, and establishes an indissoluble community between our two nations, will then afford me a double recompense.'

Article 54. (December 23, 1820, page 275)

Hezekiah Niles repeated the ominous nature of the Czar's message to Poland's Diet (i.e., parliament), known as the Sejm in the Polish language.

The emperor of Russia closed the diet of Poland at Warsaw, on the 13th of October, with a speech, by which his majesty evinces a feeling of displeasure at the general conduct of the members during their sessions. 'Examine your own consciences,' says the emperor, 'and you will know if, in the course of your discussions, you have rendered to Poland the services which she had expected from your wisdom, or if, on the contrary, misled by the seductions too common in our day, and sacrificing a hope which might have realized an expectant confidence, you have not retarded in its progress the work of the restoration of your country.'

The army assembled at Warsaw, during the emperor's stay, amounted to 30,000 men.

Article 55. (January 13, 1821, page 323)

> The following short news-brief Identified disquietudes that pre-
> vailed in Poland when it commented that:

This kingdom, as it stands connected with Russia, is officially stated to contain 3,408,000 inhabitants. The Russian yoke cannot sit
easy on the neck of Poland.

Article 56. (April 14, 1821, page 110):

> Whereas in Article 49, the June 17, 1820 issue, page 286 of *Niles'
> Weekly Register* had included the terse one-liner ("A beautiful monument
> has been erected at Janow, in memory of Kosciusko"), its issue of April 14,
> 1821, in contrast, identified the early stages of the plan to erect a massive
> Kościuszko Mound (Kopiec Kościuszki) in Kraków, as a national tribute
> to his memory, and to create a "Kościuszko Colony" of veterans who had
> served under him, to reside around the slope and base of Kraków's 1,000
> foot high Sikornik hill, atop which the Mound had been planned to be com-
> pleted in 1823. Once that objective had been achieved as planned, in ef-
> fect becoming what Poles would define as a *góra na górze* ("hill upon a
> hill"), some five years before the John H. B. Latrobe-designed Kościuszko
> Monument was dedicated by the Corps of Cadets of the United States Mil-
> itary Academy in West Point, New York on July 4, 1828, thus making West
> Point's Kościuszko Monument the world's second oldest *national* monu-
> ment raised to his memory, given that the Kościuszko Mound of Kraków is
> the world's oldest *national* monument raised to his memory.

Cracow, Jan, 30. Only 17,000 Polish florins are yet subscribed towards the monument of Kosciusko, yet it seems determined to execute
the plan on an extensive scale. The mound, or *tumulis*, is to be so large,
that the expenses of bringing and casting up the earth are estimated at
40,000 florins. On the top is to be placed a block of granite, of propor-
tionate size, to be hewn from the rocks on the Vistula, and which is to
bear no other inscription but the name, Kosciusko. It is further intended to purchase the whole mountain on which the mound is to be raised,

with a piece of the ground as far as the Vistula, to plant in a useful and agreeable manner, and to people it with the veterans who have served under the general. They are to have the land and dwellings as freehold property, and to form a little society by the name of Kosciusko Colony. It is also proposed to support two young daughters of Kosciusko's brother, who are orphans, and in narrow circumstances. In order to obtain the means for doing all this, the committee who direct the affair have resolved to apply to the admirers of Kosciusko in foreign countries, and to invite in France, general Lafayette; in England, Lord Grey; and in North America the late president Jefferson, all friends of the deceased hero, to collect subscriptions.

The referenced committee of 1820 was to be known as the Kościuszko Mound Committee (Komitet Kopca Kościuszki) which for two centuries thereafter still exists today to provide perpetual care of the Mound and its related Museum complex. On June 18, 2019, I -- Anthony Joseph Bajdek of the State of New Hampshire, USA -- had been inducted as an Honorary Member of that Committee, and as a consequence, the first foreigner to be honored as such, having had my name carved on a plaque of Greek marble in the Blessed Bronisława Chapel of the Kościuszko Mound complex, for which I am very grateful and proud. For comprehensive details and related photos of that historical event and the reason why it had occurred, please consult the current and comprehensive website of the American Association of the Friends of Kościuszko at West Point (www.kosciuszkoatwestpoint. org), under the sections, "Retrospect (2008)" and "An Uncommon Honor (2019)."

Article 57. (May 5, 1821, page 151)

This issue commented briefly on the state of affairs in Europe, and that:

...perhaps the most important of all things mentioned, *is a precipitate return of the emperor of Russia to his dominions*, having been summoned by the senate 'from motives of the greatest urgency.' *A rising of the Poles against the crusade of the kings* is spoken of, as the probable cause.

Article 58. (May 12, 1821, page 175)

> Niles' Weekly Register reported that a Polish Legion was to be formed by Poles in the kingdom of Naples, for service in support of the kingdom's independence.

A Frankfurt article of the 24th February mentions that in the number of foreigners who had tended their services to the Neapolitans, were many Poles, who intended to form a Polish legion.

At the sitting of the Neapolitan Parliament of the 20th of February, a Polish baron, son of a general of division, asked the right of citizenship, and offered his life in defence of liberty. He was declared citizen by acclamation.

Article 59. (July 28, 1821, page 351)

Certain bodies of Russian troops at Warsaw, after being reviewed by the emperor, were marched towards Italy -- they were counter ordered; their real destination unknown.

Grodno, (Poland), May 21. From the 1st to the 15th inst. Above 100,000 Russians have passed the Dwina, and are cantoned on the left bank of that river. The government of Minsk alone has received orders to prepare for the reception of 80,000 men.

Article 60. (August 11, 1821, page 382)

The grand duke Constantine is suspected of having imbued liberal principles. It is said that great care is observed to keep the troops that have been in France from mixing with the lower classes, for they are said to be infected with a revolutionary mania; and the emperor has rendered himself unpopular by abolishing the practice of wearing beards! The innovation is said to be openly reprobated at Novgorod; the Poles are reported ready for a revolt; though the emperor has done much to render himself popular, they still recollect that he has blotted the name of their country from the map. How much of these things are true, we know not.

> Czar Alexander had three younger brothers, all having been Grand Dukes, who in order of age and Imperial succession from next oldest to youngest had been Constantine, Nicholas and Michael respectively.

Article 61. (March 16, 1822, page 35)

The total amount of the military force of Russia exceeds a million men in arms! There are five large corps of 75,000 or 80,000 men each, stationed at different points, besides two armies, and, when the emperor pleases to visit Constantinople, he can easily sweep the Turks out of his way.

Article 62. (May 4, 1822, page 145)

The debates in the French legislature are still stormy. A plot to cause an insurrection in Poland is said to have been discovered by some of the arrests at Paris: the time of its breaking out was to have been when the Russians were engaged with the Turks, this is probably a manufacture to operate on Alexander.

Article 63. (June 8, 1822, page 229)

Russia. A great number of Poles who followed Bonaparte to Moscow, being captured by the Russians, were sent to the remotest provinces of Siberia. Many of them died by the fatigue of the journey, and those who arrived were subjected to the greatest hardships and sufferings that human nature could bear. The case of these men has, at last, been brought before the emperor, and he has directed the restoration of those who remain to their country and families.

> Whereas the implied likelihood of Alexander's not having been aware of the Poles who served in Napoleonic forces being condemned by Russia to imprisonment in Siberia is difficult to believe, the fact that he restored them "to their country and families" was welcome news.

Articles 64 and 65. (October 12, 1822, page 85)

> As with everything in Russia, a sobering reality of daily life always prevailed over every other consideration as these two separate news-briefs illustrate:

Russia. Previous to his setting out for the continental congress, the emperor Alexander issued the following ordinance: it marks the despotic character and rule of *the deliverer*: 'In very village or place where, unknown to the lord, a deserter or fugitive finds a forbidden shelter with a peasant, the community of these peasants shall be condemned to a fine of 2,000 rubles for every such deserter. If this shelter is given with the knowledge of the lord of the village, he shall pay the same sum, independently of that paid by the peasants. If the concealment has been effected by the lord, and if the deserter has been received by one of the villages by him, in that case the lord shall be obliged to pay alone the sum of rubles for every deserter, besides being liable to the other rigors of the law. Whoever shall denounce a deserter or fugitive shall receive a reward of 300 rubles, derived from the one imposed on the harborer'.

Poland. Among the many conjectures to be found in the French papers, is a rumor that the three great powers, Russia, Prussia, and Austria which made the division of Poland, had agreed to give up their respective portions, and to restore that kingdom, with a sovereign, who is a native of the country, and free from all foreign influence. The question as to settling the indemnities, it is thought, will prove a bar to this arrangement.

Of European people exiled by Russia to Siberia, the vast majority had been Poles.

Article 66. (November 2, 1822, page 140)

Of the number of Catholics (5,500,000) in the Russian Empire, the vast majority of whom had been Poles and Lithuanians, and their maintenance, having been reported that:

In the Russian empire the hearers are said to be 42,000,000 -- of these, there are of the Greek church 34,000,000, Catholics 5,500,000, and Lutherans 2,500,000, places of worship 24,500, clergymen 74,270, whose yearly income is 910,000*l.*

- 34,000,000 Greek church, at 15,000*l.* per million, 510,000*l.*
- 8,000,000 Catholics and Lutherans, at 50,000*l.*, per million, 400,000*l.*

Before we close, we would submit the following short statement, exhibiting the expense per thousand of the whole Christian world -- of the Catholic, of the Protestant, and of the Greek churches, for the maintenance of their clergy.

- 220,228,000 Christians in the world, per thousand, 85*l.* 4s. 9d.

Note here that the above-referenced "85l. 4s. 9d." had been equated with *85 pounds sterling, 4 shillings, and 9 pence.* The abbreviation for pence had been d rather than p because England by tradition had adopted the d in remembrance of the Roman Empire's denarius having been in use during the Empire's presence in Britain's antiquity, a point that underscored Britain's ancient origins during classical antiquity.

Article 67. (April 12, 1823, page 83):

Hezekiah Niles' persistent sarcasm both for Czar Alexander (whom Niles had accused of *moral parricide* in the murder of his father, Czar Paul, in 1801), and as well for the "peace society of Massachusetts" was clearly stated in this particular issue of *Niles' Weekly Register.*

Alexander the 'Magnanimous' and 'the deliverer.' What a change there has been in the opinion of many, who but lately hailed the emperor of Russia as a demi-god! The 'deliverer' is found to be a monopolizer, and the 'magnanimous' just as ambitious as Napoleon had been! My neighbor of the Federal Gazette, thinks that Great Britain will take part in the war should Alexander once more march his *barbarous* horde into the heart of Europe. How long is it since one of this horde was caressed in London, and almost kissed by the women in the streets, (as they kissed the old and ugly *Blucher* until he was sick of it), for the simple reason that he had 'transfixed fifteen French people on his own spear' or, that the provost of the city of Edinburg toasted the Russian lady, whose father had offered her *person*, with a large fortune, in reward to any wretch who would murder Napoleon! My opinion about this member of the 'peace society of Massachusetts,' whether right or wrong, has been the same, because the reputed assassins of his *father* were among those nearest to his person and seemed to possess the most of his confidence.

Article 68. (August 2, 1823, page 345)

> Hezekiah Niles never missed an opportunity to remind ill-informed and gullible Americans about the true nature of Russia, the Russians, and the Cossacks, all together or individually, and of Czar Alexander and his wanton grandmother, Catherine II, in particular.

The father and the grandfather of the present emperor of Russia, were assassinated, the first, no doubt through the instrumentality of his wife Catherine, the most abandoned, or, at the least, the most famous harlot of modern Europe, under whose care also, all the kindred of her husband, *happened to die*; and his father was put to death in his bed chamber, as was believed, by persons that were the immediate advisers and dearest friends of the 'magnanimous' Alexander. Gracious heaven! In what a world we live, that such actors should be at the 'top of the wheel,' and be held up as examples!

Article 69. (September 6, 1823, page 12)

> Whereas Czar Alexander may have been motivated to improve the quality of life for Russia's peasants, some members of Russia's political and social aristocracy must have thought differently about the matter.

We sometime have since copied from a Prussian paper, an article shewing that *disaffection* had shown itself in Russia. It now appears that there has not been no small amount of excitement in that country, that there have been great ministerial changes, and a large number of important persons dismissed from office. The reasons assigned are that the emperor was opposed in his project to ameliorate the condition of the most numerous class of the people, who, every body knows, are actual slaves; and it was understood that certain persons had excited dissatisfaction among the emancipated peasants, by a vigorous collection of the taxes, etc. The plot, it is said, was disclosed by a priest to the empress mother, and the removal of persons from office followed. This is, perhaps, the only account that was *allowed* to be published, and it may, or may not, be a true one.

Article 70. (March 13, 1824, page 19)

> In the right-hand column of its issue of March 13, 1824, there had been an article of news titled, "The Jews," which offered evidence that Jews had been under pressure by the Russians to celebrate the Sabbath on Sunday.

The Jews. An article, dated Warsaw, December 20, 1823 says: 'The Jewish Rabbis and Elders have met in general assembly at Plastkow, and have decided that the celebration of the Sabbath shall be changed to Sunday.' We know not how to believe this, seeing the tenacity with which the Jews adhere to the customs of their fathers.

> Czarina Catherine II ("the Great") of Russia ruled from 1762 to 1796, and had been the leader of the co-orchestrated nefarious Partitions of Poland - Lithuania of 1772, 1793 and 1795, in concert with Prussia and Austria. Centuries earlier, beginning in 1265, Catholic Poland had institutionalized

tolerance of Jews, thus becoming the kingdom which had attracted many Jews from across intolerant and largely antisemitic Western Europe. That antisemitism had been fueled principally, but not exclusively, by Roman Catholic Spain's having endured a 700-year long conquest and occupation (711-1492) by the *Moriscos* (Moslems or Moors), and the ensuing lengthy war of reconquest (i.e., Reconquista), beginning with the battle of Las Navas de Tolosa in 1212, to drive the Moriscos out of Spain, and indeed, all of Iberia, Portugal included, but were not completely driven out by Spain until 1492. During the Moorish occupation, Moslem authorities fostered freedom to Catholics and Jews alike to practice their religions openly. As Roman Catholic armies from northern Iberia systematically drove the Moors further south over the centuries, intolerance of Islam and Judaism followed liberation, and prevailed into the year 1492 when the last Moorish forces were defeated in Granada. During the final two centuries preceding 1492, large numbers of Jews in Spain sought to relocate to more tolerant areas in Europe. After 1492, Spain established an Inquisition to identify remaining Jews and Catholics, who allegedly cooperated with the Moors, for interrogation, torture and punishment. This further accelerated the relocation of many Jews to Poland.

During his reign as King of Poland, Kazimierz III (1333-1370), the only ruler of Poland to be known as "the Great" (Wielki), offered Jews a safe haven in Europe. In exchange, they helped populate his kingdom's frontier towns which had been a high priority and necessary objective he sought to accomplish. Thus, by the mid-18th century, the Kingdom of Poland, and its Grand Duchy of Lithuania, included the greatest number of Europe's Jews.

With the Partitions of the Commonwealth of Poland and Lithuania in the second half of the 18th century, Russia absorbed the largest extent of its territory, and as a consequence, the greatest number of resident Jews, of what once had been the free and independent Commonwealth of Poland and Lithuania, thus making of Imperial Russia, by way of said Partitions, the nation with the largest number of Jews, leaving a relatively small number of Jews in the Russian-controlled Kingdom of Poland where Russia's emperor (i.e., Czar) ruled concurrently as king of Poland. With the annexation of what had once been most of territorial Poland-Lithuania, Czarina Catherine II (1762-1796) forced all Jews to live within a specific territorial zone known as the "Pale of Settlement" -- also known popularly as the "Purple Pale"-- with no ability to leave that zone except as agreed and allowed by Imperial Russian authorities.

At the end of the 18th century Russia, therefore, was well on its way to becoming a totalitarian state where the evolving principal operative domestic objective of rule, would not be formally established until the final decades of the 19th century, and at which time would be known uniformly as the policy of "Autocracy, Orthodoxy, and Russification," that dictated all aspects of life for its subjects and their total unquestioned compliance.

As an example of forced uniformity, it should come as no surprise, therefore, that Jews were under pressure to celebrate the Sabbath on Sunday by Imperial Russia as *Niles' Weekly Register* had reported. Was this the result of Russification orchestrated by St. Petersburg or something else? In my view, it was the former, in keeping with Catherine's related "Pale of Settlement" policy.

Article 71. (November 18, 1824, page 170)

Thanks to Editor Hezekiah Niles, an irony of history had been placed on pages 170-171 of this issue by way of two ostensibly unrelated newsbriefs: one (Article 71), a manifesto on military recruiting issued by Czar Alexander I of Russia, in the same company with another news-brief (Article 72) from the Corps of Cadets of the United States Military Academy at West Point, New York, that announced the competition for the best design of a monument to be erected in memory of Tadeusz Kościuszko. When that Monument was dedicated at West Point on July 4, 1828 by the Corps of Cadets of the United States Military Academy, it thus became the world's second oldest national monument dedicated to the memory of Kościuszko, the oldest being the Kopiec Kościuszki (Kościuszko Mound) of Kraków, Poland in 1823.

RUSSIA. Manifesto of his imperial majesty. 'We, by the grace of God, Alexander the first, emperor of all the Russias, etc. Having judged it necessary to raise a levy of recruits this year to complete our armies and fleets in which there is a want of men caused by the ordinary reductions, and the leave of retirements, which we have granted to the veterans who have completed their time of service, and whose number was considerable, as well as to those whose maladies or infirmities rendered them unfit for service, we ordain there shall be a levy, throughout the whole empire, of two recruits in every five hundred souls, conformably to the articles of our ukase, dated the 26th of August, 1818.

Thanks to the Almighty, during three successive years, the empire has stood in no need of recruiting, and our faithful and most-beloved subjects were enabled, without having their attention turned aside from their domestic concerns, to enjoy, in the bosoms of their families, the fruits of a peace which has happily not been disturbed. The organization of the military colonies has greatly contributed to render recruiting less often necessary. It will no longer be necessary, except in time of war, when, with the aid of Divine Providence, these colonies will have received all the development which we propose to give them.

Given at Tsarskoe Selo, the 15th of August, in the year of grace, 1824, and of our reign, the twenty-fourth.

(signed) Alexander.

Article 72. (November 18, 1824, pages 170 and 171)

KOSCIUSKO. The cadets of the United States military academy, at West Point, have offered a gold medal, of the value of fifty dollars, for the best design for a monument to the memory of gen. Thaddeus Kosciusko. It is to be erected at West Point, on a romantic spot, situated on the bank of the Hudson, and known by the name of Kosciusko's garden.

Article 73. (January 22, 1825)

Despite the fact that American readers of *Niles' Weekly Register* of January 22, 1825 had been used to receiving regular intelligence (i.e., news) about the true nature of Russia's destruction of the once free and independent Poland during the 18th century era of the Three Partitions and thereafter, and although the United States and Russia were in competition for control of the of the future northwest territory of the United States, both the United States and Russia completed a bi-lateral agreement on January 12, 1825 signed in St. Petersburg, Russia to the effect that:

Hereafter there shall not be formed by the citizens of the United States, or under the authority of the said states, any establishment upon the Northwest Coast of America, nor in any of the islands adjacent, to the *north* of fifty-four degrees and forty minutes of north latitude; and that, in the same manner, there shall be none formed by Russian sub-

97

jects, or under the authority of Russia, *south* of the same parallel.

Article 74. (April 12, 1825, page 83):

Alexander – the 'magnanimous' and the 'deliverer.' What a change there has been in the opinions of many, who but lately hailed the emperor of Russia as a demi-god. The 'deliverer' is just as ambitious as Napoleon was! My neighbor of the *Federal Gazette*, thinks that Great Britain will take a part in the war 'should Alexander once more march his *barbarous* horde into the heart of Europe.' How long is it since one of this horde was caressed in London, and almost kissed by the women in the streets, (as they kissed the old and ugly *Blucher* until he was sick of it), for the simple reason that he had 'transfixed fifteen French people on his own spear', or, that the provost of the city of Edinburg toasted the royal lady, whose father had offered her *person*, with a large fortune, in reward to any wretch who would murder Napoleon!

Having reported this in the April 12, 1825 issue of the *Niles' Weekly Register*, making it added evidence of the recurring anti-Russian theme, based on sound evidence, established by Hezekiah Niles when he wrote, eleven years earlier, his first related op-ed, "The Russians and the Cossacks" of April 30, 1814, referenced earlier as Article 6 of this book.

Article 75. (May 7, 1825, page 154)

The emperor of Russia has issued a proclamation, convening the Polish diet, and admonishes the members not to spend their time in useless debates.

Article 76. (June 25, 1825, front-page)

The comparative price of wheat in Europe and the United States by ports of export, where Gdańsk (included below as Dantzic which had been a variant spelling of the German word, Danzig) was referenced; and Britain's attempts to prevent the importation of foreign wheat, thus including Poland's wheat exports, was addressed for obvious reasons, not the least of which was to satisfy Britain's wheat growers who enjoyed monopolization of high prices for their British-grown wheat established during the Napoleonic Wars, when a naval blockade by France prevented the importation of less expensive European-grown wheat into the British Isles, and threatened starvation. A decade later, following the demise of Napoleon, the British producers of wheat refused to surrender their lucrative monopoly of high-priced, home-grown wheat, which had been a topic of front-page news in this issue of *Niles' Weekly Register.*

Wheat. As Mr. Huskisson, in his late speech in parliament, would not suffer the British people to consume foreign wheat, though they might obtain it at half the price which the product of their own country costs them, it may be amusing, as well as useful, to shew what was the price of wheat at different places, during the last year, and the average price in London at the same times: the prices are in sterling money, per quarter, and taken from the returns made to parliament.

Month.	Places.	Price.	Price at London.
March,	Odessa,	15s. 9d.	64s.9d.
September,	St. Petersburg,	27 8	59 8
October,	Lisbon,	24 9	57 2
December,	Dantzic	22 5	66 9
Do. Emden,		20 8	
Do. Amsterdam,		25 8	
Do. Leghorn,		27 7	
Do. Calais,		35 11	
September,	Philadelphia,	36 0	53 11 (last week)

These are sufficient, but it is worthy of special notice that, even at Calais, which is in sight of England, the price was nearly one half less than it was in England, in December.

Article 77. (July 23, 1825, page 334)

In the opening session of the Polish Diet (Sejm in Polish), Alexander promised tax relief to the Kingdom's major landowners as well as elimination of the national debt, but prohibited news of the Diet's proceedings from being published, among other measures, and addressed the Poles serving in the Diet in the third person in one momentary "slip of the tongue" instance, as if he had been addressing a purely ethnic Russian audience.

On the 15th of May the emperor Alexander opened the session of the diet of Poland with the following speech:

'When four years ago, I separated myself from you, lamentable events had threatened to compromise the prosperity of all the nations. I wished to leave to the opinions time to become fixed, and to the passions time to subside. Your third session was deferred, but this delay, I am certain, will possess the happy result of having the better prepared your labors, and it is with real satisfaction, and with these sentiments of attachment of which I have given you so many proofs, that I find myself in the midst of you.

In the interval that has elapsed since the last diet, faithful to my duties and to the resolutions that I have expressed to you, as soon as I remarked the germ of troubles, I offered opposition to its development. To consolidate my work, ensure its duration, and guarantee to you the peaceable enjoyment of the fruits expected from it, I have added an article to the fundamental laws of the kingdom. (*The article here referred to, is that by which the publicity of the debates of the diet is prohibited.*) This measure, which removes all necessity of exercising influence in the choice of members of the diet and upon your deliberations, proves the part I take in the consolidation of your constitutional compact. This is the sole object that I proposed to accomplish in adopting this measure, *and the Poles, I have the fullest confidence, will know how to appreciate the object and the means I have employed for its accomplishment.*

My minister in the interior will lay before you the picture of the situation of the kingdom, as well as the administrative measures that have been pursued during four years. You will have the satisfaction of seeing the rapid progress of industry, and to find that if the general prosperity has not yet attained the degree of perfection to which my wishes and the efforts of the government seek to carry it, the cause must be looked for in nothing else than the almost general stagnation of trade in agricultural produce. In other respects, the most advantageous results have been obtained. The national debt approaches, to its complete acquittal.

Two conventions have fixed the part of this debt that Austria and Prussia have to support. In a short time, a new finance law will regulate the revenue and expenditure of the state. A ruinous deficit had compromised your dearest interests. It has disappeared. The excess of the receipts must be applied scrupulously to the extinction of the national debt.

The negotiations entered upon with the court of Berlin, to settle the affairs of commerce between Poland and Prussia, have been crowned with the most happy success, by means of a series of negotiations, of a frank and amicable nature, which serve as the basis of my relations with my faithful allies. The convention which I have ratified affords easy openings to your commerce abroad. That which you have with Russia acquires greater daily activity and extent. The facilities that you have been granted to it are doubly advantageous, both by the mutual welfare of which they favor the progress, and by the new ties which draw the two nations together.

The debts with which private property is burdened, have, in particular, excited my closest attention. A project for forming an association, in *solido*, of the land owners, will be laid before you. It is the result of opinions which have undergone long discussion in your council of the Palatines.

Religion, that source of every virtue, that indispensable base of all human institutions, appears to command a revision of a part of your civil code. A commission, chosen from among yourselves, has undertaken this important labor, *and the project of the first book*, which it has already discussed, will be communicated to you.

My thoughts will accompany you on the discharge of your functions and you will find me ever ready to adopt the ameliorations which may be proposed to me; but, at the same time, resolved to reject every species of concession that may be prejudicial to your prosperity.

Representatives of the kingdom of Poland, may you, free from all influence, proceed in your deliberations with calmness! The futurity of your country is in your hands. Consider nothing but its welfare, its real advantage. Render to it all the services that it expects from your assembling together, and second me in the accomplishment of the wishes which I have never ceased to form for it.'

Czar Alexander's vague reference to, at least in terms of the 21st century, "the project of the first book" is well to have been directly connected with the "Russian Bible Society" that I referenced in Article 26.

Article 78. (July 30, 1825, page 342)

Statues sculpted in salt inside the Wieliczka Salt Mines.

An observation about the truly hidden beauty of the Wieliczka salt mine, mis-identified as having been the Wielska salt mine.

SALT. It is estimated that the whole of Europe produces annually, about 1,500,000 tons of salt, in the following proportions: England 250,000; Russia 300,000; Austria 370,000; France 300,000; Spain and Portugal 200,000; the other countries 80,000 tons. From the superior advantages of engines, railways and canals, the English mines are worked with the most economy, but the mines in Wielska, in Poland, are the most interesting. The imagination is confounded at the idea of finding, after a descent of 850 feet, vast halls, (the hall of Klosky is 360 feet high and 180 feet wide), stabling for 80 horses, storehouse, offices for clerks and three chapels; the whole of the fittings, altars, crucifixes, tables, desks and seats, worked in salt!

Article 79. (August 6, 1825, page 356)

Promulgation of the Russian Empire's philosophical justification for not educating the lower classes, including those of the Kingdom of Poland, along with censorship of books, both matters of which the Czar Alexander, himself educated as a child and young man to appreciate and practice (ultimately as he saw fit in the matter of the ideals of the Enlightenment) during his reign, apparently had received his approval in the year of his death, as this report illustrates. Notwithstanding his having benefited to some extent from a superb classical and liberal education, he understood perfectly that the lower classes had to know their place in Russian society, as well as in Europe generally, if the entire despotic, hierarchal, political and social, order of divine-right rule in Europe was to survive.

RUSSIA. The autocrat, (says a London paper), is much puzzled with the problem of how to give the poor an education without giving them desires which they cannot satisfy. In short, nature is to be put on quite a new footing in Russia. We suspect there is more of his father in the emperor than people are aware of, otherwise he would have his fate more strongly impressed on his memory. The following is the article referred to: ---

'*Warsaw, May* 2. The emperor has left the capital for a few days, to view the manufactures newly established in the district of Massovia and Katesch.'

Katesch refers to Kalisz in Polish. Germans often referred to Kalisz as Kalisch which may have degraded into Katesch in popular usage.

In the speech of the minister of the interior on the state of the kingdom, is the following passage: -- 'It is to be lamented, that the want of ready money, and the poverty of the country people, have hitherto prevented the general introduction of elementary schools. *It cannot be unobserved, that a liberal and superior education given to the peasant, would, in his present circumstances, be a real misfortune for him.* He would become acquainted with much, but, unable to enjoy it, would experience many wishes, and look in vain for the gratification of them; and all this would embitter his life, and fill him with dislike for the rich, instability, and often the deceitful resolution to take up occupations without being able to pursue them; and the end of the unhappiness lies already in the child which the man prepares for himself in mature age. Circumstances have made it possible to introduce various improvements into the school system. A general committee of superintendence has been appointed, whose chief business it is to watch over the moral and religious behaviour of the students. In this manner, education is founded on the principles of morality, and where mere learning might lead to many errors, it finds its true and unerring way when led by religion. A general censorship of all the books printed in the country or abroad has been confided to the ministry for ecclesiastical affairs, under the immediate care of a counsellor of state, and the director of public instruction.'

Article 80. (August 20, 1825, page 389)

From a report on the state of the kingdom of Poland, made to the diet by the minister of the interior, inserted in the French papers, it appears that, in the *four years* that have elapsed since 1821, about 155,639 law suits have been terminated in the civil tribunals of that kingdom. In the courts of criminal justice, 120,022 sentences have been passed in the same time, of which only 23 have received the royal clemency, and 12 obtained a commutation of punishment. The next statement shows the bribery and corruption which public officers practice on the continent, 284 *functionaries* accused of abuse of power, had been condemned in the same space of time. If this number met with their deserts, how more escaped in such a country as that? The population of Poland is about three millions.

Article 81. (October 15, 1825, page 104)

The emperor has appointed by ordinance, a committee to regulate the political and civil concerns of the whole body of Jews in his kingdom of Poland, who are to be placed under a new and 'fixed' order of things. [The *Alexandria Phenix* queries whether this may not produce a quarrel between the autocrat and the governor of Grand Island, 'judge of the Jews.']

In the early American Republic, Mordecai Manuel Noah (1785-1851), a founder of New York University, had proposed to establish a national refuge for Jews on Grand Island, located near Buffalo, on the Niagara River that flows from Lake Erie to Lake Ontario. The expression, "judge of the Jews," simply meant that in biblical terms, a leader of the Jews, Mordecai Manuel Noah in this instance, was defined as a being a "judge." The Alexandria Phenix had been another American newspaper of the period.

Article 82. (October 22, 1825, pages 115 and 116)

In the October 22, 1825 issue of *Niles' Weekly Register*, its Editor and owner, Hezekiah Niles, published a news-brief about the Cossack leader Platoff, suggesting that it disproved a point in the story about Platoff that had appeared in the April 30, 1814 issue of his *Weekly Register* titled, "The Russians and the Cossacks" which constitutes Article 6 of this book. General Matvei Ivanovich Platov, or Platoff, (1751–1818) was the Hetman of the Don Cossacks.

It was stated some years ago, that the hetman of the Cossacks had publicly offered the person of his daughter, with a dowry of 20,000 roubles, to any one that would assassinate Napoleon Bonaparte; and I well recollect to have seen it published that, at a great dinner given at Edinburg, the pious provost of that venerable city toasted the lady and wished her speedy marriage, which was loudly applauded by the company present! Indeed, the fact that such reward for murder was offered, and generally believed in Great Britain at the time, and luscious engravings of the lady were exposed in the print shop, to stimulate the deed. But it now seems, by Lyall's travels in Russia, that the whole matter was a fiction -- that Platoff had not a daughter unmarried at the time (1812) and besides, that he was utterly unable to have given such a dowry, being very poor.

Though Hezekiah Niles printed the preceding news-brief of October 22, 1825, as a correction to an aspect of the related article -- "The Russians and the Cossacks" -- that had been printed in his *Weekly Register* eleven years earlier, it appears that he hadn't been fully convinced of the original story's inaccuracy, most notably expressed by his use of the phrase, "a daughter unmarried at the time." As to Platoff's being poor, he was a Count and a highly decorated General in the Russian Army who had been a commander of the Cossacks. Given that portraits of Platoff now hang in the Military Room of the Winter Palace in St. Petersburg, Russia, and in the Waterloo Chamber of Windsor Castle in England, he very likely had not been a "very poor" man. All his known children had been sons. He may have had a daughter by a mistress. Though none of this was very likely known by

Hezekiah Niles in 1825, he at least offered a clarification about the 11-year-old story he had written. Nonetheless, I suspect that there was some truth to the original story.

Article 83. (February 11, 1826, page 142)

The abbe Stanislaus Stalzic, Polish minister of state, died at Warsaw, on the 20th of January. He has left the whole of his fortune, amounting to 800,000*l.*, to public institutions.

Referenced above had been Stanisław Staszic (1755-1826), who was a leading figure of the Polish Enlightenment and a very generous civic-minded man indeed.

Article 84. (February 11, 1826, pages 352-353)

The emperor of Russia died at Taganrock after a few days' indisposition. The express that brought this intelligence arrived from Warsaw on the 8th inst. The grand dukes Constantine and Michael had not yet departed from that capital for St. Petersburg. His late imperial majesty was born December 23, 1777; ascended the throne of Russia March 4, 1801, and became king of Poland on June 9, 1815; on the 9th of October 1793, he married Elisabeth Alexiewna, princess of Baden, but has no issue. The empress mother, a princess of Wirtemberg, widow of the emperor Paul I, is still living. His majesty has left three brothers, namely, 1. the grand duke Constantine, born on May 8, 1779, married February 26, 1796, to a princess of Saxe Coburg, from whom he was divorced in April, 1801. In May of the following year, he married the princess of Lowicz, but has no issue. 2. The grand duke Nicholas, born July 2, 1796, and married July 13, 1817, to a princess of Prussia, by whom he had one son and two daughters. 3. The grand duke Michael, born February 8, 1798. The late emperor has also left two sisters, the one married to the hereditary prince of Saxe Weimar, and the other to a prince of Orange.

The death of the autocrat is said to have been caused by a sore leg, which terminated in St. Anthony's fire. His brother, Constantine, who succeeds him, is spoken of as possessing a very fiery temper and a cruel disposition. He is beloved by the army.

Although Grand Duke Constantine had been the heir-apparent to be Czar of the Russian Empire in 1825 following the death of his older brother Alexander, as fate would have it, he had renounced his claim to the throne, likely a decision that he had made two years earlier. Therefore, by default, his younger brother, Nicholas I, became Czar from 1825 until 1855.

Article 85. (February 26, 1826, page 138)

In its April 22, 1826 edition, Hezekiah Niles expressed his opinion of the late Czar Alexander I of Russia to a fellow American editor who apparently had admired the Czar.

How is this?' The editor of the *Gazette*, printed at Le Roy, N.Y. has published a large article shewing his dissent in my opinions about the late emperor of Russia, and written on the margin of his paper 'how is this, *brother Niles*?' It is thus that 'how it is' – he has one opinion and I have another, and each has a right to his own. The death of a member of the 'holy alliance' never can be a subject of regret with me, but rather one to rejoice at. Yet there is something in the *Gazette* that excuses, if it does not approve, that alliance, though intended to protect 'their *craft* (the craft of sovereigns) against the march of mind.' However, in this too, the editor has his opinion and has his right to hold it. Alexander was, probably, a very good sovereign for *Russia*, but a bad ruler for the more civilized parts of Europe. Germany, Italy, Spain, etc., have suffered more for the *backward* revolutions of the 'holy' ones, than they did by the *forward* revolutions of Napoleon. The last was ambitious, but light and improvement followed his path; the others were seen singly more moderate, but darkness and distress succeeded their operations.

The sarcasm of Hezekiah Niles about the "Holy Alliance" had been well-placed, as it applied to Russia's threat to Poland and Western Europe. On September 26, 1815 in Paris, the monarchs of Russia, Austria and Prussia, who had defeated Napoleon Bonaparte, signed the "Holy Alliance Treaty," the text of which began with the solemn Christian expression, "In the Name of the Most Holy and Indivisible Trinity," by which they pledged to act uniformly in the political and social affairs of Europe in keeping with the "sublime truths which the Holy Religion of our Saviour teaches...." Under Article I of the Treaty which stated: "Conformably to the words of the Holy Scriptures, which command all men to consider each other as brethren, the Three contracting Monarchs will remain united by the bonds of a true and indissoluble fraternity, and considering each other as fellow countrymen, they will, on all occasions and in all places, lend each other aid and assistance; and, regarding themselves towards their subjects and armies as fathers of families, they will lead them, in the same spirit of fraternity with which they are animated, to protect Religion, Peace, and Justice," they vowed to defend the existing political and social order wherein rule by Divine Right in Europe would prevail against its antithesis, which was identified to be the "systems of representative government," of which the United States, the greatest by-product of European civilization and colonization, had been the world's best example and hope.

Article 86. (November 11, 1826, page 185)

There is a great emigration from Germany to Poland, 250,000 manufacturers are said to have departed within the last few years.

Article 87. (November 18, 1826, page 182)

As usual, money speaks! At least in the matter of qualifying to hold a title of nobility in Russian Poland, but likely in other European kingdoms/empires as well.

Polish nobility. The emperor of Russia's last decree on titles, ordains, that in Poland no person shall assume the title of baron unless his income shall be 25 pounds per annum! Of count, unless he have 75 pounds per annum!! and of prince, unless he can command 120 pounds!!!

Article 88. (December 2, 1826, pages 223 and 224)

Hezekiah Niles never allowed his readers to forget the Russian massacre of the Poles residing in Praga, a suburb of Warsaw, on November 4, 1794. Clearly, he had been dedicated to keeping the memory of that atrocity alive. Thus, 32 years later, he compared the barbarities of the Turks versus those of Russia in 1794 relating to Poland.

The barbarities of the Turks and the prospect still held out that Russia, coveting more territory, would assault them, has brought the recollection of the doings of the Russians in Poland. Warsaw was gallantly defended, but 10,000 men could not hold out against 50,000, the city was taken and the people laid down their arms. In the following night, ten hours after all resistance had ceased, orders were given to fire the town and massacre all men, women and children, who attempted to flee the flames. It was done, nine thousand persons were burnt or butchered, and the 'holy men' of Russia sang *te Deums* because of the slaughter, of which the hell-bound Suwarrow was the agent of his barbarian government. The Turks have never went beyond this, and it was Christians murdering Christians.

Article 89. (June 2, 1827, page 57)

SPLENDID FOOLERY. A new and splendid mission, it would appear from the London papers, is about to proceed to Russia, in order to install the Emperor Nicholas, as a knight of the garter. The marquis of Hertford is to be at its head, and will be accompanied by his son, Lord Yarmouth, and a numerous and splendid cortege of young noblemen. The garter king at arms, sir George Naylor, and the Windsor herald, Francis Martin, esq. will accompany the mission, to assist in the ceremony of investing the emperor with the insignia of the order. The installation will, it is said, take place at Warsaw, and not at Petersburg, and be co-incident with the coronation there of Nicholas as king of Poland. (And this, when those to whom England owes her wealth, by laboring sixteen hours out of every twenty-four, cannot earn even as much of oat-meal as they can eat!)

Article 90. (June 2, 1827, page 231)

Information (it would have been properly known as intelligence in the Early American Republic) about the geographical extent of the four integral geographical components of Imperial Russia, with Poland included separately as item 2, along with their respective populations, had been provided by Niles' Weekly Register in this issue. It is interesting that Imperial Russia saw itself as constituted in four specific integral parts: "European Russia," "The Kingdom of Poland" and "Asiatic Russia" in the Eastern Hemisphere; and in its American possessions in the Western Hemisphere. Given that "The Kingdom of Poland" was neither included in "European Russia" nor "Asiatic Russia" -- one may speculate that Russia held it to occupy a very special geographical space, for better or worse, in a subservient role, wholly appropriate to Russian hatred of the Poles. Remember also that in theory as well as in practice after 1797, the very word, Poland, was not to have been ever mentioned. Later, the plan was to have it replaced by the word, Vistulaland, fully integrated in the Russian sector. Reality, however, dictated otherwise. It appears that Poland was coveted by St. Petersburg for having been the wealthiest and comparatively the most advanced part culturally and economically, indeed a special possession, both despised and coveted at the same time, conundrum-like, of the Empire.

I. EUROPEAN RUSSIA
Superficial extent   72,161 Sq. Miles
Population   44,118,600
To a sq. mile   605

II. KINGDOM OF POLAND
Superficial extent   2,293 Sq. Miles
Population   3,702,500
To a sq. mile   615
Annual revenue   8,333,333 rubles

III. ASIATIC RUSSIA
Superficial extent   276,020 Sq. Miles
Population   4,663,100
To a sq. mile   42

IV. RUSSIAN POSSESSIONS ON THE NORTH WEST COAST OF AMERICA
Superficial extent   24,000 Sq. Miles
Population   5,000
To a sq. mile   2

Article 91. (September 22, 1827, page 57)

Reported on floods in Silesia (Śląsk) stating that:

An article from Berlin says that 4,000 inhabitants of Silesia lost all their property, in consequence of late inundations.

Article 92. (September 29, 1827, page 67)

Interestingly, this brief article reported pointedly on the Russian-curtailed, small number of newspapers allowed in the Kingdom of Poland and compared it with the growing number of newspapers in the United States. Once again, Hezekiah Niles managed to keep Poland in the news for the edification of American readers.

The population of those portions of Poland which have successfully fallen to the share of Russia, is about 20 million. To meet the intellectual wants of such a mass of persons, there are but 15 newspapers, eight of which are printed in Warsaw. Our 10 to 12,000,000 are supplied by something like 5 or 600 newspapers. There is a difference here.

One early 20th century related study titled, "Growth of Newspapers in the United States," written by William A. Dill in 1928, documented the rapid expansion of the number of newspapers, from which I extrapolated the following benchmarks, beginning in 1776 until 1850:
"1776 = 37; 1810 = 393; 1840 = 1,403; 1850 = 2,526".
That further underscored the difference between living in a democracy versus an autocracy as was exemplified by Russia.

Article 93. (November 1, 1828, pages 154 and 155)

An extract from a private letter from Warsaw, under the date of August 13, received in London, states that the trial of the Patriotic Society of Poland, is drawing to a close. After three years of detention,

111

the fate of the accused has been decided by the high national court. During the first weeks of the year 1826, immediately after the attempt of the conspirators of St. Petersburg, an extraordinary commission was appointed at Warsaw, to discover any connexion which might exist between the Patriotic Society of Poland and the Russian conspirators. Numerous arrests were the consequence, and the prisons were crowded to excess. The inquiry lasted more than a year. But the mode of the proceeding being irregular, the emperor of Russia ordered recourse to measures more legal. The senate of the kingdom was declared to be a tribunal of the diet, and immediately commenced its sessions. The persons accused were authorized to select defenders from among the bar of Warsaw. At the last session the accused were permitted to speak in their own defense. In one instance, that of an octogenarian, Stanislaus Count Lotyk, who could not raise his own voice, a youthful counsellor was heard with the greatest commiseration. The judges were seen to weep, and tears were even seen in the eyes of the *gend'arms*. The affecting defense was crowned with complete success. The charge of high treason was relinquished, and the greater part of the accused were acquitted; a few only were condemned to imprisonment for a few months. The acquittal was unanimous, with the exception of one voice.

Article 94. (May 30, 1829, page 224)

The Vistula, it is related to a Hamburg paper of the 17th of April, has broken its dykes and overflowed its banks. It is not expected that the water will run off in less than fourteen days, and all hopes of an abundant harvest are at an end in that part of Prussia. The winter has been long in the north of that kingdom, and the accumulation of snow's immense, in some places, *above the tops of the highest trees*, and from the rapid thaw it is expected inundations must have taken place on the greater part of the rivers falling into the Baltic.

Article 95. (June 13, 1829, pages 255 and 256)

The journalists continue to give the most deplorable accounts of the effects of the late inundation, in west and east Prussia.

Article 96. (July 11, 1829, page 321)

POLAND. Nicholas arrived at Warsaw of the 17th of May. His coronation was to have taken place on the 25th; it will be the first ceremony of the kind witnessed by the Poles since 1764, when Stanislaus Augustus Poniatowski was crowned. The five old crowns, and the other regal relics, have been secreted for a great number of years; and in consequence it has been necessary to procure a new crown at the cost of three millions of florins. The condition of the Poles has been much improved, and they anticipated further benefits under the government of Nicholas. Constantine is accused of severity and appears to have been very unpopular.

Article 97. (September 13, 1829, page 43)

The remarkable article below titled: "THE CORONATION," had been a summary account of the coronation ceremony in Warsaw (Warszawa in Polish), of Russian Emperor Nicholas (Mikołaj in Polish) as King of Poland, and the related oath that he took on the occasion, all of which occurred in Poland's capital, and in effect, served essentially as an example, guide or script for conducting a coronation of a Russian Czar as the King of Poland in the first half of the 19th century.

Whereas Hezekiah Niles seemed to have had fluency in Latin and French, and perhaps some German as well, both he, and/or perhaps his translator, seemingly hadn't been familiar with the phrase "orb and scepter" which they surprisingly interpreted as "scepter and ball." The fact that Poland's "Order of the White Eagle" had been interpreted as the "white order of the eagle" further reveals an absence of full mastery of the German language, which implied that Niles and his staff either had attempted to translate and create a news report, taken from a German newspaper, or perhaps had been provided a translation by a weak German speaker in Baltimore. However, the translation, beginning in the second paragraph, written in the present tense, of the appropriate method (i.e., protocol, guide or script, if you will) for conducting the coronation, is generally well executed, despite its translation shortcomings. We will never know what the circumstances of the translation may have been. Nevertheless, *Niles' Weekly Register* reported the story for which it is to be commended, insofar as it provided Americans with a glimpse of a European coronation which in this particular case revealed the brief promises made by Czar Nicholas to Almighty God for being a worthy King of Poland, to rule for the happiness of his "brave" but for the most part, decidedly reluctant Polish subjects. Tsar (a variant of Czar) Alexander created the Kingdom of Poland as a constitutional monarchy which was slowly eroded away and which Nicholas soon chaffed under.

The entrance of the Russian emperor into Warsaw on 17th May, has been already announced. The ceremonies attending his coronation as king of Poland, we translate from a German paper, as given in a schedule issued at Warsaw a few days before the event occurred.

The place selected for the coronation ceremony is the senate chamber. On the day appointed their majesties and their imperial highnesses, with the whole court, will move thither in solemn procession. After his majesty has arrived and taken his place upon the throne, he beckons to the primate, who approaches and offers a prayer for the blessing of Heaven to descend upon his majesty. This being done, the primate presents to his majesty the imperial robe, with which to invest his highness saying, 'In the name of the Father, of the Son, and of the Holy Ghost.' His majesty puts on the crown, after which the primate presents to him the chain of the white order of the eagle. His majesty calls to him her majesty the empress queen, and places upon her this chain, which two maids of honor fasten upon her robe. His majesty then desires the scepter and the imperial ball, which the primate delivers to him, with the words, 'In the name of the Father, of the Son, and of the Holy Ghost.' The primate then exclaims three times, with a loud voice, 'VIVAT REX IN ETERNUM.' At the same moment the bells in all the churches begin to ring, a salute of 100 guns is fired. The clergy and assistants manifest their congratulations to his majesty the emperor and king, by three low obeisances.

Immediately after, and as soon as the ringing of the bells and thunder of the artillery have ceased, his majesty the emperor and king, after delivering the royal scepter and imperial ball to the persons who brought them in solemn procession, kneels down, and with a loud voice repeats from a royal book spread before him by the minister of religion, the following prayer:

'Almighty God! God my Father! King of Kings! Thou, who by a divine word didst create the world, and whose infinite wisdom fashioned man to govern it in the way of the truth; Thou hast called me to be king of this *brave* Polish nation. With holy reverence I acknowledge the manifestations of thy heavenly grace towards me; and while I give thee thanks for all thy kindness, I also bow myself before thy holy majesty. Enlighten my footsteps with thy grace, O Lord God, in this my elevated way, and so guide my conduct that I may fulfill my high calling. Grant that the wisdom which encircles thy throne, may be with me. Let it descend from Heaven that I may be penetrated by thy almighty will, and by the truth of thy commands. Let my heart be in thy hand and enable me to rule for the happiness of my people and the honor of my exalted predecessor, and already sworn by myself, that I not fear, on the day of thy eternal judgement, to appear before thee, to the praise and through the mercy of thy divine son, Jesus Christ, and with the grace of the beneficent and all quickening Spirit, for ever and ever, amen.'

As soon as his majesty finishes his prayer, and has risen from his knees, all present (with the exception of his majesty), will kneel, and the primate, also on his knees, will offer an earnest prayer to heaven, that its blessings may attend the reign of his majesty. Their majesties will then retire to St. John's church, where a *Te Deum* will be sung, after which they will return to the palace.

.Czar Nicholas I of Russia who reigned 1825-1855).(Painting by Franz Kruger)

Part Three: 1830 – 1839

Article 98. (August 21, 1830, page 449)

Giving credit where credit was due concerning the growth of manu-facturing in Russian Poland.

The number of manufactories in Poland, in 1815, was 100, is now 4,000. Among articles they produce 7,000,000 ells of cloth per annum. In the end of 1829, the population of the kingdom was 4,088,289 being an increase of 383,953 since 1828.

In 21st century terms, an ell is defined as "an English measure equal to 45 inches (114 centimeters)." In 19th century terms, according to the *Noah Webster Dictionary of 1828*, the ell was "a measure of different lengths in different countries"; and where "the English ell is three feet and nine inches, or a yard and a quarter. The Flemish ell is 27 inches or three quarters of a yard. The English to the Flemish is five to three. In Scotland, an ell is 37 2/10 English inches."

Article 99. (November 20, 1830, page 205)

Thanks to the interest of Hezekiah Niles in the matter of Poland and Russia, he included, in this issue among "Interesting Items," a news-brief, originally printed in the Athenaeum, on the important canals of Russia that included one involving Poland. The Windawa is the Venta River in Lithuania.

"*Important canals in Russia.* Three most important works of this kind are at present executing; the 'canal on the Windawa,' which will unite that stream with the Niemen; another canal which will unite the Niemen with the Vistula; and a third, which will form a junction between the Volga and the Moskwa. The whole of the three were commissioned in 1825, and will be shortly open for navigation."

Article 100. (November 27, 1830, page 224)

> Included under "Miscellaneous" of its November 27, 1830 issue, Niles' Register employed the word fermentation to identify the early stage of great Polish Uprising of 1830.

A great fermentation is said to exist in Prussian Poland, and some of the neighboring provinces in Russia.

Article 101. (December 25, 1830, page 303)

Travellers from Warsaw, arrived at Leipsic, state that the present ferment prevails in the whole kingdom of Poland as well as the capital. The Russians have considerable forces on the frontiers as a precaution.

Article 102. (January 1, 1831, front-page)

> Amidst the outbreak of the latest cholera mordus epidemic in Russia, the Russian government established a significant monetary award for the best treatise (but not from an ethnic Pole, of course) on ridding the world of that bacterial disease, and if not, what the unknown species of viral plague, as some speculated, it may have been; it also had been reported that the political ferment in France in July 1830 and Belgian Independence caused ferment in Poland, known as the "November Uprising of 1830" in the case of Poland, and as such precipitated Russia's hope for declaration of war against France, the perceived ongoing seat of revolution in western Europe, by way of the terms of the "congress system" agreed to in Vienna in 1815 to suppress revolt against the political status quo anywhere in Europe, for which Russian troops were to have been deployed to suppress in Paris in 1830. However, they had first to cross Poland and then the German states to get to France. Therefore, on January 1, 1831, *Niles' Weekly Register* began, with this front-page news from Poland appearing below, for what would turn out to be a very lengthy journalistic campaign first conducted by Hezekiah Niles until 1839, and then by his three successors, that lasted into 1849, to report on how Poland and Polish people elsewhere in east central Europe had been extremely ill-treated -- putting it mildly -- to an even greater extent

by Russia, Prussia and Austria than ever in the past, during which the matter of Russia's ethnic cleansing and annihilation of Poland, the Polish nationality and the Roman Catholic Faith in Poland became progressively manifest. Russian Field Marshal Hans Karl Friedrich Anton Graf von Diebitsch (1785 – 1831) was a veteran of the Napoleonic Wars, and suppressed the Decembrist Revolt in Russia and the Polish Uprising.

The *St. Petersburg Gazette* publishes proposals for a reward of 25,000 rubles to any physician of Russia, Germany, Hungary, Italy, France, England, Sweden and Denmark, who shall produce the best treatise on the origin, nature, and proper treatment of the *cholera mordus*. 'An Asiatic disease which has recently appeared in Europe, is producing fearful ravages in some of the Russian provinces, is daily spreading itself, and menacing all Europe. Late accounts say, the disease prevalent in Russia is now believed not to be *cholera mordus, but a species of plague*. Exertions were making to prevent the disease from reaching St. Petersburg, and the inhabitants of that city were laying in provisions for six months, apprehending that the stoppage of communications would last for some time.'

From London papers to the end of the 30th November. It would now seem that Europe was about to be engaged in a *general war!* Indeed, it is said, that Russia has declared war against France. This, however, is thought premature, though there are many and strong indications that such an event will take place.

Various letters from Germany say that Russia is collecting a body of 200,000 men, with 400 pieces of cannon, on the frontiers of Poland, under the command of count Diebitsch; and that, after reviewing his troops, he would proceed to Berlin, on an extraordinary motion, and gathering at the garrison towns.

It now appears that Nicholas, in acknowledging Louis-Philipe, had the 'insolence' as a French writer calls it, to say, that he should not inquire into the motives that led the latter to accept the crown, and hence there has only been a cold civility between the two courts. France is prepared for a mighty contest, and would have a *regular* army of about 300,000 men on her frontiers, besides the national guards, in the present month. The king and his government are increasing in popularity. Marshal Soult labors night and day in arranging military matters.

Austria has a powerful force in Italy, it would seem as if a triple alliance, Russia, Austria and Prussia, may be formed against France; and highly probable that the latter will be supported by Great Britain.

119

The late change in the British ministry, it is thought, will tend to the latter result, the government now being in the hands of the Whig or liberal party.

The *London Times* of the 30th, believes that much of the alleged French apprehension of sinister *holy alliance* designs, was evidently formed on the supposed inclination of the late English administration in that direction, and that the change in the British ministry will re-move it....

Another arrival brings London papers of the 1st December. They contain many letters and rumors from the continent. It is stated that the *holy alliance will interfere* in the affairs of the Netherlands, be-cause of the vote of the Belgic congress to exclude the house of Orange from the throne, or as having authority over that country.... France and England appear to have a good understanding. If they shall act togeth-er, the *holy alliance* will fail of its purposes. The signs of the times are awful, we pray we pray we may escape the whirlwind.

Article 103. (February 5, 1831, pages 401-402

American readers of *Niles' Weekly Register* had been privileged with having had access to intelligence of highly documented events, the details of which -- as is evident throughout my study -- not only amazed me but also convinced me that my investigation should become widely-known among Polish Americans (and friends of Poland) in the 21st century, lest they forget their ancestral struggles for freedom in Poland against Imperial Russia in particular. The initial comprehensive report that follows below illustrates in considerable detail, the depth and breadth of Poland's relentless cause for holding up the torch of *liberty* in central and eastern Europe, and in its plan-ning and execution. Note as well that November 9 is identified as the day the Uprising began, when in fact it had been November 29. Whether the error had been that of the *Journal de Paris* in the first place, or subsequently the London paper, Hezekiah Niles or the typesetter of *Niles' Weekly Register*, we will never know. Whatever the case may have been, it didn't detract from the overall substance of the report. Grand Duke Constantine was the brother of Alexander and Nicholas who was passed over for succession, *to which he earlier had agreed voluntarily*, and though nominal ruler of Congress Poland, he acerbated the unrest in Poland. General Józef Chłopicki (1771 – 1854) was a veteran of the Polish Partitions, the Legions, and Napoleonic Wars.

Attack on and taking of the Arsenal in Warsaw on November 29, 1830 as depicted by Marcin Zaleski (1796-1877).

By an arrival at New York, London papers to the 19th December have been received, giving the details of a revolution in Russian *Poland.* Thus, it will be seen, that the ball of revolution is still in motion. The ancient kingdom of Poland has risen in insurrection against its Russian masters, and the viceroy, the arch duke Constantine, has been compelled to retreat from Warsaw, after a short but sanguinary conflict between the Russian guards and the inhabitants and students of that city. Poland, it will be recollected, was divided between Russia, Prussia and Austria, in 1793 and in 1795. The inhabitants of the portion allotted to the first power have broken out into action; and it is to be expected with this additional stimulant to action, that those of the two latter divisions will hardly slumber.

The immediate cause of this revolution as given in the *Journal de Paris* of December 14th, is as follows:

It was in the evening of the 9th Nov. that the insurrection was commenced by under-ensigns. It was excited by the abhorrence which they had to witness the ignominious death of twelve students, who had been sentenced by a court martial to be shot for having sung the *Marsellois* hymn! The first point to which the ensigns directed their course was to the arsenal; they took possession of that post, which contained 70,000 guns, and 100 pieces of cannon. The grand duke Constantine was then at Belvedere, about three miles from Warsaw. The fight continued during the whole of the night, and on the following morning the people remained masters of the city. The regiment of engineers was the first to revolt. The French tri-colored cockade was instantly adopted, and cries of 'Vive Lafayette, the friend of Kosciusko, forever!' They went to the house of the French consul in search of the tri-coloured flag; and having found it, although the consul (M. Durand) was suspected to be a congregationist, and attached to the fallen dynasty, they joined the Polish white flag and the tri-coloured one together and hoisted them in that state. The national guard is being raised.

The *Prussian State Gazette* of December 4th, says the news of the Polish insurrection caused the greatest consternation.

'As far as we know, the plot was recently prepared, and then carried into effect by a number of young Poles, who are educated in a military school, and consequently have a military organization. The insurgents hastened to the palace and murdered the Russian sentinels. At the same time they called the citizens to arms, the arsenal was stormed, and all hastened to combat the Russian and some Polish troops, at whose head the grand duke Constantine retired fighting. The grand duke is said to have incurred the greatest personal danger.

The military students were between five and six hundred. They spread themselves through the city, calling upon the inhabitants to arm themselves. They were joined by the multitude and proceeded to the barracks and arsenal, and seized upon the arms by which the populace was supplied. Several of the regiments joined the citizens. The archduke Constantine, on the point of being surrounded in his palace, retreated towards Praga with a guard, two Russian regiments and a regiment of Polish cavalry, who followed him from a sense of honor. Forty-one colonels and majors were killed in endeavoring to keep the troops in obedience. Two aids of the duke are also said to have been slain. The general opinion is that the desertion of the Polish army will become general. The military chest, and the house of the pay-master general, had been plundered. The French tri-colour cockade was first adopted, it was however soon substituted by that of the Polish cockade. A group of national guards was organized. Many distinguished general officers had been killed. The citizens, much to their credit, were arresting those who plundered the magazines, etc. The Russian families residing in Poland, have been placed under the protection of the national honor.

Prior to the retreat of the duke Constantine, he issued a proclamation forbidding the Russian troops to interfere in the insurrection further, leaving the Poles to re-unite themselves! But at the same time he cautions the Poles to be aware of the precipice on which they stand, and exhorts them to return to order and tranquility.

As Reported in the "Niles' Register"

A provisional government had been formed, and the executive committee of the council of administration were engaged on the night of the 1st December, with the following objects:

1. With issuing an order for the opening of the barriers for all persons leaving Warsaw. They are allowed to go to the provinces without passports, first giving notice to the police.
2. With measures for the safety of the mails, both coming and going.
3. With the safety of all the money in the several public coffers.
4. With measures for the regular supply of provisions for the troops in and near Warsaw.
5. With similar measures for the regular supply of provisions for the inhabitants of the city.
6. With the organization of a committee to maintain tranquility in the suburb of Praga.
7. With new appointments for several offices.
8. With the project for the organization of a general board of public safety in the whole kingdom, and with other subjects of a similar nature.

The journals contain the decree of the council appointing general Chlopicki commander in chief of all the forces of the kingdom.

General Chlopicki was suddenly taken ill yesterday, which caused general consternation. It is, however, that he was better in the evening. Yesterday evening the general received official news that the garrison of the fortress of Modlin, after a letter of the grand duke Constantine had been communicated to it by his late aid-de-camp, count Zamoyski, had surrendered without resistance. The particulars of the capitulation are not known.

The arch duke Constantine was in retreat to the empire, and, in a proclamation, he commits all the national and public property, and persons, to the honor of the Poles. A large army, however, is on the frontiers, and the emperor may be less peaceable than the archduke. The Poles have laid the foundation stone of their regained power, and will, in all probability, succeed in raising the superstructure.

The character of the provisional government formed, may be gathered from the following proclamation:

From the *Prussian State Gazette*, Dec. 7.

The following (account from Warsaw Journals) is the proclamation of the council of administration respecting the admission of new members.

In the name of his majesty the emperor, king of Poland, Nicholas I. Considering the urgency of the case, the council of administration has invited the following persons to join in the exercise of its functions: The prince senator and Woywode Adam Czartoriski, the senator Woywode Michael Radzivill, the senator Castellan Michael Kochanowski, the senator Castellan Louis Patz, the secretary of the senate, Julian Niemcewicz, and general Joseph Chlopicki. Done at Warsaw, Nov. 30, 1830.

(Signed),
The president minister of state,
COUNT VAN SOBOLEWSKI.
The minister of finance,
PRINCE LUBECKI.
For the secretary of state,
TYMOSKI.

The *Times* of the 18th Dec. stated that their extracts from the German papers contain acts too scanty to form any decided opinion concerning the actual extent or probable result of the movements in Poland. The Courier of the same date says, the authentic accounts from Warsaw of the 4th Dec. announce that a new provisional government had been formed in that day, upon principles more hostile to Russia than those originally avowed. It is also stated that the most active measures were taken at Warsaw to repel attack.

The *London Court Journal* says that the news from Poland has not promised any marked change in the tone or bearing of the ministers of these three powers, relative to the affairs of Belgium.

At the beginning of 1829, the kingdom of Poland contained 4,088,209 souls, exclusive of the army. The increase since 1825 had been 383,983. The Jewish portion of the inhabitants had almost universally located in distinct quarters, they amounted to 384,263. The extent of property insured at the Warsaw assurance office was 420,000,000 guldens, or £33,250,000 stg. in value. Warsaw contains a population of 136,554, independently of a garrison of about 15,000 men – of this population 30,146 are Jews.

'The oppression,' says *Bell's Weekly Messenger*, 'which the Russians practiced in Poland can scarcely be believed. No man in any station of life was permitted to marry or to dispose of his inheritance; without a license from the government. Most persons possessed of any influence were compelled to live in solitude upon their own estates, and not permitted to pass even the frontiers of one province to another, without a passport obtained by the most degrading supplications. Thus, whilst the Russians were traveling in any quarter of Europe, a Polish traveler was scarcely so much as seen. Poland was imprisoned, as it were, within her own frontiers, and kept for the gloomy pleasure of Russia, who exhausted every species of tyranny and exaction upon the people.'

Whereas Sobolewski had been referenced above as "Count van Sobolewski," the use of van -- meaning of or from -- was more appropriate to Western Europe (e.g., in Denmark and Holland) than in Eastern Europe where its equivalent was von, a German word with the same meaning as van. Thus, Sobolewski should have been identified as "Count von Sobolewski," even though the use of von was superfluous in purely Polish usage. Whereas it is surprising that the *Prussian State Gazette* would not have known that (the difference between van and von), the truth of the matter may have been that the *Niles' Weekly Register*'s type-setter may not have known.

General Grzegorz Józef Chłopicki

Article 104. (February 12, 1831, page 430)

This issue of *Niles' Weekly Register* contained several news-briefs, one being about the appointment of Field Marshal Count Hans Karl Friedrich Anton von Diebitsch as commander-in-chief of the Russian army for fighting the Poles; the second being on affairs in Poland, conditions along its borders, the number of Poles killed in Warsaw, and the appointment of General Grzegorz Józef Chłopicki as dictator and commander-in-chief of the "national Polish guards", and readiness of Polish forces; the third being about the Russian Grand Duke Constantine's effort to suppress the revolt; and the fourth being Jean-Jacques Rousseau's well-known quotation about the digestibility of swallowing up Poland. Intelligence (i.e., other news) coming out of Poland wasn't easily obtained once Russia, Prussia and Austria began sealing their borders with Poland. British, French, German and Polish correspondents who often risked their lives to bring the attention of Western Europeans and Americans to the epic struggle of Poles to exist as a free and independent nation and nationality as well, in the most reactionary and totalitarian political zone of Eastern Europe, along with news from elsewhere in Europe, via a potpourri of subjects (e.g., Belgium had also risen up in revolt), yet nonetheless relevant, some of which, in the case of the latter, also appeared on this single page, that constituted a typical array of the news (intelligence) of the day, all being interesting in any editor's opinion, thanks to the competent resourcefulness of said correspondents.

RUSSIA: "The emperor of Russia had appointed *field marshal count Diebitsch* commander in chief of the army to operate against the Poles, and had determined on reducing them to subjection. It was reported in the London exchange, of disturbances having broken out in St. Petersburgh, which is said to have been confirmed by the latest letters of the date the 4th December. The Russian bonds had consequently fallen, Prince Galitzen, a minister of state, had been banished, for urging the people on to insurrection. The emperor, and most of the nobles, rumor said, had left St. Petersburgh. The military governor of that city had issued a proclamation."

BELGIUM: "The five great powers of Europe have acknowledged the independence of this country, and affairs appeared to be settling down into a state of quiet."

As Reported in the "Niles' Register"

POLAND: "Arrivals from Warsaw are to the 9th of December, and from the frontiers of Poland on the 12th, both inclusive. The number killed at Warsaw during the commotions, is stated to be about 6,000. General Chlopicki had been appointed commander-in-chief of the national Polish guards, with the title and power of *dictator*. The Poles were preparing for the conflict, and the most rigid police had been established."

PRUSSIA: "Things were quiet in Prussia, and it had been determined by the government to withdraw the Prussian troops from the fortress of Luxemburg."

ITALY: "The people of Rome were in arms and demanded a constitution."

GRAND DUKE CONSTANTINE: "The grand duke Constantine was not deficient in vigor and presence of mind in the recent revolution, but he could not be prepared, for the Polish movement came upon him as a flash of lightning. He was on horseback at the first alarm; he endeavored, at the head of four or five Russian bodies of cavalry, and several battalions of infantry, to restore the people to order; but he found it impossible to suppress so general a movement; and although he might perhaps have kept his stand at the palace outside the town for some time, he retired at daybreak."

ROUSSEAU: "'Polonaise,' said J. J. Rousseau, 'you cannot prevent your enemies from swallowing you up, but at least hinder them from digesting the meal.' It appears evident that the people of Poland of the present day, are determined to follow the advice of that celebrated writer'."

SWITZERLAND: "As to Switzerland, the Journal of Schafhausen says: 'We learn from several quarters, that the Russian Ambassador had delivered a note to the presiding canton, with the declaration that his sovereign, in concert with his allies, has resolved to maintain the present state of things in Europe, according to the treaties of Paris, and the act of the congress of Vienna'."

THE POPE: "Accounts from Rome, after mentioning the death of the Pope, say: 'Many foreigners arrive from Naples and Florence to witness the funeral of the holy father, who has left so small a fortune for his family, that they will scarcely have wherewith to maintain their rank. The sacred college is at this moment composed of 66 cardinals; 10 places are vacant. Of those 55, six are of the order of bishops, 39 priests, and 10 deacons. The chief cardinals are Pacca, who is dean of the sacred college, Cardinal Ruffo Scilla, and cardinal Albani. Those absent at this time from Italy are Robosphe of Austria, who is in Moravia; Ribera and Jevellanos in Spain; Silva, in Portugal; de Croi and Roban Chabot, in Switzerland; Latil, in Scotland; Rodnay, in Hungary; and Isoard, in France. Of the existing cardinals, 26 were created by Pius VII, 24 by Leo XII, and 5 by Pius VIII'."

ENGLISH NAVY: "An order was issued from the English admiralty office in November last, to restrict the infliction of corporal punishment in the navy. Commanders alone are permitted to direct such infliction, and are to sign a warrant previously, which is to be returned regularly to the admiralty office, and is to specify particularly the nature of the offence, and the proofs, and is to be countersigned by the flag officer, if on board of a flag ship. The number of lashes is limited even in the most extreme case, to forty-eight."

ENGLISH ARMY: "Every regiment in the British army is to be completed to its full establishment of 740 rank and file. The total will not be large, about 6,000 men."

Article 105. (February 12, 1831, page 431):

American readers of *Niles' Weekly Register* began receiving accelerated and comprehensive news of Poland's latest epic struggle to exist free and independent, and as will be aptly demonstrated, that such news subsequently produced an outpouring of American support for the Polish cause and its resolute freedom fighters.

Under our foreign head we have given an account of the recent revolutions in Poland. There have been so many partitions, and re-unions, and re-partitions of Poland within the last forty years, that it requires some attention to geography and history to understand what is meant by the term. We presume, therefore, that the following brief sketch of the modern history and present state of this ill-fated country, will at this moment prove acceptable to our readers.

Ancient Poland was a large country of Europe lying between Germany, Russia, Turkey, and Hungary. Including Lithuania, it contained 284,000 square miles, and 15,000,000 inhabitants. The partition of Poland between Russia, Austria, and Prussia, took place at three distinct epochs, 1772, 1793, and 1795; and the result of the whole was as follows:

As Reported in the "Niles' Register"

	Sq. Miles	*Population*
To Austria	64,000	4,800,000
To Prussia	62,000	3,500,000
To Russia	158,000	6,700,000
	284,000	15,000,000

At the Peace of Tilsit, (July, 1807), Bonaparte stripped Prussia of the greatest part of her Polish possessions. Of these he gave a small portion to Russia, and erected the rest into a new state, called the grand duchy of Warsaw, which he assigned to the king of Saxony. In 1809, after vanquishing Austria in the field, he compelled her to cede part of Galicia to Russia, and another part to his new grand duchy. But all the arrangements of Bonaparte were overturned by the disastrous campaign of 1812: the Russians re-occupied Poland; and the congress of Vienna, while it decreed to Austria and Prussia a partial restitution of their late cessions, confirmed to Russia all the Polish and Lithuanian provinces acquired before 1795, conferring on her, in addition, the sovereignty of the central provinces, which constitute the present kingdom of Poland. Each of the three powers was enjoined by the congress to give to its respective portion of Poland as free a constitution as circumstances should permit.

The following table shows how the territory and population were divided between the three powers at the congress of Vienna.

	Sq. Miles	*Population.*
To Prussia	29,000	1,800,000
To Austria	30,000	3,500,000
Kingdom of Poland	47,000	2,800,000
To Russia	178,000	6,900,000
	284,000	15,000,000

The *Kingdom of Poland*, as constituted at the congress of Vienna, is the seat of the present revolution. It comprises the chief part of that which, from 1807 to 1813, formed the duchy of Warsaw. It consists of the central provinces of ancient Poland, bounded all along its frontier by the respective acquisitions of Russia, Austria and Prussia. Area 47,000 square miles. The population at present is estimated at 4,000,000. This country, though subject to the same sovereign as Russia, was governed in every respect as a separate monarchy. The regal dignity is vested in the czar, represented by a viceroy, in whom, and in a cabinet of ministers, the executive government resides. The religion of the majority is the Catholic. The Protestants of different sects are also numerous; and there are many members of the Greek church. The Jews are computed to form a seventh part of the whole population.

> *Niles' Weekly Register* gave full credit to the *N. Y. Observer* as the originator of the article.

Article 106. (February 12, 1831, page 433)

> The same Niles' Weekly Register issue of February 12, 1831, contained the December 14, 1830 address of the Marquis de Lafayette to the French Chamber of Deputies on the matter of the national guard, and of Poland, the nation deemed to be the "friend of liberty."

I decline to enter into the question of cantons and communes. But if I am asked if you are now to discuss whether all France shall arm, I answer, the question is already decided; the people did not wait in 1789 or 1830 to deliberate but marched against the enemy (sensation); we must, therefore, prepare for war, as the best means of securing peace. We cannot hope to make all Europe in love with our institutions; there are those who still look with a jaundiced eye upon the accession of a citizen-king to our throne, (new movement). The revolution of Belgium, the eldest daughter of one great week may yet excite uneasiness. At this moment you see Poland, (hear, hear), ready to rival in zeal and patriotism the friends of liberty, not only in France, but in other countries, (fresh movements)! Poland, (hear, hear), is, perhaps, on the point of repairing the shame of the last year of Louis XV, and the immense fault which Napoleon committed when he neglected the occasion of restoring that fine country, after the three divisions that destroyed it, (loud acclamations *from the left*). We have announced our rule to be, that we will not allow other powers to interfere, not only in our affairs, but in the affairs of other countries. Suppose foreign powers should think proper to seize upon Belgium, or to assist Holland, could we look on in cold blood? Certainly not, (loud cheers). The same thing may happen on the side of Poland. Suppose Austria, prevailed upon by Prussia, or for any selfish purpose of her own was to make herself a party to the quarrel in Russian Poland, (violent murmurs, and marks of disapprobation.)

Article 107. (February 26, 1831, pages 461 and 462)

Considerable, copious in fact, attention was dedicated to Poland's just cause in its ongoing struggle for the right to exist as a free and independent nation and would have relatively considerable impact on American public opinion. Note as well that the correspondent who had provided the details of Russia's military operations against Poland, as having been designed to conduct operations on a "war of extermination" basis. In the 19th century, Prussian Germans, as well as other Germans, tended occasionally to employ the word, ausrotten, a word meaning "exterminate" in English, whenever they referenced the Poles living in the Prussian-controlled parts of the once free and independent, pre-1768 Commonwealth of Poland and Lithuania. (The use of the word "exterminate" as it related to ethnic Poles living in Germany persisted into the time of Otto von Bismarck of Prussia who had been known among Europeans as the German Empire's "Iron Chancellor" from 1873 to 1890). Russian Field Marshal von Diebitsch, the Russian Empire's commander-in-chief for military operations against Poland in 1831, had been Prussian born.

We have a large mass of matter concerning the affairs of Poland. Gen. Chlopicki, who had so honorably kept his word and resigned the dictatorship, has been reinstated by the diet of Warsaw in his important functions. He has refused a pension of 200,000 florins.

Warsaw, Dec. 23. The inhabitants of the circle of Random had a meeting on the 10th. They subscribed liberally, and have announced their intention of raising a regiment of cavalry. Cornelius Syko, an old Polish officer, now prior of the Carmelites, is working at the fortifications of Praga, along with all his monks. The actual abode of Vincent Krasinski is not known; but it is announced that his son Sigismund, who is now in Russia, will shortly arrive here, to raise a regiment at his own expense, and that he will enroll himself in it as a private soldier.

Russian Field Marshal Hans Karl von Diebitsch.
(Painted by George Dawe)

Lieut. Col. Geritz, *a descendent of William Tell*, forms a division of sharpshooters, which he calls his 'infernal troops.'

'It is said that the Poles of the ancient provinces of Poland, who are residing in Paris, are to place at the disposal of the Polish government considerable sums of money, and that the countess Tyschkiewitz, sister of the late Poniatowski, has distinguished herself by a large subscription.

There has appeared under the title of 'The Great Week of the Polonnaise,' a succinct recital of the Polish revolution. The bishops of Warsaw, Prazmouski and Manugiewicz, have given up for the service of their country, 70,000 florins of their actual revenues, viz. two-thirds.

Extract of a private letter from Warsaw, dated Dec. 27: 'The palatinate of Lublin, Russian Poland, has just offered the government 50,000 men. Count Zamousky is equipping a regiment at his own expense. There are in the army 12,000 soldiers who served under Napoleon, and 300 officers decorated with the legion of honor. The 24th regiment of the line which acted on the first day, has set out for the frontiers. Previous to their departure, they requested their colonel to take them to the fortifications now erecting by the citizens. On their arrival there they formed a square. The soldiers then knelt down and swore that they would attack the Russians with bayonet only, and be killed sooner than surrender. The 1st Regiment of Lancers, a fine troop, has marched. The enthusiasm is at the highest pitch, and exceeds all imagination.'

'*December 30*. Four officers of the Lithuanian corps have escaped and arrived here. They state that it will be impossible for the Russians to compel that corps to go against the Poles, and it is expected that they will be marched into the interior of Russia. We are ready with 60,000 excellent troops, and 10,000 cavalry. We have also 10,000 irregular cavalry, and 100,000 militia, but these last require to be armed with muskets, and every day there are new volunteer corps formed. The *war of extermination* which is preparing will cause torrents of blood to flow; but we can state, without fear, that Poland will not be subdued.'

'*December 31*. One of the pupils of the military school, named Zallwaki, had set out several days ago for Lithuania. All these provinces are on a volcano. We expect with impatience the details of the insurrection at Wilna. 3,000 Russians have perished there; but after three days triumph the Muscovites re-occupied it. All the youth of the university and the citizens, still full of the recollections of the revolution effected in 1794, by the celebrated Jasinski, emulated each other in zeal, we are informed.

As Reported in the "Niles' Register"

Patriotic gifts flow in from all quarters, and the amount is already near 3,000,000. The Jews alone have given above 1,000,000. Their enthusiasm is above all praise. Since the war with Turkey, Russia is very weak. It lost there in two campaigns 200,000 men and 20,000 horses. The treasury is empty; the ammunition and stores intended against France has been collected in the fortresses of Modlin and Zamosc, which are now in the hands of the Poles. These are insufficient for three campaigns. Our artillery is excellent, and it is well known that it was our officers who repaired the faults of the Russian officers at the siege of Varna and Shumla. The manufacture of arms is carried on with extraordinary activity. All the men employed sing, while they work, the celebrated *Mazurka*, of Dombrowski. Every where are seen the portraits of Kosciusko, Poniatowski, and so many other generals, whose memory was proscribed by the brutal despotism of the grand duke Constantine.'

The preceding extracts are sufficient to present a general view of the state of things. Poland is filled with enthusiasm. The fermentation had extended to the grand duchy of Posen (Prussian Poland), but all was yet quiet there.

The emperor of Russia has issued a proclamation and manifesto. The *London Times* of the 13th January says, 'All doubt or conjecture as to the course which the emperor of Russia intends to pursue respecting Poland is now at an end. The autocrat has issued a manifesto which leaves the Poles no alternative but unconditional submission, or military execution. The *hurra* of vengeance which he uttered among his warlike nobility when he first received the intelligence of the insurrection at Warsaw, is now resounded through the empire, and if echoed by the people as it was by the court, may be considered as the prelude to an *exterminating* Polish invasion.

Though prepared for a declaration of war against Poland, probably neither the Poles themselves, nor any other European nation, were prepared for the assertion of such arrogant pretensions, or the employment of such sanguinary menaces, as his document contains. The 'rebels' are spoken of as 'struck with fear of approaching chastisement, yet daring to think of victory for some moments, and to propose conditions to their legitimate masters.' These 'traitors are to be put down in a single decisive battle, and their treason is to be punished.' *When any autocrat, from Czar Peter to Czar Nicholas, appeals to God as the defender of the legitimate cause, and denounces the punishment of treason, there is no doubt of the hypocrisy is to be the cover to every excess of violence and atrocity.*

The cruel derision of demanding gratitude from the Poles for such 'peace and prosperity' as they enjoyed under the despotism of

133

the grand duke Constantine adds unbearable insult to those manifold oppressions which provoked and justified the insurrection.

The Poles are now aware of their situation. They may recall their envoys from St. Petersburg, if they are not already returned. The answer is given in this manifesto. The conditions which they are said to propose to 'their legitimate masters' are already rejected with indignation. Let them issue a counter-manifesto. Let them display their wounds and sufferings to Europe. Let them invoke assistance from every generous arm, sympathy from every patriotic heart. France and Belgium have taught them the barricades: let their cities be defended with equal heroism. Above all, let them arm their whole population, and invite all the Polish nation to join them; and then we may look forward to the shock with some confidence in the success of the cause. [*Times*]'

The manifesto of Russia seems to have provoked one general burst of indignation in England, because of the high-handed measures it threatens. But it does not appear that England or France will interfere in the affairs of Poland, at present. The best understanding appears to exist between these latter powers.

The Russian armies intended to enter Poland, will amount to 150,000 men.

The accounts from Vienna the 22nd inst., say a Frankfort date of Dec. 27th, are extremely curious. Austria is arming on all sides. The troops which have long been in Italy, and those which have lately been sent thither, will remain as a corps of observation; but all the other forces of the empire, and those of Hungary which can be spared, are going to be assembled in Gallicia and the other provinces on the frontiers of Poland. By this means it is intended, at the same time, to awe the Poles, and to repress the fermentation which has manifested itself at Lemberg, and in other provinces formerly Polish.

Lemberg was known to Poles as Lwów. Located in today's Ukraine, it is known as Lviv.

Article 108. (February 26, 1831, page 463)

There are some later accounts from Poland, they mainly go to shew the devotion of her gallant inhabitants, and the great preparations that they are making to resist the Russians. It is said that they would soon have 150,000 men fully equipped men, and 200,000 irregulars armed with pikes and pistols, etc.

Article 109. (March 5, 1831, pages 7, 8, and 9):

Czar Nicholas I addressed two manifestos to Poland, as this "Russia against Poland" article illustrates.

The emperor and king of Poland has delivered to the Poles the following proclamation: 'The odious attempt of which your capital has been the theatre has disturbed the repose of your country. The intelligence has excited my just indignation and filled me with the greatest grief.

Men who dishonor the name of Poles have conspired against the life of the brother of your monarch; have seduced a part of your army to forget their oaths and deceived the people upon the dearest interest of your country.

It is still time, however, to remedy the past, and you may yet save yourselves from greater *evils.* I will not confound those who abjure the error of a moment with those who persist in crime.

Poles! Listen to the counsels of a father; obey the commands of your king. That you may be fully aware of our intentions, we ordain:

1. That all our Russian subjects detained as prisoners be set at liberty;
2. The council of administration shall resume its primitive functions, and the authority with which we invested it by the decree of the 12th August 1826.
3. All civil authorities of the capital and of the Waywodies shall render strict obedience to the decrees issued in our name by the council of administration, organized, as we have before said, and shall not acknowledge any power illegally constituted.
4. Immediately on the receipt of these presents, all the chiefs of our Polish army shall be bound to assemble their troops, and march without delay to Plock, the point we have fixed upon for the assembling of our royal army.
5. All chiefs are to send us without delay, returns of the state of their troops.
6. Every armament formed in consequence of the disturbances at Warsaw, and not in accordance with the organization of our army, is dissolved from this moment.

Consequently, the local authorities are charged to take care that all persons found with arms illegally obtained do instantly give them up, and that these arms be placed under the veterans and police officers of each district.

Soldiers of the Polish army! In all times your motto has been '*Honor and Fidelity.*' Our brave regiment of *Chasseurs* of the horse guards have furnished a proof which will be ever memorable. Soldiers, follow this example and answer the expectations of your sovereign who has received your oaths.

Poles! This proclamation will assure those who have remained faithful to me that I know how to rely upon their devotedness, and confide in their courage. Those among you who have abandoned themselves to a momentary error will equally learn that I do not repel them if they but hasten to return to their duty.

But never shall the words of your king be addressed to men without honor and without fidelity, who have conspired against the repose of their country. Should they have dared to flatter themselves, that by taking up arms they would obtain concessions as a reward for their crimes, their hopes shall be vain. They have betrayed their country. The misery they prepared for it will fall on their own heads.

Given at St. Petersburg, this 17th December, A. D. 1830, and the 6th of our reign.

(Signed), Nicholas

The minister secretary of state,
Count Stephen Grabowski

Note that Russian Czar Nicholas (Mikołaj in Polish) was crowned in Warsaw as King of Poland on May 17, 1826, but had begun his reign as Emperor (Czar) of Russia on December 1, 1825, thus making 1830 the first, albeit partial, calendar year of his six-year Imperial reign up to that point when he had twenty-five more years left to live and reign.

RUSSIAN MANIFESTO AGAINST POLAND. As reported by that title in a newspaper of Brussels, Belgium, and re-printed by the *Niles'Weekly Register* on March 3, 1831. Please note again that Czar Nicholas had been known officially as the "emperor and autocrat of all the Russias," and not as the "emperor and autocrat of all the Russians." The word below, "Cesarowitch" is "Tsarevich" meaning, "the son of a Tsar" as it referenced Constantine who age-wise had been the expected successor to his older brother, Czar Alexander. However, Constantine chose not to become Czar, thereby making his younger brother, Nicholas, eligible to become Czar in his own right. Each of the four sons (Alexander, Constantine, Nicholas and Michael) of Czar or Tsar Paul (1796-1801) was known as a "Paulowitsch" meaning a "son of Paul."

The following manifesto has just been published: 'We, Nicholas, by the grace of God, emperor and autocrat of all the Russias, etc., to all our faithful subjects, greeting.

A terrible treason has convulsed the kingdom of Poland, which is united to Russia. *Evil* minded men, whom the benefits of the emperor Alexander, the magnanimous deliverer of their country, had not disarmed, and who, under the protection of the constitution which he had granted them, enjoyed the fruits of his solicitude, plotted the overthrow of the order of things introduced by him, and marked the outset of their crimes on the 17th (27th) of November, by rebellion, bloodshed, and criminal attempts on the life of our beloved brother, the Cesarowitsch and grand duke Constantine Paulowitsch. Taking advantage of the darkness of the night, a furious multitude, instigated by them, attacked the palace of the Cesarowitsch, and at the same time, spread to several quarters of the city false reports that the Russian troops were massacring the peaceable citizens, enraging the people, and filling the city with all the horrors of anarchy. The Cesarowitsch then resolved to take up a position in the environs of Warsaw with the Russian troops that he had with him, and the Polish troops that remained faithful to their duty, and not act offensively, in order to avoid all occasions for the effusion of bloodshed, to show clearly the absurdity and the falsehood of their reports that were spread, to give the authorities of the city time and means, with the aid of the well- disposed citizens, to recall to their duty those who had been led away, and to keep the *evil* minded in check: but this expectation was not fulfilled.

The council of administration could not succeed in restoring order, incessantly menaced by the rebels, who had formed illegal meetings and had changed its composition by removing the members named by us, and establishing others forced on it by the chiefs of the conspirators. There was nothing left for it to do but earnestly entreat the Cesarowitsch to send back the Polish troops who had left Warsaw with him, in order to preserve public and private property from further pillage. Soon this council was totally dissolved, and the whole power placed in the hands of a general. At the same time a report spread of a similar insurrection in all the provinces of the kingdom of Poland. The same means were every where employed: seduction, menaces, falsehoods, the object of which was to subject the peaceable citizens to the power of some rebels. In these serious and deplorable circumstances, the Cesarowitsch thought it necessary to follow the advice of the council of state, and he permitted the small number of Polish troops who had remained faithful to return to Warsaw, in order, if possible, to protect persons and property. He himself, with the Russian troops, quitted the kingdom of Poland, and on the 1st (13th) of December arrived at the village of Wlodaw, in Volhynia. In this manner a crime, which had been long meditated, was consummated. After so many calamities, the Polish nation was enjoying peace and prosperity, under the protection of our government; again, it precipitates itself into an abyss of revolt and misery, and troops of these credulous men, though struck with fear of approaching chastisement, dare to propose to us, their legitimate master.

Russians! You know that we reject them with indignation. Your hearts, burning with zeal for the throne, comprehend what ours feels. At the first news of the treason your answer was a new oath of unalterable fidelity, and at this moment we see in the whole extent of our vast empire only one impulse, in the hearts of all only one sentiment, the desire of sparing no effort for the honor of their sovereign, the inviolability of the empire and to sacrifice to it their riches, prosperity, and even their lives. We have contemplated with emotion the generous transport of the love of the people to our person and to the country, and we consider it as a sacred duty to answer to it by the words of moderation.

We are ready to punish the treason, but at the same time we will distinguish between the innocent and the guilty, and pardon the weak, who, through inability to resist, or through fear, followed the torrent of rebellion.

No, all the subjects of our kingdom of Poland, all the inhabitants of Warsaw, have not taken part in the conspiracy and its deplorable consequences. Several have shown, by dying gloriously, that they knew their duty; others, as we have seen by the reports of the grand duke, were obliged to return with tears of despair to the places occupied by the rebels; they form, with the victims of fraud and seduction, the greater part of the army, and of the kingdom of Poland. We addressed them on the 5th (17th) of this month (already published), in which, expressing our just displeasure at the violation of faith, we gave orders to put an end to all usurpations of power, illicit armaments, and to replace everything on its former footing. By doing this, they may still repair the fault of their countrymen, and save the kingdom of Poland from the disastrous consequence of a criminal infatuation. In pointing out this as the only means of safety, we made known to all our faithful subjects this effect of our clemency; they will see in it our resolution *to maintain untouched the rights of the throne*, and to protect the country, as well as the equally firm resolution to excuse those who have been led astray.

Russians, the example of the emperor will serve you as a guide. Justice and not vengeance, unshaken firmness in the combat for the honor and welfare of the state, without hatred towards infatuated adversaries, love and respect for those subjects of our kingdom of Poland who have remained faithful to the path taken to us, a prompt reconciliation with all those who return to their duty. You will fulfill our hopes as you have already done. Persevere in your peace and tranquility, in firm reliance upon God, the eternal benefactor of Russia, and in a monarch who knows the greatness and the sacredness of his vocation, and who will know how to maintain unimpaired the dignity of his empire, and *the glory of his Russian name.*

(signed), Nicholas.

St. Petersburgh, Dec. 12, (24) in the 6th year of our reign.

All of the foregoing can be reduced to the phrase employed by Nicholas, in closing, as being first and foremost for him and his fellow monarchs, "to maintain untouched the rights of the throne" and secondarily, "to protect the country," whereas at least the reverse should have been true. The arrogance of rule by divine right could not have been more clearly and better articulated. Ditto for the arrogance of 21st century authoritarianism worldwide.

Article 110. (March 19, 1831, page 51)

POLAND. The present 'kingdom of Poland,' the heart and center of its ancient sovereignty, is hereditary in the person of the Russian autocrat and his successors, and comprises a superfice of 6,340 square leagues, having a population of 3,850,000 souls. It is divided into eight waiwodeships -- namely, Warsaw, Sandomir, Kalish, Lublin, Plotzk, Masovia, Podlachia, and Augustowo. The national revenues amount to 2,280,000 pounds sterling, about the seventh part of which is assigned to the civil list. Its military force consists of 60,000 infantry and 20,000 cavalry. Warsaw, with 126,433 inhabitants, is its capital; and next stands in succession Sandomir, 50,000 inhabitants; Lublin, 12,000; and Kalish, 8,500. The immense tract of the country comprehending Lithuania, Volhynia, and Podolia containing 3,000,000 souls, is become part and parcel of the Russian territory. That part of Poland which is subject to Austria bears the designation of the kingdom of Galicia and Ludominia. Its population amounts to 4,379,000 souls. The grand duchy of Posen, the only part of Poland retained by Prussia, contains 538 geographical miles and 1,051,137 inhabitants. Its chief towns are Bromberg and Posen.

Article 111. (April 9, 1831, page 23)

Poland's government as well as armed forces reportedly were preparing themselves for an extended resistance against Russia.

The Polish diet, 83 to 13, placed the executive power in a commission of five members, and declared the independence of the Polish nation. Field marshal Deibitsch was advancing, filled with the hope of victory, and seemingly resolved to execute the severest punishment on the Poles. But the latter appear to have a good spirit of resistance, with many excellent officers of the school of Napoleon.

Article 112. (April 23, 1831, pages 139 and 140)

More intelligence on Poland's gallant resistance against Russian armed forces. The battle listed as Gruscho is most likely referring to the battle of Grochów.

140

As Reported in the "Niles' Register"

An arrival at New York City brings highly important intelligence from Europe, the latest dates are from London to the 20th of March.

'POLAND. The Russians have reached the Vistula, and after some hard fighting succeeded in throwing troops across the river. The Russian and Polish armies engaged in a series of bloody battles between the 17th and 18th of February. The Poles fought with great courage and desperation. The contending armies were seen from Warsaw by aid of telescopes. The Poles were at first successful but were defeated in the main battle on the 24th and 25th, before Praga. Hostilities were renewed on the 26th, on which day and the 27th, there was much hard fighting, with considerable loss on both sides. The Poles behaved with their usual bravery, but were compelled to give way. Determined, however, to make their retreat in as good order as possible, they set fire to Praga, in order to interrupt for a time the advance of the Russians. Praga was thus destroyed. Subsequently to these events, it is difficult to ascertain the real condition of affairs, though it is announced by the correspondent of the *London Morning Chronicle*, in a letter of the date of March the 8th, that the municipal authorities of Warsaw, being no longer protected by their brave army, and being unable to prevent the entry of the Russians, held a meeting at which it was resolved to surrender at discretion, and accordingly waited on the Russian commander, and signified their submission. Other accounts state that Warsaw had *not* fallen, and that general *Deibitsch*, the Russian commander in chief, had been compelled to alter his plans; that he would not again *attack* Warsaw, but *surround* it and reduce it to famine. The Polish account admits a loss of 9,000 men put *hors du combat*, and that the wounded in the hospitals amount to 3,600. The most authentic accounts in their preceding battles at Dobre, Liff, and Milosnow, state the Polish loss at 600 killed, 1,400 wounded, and 250 missing, and one six pounder; that of the Russians, in the same affairs are stated to be 800 killed, 1,700 wounded, and 300 missing. The temporary advantages gained by the Poles over the Cossacks, on the left bank of the Vistula, did not deter the forward march of the Russian army. The onward march of general Deibitsch is accounted for on the ground that the troops in the vicinity of the capital, did not present the same spirit of resistance as those of the intervening territory. Independent of the large magazines which fell into the hands of the Russians, they derive great supplies of provisions from the peasantry of the country through which they pass, who keep up an active traffic with the invaders. The successes of the gallant Poles, in their opening engagements, caused great rejoicing at Warsaw, but unfortunately for their liberty and the cause of freedom, their subsequent defeats had cast

General Jan Zygmunt Skrzynecki (1787-1860)

a gloom over the face of the country. The intelligent correspondent, however, of the London Morning Chronicle thinks that the temporary triumphs of the Russians will not avail, and that the Poles will yet be free. In a battle fought near *Gruscho*, which commenced on the morning of the 10th March and lasted throughout the day, the Poles maintained their ground, and kept the field. In the two armies, 150 pieces of cannon were in action. The Russians are supposed to have lost 10,000 men. Two Russian regiments charged with bayonets, and it is said that the conflict was so terrible and bloody that scarcely 20 men of the two regiments, escaped. At the close of the day, the Russians retired to the woods. General Dwernicki commanded the Poles, and general Geisman the Russians. The latter general very narrowly escaped being taken prisoner. The Poles killed 400 of the Russians, including one lieutenant colonel of artillery and one major, took 2,300 prisoners, including 2 captains, 1 lieutenant, 2 ensigns, many horses, a large supply of ammunition, and 11 pieces of cannon, five of the latter were immediately turned against the invaders.

The loss of the Poles was one assistant surgeon, and 15 men killed and wounded, among whom were major Rosian. The newly trained regiments of young Poles behaved with the firmness of veterans. On the right bank of the Vistula, on the 21st and 22nd of February, the outposts of the two armies came to blows. The Russians sent in a white flag, and a parley ensued, which led to a temporary armistice for the purpose of burying the dead. Several letters contradict the report of the fall of Warsaw. Accounts published in the German papers, compute the loss of the Russians at 20,000 men, and that of the Poles at 11,000 killed and wounded. The Russians lost horses from disease and want of provender. Consequently, a great part of their artillery were deprived of the means of transportation, and in all probability, in many instances must fall into the hands of the Poles.

A letter dated at *Warsaw* March 6th states the number of the Polish army, before the city for ten days to be but 40,000 strong, and with 60 pieces of artillery. The Russian army consisted of 120,000 men and 200 pieces of cannon. The weather was intensely cold; but nothing could exceed the attentions of the Polish ladies to the wounded. Stores were abundantly provided for them, whereas, on the contrary, the Russians endured every privation which cold and hunger could inflict. The want of provisions had engendered sickness which was at the above date raging in their ranks. The imperial guard which occupied Warsaw since 1815 under the orders of the Czarowitch has been entirely destroyed. Prince Michael Radziwill had resigned the command of the army, and gen. Skryznecki, had been appointed generalissimo, and had given much satisfaction. He served with Poniatowski, and it was in the hollow square of his battalion that Napoleon took shelter at Areisiaur Aube, when the regiments of the young guard gave way.

General Deibitsch had offered a reward of 500 ducats for the delivery up to him of any student of the university, and 2,000 ducats a head for members of the chamber of deputies. The several divisions of the Russian army which had been engaged were under the command of marshal Deibitch, generals Pahlen, Rosin, and Geismar, and the division of prince Schachowski had been ordered to re-enforce those already before Warsaw. General Chlopicki behaved with great gallantry and was severely wounded.

Paris, March 14.... There was a mob in Paris on the 9th of March, which attacked the home of the Russian ambassador, amid cries of 'down with the Russians' and 'the Poles forever,' broke his windows, and then bent their way towards the chamber of deputies, the members of which they assailed with insulting and seditious denunciations. The national guards acted with firmness in suppressing the riot. A general war in Europe appears inevitable.

POLAND. The Russians, at the latest intelligence from Poland, had not made any new attack upon Polish forces. The weather is said to have proved very unfavorable for military operations, in consequence of the thawing of the snow, and the breaking up of the ice in the Vistula. Field marshal Deibitsch has set at liberty the Polish prisoners of war, giving to each two ducats and a proclamation to the Poles. The governor general and vice governor of Warsaw had resigned. The central forces of Poland concentrated in the villages westward of Warsaw is estimated at about 36,000 regulars, 15,000 volunteers, 5,000 scythemen, (peasants armed with scythes), and 66 field pieces, independent of 10,000 men under gen. Devernicki, in the waiwodship of Sandomir. The loss of the Russians since the opening of the campaign is thus stated; killed, wounded, and missing 5,000 men, and 13 guns of various caliber -- sick 7,000.

It is stated that the emperor Nicholas has given directions to gen. Deibitsch not to destroy Warsaw; and a letter published in the London papers of the 22nd March states that an armistice between the Russians and the Poles had been agreed upon. The London Morning Herald of the 23rd March says that the news from Poland is cheering. The patriotic army is unbroken in spirit, with supplies of all sorts abundant, strongly posted near Warsaw, having also a large force in Praga. The Russians on the other hand, are represented as harassed by the bad roads, disappointed by the breaking up of the ice in the Vistula, weakened by diseases from the marshy country through which they marched, and to be sickly, irresolute, and dispirited.'

Article 113. (April 23, 1831, page 141)

> The fact of a Russian military commander in 1831 having placed bounties of "500 ducats for the delivery up to him of any student of the university, and 2,000 ducats a head for members of the chamber of deputies" reminds us of Vladimir Putin's imposition of bounties on the heads of American soldiers fighting in Afghanistan prior to 2021 and likely through now as well. With Russia, old habits never die. There is also another case during the Kraków Uprising of 1846 where Austrian officials supposedly paid peasants in coin and salt for the heads of Polish nobles.

A letter from Warsaw of the 10th March states that general Dworniki, had gained another victory over the Russians near Lublin, and that it was almost certain that a revolution had broken out in the Ukraine, Volhynia, Podolia and Lithuania, and that the Russian army had retreated from their position near Praga in confusion.

The official journal of Warsaw states, that the Russians who entered Putowy, pillaged the houses, set fire to the buildings, violated the women, and made prisoners of the men; *and this without any thing to enrage them,* the inhabitants having furnished them during their stay with all they demanded."

> Yet another example of Russians acting in compliance with, and indeed reinforcing, their well-earned reputation as brutish barbarians, much as they had been reported to have been decades earlier in the report, "The Russians and the Cossacks." (See Article 6). General Józef Dwernicki (Dwerniki) (1779 – 1857) fought from the Wars of the Partitions through the Napoleonic Wars.

As Reported in the "Niles' Register"

NILES' WEEKLY REGISTER.

FOURTH SERIES.] No. 9—VOL. IV. BALTIMORE, APRIL 30, 1831. [VOL. XL. WHOLE No. 1025

THE PAST—THE PRESENT—FOR THE FUTURE.

EDITED, PRINTED AND PUBLISHED BY H. NILES, AT $5 PER ANNUM, PAYABLE IN ADVANCE.

☞ To check frauds on the revenue, it has been proposed at Middletown, Con. and approved by a meeting at New York, to hold a convention of woollen manufacturers at the city of New York, on the 17th of May next—and preparatory to which a meeting of such manufacturers has been called to be held at Albany, on the 5th.

☞ There is another mass of foreign news, of which we have made a careful abstract, to keep up the history of events. It will be gladly seen that the Poles, instead of being overwhelmed as we feared, were pressing upon their barbarian invaders, who were alarmed by risings of the people in their rear, and suffering excessively from the inclemency of the season. Strength to the arm that strikes in the name of liberty—perish the invaders—let Poland be free!

We incline to the belief that some degree of "reform" will take place in the United Kingdom of Great Britain and Ireland—though, perhaps, not immediately. The public expectation is up—and something must be done. Belgium is in a much disordered state—anarchy appears to prevail. France is buckling on her armor, and, we think, will surely come into contact with Austria, in Italy, at some new and bloody Marengo. The emperor wants humbling. The small bands of constitutionalists appear to be put down in Spain. The monster of Portugal is glutting himself with the best blood of the people. The jealousy and fears of the great powers alone suffer this wretch to have dominion. The news from other states has not much interest. We regard a general war as inevitable.

There has been much alarm in the island of Antigua, because of revolutionary movements among the slaves—but they were quieted, after the conflagration of several plantations and the arrest of some of the principal actors in them. The white population was in a state of terror for 48 hours.

PRICE OF STOCKS, FLOUR, &c. On the 31st March, consols, at London, were worth only 76 3-4 7-8. Money was scarce and the market "feverish." United States 5 per cents were 85½; bank shares £26 10s. to £27. A rumor that gen. Clausel had accepted the command of the "army of the Alps," to view the operations of Austria, helped to reduce the price of British stocks, and advance that of the American in market.

The last weekly average price of wheat was 71s. 8d. so that the duty remained at the lowest point; but a fall of price and rise of duty was expected in two or three weeks. The corn market was dull and declining. Flour was worth from 34s. to 37s. for the best, duty paid. The very latest account says that it had declined from 1s. to 1s. 6d. per barrel, and was dull.

We think it most likely that the usual luck will attend speculations in flour for the British market; but, though ninety-and-nine times suffering loss, some will "go" the hundredth.

The new duty on cotton had not yet taken effect. The demand was brisk—upland 5 3-8 to 6½; Orleans 5½ to 7 3-8.

It appears rather extraordinary that exchange on England has risen considerably within a few days past—notwithstanding our increased exports to that country and the well-known desire entertained in Europe for investments in the United States. It may be caused by an expected rise in the price of British manufactures—which, indeed, has taken place in many important articles; and will become general, if there shall be an extensive war, whether England speedily embarks in it or not.

THE POLITICAL EXPLOSION. Various, and strange, and wild, are the constructions put upon the late retirement of Messrs. Van Buren and Eaton, and the dismissal of Messrs. Ingham and Branch; and it is also firmly reported that Mr. Berrien, the attorney general, will resign—leaving only Mr. Barry, the post master general, for the new "cabinet,"* being the first incumbent of that office who was considered an official adviser of the president—or "cabinet minister."

To the correspondence between Messrs. Eaton and Van Buren and the president, published in our last, we now add the letters of Messrs. Ingham and Branch, and the replies thereto—which, it will be remarked, are in the same set words to the latter. Common fame had decidedly stated for about or more than two months past, that their official days were numbered; but why Messrs. Van Buren and Eaton retired, is wrapped up in a mystery which the public mind has not yet been able to penetrate.

It might have been expected that the long letter of the secretary of state would have drawn aside the veil—but he has thickened it. The Pythia never delivered her oracles in more ambiguous terms. We have read and re-read it—it "means any thing or nothing." The doctrine of "non committal" was never more happily exemplified. The words used had better been written in the ancient hieroglyphics of Egypt—for then, at least one man, Champollion, could have given their sure interpretation to the people. Mr. Van Buren has long maintained a high reputation for incomprehensibility in his political movements—and here is indisputable evidence of his talent in the obscure. During his late excursion, the editor conversed with at least fifty gentlemen (of both parties), seeking information; and, though several of them stand high in the public estimation and are ripe scholars—one, and one only, of the whole went further than to say, that he fully understood a certain, and small, part of this official paper. But for our part, the whole is hidden from our obtuse intellect—and we must wait a moving of political elements to comprehend an event which must be regarded as an important one.

There is something very remarkable in the dates of Messrs. Eaton and Van Buren's letters compared with those of Messrs. Ingham and Branch—the first being of the 7th and 11th April, and the latter of the 18th to the 20th. Is it possible that the secretaries of the treasury and of the navy could have been kept in ignorance of the resignations of the secretaries of state and of war, the long period of about ten days—all the parties being on the spot? Yet such would seem to have been the case—or such ignorance is affected; and clearly shows that the "cabinet" was ill-tempered and in a state of open quarrel, justifying the previous reports that we had on this subject. And it is extraordinary that Messrs. Ingham and Branch, highly complimented by

*We quote the word "cabinet," and as a republican protest against the term as now used. It was not so in the days of Washington or Jefferson. It goes to show a power which the constitution never contemplated, which may relieve the president of that direct and solemn responsibility that belongs to the high office which he holds. Heaven forbid that the time shall arrive, when persons named to office by the president shall relieve the president of his responsibility to the people—and render him, like a king of England, incapable of doing wrong. We do not recollect that the words "my cabinet" were ever before officially used by a president of the United States—and cannot believe that they were; but do know that we have often offered our humble protest against even the ordinary use of the term, as a running into that kingliness that we have always hated. The secretaries are only as the clerks of the president—presumed to have no will or power in themselves, except specially delegated. Their opinion may be required, but the president has no obligation even to ask it.

VOL. XL—No. 11.

"Let Poland be free!" Hezekiah Niles had reminded Americans at the end of paragraph two in the left-hand column on the front page of this issue of April 30, 1831 some five months to the day the November Uprising began in Warsaw.

145

Article 114. (April 30, 1831, front-page)

When it came to reporting on Poland's epic struggle to exist free and independent, no one had to speculate where Hezekiah Niles stood. Indeed, he was the best-known American proponent of Poland's steadfast cause for liberty, and as such, a genuine ahead-of-his-time amicus poloniae of the subsequent 20th century when that Latin term, adopted by modern Poland, became a formal honorific recognition bestowed on "a Friend of Poland." His Niles' Weekly Resister often devoted front-page coverage to Poland's struggles for liberty. From 1811 to 1849, Niles' Register never hesitated in addressing Poland's painful victimhood throughout, as in the second paragraph of its April 30, 1831 front-page, pro-Poland news on that day! Consider his concluding statement below in the first sentence, in keeping with his stated reason for having created *Niles' Weekly Register* that I addressed in the Introduction of this book:

There is another mass of foreign news, of which we have made a careful abstract, *to keep up the history of events*. It will be gladly seen that the Poles, instead of being overwhelmed as we feared, were pressing upon their barbarian invaders, who were alarmed by risings of the people in their rear, and suffering extensively from the inclemency of the season. Strength to the arm that strikes in the name of liberty -- perish the invader -- let Poland be free!

"Siła w ramięnia które uderza w imię wolności -- zgiń najeźdźcę -- niech Polska będzie wolna!" Indeed, a sentiment compellingly stated in a free Polish translation, and would be in any language as well, as the original closing sentence stated above in English illustrated on the front-page of this issue of *Niles' Weekly Register* proclaims.

****

To its credit, Niles' Register devoted front-page reference to Poland in varying contexts as follows: Articles 50 (October 28, 1820); 76 (June 25, 1825); 102 (January 1, 1831); 114 (April 30, 1831); 150 (November 12, 1831); 162 (March 17, 1832); 227 (May 7, 1836); 241 (May 28, 1840); 242 (July 11, 1840); 253 (December 30, 1843); 254 (March 23, 1844); 255 (April 20, 1844); 257 (July 13, 1844); 258 (November 16, 1844); 259 (December 14, 1844); 260 (December 28, 1844); 264 (May 2, 1846); 267 (December 26, 1846); and 280 (January 22, 1848).

Article 115. (April 30, 1831, page 151)

It would appear since the last advices, the army of Diebitsch thought more of its safety than anything else. The *Messager des Chambres* of the 23rd March, states that provisions had failed, the roads were impracticable, and that the Russian army were perishing by degrees. Already says it flees the environs of Praga, leaves its positions in all quarters, even abandoning artillery in many places. General Kreutz and prince Adam de Wurtemburg save themselves by post-horses. The thaw of the Vistula had greatly increased the wretched condition of the Russian army. General Dwernicki is represented as pursuing the Russians with great fury; and it is stated that new levies were raising every where to give the final blow to their invasion. On the 9th of March, a corps of Cossacks , who were covering the retreat of the Russians, were dispersed. The Russians, it appeared, still occupied the frontiers with between 15 or 20,000 infantry, cavalry and artillery. The breaking up of the ice in the Vistula carried away three pontoons of the bridge over that river on the 11th of March. News had been received on the 10th of March that general Dwernicki's division of the Polish army had again broken a Russian battalion and taken two cannon. A letter says that he had captured 16 pieces of artillery. The report of insurrectionary movements in Podolia and Volhynia is again rejected, and it is added that in the first named province the nobility and their dependents had raised *en masse* and assembled 15,000 cavalry, which force advances to Kamiraz, the capital, and disarmed a Russian regiment of infantry. The direct accounts from Warsaw are to the 21st March inclusive, of which date the city was in the best state of defence, every possible means had been adopted impart strength to it. Among other preparations to insure the invaders a warm reception, mines had been strung in several of the streets, doors and windows had been barricaded, and walls built across the streets, by which the city was divided into separate fortified quarters.

Please note that in the final sentence of Article 115, it had been the original correspondent who in the year 1831 had chosen to use the words defence and insure as they appear above despite the 21st century spell-check and grammar-check computer software alerts to the contrary.

Article 116. (April 30, 1831, page 159)

This April 30, 1831 issue of *Niles' Weekly Register* included an interesting table titled, "Statistical Articles," having been the work of said President von Malchus, in which it compared technically non-existent Poland's "landed extent, population, revenue, and debt" with the other "principal states of Europe" in 1829. As such, many Europeans, von Malchus included, still held the Kingdom of Poland to be a principal European state, albeit not free and independent, a point which illustrated that the terms Vistulaland, Poznania, and Galicja wouldn't succeed in permanently replacing the term Polska (Poland). Furthermore, despite the fact of the Treaty of Partition of 1797 having vowed that "the name or designation of the Kingdom of Poland, which shall remain suppressed as from the present and forever...," some Europeans seemingly had solved the problem of Poland's ongoing dilemma, simply by referencing its extant existence, at that time at least, providing evidence that the opposite had not been true. What is also highly informative in these statistics had been the fact that most European monarchies had existed financially well beyond their means (i.e., revenues) in 1829 as the related figures on Great Britain especially, and France, the Netherlands, and Austria reveal, among others. In the matter of Russia's revenue and debt, however, I initially had lacked familiarity with the sign: l.(being a variant for pounds sterling -- £ -- as I had subsequently learned) that precedes the 17,420,000 for Russia's revenue and the 35,550,000 for Russia's debt. For the purpose of the statistical table, however, President von Malchus, it appears, simply had placed Russia at the top of the list based on the comparable magnitude of each nation's superfices and populations, with Russia's having been the most extensive.

STATISTICAL ARTICLES.
Extent, population, revenue and debt, of the principal states in
Europe, 1829.
BY PRESIDENT VON MALCHUS.*

	SUPERFICES	POPULATION	REVENUE	DEBT
Russian Empire	6,002,774	60,367,000	*l*.17,420,000	*l*.35,550,000
Austria	194,448	32,838,900	13,940,000	78,100,000
France (w/o Colonies)	161,376	32,500,000	39,020,000	194,400,000
Great Britain (ditto)	88,560	22,129,035	51,500,000	819,600,000
Prussia	80,240	12,552,278	8,149,000	29,701,000
The Netherlands	19,136	6,116,635	6,590,000	148,500,000
Sweden	126,960	2,900,000	2,170,000	
Norway	92,768	1,050,132	354,000	252,100
Denmark	16,304	1.981,014	1,238,000	3,729,000
Poland	36,668	4,035,700	1,306,000	5,740,000
Spain	135,130	13,909,000	6,420,000	70,000,000
Portugal	27,552	5,013,950	2,110,000	5,649,000
Two Sicilies	31,792	7,414,717	3,521,000	18,974,000
Sardinia	21,840	4,333,960	2,750,000	4,684,000
States of the church	12,976	2,483,940	1,238,000	17,142,000
Grand Duchy of Tuscany	6,320	1,300,000	623,400	1,834,000
Switzerland	11,626	2,037,080	448,000	
Ottoman Emp. Europe	160,000	9,476,000	2,475,000	3,667,000
Bavaria	22,160	4,037,017	2,973,000	11,311,000
Saxony	5,568	1,350,000	1,009,000	3,300,000
Hanover	11,620	1,537,500	990,000	2,384,000
Wurtemberg	5,744	1,535,400	851,950	2,505.000
Baden	4,384	1,141,727	901,290	1,670,000
Hesse (Darmstadt)	2,960	697,901	537,260	1,184,900
Hesse (Electorate)	3,328	708,000	476,000	220,000

*The table is founded, as far as possible, upon official documents; and probably no individual can have enjoyed better sources of correct information than one who was successively minister of finance to the former king of Westphalia and the present sovereign of Wurtemberg.

Article 117. (May 14, 1831, page 184)

> Two news-briefs, one being a battlefield report, and the other about the "Polish spirit" appeared in this issue. Field Marshal Fabian Gottlieb Fürst von der Osten-Sacken (1752 – 1837) was a veteran of the Turkish and Napoleonic Wars. It appears that "Cicellanow" refers to Ciechanów.

Poland. Though the dates are not later than those previously received from this country, some additional items are given. An expedition had been sent by gen. Sacken, the object of which was to re-establish the communication with Lomza, the road having been infested with partisan corps of Poles. In one affair, the Poles are represented to have lost 600 men, and in another in which they lost Lublin, their killed, wounded and prisoners are variously stated at from 500 to 2,000. A body of Cossacks had penetrated Cicellanow, but were soon driven back. Several new appointments had been made by the provisional government.

Polish Spirit. The following is one of the many incidents shewing the fine spirit of the Polish soldiers. Field marshal Diebitsch having, with his own hands, pulled the different orders of merit gained on the field of battle of major Kiwerski, who had been severely wounded and made prisoner, the major, in consequence of such an insult, being hurt to the extreme, answered, with dignity, to the marshal, 'You may take upon yourself to have us shot, but not dishonor us, for when a nation declares war upon another, there are no rebels.' The field marshal, enraged at such an answer, ordered his Cossacks to take the prisoners into the interior.

Article 118. (May 21, 1831, page 197)

In this article of May 21, 1831 titled, "Russia and Poland," Hezekiah Niles, who was the owner and Editor of the *Niles' Register*, used the occasion to reference "the cruelty which the Russians practice in Poland," being his Register's recurring theme from 1811 to 1849, with his expressed hope that it "must ultimately prove fatal to" Russia.

Accounts from Poland up to the 24th March furnish nothing new of importance but we are happy to represent the affairs of its brave and noble defenders in a comparatively prosperous condition. Never was a nation animated with a purer and more ardent spirit of patriotism, or disposed to make greater sacrifices for their liberty and independence. The Polish army, assembled in and near Warsaw, amounts to 60,000 men, and the corps of general Dwernicki and other free corps, is 20,000. Dates from Cracow to the 20th March repeat a rumor that

Polish deputies sent to the Russian headquarters have been received there, and have opened negotiations. General Chlopicki had got better. There have been no new operations with the Russian army, but it was still struggling against bad weather, scarcity, diseases and the partial insurrections of the peasants in the Palatinates of Lublin and Augustowo. It is stated in a journal of Warsaw of March 22nd that the sultan had declared war against Russia. The report is re-iterated by the French papers, which add, that a communication had been opened between the sublime porte and the Poles; that each government had sent envoys to the other, and that an insurrection had broken out in Courland. Neither of these reports rested on better foundations than rumor. *The Russians have begun to make use of frightful means to depopulate the country. They carry off all the men. The cruelty which the Russians practice in Poland, must ultimately prove fatal to them.* The Russian couriers cannot even now travel in any part of the country unless accompanied by a strong guard. Over the whole country from Pultosk to Augustowo, terror is so widely spread among the Russians, that, large detachments dared not pass the night in towns without previously entrenching themselves. In quitting Lublin, they chained the Polish col. Rielenske to a cannon, and thus carried him off. Col. Rielenske is a brave veteran officer, who made all the campaigns of Italy under Dombrowski.

Article 119. (May 21, 1831, page 198)

Cheering news from Poland was reported by *Niles' Register,* in its "Russia and Poland" article. It introduced the name of Jan Zygmunt Skrzynecki (1787-1860), one of Poland's best-known generals, whose surname rarely had been spelled correctly by non-Polish correspondents.

We are highly gratified at the cheering news from Poland. The Polish commander in chief, Skryznecki, who was raised, as it will be remembered, from a subordinate station to the chief command, for his distinguished services in the contests of February, has proven himself worthy of the distinction conferred upon him, and fully equal to important trusts confided to him.

When Victimization of Poland Was Never in Doubt

Victory of the Poles over the Russians.

The Polish generalissimo having learned that Marshal Deibitsch had divided his forces, and only left a small corps of the army to observe the capital, took the resolution to pass to the right flank of the Vistula with a great part of his troops, after previously having sent general Uminski towards Ostrolenka, to keep in check the corps of general Sacken, and the guards who were advancing there. He quitted Warsaw during the night of the 30th March and attacked, at Wawer, the corps of gen. Geismar, who were there entrenched in very strong and advantageous positions. By this bold and skillful movement upon the Russians, the Polish generalissimo was enabled to surprise their army of observation, and beat it back upon the corps of gen. Rosen, which was in its turn overwhelmed and driven upon that of gen. Geismar.

All the Russian positions were carried by storm in detail. On the 1st of April the divisions of Rosen and Geismar were brought again to battle, and an officer who set out from the camp, as early as half past one o'clock on that day and arrived at Warsaw at five, reported that before he left they had made 2,000 prisoners, among whom were many general officers. They had also taken six cannon and magazines and muskets.

Whole battalions laid down their arms in the battle of 31st March. This is supposed to be the first time that such an occurrence took place in Russian regiments.

These brilliant affairs resulted in the loss to the Russians of 6,000 killed and wounded, 6,000 prisoners, 15 pieces of cannon, several thousand stand of muskets and 2 standards, and 15 wagons filled with ammunition.

The Russian divisions of Geismar and Rosen were in full retreat, hardly pressed by the victorious army of Skryznecki, while that under Deibitsch, the commander in chief, at his head quarters at Siences was cut off by the Polish corps which had been despatched on the line of the Bug to meet it through the Palatinate of Augustowo.

There was a *report* that the Poles had obtained at Grochow a new and important victory over the Russians; that the corps of Geismar, had been entirely destroyed, that the officer was severely wounded, and among the number of prisoners; that marshal Deibitsch was closely hemmed in by the army and peasantry of the Poles in the marshes, and is thus in the most critical position; and that 6,000 prisoners and 26 pieces of cannon were gained by the Poles by this victory. This report wants confirmation.

The enthusiasm of the Poles is represented to be so great that all the nobles at Posen who could bear arms, although at risk of their prop-

152

erty being confiscated by the Prussian government, have abandoned it and proceeded to Poland. A new regiment of cavalry of 1,200 men has been formed at Warsaw, composed of volunteers from the duchy of Posen. The Polish army consists of 90,000 men, well armed, of which are 25,000 superb cavalry, and a number of scythe bearers.

The report of an *insurrection* in *Lithuania* is confirmed. The *Warsaw Gazette* has published a *proclamation* found on gen. Lermonoff, an officer decorated with the order of St. George, who was killed in a recent affair. This manifesto calls on the Russians 'to insist in *demanding a constitution* from the ultra tory of the north, the infatuated emperor Nicholas.'

An aspect of the Battle of Ostrolęka on May 26, 1831 summarized in an authentic banner carried by Polish forces which stated: "In the Name of God, for Our and Your Freedom."

Article 120. (May 28, 1831, page 222):

Here, *Niles' Weekly Register* published the article -- "Poland and Russia" (note that Willanow" is actually "Wilanów") -- wherein it had stated that:

It was rumored in Paris that Deibitsch and his army have been taken prisoners, and a letter is said by the *London Globe* of the 15th April to have been received by Estafette in the city from Paris, confirming the rumor; but the *Gazette de France*, of Paris on the 16th, says, that the report had no other foundation than supposition.

A dispatch from the Polish commander in chief dated on the 1st of April, states, that his success has been fully as great as previously represented, that he could not exactly compute the loss of the Russians, but that 3,000 men had already laid down their arms, and that the number was augmenting every moment. The Polish army had captured the hospital of Minsk, in which they found 1,000 wounded Poles. News had been received, that the 95th regiment of Russian troops had deserted and joined the Poles. The Russian troops who have thus deserted amount to 4,000.

The Russians on the 30th of March attempted by means of fire ships to burn the bridge from Warsaw to Praga, but failed; two of their fire ships were burnt and a third run aground, and the shells beginning to burst killed some of the Cossacks and obliged the others to pull back. A heavy cannonading had been heard in the direction of Willanow.

Up to 12 o'clock on the 2nd of April, 7,000 prisoners had been brought into Warsaw, and more continued to arrive; and 11 pieces of cannon taken in the battle have also been brought in.

A very large proportion of the prisoners taken are from the provinces formerly belonging to Poland.

According to the latest accounts, the several Russian corps had collected in great forces in Kaluszyn and Siedlco, and a decisive battle was shortly expected.

The Russian government has invited the nobles of Courland and Esthonia, as well as all others who have the right to bear arms, and do not belong to any associations, to enter military service.

Official accounts of the insurrections in Volhynia and Lithuania have been received and the grand duke Michael had marched with 4,000 of the guards for Lithuania. The Castilian count Plater is said is said to be at the head of the central government established by the revolutionists.

The battle of Ostrolęka of May 26, 1831 was one of the largest battles of the November Uprising. In concert with Polish infantry regiments, the legendary Polish scythe-bearers held their own against Russian forces, and were shown here pushing forward against the Russians. The official Polish flag of those days consisted of the White Eagle on a red field. This clear gravure depiction was the work of Georg Benedikt Wunder (1786-1858), a German artist.

Article 121. (May 28, 1831, page 223):

Another article, clearly written by a Pole, possibly a woman (proof of which may have been some of his/her written words printed in italics), in this issue of Niles' Weekly Register, also identified what the Polish insurgents truly needed in practical terms. The degree to which Polish women may have contributed to providing articles of news during the period 1811-1849 is a field open to long-overdue research.

The *London Times* contains a letter dated Warsaw, April 2nd, on the subject of the Polish victory of the 31st of March. It is calculated to encourage the friends of the *holy cause* in which the Poles are engaged, whatever may be the result of the present contest. It says that 'our men fought like lions; our general flew from post to post, from rank to rank, directing, animating, and encouraging. This is a glorious triumph! The barbarian has indeed felt the might that slumbers in a peasant's arm.

O, could you have seen our heroes, could you have seen the burning zeal with which the recruit hurried on with the old soldier, and even the half recovered wounded of our great previous achievement, how they hurried to the field, you would have said, this people cannot die the death of slaves, they were not born for eternal bondage.

We are tired of appealing to the great powers who were parties to the treaty of Vienna. They gave us sympathy, well, our next treaty shall be inscribed in letters of blood on the field of battle, the condition is our country's freedom: we shall achieve it ourselves, and single-handed if we can, if not, well then, we know how to perish.

The pursuit is still hot, but we have not the prompt transport which gives wings to an army; men can run for a day and night, as ours have done, fighting and struggling, but physical exhaustion will impose power, and we cannot accomplish every thing. Our country has everywhere risen, and Diebitsch will find assailants in every village. Lithuania is making her blow, and the march through Poland is not the passing of the Balkan, he will not have quite leisure enough for the use of his rich Turkish pipe and perfumed tobacco, nor even for his brandy punch. Our generalissimo, Skrzynecki, is like Napoleon; what a general he has shown himself! With a handful of men, he has thrown back Muscovite masses: 33,000 Poles have beaten back 100,000 Russians who congregated their masses under the walls of Warsaw; and now 24,000 are chasing and prostrating twice their number at the point of the bayonet, from fortified positions, deemed impregnable without heavy artillery.

Do not believe what the Berlin papers say of the humanity of our invaders, the barbarity of the Russians extends to torture. I declare to you, upon my honor, that I have seen on the skirts of fields of contest, wounded Poles, whose eyes were torn out, merely because they resisted like heroes. *Women have been, on the Muscovite line of march, brutally violated and carried off, whole families have been dispersed, and many borne into Russia under base pretenses.* They sow horror and devastation wherever they show themselves. They have even taken away a lady from Pulawy, from the very apartment of the Princess Czartoryski.

Heavens! See if it is possible to get us arms; the campaign is only begun, no fear now of a *coup de main* upon Warsaw. We do not want men, or money, or addresses, or compliments. We delight to hear of the affections of our friends in Paris and London; but this is not the season for indulging in affectionate personal recollections. We must delay all these until tranquil times; the assistance we want is what I have mentioned. Can any thing be done in this way towards Cracow? *We can pay fully for any thing of this kind, and he who gives us a musket fights with us, he is of our ranks.* Let free men, then, lend us this helping hand. Show this to our dear friend the general, if he has not set out.

There was a report of the interference on the part of England, France, Prussia and Austria in favor of the Poles. It was, however, not credited.

Article 122. (June 4, 1831, pages 241 and 242)

> Despite the fact that no technology whatsoever, other than the hand-written or printed word, supported by the speed of communications, dependent upon men traveling on horseback or in a coach, and on the transatlantic sailing ships of the times, what impressed me, was the extent and pace of intelligence of all sorts coming out of Poland as these two news-briefs were reported by *Niles' Weekly Register* on June 4, 1831, the first on page 241, and the second on page 242, illustrate. The electric telegraph was not generally deployed for use in Europe until the 1840s, Russia included (see Article 282 for telegraphy use in Russia).

PAGE 241: The Poles appear to have been successful in several minor affairs, and the following shews that a grand victory was lately won:

'Head-quarters at Siedlec, April 10, 1831, 9 P.M. To the national government. I have great satisfaction in announcing to the government that the Polish army obtained a considerable victory yesterday. We have taken several cannons, and 3,000 or 5,000 prisoners, amongst whom are nearly 300 officers of different ranks. General *Promdzynski*, commanding a separate corps, covered himself with glory. The advanced hour of the evening does not permit me to give a more detailed report.

(signed)   Skrzynecki

The Poles much wanted cannon at the beginning of the revolution, but they have captured a sufficiency, and have 40 pieces in reserve. Some of the guns that have fallen into their hands were favorites of the Russians, having been in the campaigns in France and in Turkey.

157

The soldiers called them their 'grandmothers.' It is hard to ascertain the truth, but it seems manifest that the Poles have gained many important advantages, and that the Russians have lost many men (said to amount to 60,000), and were much embarrassed by the perseverance and courage of this patriotic people. The invasion, because of the season, was also unfavorable to them, but still, the Russians are powerful, and were concentrating their force, for decisive operations.

Lithuania and several other provinces, appear in a full state of revolt, making a common cause with Poland, proper.

Austria and Prussia were lining their frontiers with soldiers. It was reported that Austria, Prussia and Russia will hold a congress at Troppau, in Silesia."

PAGE 242: "We have some further news from *Poland*. There have been several gallant affairs between the Poles and their invaders, generally in favor of the former, and the Russians, collecting their forces, it was expected, would endeavor to bring about a general estrangement. The Polish general Devernicki has much distinguished himself, a gallant second of the commander-in-chief, Skrzynecki. Marshal Diebitsch appears to have lost much of his popularity as a commander, and it is hoped that the laurels that he gathered in Turkey, may wither in Poland.

There is a report, we fear unfounded, that the Poles had totally defeated the Russians in a general battle, who suffered an immense loss, and were dispersed.

Despite Poland's military successes, the sobering reality of Poland's location in Europe as it pertained to hoped-for help from France and Great Britain, on one hand, and Russia's near-unlimited number of armed forces, on the other hand, lingered inescapably.

Article 123. (June 11, 1831, page 255)

An arrival at New York brings London papers of the 6th May. The accounts from *Poland*, though nothing decisive has happened, are of a cheering nature. The patriots have advanced upon and occupied Siedlec, late the head-quarters of the invaders, and the latter have re-crossed the Bug, which would seem to indicate weakness or apprehension. This retrograde movement has probably had its immediate cause in the general rising of the population in Lithuania, Podolia, and Volhynia, which is reported to have happened. Indeed, it is said that in Russia, proper, there is much shew of dissent. Some great effort must have appeared necessary, for the Russian troops were withdraw-

158

ing over the Pruth, leaving Wallachia open to the Turks. *It is said that 16,000 Lithuanian troops left the Russians in a body and joined the Poles,* and there is a rumor of a great battle in which the invaders perished by thousands. *But Russia, unless distracted from within, is too strong for Poland, gallant and devoted as she is, so located also that not much effectual aid can be given to her in supplies, indispensable to a vigorous support of her independence.*

The commander in chief, Skrzynecki, gives accounts of several small affairs, exceedingly harassing to the enemy, and calculated to give new stimulants to the Poles. The Polish corps of 6,000 men under gen. Uminski, was attacked by the Russian general Ugrowmow, with 20,000 men, and heavy artillery. The former bravely resisted and killed many of them, and took 500 men prisoners and 200 horses, but was compelled to retire, which he did at no great loss. Gen. Dwernicki, the *'cannon provider'* -- was fiercely attacking and severely harassing the Russians.

A quantity of ducats have been coined at Warsaw, *principally made from the wedding rings of the women of Poland!*

→ So far, well, but there are other accounts from Poland which represent the country as already exhausted, and threatened with famine, that the fields would remain uncultivated, that all sorts of business had been brought to a stand; that want had already caused sickness, the corn, cattle and sheep being consumed or destroyed by the armies, and that the general appearance of things was deplorable, indeed.

→P. S. An arrival at Baltimore last evening, brings a London paper of the 12th May. It is stated (and we are compelled to fear the news true), that, after three days hard fighting, the Poles have been defeated with a loss of 2,000 killed and 5,000 prisoners. It is estimated on the one hand, that the battle was not final, but on the other hand, that Warsaw was ready to open her gates to the Russians. The accounts are not certain....

The Russian *emperor* has ordered a new levy of 150,000 men.

A primer for pronouncing Polish surnames! Not very successfully. A daunting task for speakers of English, but correlating the article with Poland's cause for national existence free and independent, as reported in the June 18, 1831 issue, it served a dual purpose.

Article 124. (June 18, 1831, page 273):

POLISH NAMES. A correspondent of the *New York Gazette* furnishes a key to the pronunciation of certain Polish 'jaw breakers' as follows:

'To put an end to the general complaint of the impossibility, or, at least, the difficulty, of pronouncing some Polish names, I will make the brief remarks.

As we have learned from a French paper the name of the brave Skrzynecki to be pronounced Skrejinetski, I will only add that this, expressed with French characters would be written Skerzhinetski, or Skerskinetski, the accent resting, as in most Polish polysyllables, on the penultimate.

In a similar manner pronounce the *c* in all Polish names like *ts* in English (as Plock, read Plotsk); the Polish *sz* like the English *sh* (as Kalisz, read Kalish); and lastly, the Polish *cz* like *ch* in church (as Lovicz, read Lovich or Lovitsch.)

This is all that is chiefly to be noticed about Polish names, by attending to which you will preserve the true sound of the name *of many a champion of* FREEDOM.'

The *New York Standard* says: 'The Paris papers having instructed us how to pronounce the name of the *cannon provider*, Skrzynecki; we wish somebody would be good enough to walk into our office, at some cool opportunity, and pronounce, in intelligible tongue, the name of the head of his staff. It runs *spellatim*, thus -- General Chrzanwski!'

Unfortunately, as it applied to the final word of the article, that having been the near-correctly spelled surname Chrzanwski, the well-intentioned author of the article left out the letter "o" of that very old Polish surname, Chrzanowski, the source of which is the Polish word chrzan, which means horse-radish; and also, attempting to pronounce the name of the town of Łowicz located in Poland.

Article 125. (June 18, 1831, page 275)

A dispatch from the Polish commander in chief states that general Deibitsch had, on the 25th April, at the head of his advanced guard at Kuflew, attacked the rear guard of the Polish army under colonel Dembinski. The engagement lasted several hours. The Russians had 18 pieces of cannon, while the Poles had but four. General Deibitsch endeavored to surround the Polish right-wing with his main army. Col. Dembinski finding his situation disadvantageous, retreated to Koterzya. Gen. Gielgud and part of gen. Skrzynecki's corps, formed a reserve guard at Minsk, which was attacked the following morning at 11 o'clock. The Russians lost 30 men killed, and one officer, and a captain with 72 men and horses were made prisoners. The Poles lost 3 officers and 5 soldiers wounded.

Deibitsch was retreating, followed by the Poles. The Poles in a preceding affair lost 9,000 men, it was believed were dispersed in the woods or among the villages.

A dispatch of the 2nd of May speaks of the conduct of general Gielgud in very complimentary terms, and details an affair in which a regiment of Cossacks were surprised, and routed. The general in chief complains of the conduct of a part of the Russian forces in taking the physicians, who were attending to the sick, as prisoners of war, while he speaks in high terms of commendation of the generals Deibitsch and Kreutz to the officers of a Polish corps taken prisoners. At Lublin there was a great mortality among the Jews, and the Russians had converted the convent into a hospital.

The report of the defeat and capture of general *Rudiger* by general Dwernicki appears to be incorrect, though it is certain that he had gained an advantage over the Russian corps previous to the 25th of April, another account published in the evening edition of the London Times, states that general Dwernicki's corps had been defeated, and, after retreating into Austria, surrendered their arms, to the Austrians. → On the whole, the accounts from Poland are cheering, the retreat of the Russians seems to support various rumors that we have heard of their great sufferings by sickness,* [*They are said to have *left* 10,000 sick at Seidlic, on their retreat.] caused by the harassments of the Poles, who also intercept and prevent regular supplies of provisions, but we cannot see any thing in the details to justify the exultations of many that we would gladly rejoice with, as to the decided success of the Poles, which they encourage a belief has happened.

Article 126. (June 25, 1831, page 296)

The *London Courier*, on the 16th (an evening paper) gives full credit to the capitulation of the Polish army under general Dwernicki, to the Austrians, first published in the *Times* of that morning. It is thought that the event will not influence the operations of the main armies, and it is even supposed that an important object may have been achieved by rousing the people in the rear of the Russians, to arms. The corps under Dwernicki were humanely treated by the Austrians after their surrender.

Article 127. (July 2, 1831, page 312):

Some more particulars of the surrender of the Polish corps under general Dwernicki to the Austrians, are given. Their arms and munitions of war were first received by the Austrians and by them delivered to the Russians. The Poles have made a new levy of 40,000 men, and the Russians were advancing upon them in great force. There were 14,000 sick and wounded in the hospitals of Warsaw. The *cholera morbus* had made great ravages among the Russian prisoners.

Letters it was said had been received in Paris, by express, from Augsburg of the 15th of May, which state that general Skrzynecki, the Polish commander-in-chief, had obtained an important victory over general Deibitsch, and that the latter was in full retreat, and that he would be superseded by general Paskewitch. This account was not believed.

Letters from St. Petersburgh state that the emperor has rejected all accommodation as to Poland, for which France and England warmly interested themselves, and that colossal measures had been taken throughout Russia, to speedily stifle the revolution.

The Lithuanians are still in a state of revolt, and in two affairs are said to have maintained their own.

The official accounts of the Polish commanders received by this arrival, of the late affairs of the contending armies, confirm the former accounts. Gen. Skrzynecki states that on the retreat of the enemy, 'our soldiers were struck with horror to witness the traces of Russian barbarity, places of worship were pillaged and the abodes of clergymen burnt. Sometimes, however, the leaders of the army show feeling and humanity.'

Field marshal Deibitsch's official reports, published at St. Petersburgh, are in no wise discouraging to the Russians.

A Hamburg paper of May 20, states that the Austrian government has refused to allow general Dwernicki to return to Warsaw, and has made arrangements for his reception at Laybach, for the distribution of his officers in Moravia, and for sending his soldiers to Transylvania. Gen. Dwernicki has protested against the harsh procedure, and sent copies of his protest to the English and French ambassadors.

Letters have been received in London from Berlin, which state that the Poles confess they have but faint hopes of success against the Russians...

The Prussian government has formed an army, (including those in garrison), of 330,000 men; a part to form a cordon on the frontiers.

Article 128. (July 9, 1831, page 327)

Until this part was in type, it never occurred to me that I had so closely followed the ideas contained in the following extract from a

General Józef Dwernicki

letter from Kosciusko to John Dickinson dated November 29, 1785:

'In travelling through the remote parts of your continent, I learn how to compare the lives of your farmers with those of the patriarchs. It is there that misery discovers the golden age, and a poor European finds means in settling there to change his slavery for liberty, his wants for ease. Scarcely he lives two years but his ideas *enlarge*, he becomes man and almost citizen, he is forced to quit his habitudes, his prejudices and even his vices, and take the sentiments and virtues of his neighbors. Yes, I have there seen the subjects formerly of a bishop think freely on religion, and heard the natives of reason.'

This issue included Hezekiah Niles' brief report of his earlier having published Kościuszko's thinking about the benefits of liberty as has been referenced in Article 36 of this book. Clearly, Hezekiah Niles had been a lifetime admirer of Kościuszko's unfailing devotion to freedom, independence, democracy and equality for all mankind.

Article 129. (July 9, 1831, page 328)

Poland. The Poles have been successful. A corps of 8,000 men had been despatched to afford succor to the revolutionists of Volhynia. Under the command of gen. Chrzanowski, this gallant corps had passed through a body of 24,000 Russians and arrived in triumph at the fortress of Zamosc, with 800 Russian prisoners. A noble enthusiasm animates the people of Volhynia, Lithuania, and all of Poland. In the government of Vilna, 60,000 insurgents were in arms. A general battle was hourly expected between the armies of Deibitsch and Schrznecki, both armies were in motion. The Russians are manoeuvring to operate against Warsaw on the opposite end of the Vistula, and the Poles to frustrate their attempt. The country on the line of march is desolate, and the cholera prevailed to an alarming extent.

Article 130. (July 9, 1831, page 329)

FRANCE: Louis Philippe was, at the last advices, at Deppe, where he was received with the greatest *eclat*. The national guards of France, now fully armed and equipped, amount to 750,000 men.

The French government, says rumor, have sent to Vienna and Berlin, requiring either an entire or partial reduction of their present military establishments. The cabinet of Vienna is reported to have replied, that Austria desired to place her army on a peace footing, but could not do so until certain important questions, relative to Poland and Italy, were settled. France rejoined that Austria transcended its rights in controlling the affairs of Italy, and therefore, she could not be permitted to use the condition of these states as a pretext for new armaments. The report further states that the emperor of Russia had been reminded by France and England that the convention of Vienna recognizes the independence of Poland.

RUSSIA: The emperor Nicholas was determined to carry his operations against Poland to the last extremity, and the nobles were arming and equipping an army of 100,000 men at their own expense, to march against the Poles. Deibitsch is to concentrate an army of 140,000 men to move on Warsaw.

ONE DAY LATER FROM LONDON: A London paper of the evening of the 30th May, says, 'From Paris, it is stated that offers of mediation on the part of England and France, having been made to the emperor Nicholas, for the pacification of Poland, the autocrat has declared, in answer, that he will make no concessions to rebellious subjects,' and that had he been disposed to make any, *he would not have waited for advice to that effect from the west.*

Another of the 31st reports of some advantages gained by the Poles, but nothing decisive was known to have happened.

Of note, there was the matter of this article's referenced near-monopolization of trade by Polish Jews, a point which the *London Quarterly Journal* described as an "evil." Whereas the article included the statement that "the government has endeavored to check this evil," it did not clarify or identify the ultimate source of the government, whether it was purely Polish or Russian-imposed in nature. Logic would dictate that is was the latter, insofar as it had been Russia that had created the "Purple Pale" zone to which virtually all Jews had been assigned during the reign of Czarina Catherine II (1762-1796) and thereafter. However, without proof to the contrary, it must be taken as the statement of the editor of the London Quarterly Journal rather than that of Dr. Rodecki, the Polish author of the data of the original research, but not this particular article. The data, all told, traveled from Poland to the *London Quarterly Journal*, thence to the *N. Y. Mer. Adv.*, and finally to *Niles' Weekly Register*. While journalistic ethics vests responsibility in the originator of the article, it would have been difficult for readers of *Niles' Weekly Register* to deduce whether it had been by way of Rodecki himself, or the editor of the *London Quarterly Journal*, by action of the Journal's translator (and here we recall the old universal expression that "things get lost in translation"), who had commented about the significance of the tables, as they related to the word "evil" applied to the Jews, so as to create the article re-printed in the United States. Nevertheless, this otherwise comprehensively informative article reveals much about Poland under Russian Imperial rule, and for that matter, Russian censorship of the day. The matter of the word "evil" will be further addressed in Article 201 of this book.

Article 131. (July 9, 1831, pages 335 and 336)

STATISTICS OF POLAND

Yesterday we gave a brief summary of the causes that led immediately to the present revolution in Poland. The Foreign Quarterly then proceeds to speak of *La grande Semaine des Polonais* but as the particulars of that week, and the events that have since taken place, are before our readers, we pass them by. Though our readers are all familiar with the patriotism, daring, and courage of the Poles, yet we think some new light will be shown, as to the country, population and resources, by the statistical account, which as promised yesterday, follows.

Since the establishment of the grand duchy of Warsaw, we may *enpassant* remark, the peasantry of that part of Poland have been emancipated; they live on the estates of the great landlords, each family having a cabin and thirteen acres of ground, on condition of working for the owner three days in the week. They may remove themselves by giving up their tenements. Several proprietors have adopted the system of free labor and wages.

[*N. Y. Mer. Adv.*]

'From the London Foreign Quarterly.

The kingdom of Poland is divided into *eight* palatinates, viz: Masovia, Cracow, Sandomir, Kalisz, Lublin, Plotsk and Augustowo. *The populations, according to the last census in 1829 was (exclusive of the army) 4,038,290, which may be thus classed:*

By *their several races.*		By *their religion.*	
The real Poles	3,000,000	Roman Catholics	3,400,000
Rusini or Rusiniacks,		Greek Church	100,000
from eastern parts of		Lutherans	130,000
ancient Poland	100,000	Calvinists	5,000
Lithuanians	200,000	Jews	400,000
Germans	300,000	Other sects	5,000
Jews	400,000		
	4,000,000		4,000,000

The population of the towns is to that of the country as one to five.

Employed in agriculture, there are house holders	1,871,259
Their families and servants	2,221,185
Manufacturers	140,376
Their families	358,035
Tradesmen	49,858
Their families	121,331
Landed proprietors	4,205
Copyholders	1,856
Freeholders in towns	41,654
Persons employed under government	8,414
Patients in the 592 public hospitals	5,376
Prisoners in the 76 prisons	7,926

The proportion between the nobles and the plebians is as one to thirteen.

According to a verification made by the senate in 1824 there were in the kingdom 12 princes, 74 counts and 20 barons, besides the inferior or untitled nobility.

The city of Warsaw reckoned, in 1815, only 80,000 inhabitants, it now amounts to 140,000, besides the garrison. The provincial towns are Lublin, having 13,400; Kalisch, 12,100; Plotsk, 9,200; etc. The population of the kingdom has been increasing since 1815, at the rate of 100,000 individuals every year.

It appears from Dr. Rodecki's statistical tables published at Warsaw, in 1829, that there are Jews in almost every town of the kingdom of Poland; that in 14 of these, their number is equal to that of the Christians; in 114, it is greater; in three, the inhabitants are either all Jews, or almost entirely so. In Warsaw alone, they muster 30,000. Their number is fast increasing. They monopolise almost all trade, to the exclusion of the Christian population. The government has endeavored to check this *evil*, but with little success; and with this view professor Chiarini has been employed in translating the *Thalmud*, and in laying down a plan of reform for that singular people.

The Catholic religion being that of the great majority of the kingdom, is under the special protection of the government, without infringing, however, on the public freedom of the other forms of worship, and on the equality of individuals of every communion in the enjoyment of civil rights. The Catholic hierarchy consists of the archbishop of Warsaw, primate of the kingdom, and eight bishops, one for each palatinate.

There are 1,638 parish churches, 117 auxiliary ones, 6 colleges, 11 seminaries, 151 male convents, and 29 female. In 1819, Pope Pius VII suppressed by a bull 31 male convents and 13 female. The number of the clergy of the Latin Catholic church is 2,740. The Greek Catholics have a bishop at Chelm, 287 parish churches, 1 seminary, and 5 male convents. Their priests amount to 354. There are, besides, 6 churches of the Russo-Greek communion under the jurisdiction of the bishop of Minsk, 29 Lutheran and 9 Calvinist churches, having their respective consistories, 2 of the sect of Philipines, 274 synagogues, and 2 Mahomedan mosques with their imans!

The University of Warsaw was founded in 1816 in lieu of that of Cracow, and consists of five faculties, having 48 professors, and about 750 students. There are besides at Warsaw four lyceums, besides other schools, Sunday schools for mechanics, and girls' schools. In the provinces are 11 palatine schools and 14 district ones. In all the kingdom there are 1,756 professors or teachers, nearly 30,000 students, and about 11,000 female pupils.

In all chief towns of palatinates there are civil and criminal courts, besides commissions of peace in every district. The two courts of appeal and the superior court assemble at Warsaw. The senate takes cognizance of offenses against the state; there are also a court of commerce and a territorial court.

The army consisted, in 1830, of eight regiments of infantry of the line, besides the guards, four regiments of light infantry, eight regiments of cavalry, besides the *yagers* of the guard, two brigades of foot artillery, and two do. of horse; a corps of engineers, etc., in all 36,000 men. The arsenal and the foundry are at Warsaw. There are two fortresses in the kingdom, Zamosc and Modlin. Every individual from

167

20 to 30 years of age is subject to military service, except in cases of exemption provided by law. The two new military schools, formed in 1825, near Warsaw, have educated already 7,000 pupils.

The budget for the year 1827, consists as follows:

Receipts:	Florins*
Direct taxes	17,646,652
Indirect do.	40,685,630
Income of national lands and forests	7,048,265
Income from tolls, and rates on bridges, roads, etc.	3,769,955
Receipt from mines, mints, prisoners' labours, etc.	2,837,600
Total:	71,988,102

Expenses:	Florins.
Civil list reduced in 1822, from 2,324,705 to	1,508,450
Viceroy, senate, council of state	924,609
Ministry on public instruction and religious worship	3,831,821
--- Do. of justice	2,528,301
--- Do. of interior or home department	3,178,909
--- Do. of war	30,927,795
--- Do. of finances	5,155,936
Secretary of State	233,000
Superior central authorities	944,965
Commissions of administration in the Palatinates	3,665,526
Pensions, repair of roads, public buildings	11,227,000
Extraordinaries	1,866,410
Charges on separate administrations	2,837,600
Total:	69,016,030

There are in the kingdom, especially about Kielce, mines of iron, zinc, coal, and also copper and lead.

Of the 451 towns in the kingdom 353 consist more than half of wooden houses; 83 are entirely of wood; 6 have half their houses made of brick; and 9 consist of more brick than wooden houses. Warsaw contains 1,540 brick, and 1,421 wooden houses.

Besides the towns, of which 214 are national property and 237 belong to private families, there are in the kingdom 22,365 villages, 5,373 of which are national, and 16,992 private property.

The communications have been extensively improved since 1815. Two fine substantial roads cross the whole kingdom, one from Kalisz to Brzesk Litewski, another from Cracow to the Neimen, both passing through Warsaw. Diligences have been established; inns and post houses erected; 623 bridges have been constructed or repaired. Embankments, in great part of stone, have been raised to restrain the

In the paragraph immediately above, the original correspondent's reference to "yagers of the guard" is derived from the German word, *Jäger*, which was used to describe elite light infantry soldiers whose impact in skirmishes with an enemy force was deadly.

waters of the Vistula. The other rivers have been cleansed, and a canal has been cut to join the Narva to the Neimen.

The city of Warsaw has wonderfully improved since the peace. New Streets, squares, palaces, gardens, private and public buildings have been constructed either by the government or by individuals, assisted in many instances, by the public treasury. The streets are well lighted, several of them have been Macadamized. The management of prisons has been ameliorated, the convicts are employed in the public works, mendicity has been suppressed. A society of beneficence has been established at Warsaw, as well as a society of the friends of science. A new exchange, a new theatre, the new church of St. Alexander, new barracks, and a monument to Copernicus, by Thorwaldson, have been raised.

The exports of the kingdom consist chiefly in corn and cattle, besides honey, wax, timber, wool, hides and tallow. The imports are wines, tobacco, colonial produce and articles of luxury and fashion.

The manufacturers of woolen cloth, linen, carpets, and leather have thriven since the peace. While in 1815 there were hardly one hundred looms for coarse woolen cloths, there are now above six thousand, which now supply the whole kingdom, including the army. More than ten thousand families of foreign workers, chiefly German and Swiss, have expatriated to Poland, where they have built new towns and peopled districts formerly deserted. There are numerous distilleries of spirits, and the brewing trade is also very extensive; they brew porter and ale equal to them of England. By the former laws of Poland commerce was depressed, and no noble, however poor, could, without degradation, resort to it, whilst he often served in a menial capacity a richer nobleman.

The balance of trade between the kingdom of Poland and the neighboring states, in 1827, stood (in florins) as follows:

Imports from Russia	11,079,683
Exports to do.	14,548,529
Imports from Prussia	20,316,433
Exports to do.	15,544,730
Imports from Austria	8,527,480
Exports to do.	91,697
Imports from the republic of Cracow	748,857
Exports to do.	2,880,265

Agriculture, which is still the principal occupation of the population, suffers under a depression of prices. In 1827, they reaped

4,439,899 *korsces*** of rye, 3,183,023 of oats, 1,060,082 of barley, and 751,076 of wheat, besides 4,239,185 *korsces* of potatoes, and hay, flax, hemp, and honey. The cattle are improving both in quantity and quality.

In 1827 there were in the kingdom 694,728 cows; 473,946 oxen; 259,990 calves; 703,207 pigs, about two million and a half sheep, 192,841 horses, 8,771 stallions, 167,901 mares. About one half of the extent of the territory of the kingdom may be reckoned to be cultivated, one fourth of the remainder is occupied by forests, and the rest by marshes and uncultivated lands.

*The Polish *florin* is about sixpence sterling. It is divided into 30 grosc hets.

Whereas the total for the "Expenses" column above was given as 69,016,030 florins, I found, upon examination, the total to have been 68,830,332 florins, for a difference of 185,698 florins.

**A *korsce* is nearly two hundred weight. It is divided into 32 *garnices*, of four *kwartz* each.'

By virtue of the so-called "congress system" that had been created at the Congress of Vienna by the victorious allied monarchs who defeated Napoleon, the allies, but not Britain, pledged to meet again and combine their forces whenever revolutions anywhere in Europe broke out, and to suppress them before they got out of control. Prior to the Congress of Verona in 1822, the collaborating monarchs met at Aix-la-Chapelle in 1818, in Troppau in 1820 and in Laibach (Ljubljana) in 1821 to suppress threats to their monopolization of the political status quo. Of great importance, the "congress system" also stood as the declared enemy of the "systems of representative government," such as that of the United States of America. The Congress of Verona is an example of the allies' interventionist philosophy and its rationale to sustain the status quo in Europe (essentially to rule by unquestioned Divine Right), and favorable to their aims and thus applicable by extension to their "New World" colonies in north, central, and south America. The secret "Treaty of Verona" of 1822 caused the United States to promulgate a formal warning in 1823 to European powers, Russia included, by way of its "Monroe Doctrine," not to interfere in the growth of representative democracies in the New World, the antithesis of which was part and parcel of the Congress of Verona, as reported by Niles' Weekly Register. In short, Russian, Prussian and Austrian monarchs labored to prevent systems of representative government from replacing their autocratic dictatorships, and also proclaimed their related objective for eliminating "liberty of the press" as well. Indeed, national authoritarian leaders of our own 21st century continue to work for weakening representative government and eliminating the free press, the combination of the two constituting the major supporting foundation of democracies, as opposed to dictatorships. Today's authoritarians and dictators, therefore, fear the existence of the free press, and accuse it to be a source "fake news" -- or what Czar Nicholas, for example, termed to be "calumnies" -- that are detrimental to their dictatorial interests and arbitrary aspirations. (This article had initially been printed in the United States by the *National Intelligencer* newspaper and was reprinted by Hezekiah Niles.)

Article 132. (July 16, 1831, pages 355 and 356)

Among the papers lately introduced into the discussions in France, is the treaty of Verona, which having laid our hands upon a copy of, it may not be amiss at the present time to bring to the recollection of our readers. With that view we offer them the following translation of the treaty, the authenticity of which cannot be doubted, as it is recognized by Chateaubriand, one of the signers to it, in a book recently published in his own defence.

[*Nat. Int.*]

Translation. From the *Journal de Havre* of the 17th of March, 1831. Diplomatists pretend that France is bound by all the treaties, without exception, that have been concluded by the late expelled government and the other powers. Is it also bound by the following treaty, translated from an English journal or paper, published in 1823:

SECRET TREATY OF VERONA. The undersigned, specially authorised to make some additions to the *treaty of the holy alliance*, after having exchanged their respective credentials, have agreed as follows:

Art. 1. The high contracting powers being convinced that the system of representative government is equally as incompatible with the monarchial principles as the maxim of the sovereignty of the people with the divine right, engage mutually, in the most solemn manner, to use all their efforts *to put an end to the systems of representative governments*, in whatever country it may exist in Europe, and to prevent its being introduced in those countries where it is not yet known.

171

Art. 2. As it cannot be doubted that the *liberty of the press* is the most powerful means used by the pretended supporters of the rights of nations, to the detriment of those of princes, the *high contracting parties promise reciprocally to adopt all proper measures to suppress it*, not only in their own states, but also in the rest of Europe.

Art. 3. Convinced that the principles of religion contribute most powerfully to keep nations in the state of passive obedience which they owe to their princes, the high contracting parties declare it to be *their intention to sustain, in their respective states, those measures which the clergy may adopt, with the aim of ameliorating their own interests, so intimately connected with the preservation of the authority of princes*; and the contracting powers join in offering their thanks to the pope, for what he has already done for them, and solicit his constant co-operation in their views of submitting the nations.

Art. 4. The situation of Spain and Portugal unite unhappily all the circumstances to which this treaty has, particularly, reference. The high contracting powers, in confiding to France the care of putting an end to them, engage to assist her in the manner which may the least *compromit* them with their own people and the people of France, by means of a subsidy on the part of the two empires, of twenty millions of francs every year, from the date of the signature of this treaty to the end of the war.

Art. 5. In order to establish in the Peninsula the order of things which existed before the revolution of Cadiz, and ensure execution of the articles of the present treaty, the high contracting parties give to each other the reciprocal assurance, that as long as their views are not fulfilled, rejecting all other ideas of utility, or other measures to be taken, they will address themselves with the shortest possible delay, to all the authorities existing in their states, and to all their agents in foreign countries, with the view to establish connections tending towards the accomplishment of objects proposed by this treaty.

Art. 6. This treaty shall be renewed with such changes as new circumstances may give occasion for, either at a new congress, or at the court of one of the contracting parties, as soon as the war with Spain is terminated.

Art 7. The present treaty shall be ratified, and the ratifications exchanged at Paris within the space of six months.

> Made at Verona, 22nd Nov. 1822.
> Signed, for *Austria*, Metternich;
> for *France*, Chateaubriand;
> for *Prussia*, Bernstet;
> for *Russia*, Nesselrode.

Article 133. (July 23, 1831, pages 363 and 364)

Here *The Niles' Weekly Register* reported, by way of several, indeed a veritable cornucopia, important brief articles, on Polish and Russian battlefield deployments under the respective commands of Chrzanowski and Kreutz, and others as well; on Russian cruelty and vengeance in Lithuania; the incredible march of the resourceful and intrepid Skrzynecki and his Polish forces from battlefield to battlefield that involved traversing in quick succession some 130 miles of territory in a short period of time; Dwernicki's failure; and the Czar's resolve to put down the revolution in Poland even if he had to suffer the loss of 200,000 Russian soldiers to achieve that objective.

First POLAND article: "The Russian accounts of the affairs between the Russian army under general *Kreutz* and that under the Polish general *Chrzanowski*, which so gallantly cut its way through the former force and penetrated as far as Zamosc, are received. They state the loss of the Poles to be about three thousand, while they set down that of the Russians at but 400.

The Russians were *practicing every species of cruelty and outrage* against the revolting of inhabitants of Augustowa in Lithuania. The inhabitants of the district of Mariampol attacked a body of Russians on the 21st of April, but were defeated. Several officers and citizens, who took part in the revolution, were shot after their defeat, the villages were sacked and burned, houses pillaged and the proprietors imprisoned."

Second POLAND article: "It has been rumored in London that the Poles gained a signal victory over the Russians, and although nothing has been received absolutely authenticating this rumor, no doubt was entertained that great and important advantage had been obtained by the former. The editor of the London Sun had been informed that the official account had been received by the Polish legation, and that the Russian imperial guard, commanded by general Pahlen, had been almost annihilated on the 19th and 20th of May. The brave Polish commander in chief Skryznecki, had completely out-maneuvered the Russian general Diebitsch. While a Polish corps was amusing the Russians at Minsk, Skryznecki united all the corps on his left, crossed the Bug, and, taking Ostrolenka by assault, proceeded to Lomza, defeated the Russian guards at Tychosin, and in fact occupied the whole country between the Bug and the Narew.

Accounts from Warsaw on the 26th May left Deibitsch at Zocolow, apparently in the route for Ostrolenka or for Biklak or Bialistock, with no resource but to throw himself on the protection of Prussia, as Dwernicki throws himself on the protection of the Austrians. He has to cross the Bug and the Narew, surrounded by Polish corps.

By this masterly movement, the Polish general has placed himself in contact with the Samogitians, Lithuanians, and other revolted districts, by whose population his army will be indefinitely augmented, so as to leave Deibitsch no prospect of escape but within the Russian frontiers.

The march of Skryznecki is without parallel in modern warfare. From Warsaw to Ostrolenka is 80 miles, thence to Lomza 30, and from there to Tychosin 20 more, the last 50 being in the rear of the Russians. He was joined by numerous volunteers from Prussian and Austrian Poland.

At Ostrolenka, the Polish general obtained a large sum of money, the baggage of the enemy and 1,700 prisoners.

During the advance of the corps of Dwernicki in Volhynia, insurrections had broken out at the instigation of several of the nobility of Tulszyn and Batiany in Podolia, and the insurgents had even formed a provisional government. The failure of Dwernicki, however, left these brave fellows unsupported, and they were afterwards subdued by the Russian troops under general Roth.

The decision of the Austrians relative to Dwernicki and his corps, has been received. The general and his officers are to be sent to Laybach, and the privates to Transylvania. All the arms found in their possession, belonging to Russia, are to be delivered to the Russians, those proved to be Polish property are to remain in trust with the Austrians. The officers to retain their horses as private property. The whole of Gallicia has been placed under military law and a cordon formed, in consequence of the spreading of the cholera.

RUSSIA: "Capt. Dwyer, arrived at Boston from Cronstadt, reports that *very little was published at St. Petersburg relative to the Polish war,* but that it was generally acknowledged that the Russians had lost 80,000 men since the commencement of the campaign, and that the emperor had calculated to sustain a loss of 200,000 men in the final subjugation of Poland."

News Article 134. (July 30, 1831, pages 399 and 400)

A further report on Polish battlefield valor, the war's ferocious combat and slaughter, and that the Hungarians criticized their Austrian emperor for siding with Russia against Poland, the kingdom which saved Austria and Christian Europe from the Ottoman Turks 148 years earlier in 1683. Please note as well that Ostrołęka was referenced incorrectly as Ostrolenska by the correspondent who clearly hadn't been a Pole. General Dezydery Chłapowski (1788 - 1879) was a veteran of the Napoleonic Wars and was married to the sister of Grand Duke Constantine's wife. His diaries are a great source for the Napoleonic period.

In our last advices from this interesting part of the globe, the gallant Polish general and his brave army had driven the Russians, after a succession of brilliant affairs, across the Narew, and had compelled Deibitsch into Prussia for protection. This state of affairs existed on the 23rd of May, but since then a bloody engagement has taken place between the main armies of the Poles and Russians, led respectively by Skrzynecki and Deibitsch, which resulted disastrously for the former; who, in turn, has been driven back; some of the fruits of his recent victories wrested from him, and his main army was, at the last advices, resting under the guns of Praga for protection, his head-quarters again being established at Warsaw.

The Polish army under Skrzynecki was attacked by that of the Russians under Deibitsch, on the 26th May at Ostrolenska, when a sanguinary battle ensued, in which the Russian army was victorious. Ostrolenska was taken by storm by the Russians. The division of the Polish army, under gen. Gielgud, stationed at Lanrza, has been entirely cut off, by the movements and successes of the Russians. The Poles acknowledge their own loss at 4,000 men. In speaking of the battle of Ostrolenska, a writer says that the oldest generals have no recollection of so sanguinary a combat. Generals Kicki and Kaminski and lieutenant colonel Gazenski, of the Polish army, were killed. In one of the accounts it is stated that 20,000 men, on both sides, remained on the field of battle. Quarter was out of the question, and the chief work was performed with the bayonet. The Poles, though much inferior in numbers, performed prodigies of valor, and amply sustained their ancient renown. Generals Bozuslowski, Pac, Skrzynski, Malachowski, and a great many other staff officers of the Polish army, are wounded. Three Russian generals are killed.

It appears from the bulletin of general Skrzynecki, that on the day previous to the bloody affair of the 26th of May, having effected the object of his forward movement, by conveying support to the revolted Lithuanians, he gave orders, for his troops to pass to the right bank of the Narew, which was effected on the evening of the 25th May, in good order. The rear guard under general Lubienski covering the passage of the army on the heights of Zekun and Lawy. In the morning of the 26th, the Russians attacked his position with great impetuosity, under Deibitsch in person. General Lubienski retreated upon Ostrolenska, making a most vigorous resistance. His march was stopped by the city itself, which was set on fire by the mortars of the enemy. Having succeeded in passing to the right bank of the Narew, the Polish army attempted to destroy the bridge. This they were unable to effect, as the enemy were protected by a numerous artillery placed on the opposite bank. Several regiments of the Poles, under a most galling fire, attempted to arrest the progress of the Russians. The combat was for a long time one of slaughter, they fought man to man, and thousands were killed by being thrown into the dyke which passes along the marshy shores of the Narew. The Russians, it is stated in the official bulletin of Skrzynecki, towards night became exhausted and retired across the river, leaving only some sharp shooters on the right bank, who retrograded as far as the bridge, the Poles keeping possession of the field of battle. The battle did not finally end until 12 o'clock at night, when the Poles commenced a retrograde movement on Pultusk, and subsequently to Warsaw.

The *Journal des Debats* states that several of the counties of Hungary have addressed representations to the emperor pf Austria, in *which they remind him of the services rendered to that country by Poland in the wars against the Turks, and of the great mistake committed by Austria, in permitting a country that protected her against Russia, to be sacrificed.* They call also for the instantaneous revocation of the ordinances prohibiting the exportation of arms and provisions to Poland.

POST-SCRIPT: Paris appears to be the place of riot and disorder, the national guard was often on duty to put down the rioters, and had so far succeeded. Some blood had been shed. The people were calling out that aid might be given to the Poles. Much agitation prevailed.

It appears that the Polish army under general Chlapowski, gained a splendid victory on the same day that the bloody battle of Ostrolenska was fought, and have gained several other advantages. They have performed prodigies of valor. They are said to have fought a battle as bloody as that as Ostrolenska, and completely defeated the Russians under gen. Sacken, and that the army of Deibitsch had suddenly, and precipitously fallen back. The hope is freely expressed, that the Russians will be expelled and Poland be free! *Laus Deo!*

Article 135. (August 6, 1831, pages 406 and 407)

For the first and only time in all of the articles published in *Niles' Weekly Register* concerning Poland, some Jews reportedly were said to have identified Polish patriots to the Russians; and also included are news-briefs on "Paskewitsch" (Paszkiewicz in Polish) and "Kościuszko."

POLAND: Intelligence from Warsaw to the 6th June states that on the same day that the battle of Ostrolenka was fought, that general Chlapowski brought the Russians to battle and gained a complete victory. The Russians were commanded by general Sacken, and the conflict took place at Mariampol, and must have been a dreadful one, as the town was taken twice and taken thrice by assault. The Russians were finally expelled and dispersed. The Poles were greatly aided by the revolting people, who joined them in the battle of Mariampol. In several major affairs, the Russians had also been defeated and sustained considerable loss. At Bialostock, 120 Russian wagons were taken by the insurgents. In Volhynia, the fortress of Herman fell into their hands, after a well contested and sanguinary battle, in which the Russians left 1,200 dead on the field of battle. The Russian army had begun to move to the right bank of the Narew. The Polish general Lubienski, in his retreat at Chirchnowice, with 6,000 Poles, cut his way through 40,000 Russians.

The Jews at Krekiszew and Larzezow assisted the Russians, and pointed out to them the houses of the Polish patriots.

Prince Czartoryski, it is supposed would be appointed regent of Poland; by this step it is thought that greater unity would be imparted to the government.

The landowners in Lithuania, in order to render the revolution popular, had *emancipated their peasantry.* These successes of the Poles and the retreat of the Russians, will, it is said, carry the war into Russia.

A Polish commandant of artillery galloped up to the Russian infantry, during a battle, with twelve pieces of artillery, and discharged them seven or eight times at the distance of fifty paces. He is said to have annihilated twenty battalions.

The wide spread of the insurrection is proved by the late battle of Herman, on the Ukraine, nearly 600 miles from Warsaw, on the very verge of southeastern Poland. This feature of the war inspires a hope that Poland will be free.

PASKEWITSCH: "The Havre Journal of the 21st June, states that Deibitsch, the Russian commander in chief, had been superseded by general Paskewitsch, and gives as its belief that government had determined to act for Poland, in connection with Great Britain."

KOSCIUSKO: "*Memorable saying of Kosciusko.* When this brave Pole arrived at Cracow, where the revolution commenced, he made, to the little band of patriots under his command, a stirring speech that ended with: 'We are not strong enough in number to be victorious, *but we are enough to die with honor in defending'.*"

Article 136. (August 20, 1831, pages 436 and 437)

This particular article began on page 436 with brief intelligence about Russia and Austria, relatively more on Poland began on page 436, and ended with a shorter article on Russia on page 437.

RUSSIA AND AUSTRIA: "Letters received in London state that Russia and Austria have 400,000 men, armed and equipped, and ready to take the field. Some of the British journals conclude from this, that there will speedily be a convulsion on the continent."

POLAND: "Advices from this country are contradictory. A Berlin paper represents the situation of the Poles as extremely critical, the Russians having crossed the Vistula below Plock, and the corps of generals Kreutz and Rudigo, having effected a junction with the main army. Letters from Warsaw, of the 23rd June on the other hand, make no mention of these circumstances. The Polish accounts represent the insurrection in the Russian Polish provinces as spreading rapidly; that general Gielgud was at the head of 40,000 men, and that in Samogitia 20,000 insurgents are under arms. General Dembinski, with another force, had entered Lithuania, at Olitta, 50 or 60 miles west of Wilna, where he had been joined by a large body of insurgents, who had previously beaten a Russian detachment and captured two pieces of cannon and supplies near Troki. General Chlapowski had arrived at Lida. The Polish government has announced a loan of 60,000,000 florins.

The Prussians are said to be constructing a bridge for the Russians at Drewenca, to facilitate their passage over the Vistula.

The papers are loud in their denunciations against the Prussians on account of their partiality towards the Russians. General Toll derives all his supplies from them. General Schryznecki had made a demonstration upon the enemy by marching towards Siecnica, but had returned to Praga.

As Reported in the "Niles' Register"

The Poles have taken the important fort of Bobrouysek in Lithuania, which served as a Russian depot for arms and ammunition. A levy *en masse* has been decided upon in Poland, to give the Russians a mortal blow. A spirit unfriendly to gen. Schryznecki is said to exist at Warsaw, he is charged with keeping about him unskillful officers, because they belong to great families. In the midst of these private dissentions, a Russian corps is said to be advancing on Warsaw, having thrown bridges across the Narew. Lubienski, it is thought, will succeed to the command-in-chief, should Schryznecki be removed or resign."

RUSSIA: "The emperor, considering the distinguished success of general Deibitsch, has ordered that his regiment shall retain its name of Deibitsch Salbansky. The death of general Deibitsch was produced by the cholera. He left his property amounting to 1,600,000 francs, in equal portions to his brother Arnold Deibitsch, a hatter at Stettin, in Prussian Pomerania, and to his sister Albertin, a nun of the convent of St. Ulrica, at Wolfhart, on the neighborhood of Koningsburg. The appointment of field marshal count Paskewitsch, as the successor of general Deibitsch, is announced in a general order dated June 16th."

Article 137. (August 27, 1831, page 457)

This article reported on multiple topics: that Russia protested England's arms shipments to Polish Insurgents; that London denied the accusation and disregarded the protest; that Polish conspirators were proving to be relentless and elusive; that treachery had been uncovered in Warsaw involving several Polish generals; and that Polish forces under Chłapowski and Giełgud were defeated, and 600 Polish soldiers captured.

ENGLAND: "Two vessels were loading in England with 25,000 stand of arms and 48 pieces of cannon, on account of the Poles. The Russians had entered a protest against the above cargoes, but the British declined interfering."

POLAND: "The Russian army has dwindled down from 150,000 men to about 88,000, but the patriots in Lithuania were placed in a very critical situation, being pressed on all sides by the Russians."

POLAND AND RUSSIA: "Several persons have been arrested at Warsaw, charged with a conspiracy. The conspirators numbered among their ranks several generals of distinction, to the treachery of some of whom it is supposed the Russian army, under Rudiga, were enabled to make its escape. Three millions of florins were discovered at the house of one of the traitors, named Lessel. The papers discovered disclose a deep laid plot. The whole of general Skrzynecki's plans of operation had been put into the possession of the Russians, and it was intended also to deliver Warsaw into their hands. Generals Hartig, Satacki, Jackowski, and several others were implicated in these treacherous schemes, also a Russian lady by the name of madame Bazanon. This detection must prove highly advantageous to the cause of the brave and patriotic Poles. There are at Warsaw 13,000 Russian prisoners, and a part of the arrangement was, that they were to be provided with arms and to have risen in all parts of the town. General Janchowski communicated the facts to the authorities at Warsaw, in time to save that city from the horrid consequences of massacre and bloodshed.

The Poles under Chlapowski and Gailgud were defeated by the Russians, who took 600 prisoners. The arch duke Constantine (late viceroy of Poland) is dead, and is supposed to have died by his own hands. The Russians are making a new levy, which will increase their force to 600,000 men."

The referenced Gailgud had been Antoni Gielgud (1792-1830), a general in the free Polish Army, who led Polish combat forces against Russia in the November Uprising, and as fate was to have it, had been destined to be a great, great uncle of the future world-renowned British actor, Sir John Gielgud (1904-2000), who didn't use the diacritic mark in his surname, but who always identified his Polish ancestry.

Article 138. (September 3, 1831, page 4)

In this short news-brief, either an English-speaking journalist or type-setter in Britain or in the United States clearly erred when he identified "Nesbury" as a town in Russia into which cholera had spread. It likely had been meant to be Nesburg (a German-sounding word), but I had not been able to identify that location as well, which the correspondent had clearly identified to be in Russia.

Russia and Poland. The cholera is spreading over Europe. It had appeared at Tver, Jarozlaw, Nesbury, Novogorod, and in the government of Witepsh. The defeat of general Rudiger is confirmed. The death of Constantine is considered a fortunate event in Poland.

Article 139. (September 3, 1831, page 5)

An article that contained reports about: (1) social discontent in Russia, Poland included; (2) cholera mordus in St. Petersburg; (3) France, Lafayette included, declaring itself in support of the Polish cause; (4) national miles in Europe; and (5) and domestic politics in France.

This mighty empire is said to be much disturbed by the discontents of the people. The day, we trust, is at hand when the terrible despotism and abject slavery, that prevails, will be abolished. Poland may *leaven* the whole mass.

The cholera mordus, has broken out at St. Petersburg -- the imperial family had abandoned the city, and the population was in a state of complete consternation.

We translate the following address of the French *central committee*, in favor of the Poles, *to the electors of France*, from the supplement to the *Courier Francais* on the first of June last,

'*Gentlemen:* Preparatory assemblies are taking place among you, in order to fix your choice between the different candidates for the deputation; the day of election will, also, soon arrive, and you will meet in order to give deputies to France. We imagine, gentlemen, that we should be conforming to your feelings by asking of you to cause these different meetings to result profitably for the Polish cause. It is not necessary for us to explain to the flower (*l'elite*) of the French nation *the right which our Polish brethren possess to our affection. It is the desire of all in France who are the friends of honor and their country, to seize every opportunity of showing to the world our admiration of Poland, and our wishes for her triumph. By this strong claim, the committee has reckoned on your co-operation. They propose to you to open subscriptions, the produce of which shall be destined to aid the cause of the Polish heroes, in the dreadful contest which they are waging so gloriously. It will not be useless to unite with the nomination of men who are about to give a constitution to France, an action serviceable to that generous nation, who are contending so courageously for independence and liberty.'* [This address is signed by seventy-four of the most eminent names of modern France, including that of the patriarch of liberty, LAFAYETTE.].

NATIONAL MILES:

Mile of Russia	750 geometrical paces, or		1,100 yards
" Italy	1,000	"	1,467 "
" England*	1,150	"	1,760 "
" Scotland [and]	1,500	"	2,200 "
" N. Ireland	1,500	"	2,200 "
The small league	2,000	"	2,933 "
The mean league	2,500	"	5,666 "
The great league of France	3,000	"	4,440 "
Mile of Poland	3,000	"	4,440 "
" Spain	3,348	"	5,028 "
" Germany	4,000	"	5,866 "
" Sweden	5,000	"	7,233 "
" Denmark	5,000	"	7,233 "
" Hungary	6,000	"	8,800 "

*In surveying, called 80 chains.

It is reported that the French ministry intend to declare in favor of Poland after the elections are completed, and that they will give up and renounce hereditary peerage. These movements have rendered them very popular, and will enable France to assume an attitude worthy of her character and the expectations which the revolution of July 1830 gave birth to.

A proclamation had been circulated by the agents of the dutchess of Berri, in France; from Charles the X, enjoining upon the French to rally around the standard of Henry V. The Carlists were making great exertions to concentrate a force in *La Vendre*.

Article 140. (September 10, 1831, page 20)

The initial example of those Americans in Paris in July 1831 whose pro-Poland activity was reflected in the exchange of correspondence between James Fenimore Cooper (1789-1851), author of the greatest epic novel of North America in those days titled: "The Last of the Mochigans," and the Marquis de Lafayette. Being also the subsequent example of the pro-Poland fundraising resolutions drawn up by those aboard the American ship, The Swan, on route from New York to Brunswick, and which in the spirit of the pro-Poland work of Americans in Paris, resolved "that a subscription be now made, with the hope that this example will be followed throughout the union by all travelers, and that this humble commencement may be followed by a large aggregate result" to raise funds to help the Poles, that began with the "Swan Resolutions" of 1831.

There was a meeting of the Americans in Paris of the 9th July to raise subscriptions for the aid of the Poles. Mr. J. Fenimore Cooper presided, and J. A. Washington of North Carolina acted as secretary. A subscription was forthwith opened, and 6,300 francs subscribed. A spirited address to the American people was also agreed to, and has been published, on behalf of the Poles.

'Letter of the chairman to gen. Lafayette, with an abstract from the Journal enclosed.

Paris, July 10

My *dear sir,* A meeting of Americans, on the subject of the Poles, was held last evening in the Rue Richelieu, and I hasten to send you an account of the proceedings. You will see that I had the honor to preside, and it has become my duty, as an organ of the meeting, to request you will consent to receive, not only our own contributions, but any others that may be the consequences of our efforts, and to remit them to the people for whom they were intended. It was decided that an appeal should be made to the American people, in this cause, and we have dared to hope you will give the whole proceedings the high sanction of your name.

I am, sir, very faithfully and sincerely yours,

J. Fenimore Cooper

General Lafayette, La Grange'

Answer of gen. Lafayette   La Grange, July 14, 1831

'My *dear sir,* I have had the pleasure to receive your favor of the 10th inst. Including your resolutions adopted at the meeting in behalf of admirable Poland. Permit me, although I did not attend it, to proclaim my right of citizenship and to become one of the subscribers.

It is to me a source of patriotic enjoyment to see the sympathies of the United States mingle with those which the cause and heroism of the Poles have excited in Europe, particularly throughout France. Instances of American feeling on the subject we may already record. Whatever is collected in Paris, or other parts of Europe, or from the United States, I shall be happy and proud to transmit to the Polish authorities. With the highest regard, I am, my dear sir, your affectionate friend,

Lafayette

To Mr. J. Fenimore Cooper, Rue St. Dominique, Paris'

The attention of the passengers on board of the steam boat *Swan*, from New York to Brunswick, was called by *Mr. P. Ohagen* of New York, to the condition of the Poles. After explaining the object of the meeting, *B. W. Richards*, esq., (mayor) of Philadelphia, was called to the chair, and *David Hoffman*, of Baltimore, was appointed secretary, the following resolutions were suggested, and unanimously adopted:

1. *Resolved*, That we hereby sympathize with the Polish nation in their sufferings in the cause of liberty, we admire the heroism which has been displayed in the maintenance of their rights,
2. That we highly approve of the objects of the meeting of our countrymen in Paris, on the 9th of July, and trust that their call will be responded to in every quarter of the country,
3. That a subscription be now made, with the hope that this example will be followed throughout the union by all travelers, and that this humble commencement may be followed by a large aggregate result,
4. That a committee of three, consisting of *Moncure Robinson*, of Virginia, *Stephen*

James Fenimore Cooper by Mathew Brady

Baldwin, of Pennsylvania, and *Joseph Hoffman,* of Baltimore, collect the proposed subscription, and place the same in the hands of captain Degraw, to be handed over to such agents as may be appointed in New York, to transmit what may be collected there in behalf of the same cause.

5. That captain Degraw be requested to suggest similar meetings on the boat, with similar objects, during the remainder of the season.

Mr. Abraham Payne, of the island of Madeira, addressed the meeting in an animated and forcible manner, and closed his excellent remarks by tendering as a present, a pipe of the best Madeira wine, now in Baltimore, the proceeds of which will be paid to Mr. Hoffman, for that object. The pilot and engineer, and three deck hands of the steam boat Swan, gave three dollars. Total collection money about $60.

B. W. Richards, chairman
David Hoffman, secretary

→ A general meeting has been held in New York, *W. A Duer,* chairman, to raise money for the relief of the Poles. It is probable that a handsome amount will be collected in the United States."

Thanks to freedom of the press in the United States, what spontaneously occurred among sympathetic passengers aboard the Swan, as reported in the *Niles' Weekly Register* on September 10, 1831, could not have happened without them having been informed about Poland's suffering, in advance of their trip from New York to Brunswick, during which time the passengers on the Swan went on to publicize their Swan Resolutions for aiding the Polish cause in Europe. To his lasting credit and memory, Hezekiah Niles, a true amicus poloniae, published the Swan story and all the other pro-Poland stories constituting this book. Here follows the story of the now-famous Swan Resolutions:

Article 141. (September 10, 1831, pages 21 and 22)

FRANCE: "At the grand review on the last of three days, the *king* announced the reception of a report that the Poles had obtained a great victory. It produced a sensation among the troops, 'long live Poland' burst, at once, from the lips of 120,000 men, and patriotic songs were chanted by them under arms! The effect was wonderful. The soldiers embraced one another, and shouted and danced; and an abundance of wine was suddenly presented, in which they drank success to the Poles, *success to the Poles*.' The *London Sun* of Aug. 2, says, 'We have no news from Paris today. The question of peace or war mainly depends upon the fate of the election of the presidency of M. Lafitte, or the nominee of the minister. *One thing is, however, very clear, that if France does not go to war at present to support the Poles, she will be compelled in a short time to resort to it on vindication of her own institutions, which can never be deemed safe after the triumph of Russia in Poland.* If Louis Philippe thinks other wise, he will be grievously disappointed...."

RUSSIA: "The cholera was raging dreadfully at St. Petersburg and many other places. Hardly one half of those attacked with this disease survive.... Letters from St. Petersburg of July 6th, communicate some particulars of a disturbance which had broken out there among the poorer classes respecting the measures taken by the Russian government to prevent the extension of the cholera morbus. In various parts of St. Petersburg places have been appropriated for the reception of persons attacked by the disease, around which cordons have been placed. The poor people were impressed with an idea that their friends who were taken into these hospitals were unfairly dealt with, that instead of measures being adopted to restore the sick, they were buried alive or poisoned. The fact that admission was not freely granted, strengthened the opinion that something improper was going on within the hospitals. A great body of persons, in consequence, forcibly entered the hospitals, and dragged out their friends, many of whom were in the last stage of the disorder; they killed the medical men in attendance, and great disorder prevailed. An express was sent to the emperor, who was near Peterhof, and Nicholas arrived at the spot. He expostulated with the people on their conduct, and said that they ought rather to implore God to put an end to the prevalency of the malady. The emperor then fell on his knees, and was joined in prayer by all the people. Thus the disturbance was quelled without any further outrages being committed.

There was a report in London that the emperor Nicholas had died in St. Petersburg of the cholera."

PRUSSIA: "It is stated that Prussia has declared that her *inactivity* is not *neutrality*, with respect to the contest between the Russians and the Poles; and, that she will assist the former by facilitating the passage of provisions and the munitions of war. There is much speculation as to events that may grow out of this position.

Berlin was threatened with the cholera, and the people were flying from the city in great numbers."

As Reported in the "Niles' Register"

POLAND: "It seems certain that the Polish general Gielgud had been compelled to fly before the Russians in Lithuania into the Prussian territories, when he was assassinated by another Polish officer. Such appear to be the facts, but particulars are not given. The troops remain in *Prussia*, about 2,500 men. It was stated at London on the 27th of July that the Russians had crossed the Vistula, and were expected to invest Warsaw.

Much sympathy was felt for the existing condition of the Poles. There were reports of several small battles near Warsaw, in which the Russians appear to have suffered the most; but they were concentrating their forces. The Poles were resolute, gathering strength and preparing for a terrible contest.

The Russian army in Poland is not of that immense overwhelming force as to excite so serious apprehensions for the fate of that country. The whole amount is 63,000 infantry, 19,000 cavalry, and 332 pieces of cannon. Of this force are with gen. Toll, 26,500 infantry, 7,900 cavalry, and 132 pieces of cannon; the remainder of the army is in Lithuania, Volhynia, etc.

The emperor continues to fulminate his ukases against those districts of ancient Poland which have risen. Podolia, Volhynia, Grodno, Wilna and Bialystec, are all declared in a state of war. In Volhynia the insurrectionary spirit is said to be burning with great fierceness.

There was a report by way of Metz that the great battle which was expected near Warsaw, had taken place, and that the Russians were utterly defeated with the loss of 16,000 men and 80 pieces of cannon. We regret that we cannot place great reliance on this report; but it is well known that the Poles had resolved on '*victory* or *death*,' in the literal meaning of these words; and they still surely fight desperately, well knowing that a general massacre will follow the success of the Russians."

AUSTRIA: "*Vienna, July 7.* According to a report of the board of health of Gallicia, the number of persons attacked by the cholera in that province, from the first appearance of that disorder to the end of June, was 37,000; of whom 19,655 had recovered, 13,356 died, 5,989 still remained ill.

There is a strong report of a general rising in Hungary, in favor of the Poles."

At this point in the presentation of my research, it is well to remember, as noted earlier, that Hezekiah Niles who published *Niles' Weekly Register* should not be criticized for misspelling Polish surnames, along with Poland's cities, towns, villages, rivers and other locations in Eastern Europe.

Article 142. (September 10, 1831, page 24)

In this particular issue, *Niles' Weekly Register* continued to provide information of vital importance to Poland, in this case, in the news-brief titled: "Proportion of soldiers" – which interestingly, had been included and listed in random order, among other topics titled: Pyramids of Teotihualcan of Mexico; Pardoning power; Dogs; Philadelphia; Proportion of soldiers; Married; Died; The Potomac Frigate; and Russian manufactures. Appropriately, whereas Mexican pyramids, etc. are interesting in their own right, it is appropriate that I only transcribed "The Proportion of soldiers" and the "Russian manufactures" news-briefs as follows:

Proportion of soldiers to the inhabitants of various states, is nearly as follows:

In England 1 soldier to 140	
France	110
Austria	100
Russia	90
Bavaria	69
Prussia	68
Poland	60
Wurtemberg	59
Sweden	58
Denmark	57
Hesse Darmstadt	49

In the United States, there is 1 soldier to 2,074.

Russian manufactures. During the month of June there was an exhibition at Moscow of the production of the arts and manufactures, methodically arranged in eight rooms. Among a great number of machines was one by Ivan Gourekhoff, for making shawls in imitation of Cashmires, which worked in presence of the public. There were 5,800 different articles, sent by 480 artists, manufacturers and workmen.

And as well about the matter of Russian manufactures which largely had been located in the Russian-controlled kingdom of Poland:

Article 143. (September 10, 1831, page 24)

Also appearing on the same page had been a seemingly unrelated article titled in capital letters, "AMERICAN CLAIMS ON FRANCE." The report was initially published by the *National Intelligencer*, and then by *Niles' Weekly Register*.

It appears that by the subjoined article that our minister, *Mr. Rives*, has succeeded in making an arrangement with the government of France for the liquidation and ultimate payment (in part, at least, if not the whole) of the claims of our citizens for the illegal capture and confiscation of their property some thirty years ago. We expressed the opinion, soon after occurrences of the French revolution of 1830, that event was decidedly auspicious to the adjustment and final allowance of the long-standing claims, and we are now to find that our anticipations have been realized. The concession which our minister has stipulated on our part, of a reduction on the duty of French wines, however valuable it may be to France, is one which we should have been willing to see made without any equivalent; and the other, the payment of the claims of Beaumarchais, is only performing an act of justice which, in the opinion of many of our enlightened countrymen, ought to have been rendered by our government long ago.

(Nat. Int.)

The importance of that U. S. - French settlement had been highly favorable to the United States. It had been reported by yet another American newspaper, the New York Mercantile Advertiser, and reprinted by Niles' Weekly Register on September 10, 1831 on the same page, wherein it stated that:

...the amount of claims to be paid by France for spoliation of American property, is twenty-five millions of francs, payable in six yearly instalments, with an interest rate of 4 per cent per annum, from the date of the treaty being ratified by our government, which interest will swell the amount to about twenty-eight millions five hundred thousand francs. Mr. Rives has stipulated, on behalf of our government, the payment of one million five hundred thousand francs, in settlement of the Beaumarchais claims, that wines (white and red) shall be admitted in our country on the following terms.... The French government, on their part, stipulate to relinquish all the Louisiana claims....

All of which had likely been discovered by Imperial Russia's minister (i.e., ambassador) in Paris, who reported it as such to St. Petersburg which, in turn, caused Russia to begin a process for developing its own claim against France. On its part, Russia -- attentive to the success of the United States in its negotiations with France -- rationalized that since it had been the influence of the French Revolution of July 1830 that caused Poles to rise up in their own Revolution of November 1830 against Russia, followed by persistent and overt French encouragement, especially on the part of Lafayette, for the Poles to sustain their revolution against Russia, with insinuations that France might consider sending its armed forces to Poland itself in support for the Polish cause, it therefore had been the legal, if not moral, responsibility of France to compensate Russia financially for the outlay of funds it had incurred commensurate with defeating the Poles.

Article 144. (September 17, 1831, pages 40 and 41)

In this issue of September 17, 1831, *Niles' Weekly Register* included an article titled, "Prussia and Poland," and another titled "Polish Proclamation" of Prince Adam Jerzy Czartoryski, to the Polish Nation. Note as well that the European correspondent who, in a two-for-one, both misspelled the surname of Polish general Jan Zygmunt Skrzynecki (1787-1860) -- in this case, a French correspondent in Paris -- had also referred to that Polish military commander as Jean (French for John in English, or Jan in Polish), but otherwise submitted a good source of intelligence.

Paris, July 21. It is not true that the king of Prussia sent any answer to the letter of the Polish general-in-chief complaining of the scandalous violation of neutrality by the Prussian authorities; the king returned the brave general's letter unopened and in silence. This at Berlin was dignity!

General Jean Skryznecki, commander-in-chief of the Polish army, has felt himself under the necessity of writing the following letter to the king of Prussia:

'Siennica, July 9, 1831
Sire: I take the liberty of addressing you, with the hope that your majesty will deign to admit that my character of commander-in-chief of the

Polish army, and the importance of the subject to which I am about to call your majesty's attention, warrant my adopting this course.

Sire, since your elevation to the throne, justice and uprightness have never ceased to illustrate paternal reign. In appealing to those sublime virtues, I experience some relief, amidst the vexations and annoyance occasioned to us Poles by the civil and military authorities of Prussia. In conjunction with several European cabinets, you have proclaimed the principle of non-intervention, and I have no doubt but the ministers of your majesty have received instructions in accordance with your royal wishes. The Polish Army would consequently be wrong were it to complain of your majesty. They are only anxious to acquaint you with their grievances.

Every day we witness occurrences that convince us that is spite of the neutrality of your majesty officially agreed to observe towards Poland, the civil and military Prussian authorities not only violate the spirit of the laws of neutrality, but what is more, they afford direct and efficacious assistance to the Russian army, without which the latter would have been long since compelled to retire from our country:

1. The Prussian authorities supply the Russians from the magazines at Thorn, and the vicinity of that place, with provisions.
2. Prussian artillerists have been admitted into, and embodies in, the Russian army, and fight against us.
3. The Russian forces draw warlike stores from the Prussian fortresses.
4. The clothing of several Russian regiments were made in Prussia.
5. The Prussian engineer from Mariemwarder was commissioned to collect the necessary materials for the construction of bridges, to enable the Russian army to cross the Vistula at Zlotorya.

I could refer to various other circumstances to show the hostile intentions and the acts of the Prussian authorities. I confine myself to the facts that I have mentioned, persuaded as I am, that as soon as your majesty shall have been made acquainted with them, you will deign to prevent the reoccurrence of practices which, no doubt, take place unknown to your majesty, because they are directly in contradiction with the sentiments of political probity which you have ever professed.

Begging your majesty to excuse my troubling you with this dispatch, I entreat, sire, you will listen to the voice of humanity, addressed to you through the organ of those, be they ever so weak, giants would

191

be unequal to overcome, were they not secretly assisted by the civil and military Prussian authorities.'

'That letter was returned to general Skryznecki, with this declaration, 'that his majesty the king of Prussia could not enter into correspondence that was not acknowledged by the emperor Nicholas.'

Next followed Prince Adam Jerzy Czartoryski's proclamation to the Polish nation:

Fellow countrymen. In the contest which must eventually decide between the existence of Poland or her entire destruction, the nation trusts to the heroism and devotion of the army. The army has justified this confidence and has exceeded the expectation of the people anxious for the result of our exertions. From that moment the glory of Poland, which for a time had been humiliated, and even forgotten, having attained a vigour not to be produced by ages, has made itself known beyond the bounds of Europe. The enemy, irritated, has summoned forth all his energy, and become even more barbarous. We have been signally successful against him, but we must aim at his entire destruction. It is to ensure this that we must yet make further efforts. It is for this the national government invokes the Most High, who will never cease to protect us, *so long as we struggle to protect our spotless country*. We invoke our national liberty, which now stands on a point from which it may be plunged into eternity or destruction. We invoke all the kings and heroes who have ever perished for faith, loyalty or the welfare for mankind. We invoke the safety of Europe, the future race, and eternal justice; and, strong in the example of our industrious ancestors, we proclaim the levy en masse to the nation (*pos polite ruszenie*), that this appeal may be heard in the remotest parts of our beloved country, so that the inhabitants of the small portion called the kingdom of Poland, may be animated by the same sacred flame which burns so brilliantly in Samogitia, Lithuania, and Volhynia, the situation of which was infinitely more embarrassing. They have revived the deeds of our fathers: let us not allow them not to excel in this honorable rivalry.

Ministers of religion! Our struggle is for our country, for our faith, and for virtue. It is the struggle of children for their fathers, and of fathers for their children. Invoke God, that He may inspire you with his Holy Spirit, the spirit of primitive Christians, and with that spirit strengthen you in the sanctuaries, in the burying places, and on the field of battle. Do not abandon your flocks, encamp with them in the fields and the forests; suffer with them, and, by your exhortations, strengthen them.

192

As Reported in the "Niles' Register"

Prince Adam Jerzy Czartoryski (1770-1861).

Fellow countrymen. Our enemy has vowed our annihilation, but he cannot attain it by your indifference. Strengthen the ranks of our army with your sons and your brothers, revenge those that have fallen, and let every hillock, every tree, every highway, every foot path, contain for that enemy, vengeance. Perish those hordes that only seek pillage or murder, and let them not find sleep in that country which these barbarians have sullied for half a century with their crimes and our blood.

Villagers. The martyrdom of your brothers, the holy faith, and holy Poland, call you at once: it is time to put an end to this sanguinary war. The invading army has ruined your crops, has destroyed your pasturage, has destroyed your herds, has poisoned habitations with unheard-of pestilence, destroying houses by fire, and families by assassination. The survivors have nothing to expect from him. On your fields, your grain, cultivated by the sweat of your brow, has rotten. The crop is at hand, then the enemy, who can never be less thirsting for your blood, will throw himself on you to complete the catalogue of his victims. Will you await that they should dishonor your wives and your mothers, that they should exterminate your children! No: you will be more prompt than he will be. Whenever your fields do not need your labor, arm yourselves with every thing within your reach; throw yourselves on the enemy. His ranks are already thinned, and your scourge will precipitate his flight. A just God will aid you in expelling the intruders and will cause the blessings of peace to descend upon you, and liberated Poland awaits with frankness to bestow those rewards you so highly merit.

Chiefs of every rank, destined to command the levy en masse, be impressed with all the sanctity of your high calling. Here awaits you the recompense of a loyal and patriotic heart. After the example of our forefathers, your occupation should be to join military heroism with civil energy. This is what civilized Europe expects, being convinced that in her actual situation, every soldier should be a citizen and every citizen a soldier. It is the force of great national calamities that an intimate union of all classes is required, for there is no class before death, before God, and before country.

Poles. At this holy call of a levy en masse, invoke after custom of our ancestors, the all-powerful name of God. It is He who has covered with imperishable glory our heroic chivalry under the Piasts and the Jagiellons. Think of what will happen if we were now to yield. Shall those hopes be destroyed which the third generation has cherished in their hearts, which will become the glory of Poland? Relieved with so many charms, and so much blood lately spilt, consult on the means which locality, the wants and the genius present. Let the whole country become one camp, let all the energy of force and all the dexterity of intellect be combined to distress the enemy. The greatest activity and the most discerning circumspection must guide your actions, the guile of the serpent, and the desperation of the lioness. Such are the characteristics of your calling, a brotherly feeling in its most extensive sense. One for all, all for one. To arms, Poles! To arms,

Prince A. CZARTORISKI, *president*
PHIPTA, *secretary*

Warsaw, July 1, 1831"

Article 145. (September 17, 1831, pages 70, 71 and 72)

This issue of *Niles' Weekly Register* illustrated that news from Poland hadn't always been captioned as was evident throughout this publication. Indeed, one would have had to read, in this example, the entire "Foreign Articles" section which characteristically provided what I term to have been a "free flow of news-briefs" in no particular order except chronological for the most part, to find something about Poland. This issue of September 17, however, included a brief opening story, under the title, "A Polish General-ess," concerning Emilia Plater (1806-1831), the 25 year-old countess whose "pale and beautiful features are indicative of a romantic melancholy," according to the correspondent who wrote it and who had been captivated by her. Following her death after leading her Polish and Lithuanian army corps many times in combat, she was immortalized subsequently by Poland's greatest poet, Adam Mickiewicz (1798-1855), in his poem, Śmierć Pułkownika ("Death of a Colonel"), a work evoking great emotion and patriotism, that he composed in 1832. Among Lithuanians to this day, she is known as their national heroine, Emilija Pliaterytė, as well

As Reported in the "Niles' Register"

PAGE 70: "The *Hamburgh Correspondent* contains the following, dated Warsaw, July 7: 'An eye-witness gives the following sketch of the detached Lithuanian corps of countess Plater and count Caesar Plater: The countess is about 20 years old. Her pale and beautiful features are indicative of a romantic melancholy. Her duenna (lady's maid) supplies the place of aid-de-camp, and is younger than her mistress. The former is the chief of the staff, and at the same time intendant-general of the corps. No corps can be better managed. Both ladies are almost worshipped by the whole corps. They are dressed as men, and are constantly among the troops. The countess has assumed the name of M. Constantine. From *him* the soldiers receive orders, provisions, and ammunition. Count Plater is well known at Warsaw, where he spent all last winter. He is a young man of almost 21 years, of feminine features, and middling stature. When he is not engaged in military duties, he devotes his time to prayer. Both in the fields and woods, altars are erected, where a chaplain performs service, which is attended by the whole corps. Being rich, he bestows all his wealth upon his corps, and even collects considerable supplies from his numerous relations. The corps consists of cavalry and infantry."

PAGE 71: "An arrival at Boston brought London papers to the 5th August. The leading things were these: 'Very little intelligence had arrived from Poland. It is stated that the Russian grand army, 60,000 strong, had crossed the Vistula, that the Polish general Dembinski and his army had been made prisoners in Lithuania; that the Poles, at Warsaw, had made every preparation for a gallant stand. Next it is said, that the Russians had retired, re-crossing the Vistula, and would not risk the issue of a general battle."

PAGE 72: "From Poland we learn that a Russian detachment

had been defeated by gen. Muhlberg, that Warsaw was deemed impregnable, being defended by a large army, and 270 pieces of cannon. An investigation into the conduct of Schrzynecki has been had, and resulted to his honor, which gave increased strength to the Poles. The Lithuanians and Volhyniana were actively carrying on the war against Russia. The Poles were filled with the best hopes. The Russians were inactive or retiring, for causes not assigned. They had suffered several small losses...."

Emilia Plater (1806-1831)

"It seems Schryznecki kept his counsels so close, that the people became uneasy, on which some of the chiefs of the Poles were delegated to hold a *confidential* communication with him. To these he developed his plans, and they separated full of hope. There is danger in such proceedings, for among those most relied upon, traitors may be found...."

"*Berlin, August 1.* It is now ascertained to a certainty, that field marshal Paskewitsch has instructions to negotiate with Poland. It would seem also as if the negotiations were to take place under the walls of Warsaw. It is said that the Poles will be required to repeal their decrees of exclusion against the house of Romanoff; and that they will be allowed to choose from their nation a viceroy, Czar, Torisky, or Radzivill."

The above-referenced field marshal Paskewitsch had been Count Ivan Fyodorovich Paskevich-Yerevansky (1782–1856), a Russian Field Marshal who fought from the Napoleonic War to the Crimean War.   He is known to Poles as Paszkiewicz.

LETTER FROM SCHRZYNECKI TO GEN. LAFAYETTE: We translate from a Paris paper of July 22nd the following letter from the Polish commander-in-chief to gen. Lafayette:

'My Dear General: With what pleasure should I have sooner replied to the flattering letter which you did me the honor to address me on the 21st of April.

I received it, however, after a long delay. I lose not a moment in returning my thanks and expressing the great satisfaction it affords me to be so happy as to receive in this manner the favorable regard of the veteran of liberty in two worlds, of a person so eminent, whose constancy has been superior to all vicissitudes, whose character has been preserved equally grand in the dungeon of Olmutz and at the head of armies; the distinguished citizen, in fine, who has exhibited, to the world so rare an example of undeviating fidelity of principle, and disinterested regard for his fellow men!

This, indeed, is one of the most grateful recompenses to which I could aspire. You are already aware of the success that attended to throw some succors into Lithuania. On the return from that expedition, I was attacked in the neighborhood of Ostrolenka by the Russians, in great force. The combat was obstinate and at last degenerated into carnage. The Russian commander, however, in spite of every thing alleged to the contrary, was not able to prevent the object I had in view. Thus we have, up to the present date, been enabled successfully to maintain our anxious struggle against so great odds, and confident in the enthusiasm in our countrymen, and strong in the valor of our army, we will yet sustain the cause, being persuaded that the moment approaches when constitutional governments will shew less apathy concerning the outrages on public opinion, which have been committed. We think that they will interpose for our noble Poland, on which, perhaps, yet depends the safety of Europe, itself. May the prayers, my dear general, that you and so many other friends of humanity put up in our behalf, be vouchsafed! And deign to receive with kindness, the respectful assurance of the profound esteem and attachment with which I am, etc.

SCHRZYNECKI.'

Article 146. (September 24, 1831, page 71)

> This news-brief reported on the cholera in St. Petersburg, the Poles in Warsaw preparing for a gallant stand against Russian forces, and on the dangerous state of health, possibly deadly, of the Czar.

Letters from Memel of the 19th July, contain no news of importance. The cholera had not reached Memel, nor Konigsberg, on the 22nd. At Danzig there had been about 750 cases of the cholera, of which 560 had died, and the disease was spreading though the neighboring villages. The Prussian government, it appears, does not stop provisions destined for the Polish army. The disease was prevailing pretty much in like manner at Archangel, Riga, etc. Subsequent accounts inform us that the cholera was declining at St. Petersburg. The cases were much less numerous, and of a milder character. Such appears to have been the progress of the disease. Its onset is awful, but its violence appears soon to be exhausted.

An arrival at Boston brought London papers to the 5th August. The leading things were these:

'Very little intelligence had arrived from Poland. It is stated that the Russian grand army, 60,000 strong, had crossed the Vistula, that the Polish general Dembinski and his army had been made prisoners in Lithuania, that the Poles, at Warsaw, had made every preparation for a gallant stand. Next it is said, that the Russians had retired, re-crossing the Vistula, and would not risk the issue of a general battle.

Accounts from Russia say that the emperor was in a dangerous state of health, and that his decease was looked for.'

Article 147. (October 15, 1831, page 135)

News from Poland hadn't always been easy to obtain. As the situation became progressively more desperate for the Poles, contradictory, depressing and disappointing information began to appear. This issue of *Niles' Weekly Register* reflected that problem.

The Poles, if report be true, (but for the love of liberty we feel disposed to doubt it), are in a most perilous situation. The reports are, that Warsaw had been in the hands of the mob; that the command had been taken from the brave Schrzynecki; that many persons had been hung up at the lamp posts by order of certain Jacobin clubs; that prisoners were murdered in the jails; that anarchy, confusion and distrust, were the order of the day; and in the midst of all these untoward circumstances, the Polish army had retreated before the Russians, who had advanced within five miles of Warsaw. These rumors are supposed to be greatly exaggerated, if not without foundation; *we, however, fear the fate of the Poles*, as the mediation of France had failed. It us again rumored that the emperor of Russia was ill. The *cholera morbus* raged in many parts of Russia and Poland.

Article 148. (October 29, 1831, page 105)

In the atmosphere of a feared final massive Russian assault against Warsaw, more news about atrocities, including the mutilation of Russian corpses by some of the city's vengeful Poles, as well as executions, committed by Poles against perceived traitors and Russian prisoners in Warsaw, was published by *Niles' Weekly Register* in its issue of October 29, which painted an uncharacteristic picture of anarchy and bedlam among Poles. While the intelligence contained in this report had been revelatory, the correspondent struggled with Polish surnames, e.g., Krucowiecki rather than Krukowiecki, and Schrzynecki rather than Skrzynecki.

The latest intelligence from Poland is to the 27th of August. The main Polish army had retired within the fortifications at Warsaw, after having sustained a loss of 1,400 or 1,500 men in a reconnaissance, owing to the imprudence of col. Lelallois, a French officer. Two corps had been detached into the palatinates of Podlachia and Plozk. The

General Henryk Dembiński (1791-1864).

former and the stronger under French gen. Romarino, is believed in Paris to have gained a signal victory over a part of the army of Rudiger. One good effect of these diversions is, that the Poles have, in consequence, been enabled to introduce large supplies into Warsaw.

The dictator Krucowiecki had restored order within the walls of Warsaw. Four of the persons engaged in the massacres of the 16th of August had been shot. Both armies are said to be anxious to come into conflict. Paskewitsch was hastening his preparations for decisive operations against Warsaw, wishing to avoid a recurrence of those disasters consequent upon a campaign in the winter, from the effects of which, Deibitsch, his predecessor, had suffered so severely.

The emperor Nicholas is said to have determined on listening to no mediation by other powers, any terms on the part of the Poles short of absolute submission, is, therefore superfluous.

The patriot clubs of Warsaw are represented as great evils: in the excess of their zeal, in the bloody affair of the 16th of August, they perpetrated the most frightful acts of atrocity. Neither age nor sex were spared by them, and their merciless deeds were perpetrated too in the name of liberty, under the guise of patriotism. The conduct of the civic guards is represented as culpable in the extreme, and that their commander, Ostrowski, declared, on coming up to the theatre of massacre, that arms were not placed in his hands to destroy his countrymen. The palace gates were then broken, and the populace aided by some of the guards. Gen. Jankowski was seized first and hanged on a lamp post.

Soon after, generals Salacki, Hurtig and Bukowski, M. Fanshaw, chamberlain to the emperor, and madame Bazanow, were put to death in the same manner. The daughter of that lady was pierced through with a sabre for attempting to defend her mother. *These unfortunate victims were mutilated after having been killed. The details are too horrid to be related.*

The rage of the assassins continued unrelenting. They proceeded to a prison in which were confined some agents of the old police, and afterwards to the house of correction, where they recommenced the carnage. Men imprisoned on slight charges, and strangers to politics, were murdered. About 60 individuals perished on that dreadful night.

It appears that general Krucowiecki declared himself governor of the city, and that the national government confirmed him in that office the next morning. But *his efforts were insufficient to arrest the anarchists, because there were no troops of the line at Warsaw, and because the civic guard could not be depended upon.* Several murders were committed on the 16th; at three o'clock in the afternoon, a Russian officer, who had been wounded and made prisoner, was taken out of a cart and hanged in the street, because it was reported that he was a Prussian: he was, however, a native of Courland.

The dictator issued a proclamation, in which after stating that the diet had been forced by necessity to create a new government, founded upon the authority of the laws, adds, that it would act with all the vigor required by the existing circumstances of the country; that justice should be done towards all who were found guilty of having violated the laws. The count declares that *he will never sully the national glory, and will take care that with the aid of the laws, criminal agitators, who were the best allies of the enemies of the country, shall be annihilated.*

Report states that the brave Schrzynecki has entered the 4th regiment as a grenadier.

The Russians were reinforcing their army with great activity and it was thought would be able to increase its numbers from 25,000 to 30,000 in a few days; when that should be effected, it was thought that Paskewitsch would make the assault on Warsaw. The cholera was at Berlin.

Article 149. (November 5, 1831, pages 177 and 178)

Saddening news: Despite hopes to the contrary, particularly in Great Britain and France where many people hoped that their governments would send troops to fight for liberty alongside the Poles on Polish soil, Warsaw fell to the Russians.

FOREIGN NEWS. Arrivals at New York and Philadelphia, bring Dundee advices to the 24th September.

As Reported in the "Niles' Register"

'As we had been reluctantly induced to believe, by the former advisers, Warsaw, the capital of Poland has fallen. It capitulated on the 7th September, at 6 o'clock, p.m. after a most sanguinary conflict of two days duration, during which the Russians carried, by assault, all the entrenchments designed to protect the city. The Polish army followed by the diet and the members of the government, retired through Praga on the night of the 7th, and early on the ensuing day *the Russian army entered, maintaining perfect order, and respecting both person and property.* The Poles were retiring upon Modlin and Plozk, where it is said they will make an effort to maintain themselves. How far they will be able to realize such expectation, remains for time to unveil; but the hope of successful resistance, after such a blow as the fall of their capital, will prove illusory, it is a most fearful blow, and we fear will prove fatal to their cause.

On the 5th of September, the Russian commander in chief, Paskewitsch, sent a confidential officer to Warsaw, to demand the submission of the city and consequent surrender, promising in the name of his majesty, amnesty and pardon. This proposition was indignantly rejected by the brave Poles, and on the 6th, at day break, the Russians marched in the assault, made themselves masters of four redoubts which lay upon the line of attack, as well as the first line of entrenchments which surround Warsaw, and of which Wola is a perfect fortress. The task did not however end with the carrying of these; there remained a second line of entrenchments, and a broad moat around the city defended by bastions. On the 2d day of the assault, count Paskewitsch received a contusion from a cannon ball, which struck his left arm in the first quarter of an hour of the combat; he retired from the field of combat, leaving the command to general Toll. After the entrenchments and outworks were carried by the Russians, the Poles retired into the city, whereupon the former occupied the ramparts and erected batteries of 80 pieces of cannon to operate against Warsaw, should it still hold out.

In the course of the night general Kruchowiecki sent a flag of truce, informing the Russian commander in chief that the diet had dissolved itself, and that he as dictator, governed alone. At day break orders were issued to the Russian army to cease hostilities, as the capital and country had submitted to the emperor. The Russian account states that the dictator caused a report of the Polish army to be delivered to the field marshal, and that the intention of their marching on Plozk, is to await the pleasure of the emperor. The loss of the Russians is supposed to be between four and five thousand.

(next page) In this issue of November 5, 1831, Hezekiah Niles dedicated front-page news, starting in the lower right column, to the fact that Warsaw had fallen to the Russians.

NILES' WEEKLY REGISTER.

FOURTH SERIES.] No. 10—VOL. V. BALTIMORE, NOV. 5, 1831. [VOL. XLI. WHOLE No. 1,060

THE PAST—THE PRESENT—FOR THE FUTURE.

EDITED, PRINTED AND PUBLISHED BY H. NILES, AT $5 PER ANNUM, PAYABLE IN ADVANCE.

LETTER FROM THE EDITOR.

The convention adjourned *sine die* at 2 o'clock, P. M. on Tuesday last—but various circumstances will prevent my return home until after you will have been compelled to put this week's number of the REGISTER to press. The occupation of my time has been so close, that I have not had power to present even a slight sketch of our proceedings for the information of my readers. It may be generally observed, that about four hundred and fifty persons never before, perhaps, assembled in a more united and better spirit to support a cause of vital interest, (as we believe that it is), to all the American people,—or separated, after a week's severe attention to business, with greater satisfaction to themselves—mutually pleased with one another. The *moral effect* of such an extensive association of intellect and respectability must needs be powerful.

The *facts* that will be presented to the public, in consequence of this convention, cannot fail to *astonish* those who have made the highest calculations on the progress and extent of the American System. Sanguine as I have long been, and extravagant as many have thought me,—my expectations were far short of the realities about to be distinctly made known, through the permanent committee, founded on the reports of the very important and numerous committees of the convention, and other sources of authentic information,—for means have been, or will be, adopted, to collect a body of statistical facts immensely important to the people, and absolutely necessary to a discreet national legislation.

The address to the people of the United States was presented on Monday, by Mr. Ingersoll, of Pennsylvania, and the reading of it by him occupied nearly two hours. The hall was filled to overflowing—and yet the most profound attention was given during that long period, except when the reader was interrupted by the spontaneous cheers of the audience. Twenty thousand copies of this address were ordered to be printed at Baltimore, under the supervision of Mr. Kennedy. This splendid and masterly production, I understand to be the joint work of Mr. Ingersoll, of Pennsylvania, Mr. Kennedy, of Maryland, and Mr. Dutton of Massachusetts; and many good judges regard it as the ablest paper ever presented on a like occasion. Without any direct reference to the address of the "Free Trade Convention," it tears its *arguments* into tatters, and scatters them to the winds of the heavens; and, while it is generally beautiful, and often sublime, there is a plain *practicability* about it that will carry its matter to the *home* and *heart* of every friend of the free industry of the American nation; and I must think will bring many to a pause whose opinions seem to have been exclusively regulated by mistaken notions concerning slave labor. Some of these will believe that the "American System" as fully embraces their interest as that of any other class of persons in this community. As the address originated at New York, it is ordered that it shall be first *published* in that city, though to be *printed* in Baltimore. It will probably be laid before the public about the middle of next week.

I have not an opportunity to say much more. As the time of adjournment approached, the feelings of the members of the convention seemed to be greatly excited—and many new friendships formed, were promised a lasting duration. No small degree of gravity prevailed—but it was generous and kind, built upon the universal belief that a great public good would result from the proceedings just about to be concluded. Then came the brief, but appropriate and excellent address of the president, to whom the thanks of the convention had been voted, and we were dismissed with a most feeling and eloquent appeal to the AUTHOR OF ALL GOOD by the rev. Mr. Schroeder, formerly of Baltimore, all which will appear in the journals.

VOL. XLI.—No. 13.

But I must stop. Particulars shall be given hereafter. I wish you to publish the list of the members according to the copy sent herewith. Though much care has been exerted to render it entirely correct, I fear that it is not so; but errors in the list, or otherwise, will, I hope, be excused by my indulgent friends—because of the peculiar and anxious and busy situation in which I have been placed, and from which I am not even yet relieved.

Philadelphia, Nov. 3, 1831.

MR. CALHOUN. In accordance with the plan of publishing both sides of a question, we give place to the reply of this gentleman, to that part of major Eaton's appeal which related to him, and in order that a full view of the ground may be presented, we have appended the note of Mr. Evans, the brother-in-law of the latter gentleman.

BALTIMORE AND OHIO RAIL ROAD. In another part of this week's impression the reports of the president and chief engineer of the Baltimore and Ohio rail road company will be found.

Too much praise cannot be awarded to the president, directors and officers of the company for the intelligence and zeal with which they have prosecuted their arduous labors.

The subjoined paragraph, will shew the advance made in the completion of the road, since the date of these reports.

"We have the sincere satisfaction to state that the assurances given in the late annual report of the president and directors to the stockholders of the Baltimore and Ohio rail road, that the second and third divisions of the road would be opened for use by the first of November, have been realised.

"In a letter which we have seen from a gentleman who performed the trip, dated the 30th instant, he says the "Pioneer car" passed yesterday [Saturday] morning on the line as far as to the foot of the inclined plane, No. 1, at Parr Ridge, being a distance of forty miles from Baltimore.

"The fourth division of the road, which extends to the Monocacy, as well as the inclined planes over the Parr ridge, and the lateral road to Frederick, are in such a state of forwardness as to leave no doubt that the entire route to Frederick will be opened within the month of November.

"The graduation of the fifth division, extending from the Monocacy river to the Potomac, is nearly completed, except at a single point of about 2 or 300 yards, which will soon be graduated, and the travelling on the road will, without any doubt, be established to the Potomac river within a few weeks." [*Baltimore Gaz.*

FOREIGN NEWS.

Arrivals at New York and Philadelphia, bring Dundee advices to the 24th September.

POLAND AND RUSSIA.

As we had been reluctantly induced to believe, by the former advices, Warsaw, the capital of Poland has fallen. It capitulated on the 7th September, at 6 o'clock, P. M. after a most sanguinary conflict of two days duration, during which the Russians carried, by assault, all the entrenchments designed to protect the city. The Polish army followed by the diet and the members of the government, retired through Praga on the night of the 7th, and early on the ensuing day the Russian army entered, maintaining perfect order, and respecting both person and property. The Poles were retiring upon Modlin and Plozk, where it is said they will make an effort to maintain themselves. How far they will be able to realise such expectation, remains for time to unveil; but the hope of successful resistance, after such a blow

The sensation produced in London by the receipt of this unwelcome news, was great, and heavy censures were cast upon the government, for quietly witnessing the sacrifice of this brave and generous people; but in Paris it had produced a state of intense feeling, amounting to phrenzy, and a phrenzy said to be equal to that excited by the publication of the Polignac ordinances. The Parisians view it as a national calamity, as a national disgrace of which each individual must bear his share. The majority of the shops were shut, public business in some degree suspended, the ministers insulted, laughed at, threatened, and hanged in effigy, crowds thronged the streets with crape hat and arm bands; some pillaging gun makers' shops, others busy listening to the ardent apppeals of the newspapers, the theatres were closed, the black flag hoisted on some of the streets, the drum beating hourly to arms, the Marseilleise is publicly sung in the palais royal, troops of the line are in motion, to sum up all, the ministry had been twice defeated on points which it had strongly at heart. M. Casimir Perier and Sebastiani had had a narrow escape for their lives.

The above-referenced but misspelled "Kruchowiecki" had actually been Jan Stefan Krukowiecki (1772-1850), a Polish Army General in command of infantry and the head of the National Government.

Article 150. (November 12, 1831, front-page)

"LATE FOREIGN NEWS: Arrivals at New York bring Liverpool dates to the 1st October, inclusive.

FRANCE: The excitement in Paris has subsided, and notwithstanding the fall of Warsaw, the ministers still maintain a majority. The chambers have granted them 18,000,000 francs to be advanced by them on loans in aid of commerce, manufactures and internal improvements.

POLAND: The Polish army did not surrender on the fall of Warsaw; are now at Kunow under gen. Roziski, who has issued a most animated proclamation to the people of Poland, inviting them to rally. The efficient force of the Poles is between 50 and 60,000 men, determined on resistance. The loss of the Russians in the assault on Warsaw is rated at from 12 to 20,000, that of the Poles about half the number of their assailants. The cholera still raged in many parts.

GREECE: At the request of the president, Capo d'Istrias, the Russian fleet pursued the Greek fleet into Poros, where it had been burnt by admiral Miaulis, to prevent its falling into the hands of the

Russians. *The Russians pillaged Poros twenty-four hours after it surrendered.*

FROM HAMBURG: An arrival at Philadelphia brings days from Warsaw to the 13th September. The grand duke Michael, on entering Warsaw, addressed the citizens, stating, that all requests from the people were to be made to him, *direct.* He took up his residence in the royal palace, where, it is also said, field marshal Paskewitsch will take up his residence. Praga was also occupied by Russian troops. A cessation of hostilities had been entered into for a fortnight, and until the pleasure of the emperor of Russia can be received. The Polish army were still at Modlin, under the command of gen. Ribinski, gen. Malakowski having resigned the chief command.

The counsellor of state, Engel, who had been commissioned by the emperor Nicholas to organize a provisional government in Poland, was expected to arrive in Warsaw on the 13th of September."

Apparently, one could always depend on Russian soldiers to engage, like clock-work, in pillaging whenever the opportunity presented itself, as it had at Poros in the Greek world, not in the heat of battle, but 24 hours after Greek forces surrendered!

Article 151. (November 12, 1831, page 202)

Further intelligence concerning Warsaw in defeat was reported.

There is no positive intelligence of the present residence of gen. Skrzynecki, but he is supposed to be in the neighborhood of Cracow, in Gallicia. General Wilt has been appointed governor of Warsaw, and baron Korff, city commandant. The governor issued a proclamation, directing the inhabitants to deposit all arms in their possession in the arsenal, within 48 hours, under the penalty of being tried and punished by a court martial. The *Warsaw Gazette* of the 10th of September, re-publishes the proclamation of the emperor of the 29th of July. There was, on the 13th of September, 60 Russian generals in Warsaw. The municipal council still continue to perform their official duties.

On the night of the 10th, between 11 and 12 o'clock, the criminals imprisoned in the inquisition house, called the powder house, attempted to execute a plan they had formed to liberate themselves. The police guard there, assisted by many citizens of the national guard, made exertions in overcoming the prisoners. Some shots were fired, which wounded 4 and killed 1 prisoner.

It is expected that bank notes will continue in circulation. The price of *hypothaques* (public funds) has advanced, and are now selling again at 87ft, for some months past no silver coin has been seen in Warsaw; much is again in circulation.

For the week past, the cholera has demanded but few sacrifices, many soldiers of the Polish army, fully cured, left the hospitals on the 9th. But subsequently several persons were attacked with the disease. In all the military hospitals, the wives of the citizens, and the inspectors still render the most active assistance. A great many Polish families are still at Krahan; the communication between Gallicia and Krahan will be again opened; a great number of the wounded have been at Krzeszowie during the summer.

A great part of the barricades and palisades were destroyed on Thursday. Forty-eight homes were burned in the suburbs of Warsaw during the battle of Tuesday and Wednesday.

Note the reference above to "the wives of the citizens" which implied that in Europe, and in Poland as well as in the United States for that matter, only men could be termed to be citizens.

Article 152. (November 19, 1831, page 231)

According to Roziski, actually General Karol Różycki (1789- 1870), all was not yet lost because Warsaw alone, he proposed, did not constitute the entire Polish nation. In addition, please note that the Krukowiecki surname had been accurately spelled in this report. Clearly, accuracy depended on the initial reporter's (i.e., correspondent's) capability, or lack thereof, in the Polish language.

Poles! Four days ago a most sanguinary and obstinately contested battle was fought under the walls of our capital. Before the eyes of your wives, sisters and mothers, under the view of the whole city of Warsaw, the Polish troops have slain more than 20,000 of the enemy, and the entrenchments which are formed by the labor of your fellow-citizens have now become the grave of her invaders. To save the town from destruction, to weaken the force of the enemy, our troops have evacuated the capital.

The cannon, ammunition and all implements of defense, the government, the deputies, all the magistrates have withdrawn with the

General Jan Krukowiecki (1772-1850).

commander-in-chief and the army to Modlin. General Krukowiecki is no longer president of the government.

In consequence of an armistice, hostilities are for a moment suspended; but, my countrymen, let not that moment be for you a period of repose which might divert you from the great object of the deliverance of your native land; employ it rather to redouble your strength in new efforts to establish the existence and independence of Poland.

Is Warsaw for us all our country? Do its walls and inhabitants within so narrow a circuit form the limits of the nation? After so many great sacrifices, after so many dearly achieved victories, which have justly astonished the world, shall our high thoughts, our feelings, our hopes, shall all these be at the last moment expectation dissipated, as if the waters of the Warthe, Vistula, the Dnieper, the Bug and the Dwina, did not present to us the inheritance of our fathers, which, again reconquered, we will convey to our children? Who then would treacherously violate the sacred oath we have sworn, to shed the last drop of our blood in defense of our native land? No! The Pole is too proud to fail in a pledge given in the face of the whole world, or to look forward with a doubt of victory while he is still able to lift an arm. He who can value liberty, who calls himself free man, will also know how to break the fetters attempted to be imposed upon him.

Poles! Yet the moment more of endurance and resignation, and the end of the glorious contest, whose result will be the restoration of our freedom, independence and rights, is at hand. The scale of victory must preponderate in favor of the zeal, and resolution of our soldiers, and the sacrifices of our citizens. History exhibits no example of a united nation, striving to obtain one great object, being deceived in its hopes. Did not our enemies, 19 years ago, lose their capital, and not withstanding, was not their nationality and independence secured? *Never let us forget that we owe every thing to our country, our common mother. Her existence is ours; we wear her chains.* Then let us once more renew in our heart the already sworn oath, that we resolve to be a free people; that we will not lay down the sword of our fathers until we recover liberty and independence. Henceforth let our motto be, 'Death or Victory!' and when we shall stand in the order of battle, we will meet the enemy with the cry -- 'Live the country!' -- and thus we will conquer.

ROZISKI

Article 153. (November 26, 1831, page 241)

It must have been painful for Hezekiah Niles to print the particular "Poland and Russia" news-brief of the defeat of the Polish army, after which, in Warsaw, Russian troops slaughtered Polish prisoners in their prison cells, most of whom had been political, rather than military, prisoners. That issue carried this story as it appears below. Indeed, as students of history know, the murder of political opponents and prisoners became a characteristic of Russian conduct during periods of war, and in peace, well throughout the 19th and 20th centuries, and still continues to this day in the 21st century, worldwide as well as in Russia itself. Please note that a variant of the Róży-cki surname appears in this news-brief, but this time is spelled as Rozyski.

As was to have been anticipated, the army of Poland has been dispersed, and the triumph of her emperor may be said to be complete. Rozyski retreated from Modlin into Gallicia, being unable to keep his army together. The troops at Modlin had surrendered, so that all hope of Polish liberty, for the present, must be deferred. The emperor of Russia has organized a provisional government at Warsaw, and placed field marshal Paskewitsch at its head. Upwards of 1,500 of the most distinguished leaders of the Polish revolution had been arrested and imprisoned at Warsaw -- and, to complete the picture of oppression, the Russian troops had fired upon the prisoners confined in one of the wings of the prison, under the pretence of revolt among the malefactors, though it was known that three fourths of those there were imprisoned for political offences. The cholera continued to spread.

Article 154. (December 10, 1831, page 258)

As 1831 approached an end, the oppressive and painful military and political situation in Poland was further exacerbated, in the final analysis, by the seemingly viral-like spread of cholera into Europe, as reported in this issue of *Niles' Weekly Register*.

Several Polish officers had reached Paris. They complain most bitterly of being the victims of intrigue and treachery. Krukowiecki, who was the last commander (dictator) in Warsaw, is charged with having acted the part of traitor, in the surrender of that place. Prince Czartoryski, general Skrzynecki and count Malachowski had retired into the Austrian territories. Gen. Chlopicki, whose wounds were not healed, still remained at Cracow. Joseph Ullerman, a citizen of Warsaw, had been shot for having ammunition in his house. Field marshal Diebitsch was buried with great ceremony at St. Petersburgh, on the 27th September. The cholera was increasing at St. Petersburgh, and had broken out at *Hamburg*; and the *Liverpool Times*, says, that there is now only too much reason to fear that it will reach England in a few weeks.

Article 155. (January 14, 1832, page 259):

Poland and Russia. The accounts from Poland are filled with gloom, scarcely a family that has not lost some relative by the war; prosperity is destroyed, and trade is in a wretched state of depression.

The emperor of Russia, upon whom a demand was made by the Prussian government, has refused to pay the expenses of the Polish army in passing through Prussia; he has also forbidden the officers of the several corps who sought refuge in Prussia, from either returning to Russia or Poland.

The brave Schryznecki, Dembinski, and a number of other Polish generals, together with the countess Plater, has determined on seeking asylum in Paris. The first named had reached Berlin on his way thither.

Article 156. (January 14, 1832, page 371)

Although the Polish civil national air, "Poland is not yet lost" (*Jeszcze Polska nie zginęła*), and its religious national air, "God! Who through the many ages" (*Boże! Coś Polskę, przez tak liczne wieki*) served as sources of hope for Poles during the 19th century as this particular report implies, yet despair had been a recognizable reality as well. Warsaw's population had decreased by 25,000 persons.

It appears that a census lately taken, that the number of the inhabitants of Warsaw is now 113,948, not including the persons arriving daily. The population has therefore been diminished in the course of this year by 25,000 -- namely, 15,000 males and 10,000 females. Among the present population are 28,214 Jews; in the third quarter of the city they are most numerous, and exceed the Christians. The number of females now exceeds the males by 7,423.

The Polish refugees who have been able to reach Paris have found an asylum, chiefly through the efforts of general Lafayette. They exhibit letters which reach them by every post from the Prussian border, describing the cruel treatment of their unfortunate brethren by the Russian authorities. Those who, after the fall of Modlin, returned to seek their former homes and families, and who relied upon the amnesty of the Russian generalissimo, have been, according to these letters, treated with the utmost harshness when they sought the restoration of any portion of the spoliation perpetrated upon their property while in the occupation of the Russian soldiery. Indeed, generally, all who have not prostrated themselves before the conqueror, have been treated with disdain and contumely.

Article 157. (January 14, 1832, page 371)

> Understandably, despair fueled thoughts of leaving Europe for America as well.

Address to the Poles by their countrymen in England and France.

'Poles! – Confident in the enlightened spirit of the age, and in the sanctity of your cause, you rose to throw off the yoke of the oppressor. The world, in astonishment, has witnessed your achievements; but nations whom honor, duty, and even interest, commanded to assist you, have pusillanimously betrayed the common cause. Future ages will show how base was their conduct, how short sighted their policy. The contest is at an end: the sword of the Autocrat has triumphed. Europe, by her callous indifference to your misfortunes, participates in the unhallowed act. Poland is no more: erased from the list of nations, she is doomed anew to a long slavery.

Countrymen! What can we expect from the conqueror? His rage and fury we have already defied, and if an unexpected effort of humanity should attempt to spare our sufferings, feelings of patriotism would be more deeply wounded than they have ever been by every cruelty and torture formerly devised to suppress them; for what, short of the independence of Poland, can satisfy men who have sworn to die for her freedom!

Poles! You have hitherto done all that became a great and noble nation. You have spared no sacrifice to attain your great and noble object; thousands of your brave brethren have already sealed with their blood their greatest compact with heaven to die for their country. But if the sword of the enemy has spared our lives, let us remember that we are bound to devote every hour that remains to us to emulate the heroes that have fallen, and whose honor and glory are our most sacred trust. No inducement of fortune, rank, or interest shall betray us into any act unworthy of our most solemn vows; *these must be guarded as spotless as the name of Pole,* which will henceforward be left to Europe as that of patriotism and devotion.

Poles! Let us leave that wretched country, now no more our own, though soaked with the best blood of her defenders, let us leave Europe, a heartless spectator of our struggle and despair. America is only country worthy of providing asylum to men who have sacrificed everything for freedom; there Poland will be enshrined in our hearts, and heaven will perhaps bless our devotion.'

Article 158. (January 14, 1832, page 372)

Whereas the same issue of January 14, 1832 had continued from the final sentence of page 371 onto page 372 ("We have seen some attempt to rescue the character of the late duke Constantine from...") which recounted -- thanks to the *Albany Daily Advertiser*, that originally published the story in the United States, followed by *Niles' Weekly Register* publishing it as well -- Russia's cruel conduct of its imperial affairs in Poland during the period of its governance by the erratic and sadistic Prince Constantine (1779-1831), the younger brother of Czar Alexander, who served essentially as the unofficial viceroy of Poland and the official commander of its armed forces. Of interest and worthy of mention, is that, whereas Prince Constantine had ordered 500 lashes be given a soldier for an infraction involving the seams of the soldier's gloves, in England at the same time, Royal naval officers were limited, it should be remembered, to no more than 48 lashes (see Article 104 for details) given to any sailor, regardless of the magnitude of the infraction. Stark differences in civilizations indeed!

We have seen some attempt to rescue the character of the late duke Constantine from the charge of barbarity toward the Poles. A recent work of authority, however, states that his temper was truly ferocious. He was known to have a soldier given 500 lashes for having the seams of his gloves sewn inside instead of outside. A lady and gentleman having passed him one day in their carriage without recognizing him, were forced to labor on public works, trundling a barrow along with convicts and deserters. An officer of lancers was commanded to perform some manoeuvres of great difficulty, which his horse's lack of training prevented him from executing. Constantine cursed both man and beast. He called for muskets, and had a pile of them with bayonets fixed, set upon the ground, of the width of twelve feet, and then ordered the lancer to leap over them. He succeeded in accomplishing the frightful task, only to be compelled to do in a second and third time, to the astonishment of all present. One of the generals then interfered, representing the exhaustion of the officer and animal. Constantine, in a rage, again commanded the leap to be made. The noble animal cleared the bayonets with the fracture of two of his legs; the lancer escaped unhurt. He advanced to the duke, and thanking him for the honor he had hitherto enjoyed as an officer in the emperor's army, tendered his resignation. He was ordered to the guard house, and was never seen again, doubtless assassinated, as others had been before, by order of the grand duke. This was the rule, *this the government which the heroic Poles attempted to overthrow*; and which they would have succeeded in overthrowing, if the treachery of the late commander had not rendered their valor unavailing. To such oppression they are again doomed, since in the memorable language of the French minister, 'ORDER' again reigns 'in Warsaw.'

Article 159. (January 21, 1832, page 380)

The Poles. At a meeting of the Americans in Paris on the 22nd October, J. F. Cooper, esq. in the chair, a letter was read from gen. Lafayette, asking advice and assistance in the disposition of the money which had been remitted to him from New York, etc., for the relief of the Poles, and a committee of twenty, of which Dr. Howe was made the chairman, was appointed to act in this matter, under the revision and approval of gen. Lafayette. This committee had addressed a circular to the citizens of the United States, contributors in favor of the Poles, informing them that the funds will be distributed for the present relief 'of the barefoot and hungry' Poles who have already arrived at Paris, or are begging their way thither. Their number is not stated, but they have formed a national re-union, and 'Leonard Chodzko, a member of the Polish committee,' will give a list of their names, and of such as may hereafter arrive, to the American committee.

As an early 21st century quality-control test of the accuracy of the preceding *Niles' Weekly Register* news-brief of January 21, 1832, and indeed the entire contents of this book, one may ask, "Who was Dr. Howe?" The answer is corroborated in a biography titled, "The Manliest Man: Samuel G. Howe and the Contours of Nineteenth-Century American Reform" authored by James W. Trent, Jr., © 2012, by the University of Massachusetts Press, Amherst and Boston, in which Trent states that: "In May 1831 Howe also had met with the American Polish Committee, which was supporting Polish revolutionaries in the midst of a rebellion begun in Warsaw on 20 [sic] November 1830 against Russian domination. Encouraged by communication from Lafayette and James Fenimore Cooper in Paris, the committee met again in Clinton Hall on Monday evening, 5 September 1831. Quite familiar with Howe's exploits in Greece, Paris and Brussels, the committee entrusted Howe with funds they had raised for Polish national forces in Warsaw. Thus, Howe left for Europe with two humanitarian missions: to study educational methods for the blind in preparation for his new position in Boston, and to deliver American funds to the Polish Committee in Paris for distribution in Poland. What neither he nor the American Committee in Paris knew when he sailed for Europe was that Polish revolutionary forces were about to surrender to Russian authorities...." In France, "Howe visited Versailles in December and... met the Polish scholar and patriot, Joachim Lelewel, who had only recently fled to Paris. In February 1832 Howe visited schools for the blind in Belgium and Prussia, where he began carrying out his second European mission, bringing aid to Polish revolutionaries.... During the last two weeks in February, Howe travelled to Elbing and Marienburg in eastern Prussia and visiting schools for the blind and distributing the funds which he had received from the Polish Committee.... When he returned to his

Dr. Samuel Gridley Howe (1801-1876) of Massachusetts.

hotel on the night of 3 March, Prussian police were waiting to arrest him.... He remained in solitary confinement for four weeks." American State Department minister William C. Rives, "a Virginian appointee of Andrew Jackson's, and former law student of Thomas Jefferson's, who had known Howe in Paris and was in sympathy with what he considered Howe's humanitarian efforts for the Poles, brokered Howe's release."

Samuel Gridley Howe (1801-1876) of Boston, was an alumnus of Boston Latin School, Brown University in Providence, Rhode Island and Harvard Medical School, Class of 1824, who had fought as a volunteer both as a surgeon and as a battlefield commander in the Greek army against the Ottoman Empire, and eventually went on to become the Executive Founder of the Perkins School for the Blind in Watertown, an immediate western suburb of Boston, on the shore of the Charles River. The School sustains its mission to this day and remains in its original location.

Article 160. (February 11, 1832, page 438)

The proposals of gen. Lafayette to grant civil rights to the Polish refugees in France, has been *rejected* by an immense majority in the bureau, and will, therefore, not be read in the chamber.

The whole loss of the Russians in the late campaign in Poland, is put at 180,000 men, of which the capture of Warsaw cost 30,649. The Russian army in Poland is 150,000 strong. The Poles are governed with a high hand. The number of Poles at present in banishment amount to 62,000.

Contrary to Poles being held in high esteem by Lafayette and his supporters, and indeed, by a majority of the French population, some members of the French government began looking differently at the influx of Polish exiles, amounting to several thousand, not the least consideration of which had been that the Poles had become viewed as a financial, and thus, a civil burden to France as well, in their opinion.

Article 161. (March 10, 1832, page 23)

Some efforts were making by the Russians in *Poland* for the relief of the Polish officers, and the widows and orphans of those who fell in the late struggle.

Russians reportedly had been engaged in helping Polish widows and orphans? To say the least, it seems to have been very much out of character, if in fact it had occurred by ethnic Russians. Nonetheless, it may have occurred. It may also have been true, however, that the Russian officers actually may have been "unpatriotic" ethnic Poles in service of the Czar against the Polish cause but who had neither forgotten nor abandoned their Polish origins.

Article 162. (March 17, 1832, front-page)

The *Moscow Gazette* of the 27th December contains an article strongly indicative of the bad feeling entertained by the Russian government towards England. It states that the Russian government is indignant at the part which England took in the troubles of Poland, and says 'that we shall have our turn. We will strip off its mask, and will show the entire world how a people is rescued from slavery. How,' it asks, 'can this Albion, loaded with debt, and now imbued with the most perfidious principles, dare to rouse the bear, which was near devouring Napoleon with the first army that ever entered its territory, and then went to punish his territory at Paris itself. No, its turn, must come, and then we shall make a treaty with that people, except in Calcutta. We barbarians, as it calls us, will give it a lesson.'

Preparations were making at Riga for the reception of the emperor, on his journey to the Polish provinces.

The Poles banished to Siberia, are divided into two classes, and their punishments graduated accordingly. Those who sought refuge in Prussia, would be allowed to return to Poland.

What follows here was front-page news in this particular issue. Russia warned England in particular of the consequences for its allegedly having been engaged in the matter of helping Poland, and threatened to teach the British "a lesson" for having done so; and as well, criticized and characterized England (i.e., Albion) interestingly, as a country "loaded with debt," a point that had absolutely been true, and will be addressed as this book progresses.

Article 163. (April 7, 1832, page 94)

The Russian dominion over Poland, is perfect, and all sorts of tyranny practiced. The fate of this nation is sickening. Many of the Poles were abandoning their country. They are such persons as we shall gladly receive in the United States. The white eagle of Poland has been superseded by the black eagle of Russia, which shows an incorporation with the latter.

Article 164. (June 2, 1832, page 264)

Czar Nicholas I of Russia proclaimed "The End of Poland" on February 26, 1832, and as well issued his "Organic Statute" for Poland, as reported in this issue of *Niles' Weekly Register.*

The *Berlin State Gazette*, under the head of Warsaw, March 25th, contains the following important manifesto:

'By the Grace of God, Nicholas I, emperor of Russia, king of Poland, etc. When by our manifesto of Jan. 2nd, last year, we announced to our faithful subjects the march of our troops into the kingdom of Poland, which was momentarily snatched from the lawful authority, we at the same time informed them of our intention to fix the future fate of this country on a durable basis, suited to its wants, and calculated to promote the welfare of our whole empire. Now that an end has been put by force of arms to the rebellion in Poland, and that the nation, led away by agitators, has returned has to its duty, and is restored to tranquility, we deem it right to carry into execution our plan with regard to the introduction of the new order of things whereby the tranquility and union of the two nations, which Providence has entrusted to our care, may be forever guarded against new attempts. Poland, conquered in the year 1815 by the victorious arms of Russia, obtained, by the magnanimity of our illustrious predecessor, the emperor Alexander, not only national existence, but also special laws sanctioned by a constitutional charter. These favors, however, would not satisfy the eternal enemies of order and lawful power. Obstinately persevering in their culpable projects, they ceased not one moment to dream of a separation between the two nations subject to our scepter, and in their presumption they dared to abuse the favors of the restorer of their country, by employing for the destruction of his noble work the very laws and liberties which his mighty arm had generously granted them. Bloodshed was the consequence of this crime. The tranquility and happiness which the kingdom of Poland had enjoyed to a degree until then unknown, vanished in the midst of civil war and a general devastation. All these evils are now passed. The kingdom of Poland again subject to our sceptre will regain tranquility, and again flourish in the bosom of peace, restored to it under the auspices of a vigilant government. Hence, we consider it one of our most sacred duties to watch with paternal care over the welfare of our faithful subjects, and to use every means in our power to prevent the recurrence of similar catastrophes, by taking from the ill-disposed the power of disturbing public tranquility. As it is, moreover, our wish to secure for the inhabitants of Poland the continuance of all the essential requisites for the happiness of individuals and of the country in general, namely, security of persons and property, liberty of conscience, and all the laws and privileges of towns and communes, so that the kingdom of Poland, with a separate administration adapted to its wants, may not cease to form an integral part of our empire, and that the inhabitants of this country may henceforth constitute a nation united with the Russians by sympathy and fraternal sentiments, we have, according to these principles, ordained and resolved this day, by a new organic statute to introduce a new form and order in the administration of our kingdom of Poland.

St. Petersburgh, Feb. 25, 1832.

NICHOLAS
The secretary of state,
Count Stephen Grabowski'

And Hezekiah Niles went on to print the Czar's related "Organic Statute" as well.

After this manifesto, the organic statutes of Poland are given. The principal provisions are as follows:

'Poland is forever united with the Russian empire, of which it forms an integral part. The kingdom shall have its separate administration, its own code of civil and criminal laws, and the privileges of towns and communes shall remain in force. The *coronation of emperor of Russia and king of Poland in future will take place at Moscow by one and*

216

the same act, in the presence of special deputies appointed for the occasion. In the case of a regency in the empire, the power of regent will extend over the kingdom of Poland. The liberty of worship is guaranteed; the Catholic religion being that of the majority of its inhabitants, will be under the special protection of the government; personal liberty is granted; no one shall be arrested except in cases provided for by the law and under the regular formalities, and must be brought before a competent court of justice within three days. The punishment of confiscation can only be applied to offences against the state of the first class. The press will be subject to some indispensable restrictions. The kingdom of Poland is to contribute to the general expenses of the empire in due proportion. The taxes which existed prior to November 1830, shall be maintained. The commercial relations between the kingdom and the empire are to be regulated by the mutual interest of the parties.

For the future there will be but one army for Poland and Russia, and the emperor reserves to himself to fix hereafter the part which Poland is to contribute to its composition. The inhabitants of either country may become mutually naturalized. The high administration is composed of the council of government, presided by the governor-general, and other members appointed by the sovereign. The council of government proposes the candidates for archbishops, bishops, directors-general, etc., who are to be chosen from among all the subjects of his majesty without distinction. There is also a council of state; to which is entrusted the care of administrative laws. All generally important laws, such as the budget, are to be sent into the council of state of the empire for revision and sanction. All administrative business is to be transacted in the Polish language. The old division of the country continues the same, as well as the committees of the Palatinates. The assemblies of the nobility, of the communes, and the councils of the Palatinate shall also continue.

Article 165. (June 23, 1832, page 303)

In addition to being engaged in the life and death struggle against the Russians for the right to exist as a free and independent nation, Poles also had been engaged in the European-wide existential struggle against the dreaded cholera mordus disease that spared no one at that time in Europe, as is illustrated in this news article that appeared in Niles' Weekly Register.

CHOLERA IN EUROPE: The following analytical table of the ravages of the cholera in the various European countries which it visited *previous to* its appearance in France and England, has been published by a German paper.

Places	Inhabitants/Cases	Deaths	Of 1,000 inhabitants were attacked	Of 1,000 attacked, died	Proportion of the sick to the living
Moscow	350,000 8,576	4,690	24,5	546	40
St. Petersburg	360,000 9,247	4,757	26,4	514	37
Vienna	300,000 3,984	1,809	13,2	477	75
Berlin	240,000 2,200	1,401	9,24	631	108
Hamburg	100,000 874	455	8,75	521	114
Prague	96,600 3,234	1,333	33,4	413	29
Breslaw	78,800 1,276	671	16,4	525	61
Koningsburg	70,000 2,188	1,310	31,2	699	32
Magdeburg	36,600 576	346	15,7	600	63
Brunn	35,300 1,540	604	46,2	327	21
Stettin	24,300 366	250	15,06	699	66
Halle	23,800 303	152	12,7	503	78
Elbing	22,000 430	283	19,5	658	51
Hungary	8,750,000/435,330	188,000	4,9	439	20

It was remarked at Moscow, St. Petersburg, and in many other places, that previous to the breaking out of the cholera, the atmosphere was obscured by clouds of insects. The city of Lille is at this time completely covered with gnats. A calculator has amused himself with ascertaining the number collected upon one square *metre* of a wall in the town. The whole of these walls comprise a surface of 3,750,000,000 square *metres*, (about 4,485,114,000 square yards), each *metre* having, on an average, a *milligramme* in weight of gnats, the result of which is, that the aggregate of these insects, when dead, formed a mass of putrid matter, weighing 3,750 kilogramme, or 8,271 lbs., a weight equal to that of least fifty human carcases, and which remained in this state in the streets.

It should come as no surprise that there was no related information from all once-Polish cities, other than Breslaw (Wrocław) and Stettin (Szczecin), Koningsburg (Królowiec) and Elbing (Elbląg), for example, in revolt during this period. It is safe to say, in my opinion at least, that from our vantage point in 2021, the cholera must have also taken its vicious toll in Warsaw and Wilno, and in other cities of the former Commonwealth of Poland and Lithuania, especially so if one compares the population of the Kingdom of Poland, under Russian rule, to that of Hungary under Austrian rule at the time, as is illustrated in the table above.

Article 166. (July 21, 1832, page 374):

The Polish exiles are yet pursued with the vengeance of Russia. The count of Dresden has received bullying notes from the Austrian and Prussian ministries, insisting that they shall be expelled from Saxony. In Europe, they can find no asylum, except in France and Great Britain. Many, we hope, will come to the United States.

Article 167. (August 11, 1832, page 422)

We have mournful accounts of the oppression of the Poles by their Russian masters. A black and bloody despotism prevails over the land.

Article 168. (August 18, 1832, page 437)

The majority of articles published by Hezekiah Niles for inclusion in *Niles' Weekly Register*'s ongoing dramatic story of Poland's suffering at the hands of Russia evoked images of the eternal struggle of good versus evil, and of Russia as the perennial ogre standing by choice on the wrong side of human history and the dignity of mankind. The following "Wretched Poles!" article reveals but one example of many instances of the flagrant ethnic cleansing of Poland practiced by Imperial Russia, subsequent to the failure of the November Uprising, and documented in my research for this book.

Gallignini's Messenger of the 23d June, contains a letter dated Bamberg, June 6th, which states that on the 3d of that month, an officer of high rank, formerly belonging to the Russian army, had arrived at that city, having by artifice escaped from Siberia, whither he had been perpetually banished. At Bamberg he was received with great kindness and attention. He states that on his journey, he saw *forty-eight thousand Poles*, persons of all ages, sexes, and condition, CHAINED, and marching to Russia. The general officers of the late Polish army were not exempted from the heaviest shackles! Such are the blessings of an autocratic government! Where was France, whom Lafayette recommended her interference in behalf of this noble, but ill-fated country?

Lord Durham has proceeded in a line-of-battle-ship from England, on a special mission to Russia, for the supposed purpose of remonstrating against the barbarities practiced on the unfortunate Poles.

Article 169. (August 25, 1832, page 453)

Another example of overt, flagrant and "detestable" but undefined ethnic cleansing by Russia, applied to Polish children. Indeed, as an attribute of a future century's ethnic cleansing it also had been manifested by the removal of the library of the University of Wilno (Vilnius in the Lithuanian language) to Russia that had sought to obliterate the history of that Library which had stood as a model of academic excellence of the similarly obliterated and not-to-be-remembered Commonwealth of Poland and Lithuania. The same issue addressed the matter of the Polish exile "chiefs" in Paris having been ordered by French authorities to leave Paris and France as well.

RUSSIA AND PRUSSIA: "The military arrangements of the emperor and king cause much speculation. The first has a great army in Poland, and is increasing it, the army of the second seems to be on the highest war establishment."

POLAND: "The Warsaw Gazette contains three imperial ukases, condemning many gallant officers of the Polish army to be degraded from their ranks of nobility and sent to Siberia, with a confiscation of their property.

Posen, June 19. The late statement, that *in all Poland children are taken and carried away to Russia*, is confirmed by letters from all quarters. This detestable measure was largely to be carried into execution by Ralisch, and when the inhabitants refused to obey orders, general Sabolew, the governor, issued a summons to them, to obey, or to expect more severe measures. *The citizens, joined by their wives, feeling the injustice of the proceeding, were resolved rather to bear the worst that could happen, and an affray attended with bloodshed took place, in which 90 Russians and a not inconsiderable number of citizens, were killed.* No doubt arrests will take place. But meantime the removal of the children has been deferred and a report sent to Paskewitsch. It is hoped that the Russians will abandon this terrible measure, as it is said that great disapprobation of the proceeding has been manifested by the people of Russia itself. From time to time, new emigrants from the neighboring provinces of Poland arrive, but they are immediately delivered up, without distinction, to the Russian authorities."

LATER NEWS: "The destruction of Poland continues: the fine university of Wilna has just been dissolved, and its splendid library of 200,000 volumes, is ordered to be removed to Russia. An insurrection has broken out in Lithuania, and a large detachment of Cossacks had been cut to pieces, by the peasants, driven to despair.

The sentences of marshal Francis Bilgorayski, the demissionary lieut. Tripolski and the canon John Siercaonski, by which they were degraded from their several ranks, and made soldiers in the line in the battalions in Siberia, and their property confiscated, are published in the English papers, with the approval in full by the emperor....

Three Polish chiefs had been ordered to leave Paris and France, in five days. The reasons are not distinctly assigned, but it would seem that they had interfered in the political affairs of France. The anniversary of the 'three days' was regarded with some alarm in Paris."

The referenced anniversary of the "three days" (Trois Glorieuses) in Paris pertained to July 27-29, 1830 which marked, among other things, the abdication of King Charles X of France, and his replacement by Louis-Philippe who declared his title to be "King of the French" rather than "King of France," the latter of whom Russia did not view as the "legitimate" ruler of France. Those events in Paris ignited Poland's subsequent November 29, 1830 Uprising against Imperial Russia.

Article 170. (September 1, 1832, pages 7 and 8)

This issue of the *Niles' Weekly Register* devoted nearly two full pages, likely written by a Pole, (and if not, then by a non-Pole who championed Poland's cause via his news reports) on the state of affairs in Poland wherein it stated that, as the sole responsible person for Russia's brutality against Poland, "Nicholas stands prominent, as in him the soul of the infanticide Herod is metamorphosed." Strong words indeed, but highly appropriate and well-placed. It also included the text of the letter sent to President Andrew Jackson of the United States by the exiled Polish National Committee in Paris which appealed to the United States government to accept some 3,000 to 4,000 Polish exiles as immigrants from France where they were no longer welcome. Here included as well had been a vivid description of Warsaw under Russian occupation and control:

POLAND: "Those of the Polish troops who had the misfortune to become prisoners of war, did not return from Russia, and all those who were either deluded by the amnesty solemnly promised them by Nicholas, or compelled by force or deception to re-enter, from Prussia or Austria, their country, were immediately conducted into the interior of Russia, where they will be embodied with Russian regiments. Their number amounts to 50,000. The appearance and the population of Warsaw has undergone a complete change. The eternal parades of the Russian military, the shrill voices of the bearded Russian coachmen driving furiously through the streets their haughty and starred masters, the oriental gorgeousness dazzling the eyes and stunning the ears, they have altogether given other features to the capital, which, not long since was the charming abode of simplicity, elegance, and harmony, and represented, as it were, a single united family. Warsaw is now crowded with Russian families, which can scarcely deserve the name of European population. In every house the first floors are monopolized by them. Dirty uncouth Russian dealers and victuallers, with their unshaved long beards, infest every where the public places. You see them surround the column of king Sigismund, and the statue of Copernicus, with their little shops and provision wagons. Our inhabitants are hardly seen in public, children not at all. They are fast clinging to the bosoms of their unhappy mothers, as if frightened by wolves, wild beasts, or monstrous spectres, *at whose head Nicholas stands prominent, as in him the soul of the infanticide Herod is metamorphosed.* Still the metropolis bears her misfortunes with dignity and calmness, approaching on sublimity; like Laocoon encircled, with serpents, she looks up to heaven vanquishing her grief.

Warsaw, June 2. My former information of the existence of a revolt in a part of Lithuania is daily gaining ground. The experienced people have made the large forest of Bailowies the abode for their security. The body of insurgents is mostly composed of the inhabitants of the surrounding country, who being the constant objects of Russian persecution, oppression, and deportations to Siberia, saw in the revolt the only means of rescuing themselves from cruel fate impending over them. Among the number are many citizens of wealth and respectability, with their families, and the peasantry of adjoining villages. The Russians themselves do not conceal the existence of the fact, which they gave out to be 20,000 men. It is not long since a whole regiment of Cossacks was cut to pieces in an engagement with these desperate men. They are said to possess 12 pieces of cannon which they had captured from the Russians, but to be in want of ammunition. They gave no quarter to Russians, the terror thereof is great, and their number is increasing by deserters from the army. *Russia already appropriates to herself the revenue of the kingdom, but her army is paid from the Polish treasury, and the Poles have further to defray the expenses of the new fortifications erected to keep them still more in bondage.* Up to this time, upwards of 10,000,000 florins have been disposed of in this way, and considerable sums have been drawn on the bank, in the shape of loans. *All vestiges of our nationality, even in the most trifling particulars, are made to disappear before the cruel jealousy of the public enemy.* The outworks of the citadel are proceeding rapidly; the first edifice erected in it is the state prison. Up to this moment, not more than 150 Polish soldiers have voluntarily entered the Russian service; the last were enrolled by compulsion, or by holding out to them promises which will never be realized. They were immediately marched off into the interior of Russia. The volunteers, however, were introduced to field marshal Paskewitsch, which was done on account of the singularity of the case; on which occasion each received two Dutch ducats from his own hand. A levy of 25,000 recruits has again been ordered, *which will considerably thin the young population of Poland.* They will be put among Russian regiments."

NATIONAL POLISH COMMITTEE: Paris, May 9, 1832. To his excellency, general Jackson, president of the United States of America.

General: The Poles, exiled from their unhappy country, which their efforts and their sacrifices were unavailable to save from the fangs of treachery and the frightful consequences of conquest; the Poles, persecuted by all the sworn enemies of liberty, bearing nothing from their native country saving hope and misfortune, confidently address the government of the happy people of America, whose power and dignity the old hemisphere delights in contemplating; whose wise institutions have taken deep root in the soil, and sent forth vigorous shoots of freedom, and who has realized the sublime problem of social welfare united to liberty.

Europe knows our rights and vicissitudes. Her nations, in their progress towards general emancipation hailed our successes with raptures and joy, and shed tears over our reverses. The country of Washington, still revering the memory of the intrepid Pulaski, and the virtuous Kosciusko, resounded with unanimous acclamations at our last efforts, and neither the immense space of the ocean, nor the charms of social comfort which they so plentifully enjoy, could deter its happy citizens from sympathizing for our cause. Those circumstances, together with the consciousness of having done our duty, induce us to make an appeal to popular feelings, which alone are capable of ministering to the sufferings of the proscribed of a once free and great nation.

Ten months of an independent existence, of which the insurrection of the 29th of November, 1830, was the signal, were passed in a bloody contest with a powerful enemy, *possessed of all the advantages derived of material force aided by the allies who shared in the criminal dismemberment of the Polish republic, and assisted by secret agents in the interior.* Poland fell a victim to the league of kings. Her armies divided for the purpose of facing the enemy on all sides, having to contend with overwhelming forces, increasing every moment and suffered to want for nothing by all ill-disposed neighbors, were obliged to take refuge in a country which belonged to Poland before it became the booty of invaders. Meanwhile, France remained an indifferent spectator of their struggle. Lulled with the vain hope of preserving peace, and led astray by a mistaken policy founded on moderation and concession, her government disregarded the old friendship existing between both nations, the brotherly ties that once united them, and the fact of Poland having stopped the crusade of the northern despots directed against the principles proclaimed by the revolution of July. Poland has undergone the yoke; she can no longer boast of a political existence, being entirely ruled by ukases, in violation of the very treaties and engagement which it had pleased her masters to impose on her fifteen years before. *The Poles, outlawed in the empires, kingdoms and principalities of the holy alliance, had to choose between chains, dungeons, death, or transportation to the icy deserts of Siberia, and exile and the confiscations of their properties.* The remains of the army, whom it was attempted after they had witnessed the murder of their disarmed brothers to induce to accept a perfidious amnesty, together with the members of the diet and of the revolutionary government, preferred going into exile, there to devise means of asserting some day their country's rights; for be their losses and misfortunes ever so great, the *Poles shall never cease entertaining in their hearts the secret assurance of the triumph of their cause, and of the establishment of a free and independent Poland. They sought a secure asylum where they might vindicate their common interests, and support and preserve their nationality.* A constant amity and recollections of former glory and reverses, shared and borne at different periods with the French people; zeal and repeated service rendered by Poland to France; solemn assurances given at a moment when other states remained silent, by the chief of the government and of the representatives of the French people, a country in which the Poles thought that the Polish nationality should not perish, pointed out France as the only country in which Poles could expect to meet with hospitality and protection, religiously preserve their nationality, and prepare the way for the regeneration of their country.

As Reported in the "Niles' Register"

The dispersion of the last members of the national government, and of the representatives of the last diet, left no hope of their being able to muster on any point the number required by law to transact business. The absence of national representation at so critical a moment, suggested to the Poles who arrived first in Paris, the propriety of appointing from among themselves a national committee. By degrees, as the number of refugees increased in France, the committee entered into communication with them, and took upon itself, to act in their name. It is in that quality they now apply to the president and government of the United States of America. The French people received with enthusiasm their unhappy brothers. Confiding in their generous feelings, and in the solemn assurances of France, we expected to find among them a harbor in our adversity, and the guarantee of a sort of political existence. Such were our hopes in coming to France. But the government has been deaf to the just application of the Polish refugees, nay, it has even persecuted them: and both chambers have sanctioned their system by enacting the law of the 9th of April last, which is particularly aimed at the Poles, whom it places at the mercy of a hostile administration.

The political horizon of Europe is assuming every day a more sombre aspect, and France may fall a prey to factions or invasion. Then the Poles shall be left without this last precarious asylum. Impressed with the deepest concern at the thought of the present uncertain situation of the refugees, the national committee could not but take into serious consideration their future prospects, and devise some plan for their safety in case of the exceptional laws of France being carried into execution, or that the Poles should again become the victims of a mistaken policy. They are perfectly aware of the difficulties and dangers they would have to encounter should they be compelled to quit the hospitable land of France; *in their perplexity they look up to the United States, without, however, concealing that to seek a refuge in a friendly country so far from theirs would be very painful to their feelings, since it would be attended by a long exile.* But on the other hand, their republican minds would derive some consolation in their misfortune, from breathing the air of a pure hemisphere; they flatter themselves that the government of the United States will not belie their hopes and the high opinion which the world has conceived of its dignity and liberality; and that their illustrious president, raised to that proud station by the voice of his fellow citizens and partaking their sentiments, will favorably receive the application of the remains of a nation assailed by the most cruel fortune.

We already have flattering proof of the friendly disposition of the Americans towards us. On the anniversary of the Declaration of Independence of the United States, on the 4th July, 1831, the citizens of that republic present in Paris met under the presidency of Mr. F. Cooper, and subscribed a considerable sum in favor of our cause. Mr.

S. Howe having brought us two banners and additional patriotic subscriptions, most of the American citizens in Paris formed into a committee, under the patronage of gen. Lafayette.

So much sympathy shown in the Polish cause, emboldens us to hope that the government of the United States will not deny us its assistance. If it should happen through a fatality without example in the records of the world, that the Poles, persecuted in Europe, should be under the hard and cruel necessity of directing their last course towards a *transatlantic shore*, they would demand friendship and hospitality of the people of the United States, in whose country they know misfortune is ever sure to find a refuge. *Nevertheless, as the number of our countrymen might amount to between 3 and 4,000 men, destitute of arms and resources, and consequently in imminent danger, they deem it expedient to warn the government of their determination, and to claim its aid.*

Under these circumstances, it is important for them to be informed with all possible dispatch, to what extent they may rely on the protection and support of the United States, what condition would be required of those who would seek an asylum in the republic, what would be the nature of their relations with and duties towards the states of the union, and how far their nationality could be guaranteed without interfering with the institution and interests of the country? They further request to be informed, would the government secure a safe passage across the ocean, by providing them with a safe conduct which would preserve them in their navigation from dangers they would otherwise have to encounter?

Such are questions which the Polish national committee take the liberty to address to the supreme chief of the United States. They consider it a most fortunate circumstance that their sentiments and wishes should be conveyed to him through the medium of Dr. Howe, who by his zeal and exertions in our behalf, has acquired additional right to the gratitude of the Poles.

We remain, general, with the most profound respect, your excellency's most obedient servants.

The president of the national committee.

(Signed)

LELEVEL JOACHIM,
LEONARD CHODSKO,
ANTONY BLUSZUCEWIDZ,
JOSZEF ZALIZOSKI,
ANTONY FOZCUISWOSKI,
E. RYKARZEWSKI,
MICHEL STUDE,
EDWARD WODZINSKI.

Once again, I remind readers of this study and book not be critical of the misspelling or confounding of a surname with a given name (e.g., Lelevel Joachim incorrectly versus Joachim Lelewel, as noted above, and as well earlier) in this instance among all the Polish-surnamed co-signers of the letter from the Polish National Committee in Paris, to the United States President, Andrew Jackson (1767-1845), who led the Executive Branch of government from 1829 to 1837, and whose major interest in "foreign relations" for the most part ostensibly concerned Mexico, the annexation of Texas and the Indian Removal Act in North America, and the vastly more contentious matter of claims of the United States against a European power for damages to American commercial shipping caused specifically by France during the Napoleonic regime. Happily for all concerned, France, the first ally of the United States following the American decisive victory over British forces at Saratoga in October 1777, settled for a mutually-acceptable claim in the final month of 1835.

Thus, initially at least, and as fate might have had it at the time, there would have seemed to be no hope for the "Polish cause" and its related appeal to President Jackson from Paris for assistance by temporarily re-settling 3,000 to 4,000 Polish exiles from France, as a community intact and apart from American life, in the United States.

By bluntly stating their position -- the essential points being that they not be required to expend personal financial cost for transatlantic passage to and from their American exile, and no cost in the matter of sustaining themselves in their apparent temporary American exile as well -- had been no minor consideration. Added to that, they neither offered a frame of reference for the estimated number of years (admittedly a very difficult task) for their American exile, nor any expression of interest in becoming citizens of the United States -- President Jackson's response, if any, would likely not have been favorable. Niles' Weekly Register did not reference a response from President Jackson. If he had agreed to grant them refuge in the United States, it would have been "big news" as the expression goes, considering that the Poles numbered several thousand as a body.

However, *Niles' Weekly Register* did provide evidence of the arrival of Polish exiles, one of whom reportedly had been a nephew of Kazimierz Pulaski, in New York City, in 1832. (See Article 177.) Also included among those 300 Polish exiles from Austria who arrived in New York city in 1833, were the 235 who brought their appeal for assistance to the attention of United States Senator George Pointdexter of Mississippi, and about whom President Andrew Jackson took an interest as will be seen, on a relatively "big news" basis.

Subsequently as well, *Niles' Weekly Register* provided comparably extensive coverage of the large group of said Poles, all of whom had been exiled from Austria, as arranged in 1833 by order of the Austrian Kaizer (Emperor), and who left Europe for exile from the port of Trieste on the Adriatic Sea and disembarked at the port of New York City with reportedly $50 in cash provided to each of them by the Austrian government. The number said Poles had been 300, consisting of 299 men and 1 woman. (*Articles 198, 201, 202* and *203* of this book will relate their story in America during the period, 1833-1834 and in 1842.)

Article 171. (September 22, 1832, page 53)

Of Poland, Hezekiah Niles commented in this issue, that its "struggle is hopeless" -- but that "death is not the greatest of evils." He also looked for a "chosen curse" for Russia's "export" of Polish male children to the Empire's interior and beyond to Siberia and other remote hellish locations where many of them died of starvation and/or from the harsh elements of nature. Russia's typical responsive accusation in those days had been that such articles of news had been "calumnies" (i.e., lies or what some in our 21st century deem to be "fake news"). Hezekiah Niles' news-briefs on Poland and Russia transcribed below are succinct but powerful, and illustrative of Russian efforts for the final completion of the *ethnic cleansing* of Poland by reducing the number of its children on a planned and extended basis.

Driven to desperation by the *ruthless despotism -- the cold-blooded and beastly barbarity of the Russians --* many *Poles* are in arms in the forests of Lithuania, to kill or be killed, rather than submit. The struggle is hopeless, but 'death is not the greatest of evils'.

It is stated that several strong corps of the Russian army are posted in the neighborhood of the German frontier.

The *export* of young male children from Poland to Russia proper, is one of the most affecting and *rascally* doings in modern times. In some parts, this infernal business extends to carrying *19-20ths of the boys, and thousands of them perish through grief or hardships.* One half die on their journey from their mothers and homes. Is there not *'some chosen curse to blast'* such doings!

Article 172. (October 6, 1832, page 95)

Polish heroism. At the storming of Warsaw, the principal battery was defended by only two battalions, but with such bravery as history can hardly parallel. When it was evident that it could no longer hold out, several privates of the artillery seated themselves on the powder barrels and blew themselves up. But the conduct of gen. Sowinski was truly heroic; having lost one foot, he was, at his earnest request, seated on a chair, and placed on the altar of the desperately defended church, where he continued to give orders until the last of his comrades was cut down, when, drawing forth two pistols, he with one, shot a Russian who was rushing upon him, and, with the exhortation -- 'so dies a Polish general!' -- fired the other through his own heart.

The referenced 'Sowinski' in the article had been Józef Sowiński (1777-1831) who was a Polish General in command of field artillery. According to the 19th century Polish poet, Juliusz Słowacki (1809-1849), in his poem, "Sowiński in the Trenches of Wola", the Polish general's life ended differently. He was bayoneted to death by Russian soldiers after the agreement to surrender. Modern historians tend to agree with Słowacki. The 19th correspondent who wrote the news-brief could not have known that in life Sowiński reportedly had been fitted with a wooden leg.

Article 173. (October 20, 1832, page 119)

News about Poland appears directly as well as inferentially in the October 20, 1832 issue of *Niles' Weekly Register*, in three brief paragraphs, as follows:

Lord Durham was about to return from St. Petersburg. Nothing is stated as to the result of his mission....

In Germany, 'the Baden government has dissolved all the committees formed in that duchy for the relief of Polish immigrants, declaring those brave but unfortunate refugees in future be maintained at the expense of the state.'

In Portugal, 'a large body of Poles, and other recruits' were about engage at Oporto likely on the side of King Dom Pedro the Liberator in a war against his brother Miguel.

Article 174. (November 3, 1832, page 149)

We hear much in recent years that Poles tend to exaggerate their history of relentless victimization and suffering as a nation. Americans from 1811 to 1849 didn't think so thanks to *Niles' Weekly Register* because of what this issue and others continually reported as harsh truth.

Poland. It is stated that 'the pope in compliance with the wish of the emperor Nicholas, has just signed a brief, in which he declares to the clergy and the Catholics of Poland, that all the faithful are bound to obey the Ukases issued by their lawful sovereign of Poland.'

Great numbers of Poles were being sent off to Siberia. The population of Warsaw has been much decreased; and it is said that the licentiousness of the lower classes of women is without bounds.

A perspective on the matter of the alleged licentiousness reported above is in order. With husbands away serving as soldiers, or perhaps being held as prisoners of war or exiled to Siberia, or killed in action, and with their wives confining their male children, especially, to homes, lest they be kidnapped by Russian forces as part and parcel for the "ethnic cleansing" of future Polish generations, and the necessity of foraging for food, without money to pay for it, sadly left Poland's "women of the lower classes" with no choice if they expected to survive, along with their children, thereby being forced into unfairly perceived "licentiousness."

The Poles who sought an asylum in Prussia have been given up, some however, had escaped to France. They were marched to the Russian frontiers in detachments of some 200 to 500 men, by Prussian soldiers, supplied with clubs, to beat those who might be refractory, the Russians, as they received them, subjected each man to 50 or 100 lashes of the knout. In some cases, rendered desperate by personal sufferings and indignities, they resisted, and were trampled to death by the cavalry or hewed down. Others were chained and sent to work on the fortifications as felons.

> The brutal graphic symbolism reflected in the paragraph immediately above is breath-taking.

Article 175. (November 17, 1832, pages 191 and 192)

> This issue contained two full pages of intelligence about Poland that had been remarkably comprehensive, in which the story about the Grand Duke Constantine and the Polish lancer (reported earlier in Article 158 of January 14, 1832) was published again. Both articles drew attention to Constantine's grossly sadistic tendencies; the speech of Count Plater at Leeds, England; the flagrantly imposed, ongoing painful *ethnic cleansing of Poland's children by Russia*; and the tar and feathering, by order of the Grand Duke Constantine himself, of the shaved heads of Polish women, are instructive, if not alarming and disgusting.

CONDITION OF POLAND: We insert the following articles to shew the condition in which the unfortunate Poles have been placed by their Russian masters, and that the latter may be held up to public execration, though means of redressing the wrongs inflicted by them are wanting.

'From *Campbell's Metropolitan*

The grand duke Constantine, who has played so conspicuous part in the affairs of Poland, is worthy of something more than a passing notice. Though possessed of very considerable talents, he is in fact an untamed tiger, giving way on all occasions to the most violent paroxysms of temper. He has a deep sense of the rights of his order, and holds the feelings of every class of human beings as naught. So soon, therefore, as he found that his imperial brother was no longer the liberal patron of the constitutional rights, he gave the most unrestrained license to his capricious and violent injustice. A few instances are better than general assertion. A most opulent and respectable man, Woloski, the principal brewer of Warsaw, had through some of his people, hired as a servant, in his establishment, a Russian deserter. The offender was detected, and proof of innocence on the part of his employer being disallowed, the grand duke by his individual decree, ordered this respectable individual to be fettered, and in that condition to work with a wheel barrow in the public streets. His daughter, an amiable young lady, ventured to appeal to the mercy of the grand duke in behalf of her parent; and the unmanly monster kicked her down stairs, using at the same time the most abusive language.

A boy nine years of age, a son of count Plater, had, in the playfulness of childhood, written with chalk, on one of the forms, '*The third of May forever!*' that being the anniversary of Kosciusko's constitution. The fact was discovered by some of the innumerable spies employed even among these infants, to Novozilyoff, who instituted an inquiry among the boys, not one of whom would betray poor Plater; they were all ordered to be flogged with the utmost severity. The unhappy offender declared that he had written the offensive words. The grand duke condemned him to be a soldier for life, incapable of advancing in the army; and when his mother threw herself before his carriage to implore for her wretched child, he spurned her like a dog with his foot.

Shaving the heads of ladies of rank who displeased him, was a common occurrence; and on one occasion, four soldiers were hanged because they abstained from carrying such an order into effect, as they found it impossible to do so, without using personal violence. Tarring and feathering the shaved heads of the offenders, was also a favorite recreation of the commander-in-chief.

One day an officer of the lancer guard was going through his exercise before the grand duke. He had performed all the usual evolutions in the most satisfactory way, until, when at full gallop he was suddenly ordered to turn, his horse proved restive, and refused to obey either bridle or spur. The rage of the grand duke had vented itself in furious imprecations, and all present trembled for the consequences. Halt, he exclaimed, and ordered a pyramid of twelve muskets with fixed bayonets to be erected. The order was instantly obeyed.

The officer who had by this time subdued the restiveness of his horse was ordered to leap the pyramid, and the spirited horse bore his rider safely over it. Without an interval of delay, the officer was ordered to repeat the fearful leap, and to the amazement of all present the noble horse and his brave rider stood in safety on the other side of the pyramid. The grand duke, exasperated at finding himself thus thwarted in his barbarous purpose, repeated the order for the third time. A general, who happened to be present, now stepped forward, and interceded for the pardon of the officer; observing that the horse was exhausted, and that the enforcement of the order would be to doom horse and rider to a most horrible death. This humane remonstrance was not only disregarded, but was punished by the immediate arrest of the general who had thus presumed to rebel.

The word of command was given, and horse and rider for the third time, cleared the glittering bayonets. Rendered furious by these repeated disappointments, the grand duke exclaimed, the fourth time, 'To the left about! – Forward!' The command was obeyed and for the fourth time the horse leapt the pyramid, and then with his rider, dropped down exhausted. The officer extricated himself from the saddle, and rose unhurt, but the horse had both his fore legs broken. The countenance of the officer was deadly pale, his eyes stared wildly, and his knees shook under him. A deadly silence prevailed as he advanced to the grand duke, and laying his sword at his highness' feet, he thanked him in a faltering voice, for the honor he enjoyed in the emperor's service. 'I take back your sword,' said the grand duke gloomily, 'and are you not aware of what may be the consequence of this undutiful conduct towards me?' The officer was sent to the guard house. He subsequently disappeared, and no trace of him could be discovered. Against a thousand like actions, the Poles rebelled'." {Harring's Poland}

"Extract from the speech of count Plater, at Leeds, England: 'And after so many years of most cruel oppression, Poland rose to vindicate her right, to be free and independent. (Cheers.) There are no sacrifices that she has not submitted to, no effort that she has not made. Old men, women, and children, every one indeed has joined most bravely in the national struggle, every where the same efforts, the same love of the country; and if the brilliant victories of Poland did not longer continue, we must ascribe it to the indifference of some powers who guaranteed the Polish nationality, and who did not prevent the shameful secret assistance given by Prussia to Russia! (Hear, hear.) Without this intervention, and with a more energetic exertion on the part of its government, and less confidence in any favorable assistance, Poland would have been saved, and with the Russian despotism crushed forever. At present the barrier between barbarism and civilization, between liberty and oppression, is destroyed, and Poland being sacrificed, let us see into what state the indifference of the European powers towards Poland has plunged that country; let us see what are her sufferings. (Hear, hear.)

Will you believe, gentlemen, that at this very moment, many thousand citizens are sent in a most atrocious way, attached to a bar of iron, on foot, in the way to Siberia, that infants are torn from their parents and sent by thousands (boys to the military schools, and girls to the manufactories, in the interior of Russia), where they lose forever their nationality, that even the women are sent to Siberia, that many mothers, in their despair, have plunged the dagger in their infants' breasts and have with the same dagger killed themselves, that those unheard of cruelties are perpetrated without any consideration for age, for sex, or the rank of the inhabitants, people die on their way in consequence of the most barbarous treatment, that Poland, in a very short time, will *be peopled by the Russians, and Siberia by Poles, that the language, religion, civilization, are destroyed, many of the churches in ruins, many occupied by the Russian priests, the universities and schools abolished, all fortunes confiscated, and the Polish villages peopled by the Russian peasantry, committing the most enormous enormities, that by Russian intrigues the greatest part of the Polish army, who had taken refuge in Prussia, was, after many murders, compelled to return to Poland, and then sent to Siberia, or compelled to be common soldiers in the Russian regiments for all their lives. (Shame, shame.) This is the wretched state of Poland, perishing under the despotism of Russia. And what hope can we have for her future recovery, if the free governments of Europe will not put a stop to those cruelties? (Cheers)'."*

Count Plater's remarks are instructive to a modern 21st century reader. Not only do they convey the image of Imperial Russia's actions in support of the flagrant, premeditated ethnic cleansing, perpetrated in extremis, of Poland and the Polish nationality during the fourth decade of the 19th century on an unquestionably apocalyptic basis, particularly during the reign of Nicholas I, but also presage the 20th century's genocides of Armenians by the Turks and of Jews by the Germans. Where, one may ask, does the very fine line separating ethnic cleansing from genocide manifest itself, if in fact it exists? In this regard, consider the following about the exportation (i.e., kidnapping) by Russia of young Polish boys to the interior of the Empire as reported by a German newspaper:

The *Brunswick German National Journal* contains, under the head of 'the present state of Poland,' the following accounts: 'The intercourse with Poland is now so difficult that the communications on the subject furnished by the public papers either give a general view of the misery of the country, or describe only isolated facts that are soon forgotten, so that it is impossible to form a correct idea of the entire system which Russia is now preparing in Poland. We have lately received letters of the 1st, 4th, 5th, and 30th of May, which bring various, numerous, complete, and important statements founded on public documents, and the evidence of creditable persons. We here give extracts from them. We abstain from all personal reasoning, confining ourselves to the quotation of naked facts, dates, names, and documents. *It appears certain that Russia has wholly renounced the idea of attaching the Polish nation by benefits and institutions; it has now recourse to a severe, perhaps, last means – viz: the system of the depopulation of the country; it desires the Polish land, but not its inhabitants.* In consequence of this system, the following orders have been issued:

234

As Reported in the "Niles' Register"

The confiscation of the children. This takes place in the provinces previously incorporated with Russia – viz: Lithuania, Volhynia, Podolia, and the Ukraine, without any previous orders, merely according to the general ukase; the exceptions depend on the will of the military governor. It extends to children of both sex. In the kingdom of Poland which is nearer to Europe, it embraces only the male children, of the poorer class – that is to say, 19-20ths of the male children. This measure first was announced as an ukase of the emperor, communicated by prince Gerezakow, chief of the staff of the army to M. Tymowski, secretary to the council of the administration of the kingdom, who stated that it was his majesty's pleasure that boys wandering about the streets, orphans, those who are destitute of means of subsistence, shall be collected together, sent to Minsk, and delivered to the commander of the garrison, to be placed in the battalions of the military cantonments, and to be afterwards sent to the divisions assigned by the chief of the staff for the military colonies. The commander-in-chief, it adds, has received orders for the punctual execution of his majesty's will, and a fund was assigned for the support of the boys, and for the expense of vehicles to convey them to Minsk.

The prince marshal accordingly sent directions to the military governors and intendents general in the provinces. A subsequent order of prince Paskewitsch, recapitulating the heads of the ukase, is addressed to the counsellor of state, Fuhrmann, president of the finance department, informing him that the intendent-general of the army has been ordered to have clothing made of three different sizes for boys from the age of 7 to about 15, to the number of 100 for every waiwodeship. The clothing, of which patterns have been sent in, consists of gray cloth with yellow collar and plain buttons, gray pantaloons, short boots, two shirts for each and socks. This uniform, resembling that of the cantonists, amounts for the whole reckoning, 100 for each waiwodeship, to 38,222 Polish florins. The field marshal adds that he has approved of the pattern and prices, and desires the president of the finance department to furnish the above sum from the revenue of the kingdom, and to bring it to account in the budget, under the title of extraordinary military expenses.

'These orders, the contents of which are so threatening, and which are still more terrible in the execution, excited general fear in the whole kingdom. The terrified mothers ceased to send their children to the schools, still existing, which indeed were very indifferent, and this went so far that the municipality of Warsaw found it necessary to publish a proclamation which was immediately made known to the Prussian State Gazette, that the emperor took only poor and orphan children under his protection. But it depends on the military

governor to decide, which child is to be called poor or an orphan. Up to 6th May, four convoys, each 150, had been clandestinely sent out of Warsaw alone.'

On the 17th May, the 5th convoy, consisting of more than 20 wagons full of Polish children, from the ages of six years to 17, was away, not in secret, but quite openly. *The scene was heart rending.* 'For some days past,' writes an eye-witness, 'the weather had been very bad and cold, and on that day, 17th May, there was a heavy rain. Nobody was seen in the streets, all at once, about one in the afternoon, there was heard an extraordinary rumbling of wagons, trampling of horses, cries of women mingled with sobbing. It was the caravans with the stolen children rolling from the Alexander's barracks to the bridge. Every body who had any provisions, clothing, or money, in the house, sent or carried it out, put it in the wagons, or gave it to *the innocent creatures forever lost to their mothers and their country.* The mothers running after their children rushed among the wagons to stop them; other women join in their grief; a general lamentation is heard, with loud curses of the *gend'armes*, but without effect. The better informed could not help recollecting the story of the lion of Florence, that prowled the street, seized a child, and bore it off to the desert. Alas! The despair of the mother disarmed the cruelty of the wild beast, but it could not disarm the cruelty of the men at Warsaw.'

Those Russians who felt how dreadful the orders of their government were propagated in Warsaw, as an apology, that *this was done in consequence of the principles adopted with regard to Poland by the three allied courts of Russia, Prussia, and Austria.*"

{*Allgemeine Zeitung,* Aug. 22}

"*Environs of Kalisch, July 6.* The estates of those who have quitted the country will very shortly, in spite of the constitutional guarantees, be confiscated, and given to the Russians. We expect a very bad harvest; it rains incessantly. *The levying of recruits and the carrying away of the children destroys our agriculture. Even dwarfish, deformed, crippled persons are taken for recruits; the number is to be in all 70,000. As a great many of them run away, new levies are continually made, and thus the country becomes more and more depopulated.* Another levy of 7,000 men is said to be raised in September. War continues to be talked of."

There are references to "waiwodeship" which is "Voivode" or "Wojwode" -- an administrative area or province known in Polish as a województwo. The foregoing short paragraph clearly identified an example of what became known as "ethnic cleansing" during the latter decades of the

20th century. It referenced Kalisch which was the German word for the Polish town of Kalisz which remains as a city in Poland today. Kalisz is located about half-way between Poznań and Warszawa. Within the framework of the yet-undefined "ethnic cleansing" of that era, Russia's energetic levying of Polish recruits of all physical types, including those with physical disabilities, likely was designed to provide "cannon fodder" troops for its armies, on a *better-to-suffer-Polish-casualties-rather-than-Russian-casualties* on a front-line combat basis, particularly against the opening rounds enemy artillery fire.

Cracow, July 15. General Chlopicki has obtained permission to remain at Warsaw. A great number of peasants fly out of the kingdom, and either come hither or go to Galicia. In the woody parts of the country the peasants desert their villages, and go with their axes into the forest, to defend themselves against the levy of the recruits *and the carrying away of the children.* The insurrection in Lithuania is said to continue, and if the Russians do not renounce their dreadful system, it will spread. The Lithuanian insurgents kill all that fall into their hands. There are scarcely any Russian troops left in Podolia. All are concentrated in the kingdom, and ready to march. *Countess Bronzitska, a lady in the Russian interest, has presented to the emperor 2,000 young girls for the colonies.*

So that the final sentence of the preceding paragraph does not pass by unremembered, it had been reported essentially that Russia treated young Polish girls as commodities, if not cattle, to be given away by the Countess Bronzitska, for example, as gifts to Czar Nicholas for breeding purposes, it would appear, in his far-flung military colonies garrisoned by Russians, Cossacks and others. In what appears immediately below, Polish women had also been selected for expatriation by categories ranging from the most desirable to the least desirable, but all of whom were removed from the Kingdom of Poland. Undeniably, the entire scene had been one of the most flagrant examples of 19th century ethnic cleansing in Europe. Yet no one in the 21st century has referenced it as such, as far as I know. By way of my book, I hope that this will be henceforth likely to change.

Accounts from the frontiers of Poland, of July 20, state that no fewer than 20,000 Polish women will be very shortly *expatriated.* They will consist -- 1stly, of all women married to Russians --and *Russian officers are encouraged to take Polish wives by grants of rewards*; 2ndly, of the wives of the Polish officers taken prisoners, and are ordered to join their husbands in Russia; 3rdly, the wives of all Polish officers who were killed during the revolution; 4thly, the wives of all Polish officers killed; and 5thly, all the public women.

{French Paper.}

Augsburg, Aug. 21. We published some time ago an article from the *Brunswick German Nation Journal* on 'the present state of Poland.' The *Volksblatteaus Plamen* (popular journal of Plamen) gives the following continuation of it:

'Another measure against the Polish nation is the system of recruiting. The ukase of the emperor Nicholas, by which all officers and subalterns of the ancient Polish army are to be incorporated in the Russian army, is known to all Europe. This measure is extended to all those who were taken prisoners during the war, or who returned from Austria or Prussia, trusting to the amnesty and to the assurance that they should remain unmolested in their own homes. If the amnesty contains any tranquilizing expressions they refer only to the landowners, but as in Poland the soldier either has no landed property, or has left it to enter the service, the number of land-owners is scarcely 100 out of 30,000 that composed the army. The following is the order of field marshal Paskewitsch, which he issued for the execution of the imperial ukase: 'In conformity with the will of his imperial majesty, which was notified to the prince of Warsaw in the letter of the 26th of February (O. S.) of the present year, and considering that according to article 20 of the organic statute, graciously granted to the kingdom of Poland, the Russian imperial and royal Polish troops are henceforward to form one body; we order:

A. All subalterns and privates of the former Polish army and the military who have returned, as well as the civil officers who enlisted in the army of the insurgents, whether they were made officers or not, are to be incorporated in the Russian regiments, and be employed accordingly as they are qualified in the field or the garrison; those who were subalterns before the revolution retain their rank in the Russian army: all the others enter as privates.
B. From this conscription are accepted not only the invalids, and those who possess landed property, and are inscribed in the list of the communes, as land owners and if they returned to their agricultural pursuits immediately after the troubles were quieted.
C. The time of military service is 15 years. The subalterns and

privates of the former Polish army will have the years which they served before the 29th Nov., those who first entered the service during the revolution are to serve fifteen years from the time of their entrance into the Russian service.

D. The present levy, which must add at least 20,000 men to his majesty's troops, must be completed by the 1st of August this year.

(signed)   THE PRINCE OF WARSAW.

To this decree are annexed directions to the recruiting commissioners who are to begin their proceedings on the 1st of May, under the directions of the military governors of the palatinates. These commissioners consist of officers of the army in active service (Russians), and of the officers in garrison and veterans (Poles). These officers had to make their preparations in the middle of April. The Polish military intended for service are kept for the present in the depots of the regiments now cantoned in the kingdom. During their stay in these depots their conduct will be strictly watched; they receive food and clothing like others of the same rank, and from the day of their entrance into the army they are answerable for all their actions to the military tribunals, according to the regulations of the Russian army. The oath which they have to take contains an infinite number of obligations with respect to the use of arms and an engagement to lend their assistance in adding to the Russian dominions, and to the number of his majesty's subjects. By all those regulations with the new levy, the number of conscripts amount to 25,000 men; *and the greater part of the male population, and almost all the young men of education are lost to their country.*

It is impossible, (says one letter), to describe the situation of families on the publication of this order; despair and shame are on every countenance. All those who were taken prisoners during the campaign, and have since been sent to the interior of Russia, were obliged to enter the different corps situated in Siberia.

A letter has reached Warsaw from a young man of good family, whose parents are very rich. He was taken at the beginning of the war, and is now a common Cossack, 4,000 wersts from Warsaw. The Polish officers who returned, confiding in the amnesty, are still left unmolested; they receive a moderate pay, and are allowed to enter the Russian army, a permission of which they do not avail themselves. At the beginning of April, gen. Rautenstranch issued an invitation to all officers of the engineers to accept places in the Russian service, holding out to them the most advantageous prospects of rapid promotion, giving them to understand that they would be employed only in directing the works of the fortress of Modlin and the citadel of Warsaw. Not one answered to the invitation. They have all declared that they would not wear any Russian uniform; but they offered their services in civil employments.

The same proposal was made to 26 Polish officers, who returned from Russia where they were at the beginning of the war, and had been detained, so that they could not be implicated in the revolution; they refused in like manner. So much offence was taken at this in a high quarter, that each of them was called upon to give a declaration in writing of the motives of his refusal.

{*Allgemeine Zeitung*, Sept. 1}

Article 176. (December 1, 1832, page 205)

Niles' Weekly Register in its issue of December 1, 1832 had included another update about affairs in Poland. Here under the caption, "Foreign Articles," is the terse statement that:

Lord Durham's mission to Russia is accounted a failure, but that the particulars have not transpired.

Lord Durham, to his credit, acting on behalf of Great Britain, sought if not to mediate an end to hostilities, then at least to mitigate Russia's excessively harsh treatment of Poland and patriotic Poles who refused to become Russians.

Article 177. (December 1, 1832, page 212)

The condition of Polish immigrants, one of whom purported to be a nephew of Kazimierz Pulaski, who had served as officers in the Polish army fighting against Imperial Russia, and who arrived in New York City, along with their wives and children, caused the author of the article, reprinted in its issue of December 1, 1832 by the Niles' weekly Register, from the New York American newspaper, to propose that the United States Congress should act to help Polish exiles in the United States.

The *New York American*, speaking of the number of Polish exiles in that city says: 'Many of them, after pledging the few valuables with which they escaped from their country, have finally been compelled to have recourse to their scanty wardrobes, and pawned the very coats off their backs, to provide themselves wherewith to subsist upon.

And after stating that the nephew of Pulaski is among them, he adds:

'We are told, too, that some of these officers have brought their families with them, and that females, whose heroic dispositions bore up with more than manly fortitude against the horrors of civil war, are now exposed to the more harassing, because inglorious, ills of poverty, under circumstances the most aggravated and disheartening. The silent appeals as such as these will not remain unanswered, and those fair hands which are always so active in turning a harmless taste for nicknacks into account, by manufacturing and selling elegant trifles for the benefit of the poor, will not remain idle when it is the wives and sisters who have done everything for their country, that are the objects of their bounty and care. Let something be done at once by all parties; and the moment congress meet, *let a resolution be introduced for a grant of land to the heirs of Polish officers* who served in the armies of the American revolution, so that countrymen shall at least have one asylum and homestead in the land that Pulaski and Kosciousko helped to redeem.'

Article 178. (December 1, 1832, page 216)

In its same December 1, 1832 issue, the Niles' Weekly Register noted that England and France had been engaged in a near-warlike confrontation with the "Holy Alliance" of Russia, Prussia and Austria, caused by England's actions to mediate the matter of Poland, and with Russia's having disallowed England's "interference" in favor of the Poles, which in turn caused England to disallow Russia's trading ships from having access to the navigation of the Scheldt River for commercial purposes in western Europe, along with other news from Poland as well.

The *London Morning Herald* of the 16th Oct. says: On Friday night, earl Grey directed a circular to be sent to all foreign ambassadors, acquainting them with the resolution of the British cabinet to eject the Dutch *vi et armis*, from the citadel of Antwerp, which is said to have alarmed none more than the Dutch ambassador himself. Austria, Prussia and Russia having signed the protocols to that effect, cannot, and will not support Holland now. During Lord Durham's embassy to St. Petersburgh, that court would not admit the interference of England in favor of the Poles, that being a Russian or continental question, and

241

now England retaliates, and declares the navigation of the Scheldt a British question in which she cannot admit of any continental interference. Her fleet and that of France, are therefore immediately to sail for the Scheldt, a measure that none of the continental powers can prevent.

In the 21st century, "fables" and "calumnies" are best understood by the expression, "fake news." Finally, this Article includes a report that brave and well-placed Polish women and their families staged boycotts of Russian-organized social events in Warsaw, particularly those of General Paskewitsch, who held the title, "Prince of Warsaw," granted him by Czar Nicholas. The Article's use of the Latin expression, vi et armis, in its opening sentence in free translation means "with force and arms."

An article from Warsaw says that the 'representations of the present state of Poland, are much exaggerated, and calls them fables or calumnies'.

Letters from the frontiers of Poland say: 'The 8th instant, being the anniversary of the surrender of Warsaw, was a day of mourning for its inhabitants. Prince Paskewitsch, however, gave a ball on the occasion, to which he invited numerous guests, but many of the cards of invitations were found thrown into the streets, and none but Russian military and civil officers were present. The women, as on all former occasions, display their patriotic feelings, and filled the churches throughout the day, dressed in mourning.'

Article 179. (April 13, 1833, page 103)

In this article, Hezekiah Niles, utilizing a report from a European correspondent, provided a comprehensive commentary on the matter of Russia's audacity in its having defiled the church housing the miraculous image of Our Lady of Częstochowa (identified by Hezekiah Niles as 'Chenstokow'), and then proceeded to the matter of the well-known Russian plan for the "annihilation" of the Roman Catholic Church in Poland, and indeed to render the Polish nation "extinct," and openly swearing to do so, while at the same time, contradicting and denying its related intentions in the foreign press.

POLAND. The latest intelligence from this ill-fated country is contained in the following article.

'Since the press in Germany is under the severe control of Russia, Austria, and Prussia, *no information from Poland can be obtained but with the greatest difficulty.* I must add that the Russian government takes the greatest care that its cruel ukase should not be known in foreign countries. I find, however, the means of informing you that the establishment of the mint and its steam engine have been carried away to St. Petersburgh, that the prisons are still full, and the fate of the imprisoned is not as yet known. Every thing indicates great poverty in the Russian finances. The increase of taxes, and the confiscations, without waiting for the sentence of the courts, is going on with great vigor. Prince Czartoryski's magnificent country seat at Pulway has been announced in the Warsaw newspaper as confiscated, and offered for sale; and in Volhynia and Podolia the confiscations are almost general, without paying the mortgages on those estates. *The system of transplantation continues to carry away to Siberia and the Caucasus the peasants and the small gentry.* The measure which provoked the whole population was the violation of the church at Chenstokow, held in the greatest veneration. There was in that church a miraculous image of the holy Virgin. For many centuries, kings, princes, the wealthy, and the poor, carried to that church their offerings in diamonds, gold, silver and most rich *exvotos.* It was respected during the invasion of the Turks and Tartars, but not by the Russians. That rich treasure, amounting to millions, has been robbed and carried away to St. Petersburgh. *The annihilation of the Roman Catholic church, the introduction of the Greek schismatic religion, the extinction of the Polish nation, is openly declared and sworn! The most provoking circumstance is the audacity with which the Russian government, in perpetrating these barbarous cruelties, denies, and contradicts them in foreign newspapers.'*

Article 180. (April 13, 1833, page 103)

> Appearing as well on page 103 of the same April 13, 1833 edition of Niles' Weekly Register had been the July 29, 1832 letter from Lafayette "to the inhabitants of Bogotá," Columbia, in South America, in which he recognized the second anniversary of revolution there and included a somber reference to Poland.

On reading your valued letter, which I shall preserve through life as a treasure dear to my heart, I cannot but compare your hopes then expressed with the present state of Europe. Be convinced, however, that our popular week, so justly celebrated by you, has already greatly favored the emancipation of this part of the world, and that, in spite of obstacles, both foreseen and unforeseen, the principles and practice of true liberty will triumph in Europe, over the pernicious influences which are exerted to retard its progress. Thus, we also count, I confidently assure you, on the independence of noble Poland, whose efforts you admire, and whose misfortune we have now to deplore.

Izabela Flemming Czartoryska leaves Puławy. After rebuilding the palace, Izabela, a patriot, and Princess in her own right, had been forced to flee to France as Poland's valiant November Uprising failed to succeed against Imperial Russia.

Article 181. (April 20, 1833, page 115)

Twenty-first century Americans are generally unaware that Imperial Russia maintained two diplomatic legations, one in Washington City, now known as Washington, DC, and the other in New York City during the period -- 1811 to 1849 -- upon which my study is based, as well as prior to and following that period. One can only speculate as to the number of said sane Poles in the United States at the time who would have visited the Russian Legation in Washington City or the Russian Consul General in New York City, so as to comply, in writing and in person, with the Imperial Russian Legation's soft surveillance protocol request of the day.

As Reported in the "Niles' Register"

Russian legation, Washington. April 15, 1833. Notice is hereby given to all subjects of the kingdom of Poland now residing in the United States, who have taken no part in the Polish rebellion, and who intend to return to Poland, or wish to prolong their stay in this country, that they are required to express such intention, and obtain permission to that effect, by addressing their request in writing, to the Imperial Russian Legation in Washington or Consul General in New York, within three months from the present date. It is understood that this notice does not apply to those subjects of Poland who, since the restoration of legal order in the kingdom, have received permission to go or to continue to reside abroad, and who are furnished with the proper passports for that purpose.

Given that there had not been a "Polonia press" at that time in the United States, the fact that the Russian Ambassador issued the above-referenced notification in English suggests that there had been some Poles, likely a small but growing number, who had fluency in the English language. This becomes clearly evident as my book progresses.

Article 182. (June 8, 1833, page 238)

A report about Poland under the "assiduous care and paternal solicitude" of Czar Nicholas and the Russian government! A nightmare for Poles.

POLAND. The *Augsburg Gazette* of the 18th of April states, that an insurrection of the Poles had taken place at Cracow, who had cut to pieces some detachments of Russian troops. Considerable bodies of Poles are represented to be organized in the forests, and the Russian government is said to have had recourse to severe measures to suppress the spirit of revolt that has been manifested.

The emperor of Russia has issued a manifesto, relative to the state of things in Poland, and the czar has the effrontery, at the commencement of it, to assert 'that every body knows the high degree of prosperity to which Poland had been raised by fifteen years' *assiduous* care and *paternal solicitude* on the part of the Russian government.'

The autocrat has issued a more rigorous prohibition against Poles and Russians travelling to France. His 'paternal solicitude' for their welfare is such that he chooses to retain them within the reach of the knout.

Article 183. (June 15, 1833, pages 261 and 262)

> Circumstances of Polish parents, in this case, those of the nobility of Podolia, desperately concerned for the safety and welfare of their children, necessitated sad parental expressions of groveling loyalty to the Russian Czar as noted by Hezekiah Niles who observed, "This alas! is the language used by people who were once the freest in Europe!"

The nobility of Podolia have summoned the courage to supplicate mercy from their barbarous oppressors, though they only venture to do so in the humblest tone and on their bended knees. The following is an extract from their address to the emperor Nicholas. Permission to use their own language, in courts of justice, protection in their national religion, and an exemption from the horrors of perpetual imprisonment and exile, is all they venture to ask, and far more than they will obtain. They say:

'Your nobility, O sire, sees with fearful apprehension the difficulties and losses to which the prohibition of our native language in the judicial courts will expose us; and we Poles, like other Sclavonian nations, have our own distinct language, have for so many centuries become natural, rich in remembrances, common to millions of your subjects, preserved to us by your ancestors, indispensable in our social occurrences; in that language we had all our deeds, contracts, conventions. It explained our wants, it became indispensable, and incorporated with us. Gracious lord, leave that language to us, that in it we may pray to God for you and your blessed family.

With our persons we carried our Roman Catholic religion under your sceptre. Religion, watching on human frailties, wants the guidance of the ministers of God; the neglect, the fall of religion are forerunners of general corruption. The religion of our ancestors has left to the sovereigns its protection. In your high wisdom, your majesty has found it necessary to abolish the convents and confiscate their estates; but sire, those convents fulfilled likewise parochial duties. Great scarcity of curates and priests is felt already; the conscience and morality of your people in such general subversion, wanting the assistance of religion, will prove most detrimental. As our common father, we beseech thee humbly, O lord! Have mercy upon us, advice as to those impending evils.

In all countries the nobility is aware that its duty is to support the throne. The difference in fortunes, poverty even, did not deprive them of their privileges. We humbly beseech your majesty to stop orders by which beings without any guilt are carried away from their homes into most remote countries. In every corner of the world they will prove faithful subjects to your majesty; but sire, the poorest man loves the country where he was born. That universal instinct, witnessed by tears of thousands of families, emboldened us to entreat, sire, your humanity for them.

Our brothers have offended you, seeking relief from their sufferings, not by prayers addressed to you. But, sire, as an image of the Almighty on earth, you shall not always remain provoked, you shall not always punish us. Parents, with a ghastly bewildered eye, look for their children carried away from them, sent for ever to impervious regions; others seek an asylum in foreign countries, remote from their relations, in want and poverty. Few of them you have pardoned; jointly with us, they beg you to extend your clemency to others. We lay, sire, these most humble prayers at the footsteps of your throne.'

It followed with the "signatures" of all the marshals of the different districts.

'Kamieniec, the 12th day of September, 1832.

This, alas! Is the language used by a people who were once freest in Europe!

London, April 14 – In spite of the remonstrances which we are willing to believe have been made by the only two powers of Europe that still remain undistempered by the pestilent influence of Russia, the work of confiscation is still carried on in Poland with an unsparing hand. *The greediness with which the barbarous oppressors of that ill-fated land pursue their course of rapine shows that their appetite for Polish plunder is as inordinate as their thirst for Polish blood.* It is now nearly three months since the publication of an official notification of the Russian governor specifying in detail the estates and property of every description confiscated in the single government of Volhynia. Recent disclosures of the sufferings of the Polish refugees in this country, and the consequent appeals on their behalf to the generosity of the British people, have brought this document once more under our observation, and we reproduce it here.

The referenced "document" in the final sentence of the immediate paragraph above was the Russian governor's related comprehensive list of confiscated properties. And here, worthy of note, that "serf-peasants" attached to "confiscated property" estates were valued at *£25 per head!* (This is the equivalent of £2,817.43 in modern money.)

1. Peasants, 37,218, estimated, agreeably in the custom of the country, (where, in selling estates, they are valued according to the number of serf-peasants inhabiting them, and who are attached to the glebe), at £25 a head: £930,000
2. Movables, cattle, manufacturing and agricultural machines, articles confiscated along with landed estates, computing them at one-eighth of the value of the estates: 115,000
3. Roubles (in silver) 266,853   50,000
4. Ducats, 16,738   9,000

Amount of confiscations in the single government of Volhynia:1,104,000

The civilized world has not been outraged by a second official record of the progress made by the commissions appointed and authorized to superintend the spoliation of a land which the sword, the scaffold and the deserts of Siberia, have already nearly depopulated. That the members of these commissions, however, have not been idle, that they have been unceasingly occupied in the prosecution of the objects of their disgraceful mission, is unhappily but too well known by the raggedness and poverty of their victims, who, but for the charity of strangers, would have wandered naked on foreign shores until sheer starvation put an end to their miserable existence. Nor is there any great difficulty in forming something like an estimate of the gross amount of plunder which these commissioners will purvey to the imperial coffers at St. Petersburgh. Let the amount of the confiscations in Volhynia, be a criterion, and then, in the six governments (namely those of Podolia, Volhynia, Kijev, Vilna, Grodno and Minsk), the amount will be: £6,894,000.

The kingdom of Poland, in which the insurrection was almost general, will furnish about an equal amount of confiscations, making altogether about: £12,000,000.

Whether this sum of £12,000,000 be destined for the support of new attempts to bring freedom and civilization beneath the yoke of barbarism and tyranny, it is not our present purpose to enquire; all we were desirous of showing was the probable amount of gain which will accrue from the subjugation of Poland, besides blood-guiltiness, the widow's and the orphan's curse, the hostility and hatred of every honest heart, and all else that follow in the train of wanton aggression on the land and liberty, and life, of a brave and deserving nation.

Warsaw, April 2. The *commissioners for quartering the troops give notice,* that if several of the house-holders of Warsaw, notwithstanding repeated summonses persevere in their negligence, and will not prepare lodgings for the Russian officers, especially those of high rank, the commissioners will hire such lodgings at the expense of the persons in question, and at the same time invite all those who have lodgings to let, to apply to their office'.

Article 184. (June 17, 1833, pages 329 an 330)

POLAND: A Berlin paper of May 14th, says: 'It seems that new fears are entertained respecting the maintenance of tranquility in Poland. The Russian government has received information from Paris, that a conspiracy has been formed to make a fresh attempt at revolutionizing that country. It is even said that letters have been intercepted, in which a plot has been discovered against the life of the emperor Nicholas. This last report wants confirmation. The emperor Nicholas has postponed his journey abroad, because the affairs of the east require his presence at St. Petersburgh.

Article 185. (June 22, 1833, pages 268)

The Chains of Poland. The administrative council of Warsaw, by a decree dated March 1st, has regulated the weight of the chains by which Polish prisoners are to be fettered. All male convicts are to drag seven pounds weight of iron -- women six.

Article 186. (June 29, 1833, pages 287)

This issue reported two separate news-briefs, the first on Russia's purchase of two ancient "sphynxes" from Egypt for re-location in St. Petersburgh, and then in the second, that: "a conscription of troops has been ordered in Poland, four out of every 1,000 inhabitants of the district," perhaps to be used to augment Russian forces in preparation for war against the Ottoman Turkish Empire, or perhaps against rebellious Poles.

The two sphynxes recently discovered near the statue of Memnon, among the ruins of ancient Thebes, have been purchased by the Russian government for 64,000 roubles. The expense of their transport to St. Petersburgh will amount to 28,000 roubles. These sphynxes are destined to adorn the Russian capital, where they will be placed on pedestals."

"A letter from St. Petersburgh, dated 25th April, states, that gen. Orloff has been ordered to proceed to Constantinople to take command of the Russian land and sea troops there, and it has been naturally concluded that the war will be continued. All the numerous disposable regiments were concentrated on the Turkish boundaries. Prince Paskewitsch has prepared a plan of military operations against Ibrahim.

A conscription of troops has been ordered in Poland, four out of every 1,000 inhabitants of the district.

Article 187. (July 6, 1833, pages 309 to 311)

This issue contained brief reports: on the Poles attempting to leave Russian Poland for entry to Austrian Poland's Galicja province; the grand council of Switzerland's consideration for sending Poles in Switzerland back to France from whence they came after escaping Poland; the response of the Polish "fugitives" in Switzerland; the order of the Czar to impose punishment for political offenses such as spreading "false news"; and the death sentence for any Poles who deserted from the Russian army.

From page 309: "The people, made mad by oppression, have again appealed to force, on the frontiers of Galicia, in large numbers, but they cannot hope to accomplish any good purpose. All that are able, and are willing to labor, should leave it.

Paris, 20th May. The grand council of Berne, has proposals under consideration, the purpose of which is, that permission shall be asked for the Poles to return to France who left that country on the news of the disturbances at Frankfort, and that, in the meantime, a specified sum shall be allowed for their support."

From pages 310 and 311: "*The Polish Fugitives*: The following is the answer of the Polish fugitives to the council of Berne, on the proposal that they petition the government of France to be readmitted into that country:

'Consider yourselves, gentlemen, whether it is possible that we can take this step without injuring the dignity of our nationality, whose guardians we are. When we left France, in order to withdraw ourselves from the oppression of that government, we did not do so with a view of returning under the same yoke, if we might obtain asylum there. We could willingly spare the noble Swiss nation the burden which the presence of a corps of 50 persons impose on it; but we cannot return to France with the sacrifice of our honor, and to induce us again to enter

France, the inhabitants of which country sympathise with us, the law which makes exceptions to our advantage must be first repealed. This is our resolution which I hope you will approve. Accept, etc.'

(The signatures.)

Saignclegier, April 25, 1833.

Finally, more examples of the nightmare for being Poles, of all ages, defeated in their existential struggle to defend Poland and their ancient nationality.

Hamburg, May 17: "The Russian government in Poland has published an ordinance of the emperor, dated the 22nd ult. by which persons accused of certain political offences *including the publication of false news*, are ordered to be tried before courts martial, the sentence of such courts to be carried into execution as soon as they have received confirmation of the viceroy.

The Warsaw papers also contain an account of 25 individuals belonging to the late Polish army, who were concerned in a recent unsuccessful attempt at insurrection. Five of the party were taken by the Cossacks on the frontier; one of them poisoned himself, but the other four were brought before a court martial and sentenced to death. The sentence was carried into execution of three of the surviving prisoners; *with respect to the fourth, on account of his extreme youth, the sentence was mitigated into corporal punishment and hard labor.*"

As implied in the foregoing paragraph, "extreme youth" must have equated with the fourth alleged Polish insurrectionist having been a child, not a teen-ager, but a child, whose age, one may speculate, had been somewhere in the range of 7 to 12, for whom the death sentence had been inappropriate, but yet quite appropriate, in the opinion of those responsible for the administration of Russian-imposed justice, for the mitigated sentence of corporal punishment and hard labor (of a child!). So much for the happy days of childhood in the Russian Empire.

Article 188. (August 3, 1833, page 377)

Of the next two articles (188 and 189) appearing in this issue on separate successive pages of Niles' Weekly Register, the first underscores Russia's cruel policy, as enforced by Prince Paskewitsch, of making war on Polish women, i.e., "respectable mothers (now bereaved of their sons)" by whipping them in public; and the second news-brief relates to a memorial service honoring Kościuszko's memory held by Poles in Soleure, Switzerland.

RUSSIA: The czar received that portion of his troops, at Dunaberg on the 31st, which were under the command of count Pahlen. He has also visited a number of fortifications that have been recently erected. The numerous new public buildings in St. Petersburgh are proceeding rapidly. But no works of art, no splendid dome, or costly towers, can relieve him from the execration which his conduct has justly drawn upon him, in relation to the Poles.

A letter from Warsaw, in March, states, that by order of the czar, prince Paskevitch, has declared to *respectable* mothers (now bereaved of their sons) that should they be discovered to have written to their exiled children, they would be publicly whipped in the public market place.

Article 189. (August 3, 1833, page 378)

TOMB OF KOSCIUSKO (From the *Swiss Patriot*.): 'Soleure, Switzerland. At a short distance from Soleure, on the high road to Lucerne, is situated the village of Zukwill. It is there, in the vicinity of a chapel, that repose the remains of Kosciusko. Kosciusko! At this revered name Poland should arise and threaten the tyrants oppressing the land of liberty. At this very name the glorious achievements of a great general burst on our minds.

On the 3rd of May, 25 Poles proceeded in military procession to Zukwill, to prostrate themselves at the altar of the Almighty, to salute the ashes of an illustrious countryman, and to celebrate the anniversary of the constitution granted on May 3, 1791, to the people of Poland.

The sun gave the light of its glorious rays to the noble remnant of the nation as illustrious as unfortunate.

The hospital chaplain, M. Saaner, was at Zukwill to give his pious assistance to the noble refugees.

The religious ceremony over, the Poles left the temple, and knelt before the tomb containing the ashes of Kosciusko. It would be difficult to describe the solemnity of the scene, Grochen and Ostralensky bathing with their tears the stone containing the ashes of the hero of Poland, and swearing to march in his footsteps. Perhaps at that very moment the vile slaves of despotism were insulting with their sardonic grin the unfortunate Poles who, on the borders of the frozen ocean are painfully eating the bread of slavery.

As Reported in the "Niles' Register"

A Polish officer, in his mother tongue, briefly mentions the deeds of Kosciusko in behalf of his country, and gives out that noble warrior as the model they are to imitate. 'Poland,' says he, 'is not yet annihilated; wherever beats a Polish heart, still exists the nationality of Poland.' He then, in French, stated his satisfaction at being able to speak of liberty in the land of freedom; and to offer, in the name of his countrymen, his thanks to a nation that has given them welcome and entered unto their pain and suffering. And, like the people that always turned their eyes towards Sion, the children of Poland turned their faces towards the north, and saluted their country from afar.

An inhabitant of Soleure replied to this speech; he expressed the wish of the Swiss population: union, fraternity, liberty, and devotedness for those who have shed their blood in defense of freedom. Thus terminated a ceremony which affected the numerous spectators it had called together.'

Kosciuszko's tomb in Wawel Cathedral

The referenced ashes of Kościuszko that appeared in this particular article had been those of his entrails which remained in Switzerland. By that time, his heart was in Warsaw's Royal Palace and his remaining corpse was enclosed in his sarcophagus in Saint Leonard's crypt beneath the main floor of Wawel Cathedral in Kraków. All told, this had not been an uncommon practice in Europe generally at the time.

Article 190. (August 17, 1833, page 403)

During the decade of the 1830s, acts of Russian brutality against Poles had been boundless, as this horrid example of execution by a Russian firing squad of an 18-year old noblewoman painfully illustrated. Contrary to civilized convention of that era, it had been Russian policy to inflict capital punishment on Polish women as well as to degrade them by rape, public whipping, tar and feathering their shaved heads, imprisonment and execution by firing squad. However, it appears that that Russian justice mercifully exempted women from punishment by "strangulation" (the act of being hung by the neck) and decapitation.

The Russian accounts from the frontiers of Poland are still harping upon the discontented impatience which is but ill suppressed in that country, and ascribing it to the machinations of the propagandists of France. The 'leniency,' as it is called, with which the Poles have hitherto been treated is now thought to have had a bad effect upon them, and henceforth a new system is to be adopted, under which even the nobility are not to be exempt from the degradation of corporal punishment. This, no doubt, will be a refinement in the tactics of the cruel autocrat.

Several letters from the frontiers of Poland announce that the young Lady Hawecker, aged 18, was recently shot at Lubin by the Russians, accused of having furnished provisions to the insurgents; she proceeded quietly to the place of execution between a file of Russian soldiers. Count Michael Wollowicz having returned from France put himself at the head of the insurgents in the environs of Grodno; engaged in a skirmish with the Russians, was wounded, taken prisoner, and immediately hung at Grodno.

The citadel of Warsaw was nearly completed, and Kiew was also to be strongly fortified.

Lubin, not to be confused with Lublin in eastern Poland, is located in lower Silesia (Śląsk) in western Poland. Founded in the 13th century, it is situated some 44 miles northwest of Wrocław. The fact that Russian soldiers executed the 18-year old Polish noblewoman in Lubin also illustrates that the Russians troops ranged near-freely throughout what once had been the Commonwealth of Poland and Lithuania. The only exception had been Galicja, that province having been integrated with the Austrian Empire.

Article 191. (August 24, 1833, pages 424 to 426)

> This issue included articles about: (1) a British resolution in Parliament which refused to recognize the state of affairs in Poland, that was defeated for fear of having to go to war with Russia; (2) an alleged plot against Czar Nicholas; and (3) Wodzyński's letter thanking the United States, and his comments about exiles in France and the attitude of other countries towards the Poles. Of great interest, some 14 years later in 1847, Lord Palmerston of Great Britain would express similar anti-interventionist sentiments in the matter of defending the Republic of Kraków which Russia would seek to terminate. (*See Article 273.*)

Mr. Ferguson has moved in the house, 'an address to his majesty that he will be graciously pleased not to recognize, nor in any way give the sanction of his government to the present political state and condition of Poland, the same having been brought about in violation of the treaty of Vienna, to which Great Britain was a party.'

Lord Palmerston, in reply, admitted the truth and justice of all the observations and details made by the hon. mover; but, at the same time, deprecated the pressing of the motion, on the ground that, if carried, a war with Russia would be inevitable.

Lord Althorp followed in a similar strain, and moved the previous question.

Lord J. Russell hoped, that though ministers might concur in the sentiments of the mover, he would withdraw the motion, on the ground that when the unanimous opinion of the house went forth to the world, it would have more effect than if a division took place and a large majority voted against it.

He was followed by Mr. Hume, Mr. Attwood, Mr. O'Connell, Mr. Sheil and several other members, who argued in favor of the motion, as being due to the character and feelings of the country; and by lord Palmerston and Mr. Stanley, who, along with Mr. Warburton and sir Robert Peel, *argued against, as being likely to involve the country in a war, for which it was not prepared.* Mr. Cutlar Fergusson replied, and the house divided, when the numbers were, for the previous question, as moved by lord Althorp, 177; against it, 95; majority, 82...

Mr. Bulwer moved an address to the king calling for papers respecting the *measures pursued by Russia in her interference* with the state of Turkey. He asked if there was any government in the country. (Lord Althorp, here we are.) It did not follow said Mr. B. that because they were here, that they constituted a government. He condemned ministers for having taken no share in the affairs of Turkey, Russia and Egypt. No one could doubt that the object of Russia was to reduce Turkey under her dominion.

Lord Palmerston replied and said a correspondence was now going on, on the subject, and the motion would be productive of inconvenience; he doubted not Russia would preserve her faith, and hoped that confidence might be reposed in government, on this subject, for a very short time longer.

The story above concerning Poland and Lord Palmerston in 1833 deserves our special attention. Despite the fact that in 1833 Great Britain had allowed shipment to the Poles of weapons from London to be used in combat against Russian forces, the August 24, 1833 issue of *Niles' Weekly Register,* carried the story displayed here of the discussions and vote in Parliament which, unknown at the time, of course, would find Palmerston holding to the same position about Poland some 14 years later in 1847 (again, see this book's *Article 273*), that being, reluctance to engage British forces to help the Poles in the Republic of Kraków because Great Britain had *not been prepared for a war* with Russia "despite the feelings of the country" to the contrary.

Clearly, The British position had been welcome news in St. Petersburg both in 1833 and again in 1847. The article continued with several more Polish-related news articles of importance:

RUSSIA: Despatches from St. Petersburgh, as also the *St. Petersburgh Gazette*, received in London on the 14th of July, mention a plot against the life of the emperor of Russia, on the part of some Polish exiles, who left Paris a short time ago, and bound themselves by an oath to effect his assassination. It was first made public by a journal which gave an account of the reception of a deputation which waited upon the emperor in Finland to congratulate him on the frustration of the conspiracy. It seems that the Russian authorities did not wish the matter made public, but on this account appearing deemed it right to allude to it in the Gazette. The sensation created throughout Russia is very great, and all sorts of precautions are employed to protect the emperor in his various visits to the frontier towns.

"LETTER FROM A POLISH OFFICER: The following extracts are translated from a letter of a gallant Polish officer, to a friend in Boston, who has for years past felt a deep interest in the affairs of that brave and unfortunate nation. The name of *Wodzynski* is a sufficient guarantee for the truth of what is said. (*N. Y. Com. Adv.*):

'Chateau de Montargis, April 1, 1833

My dear friend -- *You will have learned by the journals, that since my last, the national Polish committee, presided over by Lelevel, has been dissolved by an arbitrary order of the French ministry, on the formal demand of the Russian ambassador.* Subsequent orders, entirely in the Russian spirit, obliged all of us exiles, to leave Paris, and to abandon entirely the affairs of our brethren in exile as a body. But a new committee has been attempted under the presidence of our gallant friend Dwernicki; unhappily, however, the choice was made in haste, just before the breaking up of the committee, only a few members being present, and those the ones whose conduct had been so unpopular with the exiles that they were obliged to resign. *Still, we hope we shall soon succeed in forming a new committee, that we may preserve at least a rallying point, and the shadow of a political existence, which, however, the Russian ambassador is striving to destroy, even on the soil of France.*

You know how shamefully we have been treated: how, cooped up in small and retired places, it has been forbidden us to leave them; how our unfortunate youth, who wish to profit by the advantages of Paris, in finishing their education, have a thousand and thousand difficulties thrown in their way. But alas! This is not the worst: it seems that the *coup de grace* is to be given, for the minister of war has published a circular to the Polish officers, saying that the French government will endeavor to obtain an amnesty for them *so that they may return to their homes!* You know, my dear sir, the cruel tendency of this measure, which the world will call a generous and magnanimous one! *Oh God!* It boots man to have more than a soldier's patience, to support such a horrible situation; and yet, my countrymen seem to have it, I know not how, but yet they keep up their hearts and their hopes; they have got up little schools among themselves, and seem determined to make the most of their sad exile.

I will spare your sensibility, and not give you the detail of the sad and sickening news we receive from our unhappy country; enough, that it is the same old system, the same persecution, the same confiscations, the same outrages and *transportations*, which freeze the blood to think upon, and which our ruthless tyrants follow up with hellish perseverance. One must have much faith, much strength of mind, when with thousands, innocent as himself, he is suffering such persecution not to doubt the existence of eternal justice.

It is the tyrant of the north, who has revivified the spirit of the *holy alliance*, for it is this spirit which governs and oppresses all Europe.

You know the state of France, and the men who have seized upon the reins thrown down at the revolution of July, men who have done nothing during the past year, but made bad worse. There is no meanness, no cowardice, no deception, which Louis Philippe has not practiced to strengthen his seat on the throne of the barricades; and at the same time to make the other thrones forget the popular origin of his own, and to unite it more firmly with theirs.

Public opinion in France seems to be in the state of complete lethargy: men seem almost in despair of better things, for although the present ministry is condemned and hated by the vast majority of the people, it still exists, and still goes on its course, unopposed by aught but silent indignation. This state of things cannot exist long, but it is impossible to know when it will terminate.

In England, where public sympathy was at one time so strongly awakened in our favor,   every one is occupied at present with more intense interest about their own internal affairs, and more fully awake to the true character of the *soi disant* ministry of lord Grey; the late measures against Ireland seem to arouse the people to observation at last. On the whole, the political situation of England does not differ from much that of the rest of Europe.

Soi-disant is a French expression meaning "pretended" or "would-be."

As for us, our minds are made up upon the course we must follow. There seems nothing to hope from the actual state of things, nothing from the darker policy of Europe, which seems to be arresting the march of mind, and of retarding the progress of civilization and humanity. We agree perfectly with what you tell us, that there is little to hope for our country, but from a general effort which shall break up, which at present broods incubus-like over all Europe; and we believe, too, with faith, that although appearances are now against it, it must be broken up; that the progress of light and reason, founded as they are on the immutable laws of God, must work its effects, in spite of the artificial barriers erected against them.

That which you tell us about the empathy of the American people for our sufferings and for our cause, seems to confirm us in our hopes, while it consoles us in our misery. We know that the American people can do nothing for our country, until the knell of vengeance have tolled, and the day of struggle shall have again dawned. They have done for us already, much more in proportion, than those nations of Europe ought to have succored us as much, in gratitude for services done them, as in regard of their own interest; and they have done it from pure sympathy, and noble sentiment, for, not for America, as for France, have two hundred Poles given their best blood. The Americans have not partaken of the hospitality and eaten the bread of Poland, as did the French emigrants and the soldiers of the grand army; the liberties and commerce of America were not menaced by Russia, as were those of France and England. In counting, then, upon the sympathy of the American people, we shall never forget what we owe them for the voice of sympathy and the welcome supply sent in the dark hour of our agony. We shall not forget what her agent suffered in the prison of Berlin, for having carried consolation and hope to our poor soldiers in the forests of Posen, nor shall we forget that even to this hour, they interest themselves, in our situation, and pray for our deliverance.

WODZYNSKI."

The American 'agent' that Wodzyński (possibly a Polish *nom de guerre*) had referenced in the final paragraph of his letter was Samuel Gridley Howe (1801-1876), the Harvard-educated physician, abolitionist, admirer of Polish revolutionists as well as Greek revolutionists of that period in history, and importantly, the founding director of the Perkins School for the Blind in Watertown, Massachusetts. *Article 159* of this book referenced his story as well.

Interestingly, the only Wodzyński-surnamed person I came across had been Józef Wodzyński whose name appears in *Article 205* of this book which identifies him as number 219 on a document titled, "List of the Names of Polish Immigrants that Remain in the United States of America" (Lista Polskich Emigrantów Zostających w Stanach Zjednoczonych Ameryki, rkps, 5313, k. 335-338), that was created in 1835 in Poland, the original copy of which is in the collection of Kraków, Poland's Czartoryski Library. I will address the source of that List in Kraków's Czartoryski Library as this book progresses.

Article 192. (August 31, 1833, page 9)

Large bodies of troops were collected on or near the Turkish frontier, waiting for orders. The Russian fleet had left the roads of Bajukderen for the Black sea, and the English squadron had also departed for the Dardenalles. The emperor Nicholas has issued an edictal summons, through lieutenant general Sulina, president of the supreme criminal court, requiring the appearance of all those Polish subjects who were excepted from his gracious amnesty, in order to await their trial, and in the event of their non-appearance, the court would pass sentence upon them *in contumaciam*. Two hundred and eighty-six names are contained on the list.

Article 193. (September 7, 1833, page 28)

In Poland and in Germany order reigns under the influence of the bayonet.

Article 194. (September 14, 1833, page 40)

> This issue Included a very informative summary report on the Republic of Kraków.

THE REPUBLIC OF CRACOW: According to *Bell's Geography*, the territorial extent of this little republic, does not exceed 500 square miles, with a population of 100,000 souls, 30,000 of whom reside in the capital.

In 1815, when Russia and Prussia both laid claim to the town and territory of Cracow, the dispute gave to its comparative independence, and Cracow became a republic under the protection of three surrounding powers.

A small district of very fertile land, running about 20 miles on the left bank of the Vistula, was on this occasion added to its territories.

Cracow, or Krakow, consists of a plain running along the banks of the Vistula, which becomes navigable immediately under the walls of the capital. Principal production is grain. No manufactories, with the exception of the iron works of Krzessovice. The peasants manufacture their own cloth and linen, and a few weavers supply the capital, which is the only commercial mart. Bulk of inhabitants, Poles. Religion, Roman Catholics. No political distinction among the inhabitants, with the exception of the members of the chapter of the cathedral and of the university, who possess a few unimportant privileges. Bishop of Cracow, primate. Free toleration.

The constitution is called democratic. But notwithstanding the nominal independence of the republic, no criminal belonging to Russia, Prussia and Austria can be protected within its limits. The legislative power is in the hands of a popular representative assembly, which meets towards the end of each year, the sittings never exceeding four weeks. On these occasions, laws are discussed, the administration reviewed, and the budget drawn up. The assembly likewise elects the senators and magistrates, who are responsible to it. Each community or parish, sends a deputy to the assembly, which likewise contains three members from the senate, three prelates from the chapter, three doctors from the faculties of the university, and six judges of equity. The president is chosen from the three members sent by the senate. No change of any existing laws can be proposed in the assembly which have not previously received the sanction of the senate. The executive power is vested in the senate, which consists of a president and twelve members, who must be thirty five years of age, and contribute at least 150 Polish florins to the public revenue. The president and eight senators are elected by the popular representatives, the university elects two, and the chapter the other two. Six of the former class of senators, and two of the latter, retain their office for life; the others are changed annually. The president is changed every three years, but may be re-elected. The senate exercises the patronage of the republic. The political divisions are into town and country communities; the former containing at least 2,000, and the latter 2,500 inhabitants. Every community is governed by a *starost*, or mayor, and in every district of 6,000 inhabitants is a judge of equity, or a kind of justice of the peace. The electors include all who pay 50 florins to the public service, or belong to a liberal profession. The military force consists of a town militia and a body of *gens d'armes*. In 1817, revenue was 301,072 florins; expenditure 286,440.

Cracow, the capital, and the ancient capital of Poland, and the place of coronation of her kings. University once called the *schola requi*, the most ancient of the old kingdom. In 1817, 131 students. The country divided into 10 districts, containing 1 town, 2 boroughs and 77 villages and hamlets.

Article 195. (September 29, 1833, page 67)

This article written by Hezekiah Niles, a true Friend of Poland, correlated Poland's ordeal with the near-elimination of the press and its defiant existence despite persistent Russian surveillance and other measures of control. In the 21st century, elimination and curtailment of the free press, substituting a government-controlled press, as well as other media sources, continues to be a characteristic of authoritarian and/or totalitarian regimes world-wide.

As an evidence of the trifling value of a newspaper in those parts of Europe where they are under government control, we may instance the recent sale of the *Berlin Gazette*, with 11,000 subscribers for 11,000 dollars. In New York, a daily paper, with such a subscription list and a corresponding advertising patronage, would be worth more than $100,000, and in London might be sold for something like 350,000. The *Morning Chronicle* was purchased by its present owner for a little less than $250,000, and had a circulation of less than 3,000. The annual profit for the *Times* (which circulates about 6,000), averages between 80 and $100,000. The secret of this vast difference between Prussia and England, or America, is that the despotic governments of the one can suppress every journal in the kingdom instantaneously and with impunity, whilst under the free governments of the other, editors laugh at ministers and fear nothing but the laws.

The population of those portions of Poland which have fallen successively to the sphere of Russia, is about 20,000,000. To meet the intellectual wants of such a mass of persons, there are but 15 newspapers, eight of which are printed in Warsaw. Our 10 or 12,000,000 are supplied with something like 5 or 600 newspapers. There is a difference here.

Article 196. (October 19, 1833, pages 120 and 121)

Clearly intended for the ongoing edification of its American readers in the matter of Poland's never-ending and yet-undefined *ethnic cleansing* by Russia, Hezekiah Niles included a startling article under the benign caption, "STATE CATECHISM -- RUSSIA," the objectives of which were manifold, and not the least of which focused on the person of the Czar *who was to be worshipped and obeyed* by way of systematically-based and cleverly-elaborated doctrinal and liturgical underpinnings, some of which bordered on the outrageous, having been the product of uncontrolled and culturally-deadly-for-Poles *caesaropapism!* The essential elements of the *Russian Catechism* were to be delivered on a question-and-answer basis during mandatory gatherings of Roman Catholic congregants in Poland.

Consider as well that the long-range master plan of Russia had been to eliminate by "annihilation" of Roman Catholicism in favor of imposing Russian Orthodoxy on all Poles in its place. One of the plan's manifold related objectives was to declare that *"irreverence, disobedience, malevolence, treason, mutiny and revolt"* against the Czar, constituted grave sins against the will of God, punishable on earth as well as in hell.

The following is the new catechism prepared for the use of the schools and churches in the Polish provinces of Russia. It is published by special order, and printed at Wilna, in 1832:

Quest. 1. How is the authority of the emperor to be considered in reference to the spirit of Christianity? *Ans.* As proceeding immediately from God.

Quest. 2. How is this substantiated by the nature of things? *Ans.* It is by the will of God that men live in society; hence the various relations that constitute society, which, for its more complete security, is divided into parts called nations; the government of which is trusted to a prince, king, or emperor, or, in other words, to a supreme ruler. We see then, that as man exists in conformity to the will of God, society emanates from the same Divine will, and more especially the supreme power and authority of our lord and master the Czar.

Quest. 3. What duties doth religion teach us, the humble subjects of his majesty the emperor of Russia, to practice towards him? *Ans.* Worship, obedience, fidelity, *the payment of taxes*, service, love and prayer, the whole being comprised in the words worship and fidelity.

Quest. 4. Wherein does this worship consist, and how should it be manifested? *Ans.* By the most unqualified reverence in words, gestures, demeanor, thoughts and actions.

Quest. 5. What kind of obedience do we owe him? *Ans.* An entire, passive and unbounded obedience in every point of view.

Quest. 6. In what consists the fidelity we owe the emperor? *Ans.* In executing his commands most rigorously, without examination, in performing the duties that he requires from us, and in doing every thing willingly without murmuring.

Quest. 7. Is it obligatory on us to pay taxes to our gracious sovereign the emperor? *Ans.* It is incumbent on us to pay every tax in compliance with his commands, both as to amount and when due.

Quest. 8. Is the service of his majesty obligatory on us? *Ans.* Absolutely so; we should, if required, sacrifice ourselves in compliance with his will, both in a civil and military capacity, and whatever manner he deems expedient.

Quest. 9. What benevolent sentiments and love are due the emperor? *Ans.* We should manifest our good will and affection, according to our station, in endeavoring to promote the prosperity of our native Russia as well as that of the emperor our father, and of his august family.

Quest. 10. Is it incumbent on us to pray for the emperor, and for Russia, our country? *Ans.* Both publicly and privately, beseeching the

Almighty to grant the emperor health, integrity, happiness and securi-ty. The same is applicable to the country, which constitutes an indivis-ible part of the emperor.

Quest. 11. What principles are in opposition to this duty? *Ans.* Irreverence, disobedience, infidelity, malevolence, treason, mutiny and revolt.

Quest. 12. How are irreverence and infidelity to the emperor to be considered in reference to God? *Ans.* As the most heinous sin, the most frightful criminality.

Quest. 13. Does religion, then, forbid us to rebel, and overthrow the government of the emperor? *Ans.* We are interdicted from so doing at all times, and under any circumstances.

Quest. 14. Independently of the worship we owe the emperor, are we called upon to respect the public authorities emanating from him? *Ans.* Yes, because they emanate from him, represent him, and act as his substitutes; so that the emperor is everywhere.

Quest. 15. What motives have we to fulfil the duties above enu-merated? *Ans.* The motives are twofold; some natural; others revealed.

Quest. 16. What are the natural motives? *Ans.* Besides the mo-tives adduced, there are the following: the emperor being the head of the nation, the father of all his subjects, who constitute one and the same country Russia, is thereby alone worthy of reverence, gratitude and obedience; for both public welfare and individual security depend on submissiveness to his commands.

Quest. 17. What are the supernatural revealed motives for the worship? *Ans.* The supernatural revealed motives are, that the emperor is the viceregent and minister of God to execute the Divine commands, and consequently disobedience to the emperor is identified with dis-obedience to God himself; that God will reward us in the world to come for the worship and obedience we render to the emperor, and punish us severely to all eternity should we disobey and neglect to *worship* him. Moreover, God commands us to love and obey from the inmost recesses of the heart every authority, and particularly the em-peror, not from worldly consideration, but for apprehension of the fi-nal judgment.

Quest. 18. What books prescribe these duties? *Ans.* The New and Old Testaments, and particularly the psalms, gospels, and apos-tolic epistles.

Quest. 19. What examples confirm this doctrine? *Ans.* The exam-ple of Jesus Christ himself, *who lived and died in allegiance to the emperor of Rome, and respectfully submitted to the judgment which condemned him to death. We have, moreover, the example of the apostles, who both loved and respected that; they suffered meekly in dungeons conformably to the will of the emperors, and did not revolt like malefactors and traitors. We must, therefore, in imitation of these examples, suffer and be silent.*

Quest. 20. In what period did the custom originate of praying to the Almighty for the prosperity of the sovereign? *Ans.* The custom of publicly praying for the emperor is coeval with the introduction of Christianity; which custom is to us the most valuable legacy and splendid gift we have received from past ages.

Such is the doctrine of the church, confirmed by practice, as to the worship and fidelity due to the omnipotent emperor of Russia, the minister and vice-regent of God.

[London Paper]

Despite the fact, for example, that the once Roman Catholic King of England, Henry VIII (1509-1547), who rejected the authority of the Pope by divorcing his wife, thereby making himself an unintended "protestant" *Protector and Supreme Head* of the Church and Clergy of England, known as the Anglican Church, which he created by his willful act of divorce from his first wife, yet unlike the monarchs of Russia, the Anglican Church likely never asked that he and his successors as monarchs be worshipped!

Article 197. (November 16, 1833, page 178)

On the European balance of power, war and peace, and the place of the "Polish question," among others, in Europe:

"Bell's London Weekly Messenger, and some other British newspapers, contain many speculations of a warlike character. We do not see any present reason why an extensive war in Europe should be just now expected, but the truth is, that every nation is oppressed, because that peace exists like a war, in the weight of the military establishments which are kept up.

Austria, however, seems determined to possess herself of the command of all of Italy, and will probably be supported by Russia and Prussia, and opposed by France and Great Britain. The Belgian, Portuguese, and Polish *questions,* too, are unsettled, and the influence of Russia, in Turkey, is a subject of jealousy. It is said that the emperor Nicholas has resolved not to acknowledge Donna Maria. And we have just now heard of the death of the petticoat-making sovereign of Spain, which may bring about a contest for the succession, and perchance, cause the formation of a *holy alliance* between Don Miguel, Don Carlos and the duchess of Berri!"

> Whereas *Article 177* had identified an unknown number of exiled Polish soldiers who arrived in the port of New York City in 1832, along with their wives, and perhaps some children, the nearly-precise additional number of 300 (one of whom was a woman), being the much-publicized later Polish exiles to the United States in 1833, by order of the Austrian Emperor, with supposedly free passage to New York City and $50 in cash for each member of the 300-person exile group, had been destined to attain national notoriety and support in the halls of the United States Senate and House of Representatives in 1834.

Article 198. (November 16, 1833, page 183)

'THE POLES. The '*Globe*' says, 'We are informed that a number of Poles, when, at the close of the late contest with Russia, took refuge in Galicia, where they have been supported by the Austrian government, having expressed a wish, in compliance with a proposal by the emperor, to emigrate to the United States, he has offered them a conveyance to our shores without expense. Two national vessels have been assigned to that service, and are probably now on their voyage, from the port of Trieste, to this country. This unfortunate people, deprived of the asylum which had been afforded them within the limits of Austria, and fearful of encountering the penalties which awaited them on their return to their own country, at first determined to seek protection in France; but in consequence of the sudden departure into Germany of some hundreds of their countrymen, from the depths which had been established by the liberality of the French government, that door was closed against them.' {'The number of these Poles is about 300. It is said that they will each receive 50 dollars, from the Austrian government, on landing in the United States. They will have a kind reception, but we fear are not of the classes best fitted to thrive in our country, where the habit of labor is the best capital of immigrants.'}

> Given that the author of the original article printed in the Globe newspaper, and reprinted in *Niles' Weekly Register*, had been pessimistic about the Poles "fitting into" American society because he had assumed that they had not only been officers but also noblemen rather than workers and laborers, causes me to add the following related story as author and compiler of the research upon which my book is based.

Of the 300 Polish soldiers exiled to New York City in 1833 by the Austrian Emperor had been Lieutenant Władysław Sokalski of the Polish Army, a point that is confirmed by Kraków's Czartoryski Library (Biblioteka Czartoryskich w Krakowie), in its related "List of the Names of Polish Immigrants that Remain in the United States of America" (Lista Polskich Emigrantów Zostających w Stanach Zjednoczonych Ameryki, rkps, 5313, k. 335-338), that was recorded contemporaneously. (That list appeared as an integral component of an article in 1969 written in Poland by Florian Stasik titled: "Activities of Charles Kraitsir During the November Uprising and in Exile (1830-1842)" -- *Działalność Karola Kraitsira w czasie powstania listopadowego i na emigracji (1831-1842)* -- that was published in Poland, in the journal, "Historical Review" (Przegląd Historyczny; 60/1), in the Polish language, pages 114-129.)

Some six years later, Władysław Sokalski, by then was a married man, at which time his wife gave birth to a son, George Oscar Sokalski. Following graduation from high school in the United States, George O. Sokalski, a Polish American, went on to become a Class of 1861 graduate from the United States Military Academy in West Point, New York. As such, he had been *the first Polish American to graduate from West Point*, served in the Union Army during the American Civil War, advanced to the rank of Lieutenant Colonel, and fought with patriotic distinction in fifty Civil War engagements.

Though Lieutenant Colonel Sokalski, to repeat, had been *our nation's first Polish American to graduate from West Point*, and survived the combat horrors of the Civil War that produced a staggering count of battlefield deaths, he died in Fort Laramie, Wyoming while on duty at the age of 28 in 1867, just six years following graduation from West Point. Young Lieutenant Colonel Geroge Oscar Sokalski was likely taken to West Point as a child by his parents, who lived in the greater New York City area, to view the Kościuszko Monument of 1828 as the means by which to educate him about Kościuszko's heroic service to Poland as well as to the United States. They taught their son well.

I mention the story of George Oscar Sokalski (1839-1867) because he would assuredly have taken part at some point as a Cadet in an annual ceremony commemorating Kościuszko in front of the Kościuszko Monument at West Point that had been dedicated on July 4, 1828, by the United States Military Academy's Corps of Cadets, to honor the memory of Poland's greatest hero and champion, and because of Kościuszko's highly important service to America at Saratoga and West Point, as well.

Indeed, Kościuszko had been held by informed Americans of those days of the early American Republic, to have been the patron saint of West Point. (See *Polish American Studies* of the University of Illinois Press, Volume LXXVI, No. 2, Autumn 2019, pages 47-64, for the related article, "The Patron Saint of West Point: Tadeusz Kościuszko and His Academy Disciples," written by me, Anthony Joseph Bajdek.) Needless to say, that those Poles, exiled by the Austrian Emperor, adjusted to American society, and had been a credit to their Polish upbringing, as were their children, particularly in the case of the Sokalski family.

One can only speculate about what United States Army Lieutenant Colonel George O. Sokalski's life would have been, had he not have died at a relatively very young age, as a potentially iconic Polish American leader of the small but growing community of *Polonia* (i.e., persons of Polish descent living in the world apart from Poland) in the United States.

I consider it a privilege and obligation to recognize and honor, in the pages of this book, the memory of United States Army Lieutenant Colonel George Oscar Sokalski's American patriotism in combat against the traitors of the Confederate States of America, as his father had done earlier, under diametrically-opposed combat circumstances, as a Polish patriot soldier and freedom fighter in combat against Imperial Russian forces during the November Uprising of 1830 and thereafter.

In my opinion, the story of the United States Army's Lieutenant Colonel George Oscar Sokalski -- the first Polish American to graduate from the United States Military Academy at West Point, the Academy having been included as an integral entity among our early American Republic's leading institutions of higher education -- deserves and should be taught to 21st century Polish American children with the same level of intensity as is devoted to the worthy stories of the early 17th century principals of the Jamestown Colony in Virginia, and later in 1854 those of the first permanent Polish settlement in Panna Maria, Texas. In short, let it be done.

United States Army Lieutenant Colonel George Oscar Sokalski (1839-1867), a Civil War combat veteran, was the first American of Polish descent to graduate from West Point with the Class of 1861. He is shown here in the uniform of a West Point cadet. His father had been a Lieutenant in Poland's Army during the November 1830 Uprising against Russia, who was exiled to New York City by the Emperor of Austria.

Article 199. (January 25, 1834, page 367)

Of Poland, Hezekiah Niles informed his American readers in this issue that:

The fate of this brave people is, we fear, fixed for the present, Russia, Austria and Prussia having signed an offensive and defensive treaty respecting Poland, each party bound to furnish 35,000 men to put down any revolt.

Article 200. (February 15, 1834, page 411)

RUSSIAN PUNISHMENT FOR POLISH HEROISM AND PATRIOTISM WAS INFLICTED ON WOMEN AS WELL AS MEN and reported to Americans by Hezekiah Niles. Of significant note, readers are reminded that in England's Royal Navy at approximately the same time in history, no more than 48 "stripes" (lashes inflicted by a whip) could be inflicted on a sailor regardless of the level of his transgression, whereas in Poland under Russian authority and control, Polish women could receive as many as 200 to 300 "stripes" per woman as punishment for having been Polish patriots.

Polish Heroism. Three of the confederates of Dziewicki, who has poisoned himself, have been shot at Warsaw, in the public square of execution, without the walls. They all died with a display of courage, hoping that their deaths might be useful to their unhappy country. Olkowski, in particular, showed great self-command. While on his way to execution, he gathered up a handful of the soil, and exclaimed – 'For this we have fought, and for this we are willing to die!' The tombs of these young heroes have become objects of veneration to the people, who strew flowers and garlands upon them. Many women have compromised themselves. *A young lady, Helen Nowakowska, has received 200 stripes, for having sent provisions to some unfortunate insurgents who were dying of hunger in the woods. The horrible punishment was inflicted in one of the barracks of Lublin, to the sound of military music; and to render it more severe, they afterwards shaved her head, and confined her to a convent, and no one can tell when she will be released. The wife of Orlowski has been condemned to receive 300 stripes for having sheltered one of her relations. She entreated that her punishment might be inflicted publicly at Warsaw, in order that it might inflame the courage of the patriots. This, however, being denied her, on the day her sentence was to have been executed, she was found dead in her prison, having forced pins into her bosom.*

In those days, long hair had been the basis of hair styles for women. When the occasion demanded that the hair be worn up so that it could fit under a wide-brimmed hat, for example, at least one long wooden or metallic "hair-pin" (szpilka do włosów in the Polish language) as it had been termed to be, was used by women to keep their long hair in place so as to fit into the crown of the hat. The pins ranged in length from eight inches or more as I understand it.

Article 201. (April 5, 1834, page 85)

Unfortunately, Poles arrived in America during a period of considerable unemployment, provoking resentment in some quarters among Americans seeking employment.

Two Austrian frigates have arrived in New York with 245 Polish exiles. They have come to us in *evil* times. Thousands and tens of thousands of our own people are hard put to it to get a living, and make heavy claims on those yet able to do deeds of charity. The Poles at Harwich, in England, and Havre, in France, and also 212 who lately arrived at Portsmouth, Eng. on their way to the United States, have obtained liberty of the French government to settle in Algiers. There is a great field of honest labor in *that* country -- as well as military employment, if preferred.

Article 202. (April 12, 1834, page 101)

Despite the problem of unemployment in the United States at the time, on April 12, 1834, the *Niles' Register*, page 101, reported that:

A considerable subscription has been made in New York for the relief of the Polish exiles, who have arrived in that city. One person, unknown, contributed $200.

Article 203. (May 8, 1834, pages 166 and 167)

Re-printed below is this considerable new-brief about the Polish exiles deported from Austria to New York City, that included a brief summary of the circumstances that brought them to America, which had been validated by statements from one of the exiles who, apparently but not surprisingly, had been fluent in English; the rejoinder from the Austrian consul general in New York City; and of the precarious condition of Polish exiles in Switzerland, as reported in this issue of *Niles' Weekly Register:*

As Reported in the "Niles' Register"

POLISH EXILES AT NEW YORK. *From the New York American.* 'The Polish exiles, who have come hither in the Austrian frigates, not only without their own consent, as it is understood, but protesting solemnly against being forcibly torn from Europe and thrown destitute upon a land whose language they are ignorant, and where they will be without any means of existence, are entitled to the sympathy of this community.

These unfortunate men, as we learn from the writer of the annexed letter, one of their countrymen, were gathered together from different parts of Austria, passed from brigade to brigade, down to Trieste, and there, each being furnished with a great coat, a pair of trowsers, and one or two other accessories, sent on board the frigates, and thus were brought away forcibly from Europe. They are each to receive here a sum of $22; there is one female, seven or eight officers, and the rest soldiers.

The first steps should be to provide these people with some clothing, and an asylum, so that they may not be obliged to prowl about the streets, or be stripped of their little money by persons taking advantage of their ignorance of our language, etc. Then time may be taken for making ulterior arrangements.

Among these people are some who have been farriers; they may find employment, we presume, with our blacksmiths. The great mass, however, have only their stout arms to rely upon. Their case, we are sure, will excite the sympathy of our citizens, to whom we recommend the annexed appeal of Mr. Gerard.

'To the editor of the *New York American.*

Sir – It is in the name of 249 Polish exiles, that I ask through your journal, the opportunity of making an appeal to your fellow citizens. Emboldened by the recollection of many kindnesses which many Americans have lavished upon me, during the eighteen months that I have dwelt among them, I address myself to their hearts, in the full conviction that they will not be insensible to that compassion, which constitutes now the whole dependence of my ill fated countrymen. May they in their turn experience the blessed fruits of that benevolence which has so much contributed to ameliorate my condition. Especially, may they be permitted to draw upon that source, which the charities of the ladies of New York so abundantly supplies. Soon, then, would the wretched state of destitution in which they now are, be changed for one less discouraging, and on our part, we Poles, will know how to acknowledge the aid that shall be extended to our misfortunes.

I have the honor, to be, sir, with the highest consideration, your devoted servant,

GERARD, *ancient Polish officer,*

New York, 31st March, 1834.'

Please note that the letter from "GERARD, ancient Polish officer," was very likely a *nom de guerre* that one of the Polish exiles used in the war against Russia. The name Gerard neither appeared as a surname nor a given name recorded in the initially-referenced (in *Article 198*) "List of the Names of Polish Immigrants that Remain in the United States of America" (Lista Polskich Emigrantów Zostających w Stanach Zjednoczonych Ameryki, rkps, 5313, k. 335-338).

'On which the Austrian consul issued the following card:

As it appears from several articles published in the daily papers that the true nature of the transportation of the Polish passengers, in the frigates of his majesty the emperor of Austria, is not understood, the undersigned thinks that the following statements of facts will give every explanation on the subject.

In the years of 1830 and 1831, during the last revolution in Poland, a number of those who had taken an active part in that revolution, took refuge on, or were driven into the Austrian territory, where the government not only received and granted them an asylum, but even generously maintained them. By far the greatest number of them expressing a wish to go to France, and others to avail themselves of the amnesty offered by his majesty the emperor of Russia, every facility was afforded them execute these their purposes.

There remained, however, a number, who could not or would not return to their country, and could neither obtain passports for other countries of Europe, all of which were shut to them in consequence of sundry events well known. Under these circumstances his majesty the emperor of Austria offered them a free passage in national vessels to this country, which they accepted, and signed for that purpose their determination. On their landing here, after having paid the usual charges for passengers, the undersigned, by command of his imperial majesty paid each of them forty dollars, and all of them, on parting from the ships, manifested feelings of gratitude for the generous conduct of his majesty, and the good treatment on board of the two frigates.

It affords me great pleasure to hear testimony to their general good conduct, and having contributed all that I have been authorized to do by my government, it will afford me additional satisfaction to offer them all the advice in my power, and it is particularly gratifying to witness the generous feeling manifested by the inhabitants of this city, towards them, as I feel satisfied they are deserving of every friendly aid and assistance.

L. BARON LEDERER, *consul general*
Austrian consulate, April 4, 1834'

The following reply has been made on behalf of the Polish exiles to the preceding statement:

'It is but too well known in all of Europe what reliance is to be placed upon the amnesties of monarchs in regard to the combatants for liberty; and particularly upon that of the Russian cabinet. In spite of repeated oaths, the regulators of the fate of nations, only do what their interest suggests. The amnesty of Modena, of Spain, of Naples, are but the first fruits which flow from the cornucopia of the paternal benevolence of the kings and petty rulers of the other hemisphere. The Polish patriots who have the weakness to trust to the emperor of Russia's forgetfulness of the past, are expiating their credulity in Siberia, in prisons, or in the regiments of the Muscovites.

We have in vain protested against our deportation, as contrary to the rights of nations; there remained to us no alternative but to return under the reign of the *knout*, or to proceed to America. There were yet but two chances remaining: either to go to the United States or to be conveyed to South America. After having endured a course of treatment *a La Metternich* in the garrisons of Brunn and Trieste, destitute of the means and of permission to go to France and England, we were constrained to make a virtue of necessity, and to become burdensome to this free country. What could be more natural than what the Austrian consul has recently declared? He has resided so many years in this country as to forget the blessing of monarchical paternity; he is not acquainted with the last catastrophes in Europe; and he only does his duty in representing things according to the well calculated instructions of his court. Could he, with his hands on his heart, putting himself in our place, conscientiously say that he would have us follow any other course than that which has rendered us free from all persecution in this hospitable land, under the protection of that constitution which has been the guide of the Poles for half a century?

With respect to our treatment on board of the Austrian frigates, it was not of a nature to make a parade of it in the port of New York.

We abstain both from praising and from blaming certain officers, for fear that the praise may turn to the injury of those who are worthy of it, and the blame to the profit of the inhuman. We are too deeply sensible of the solvency of the *holy alliance* to be able to believe a single moment that the entire expenses of our deportation are not furnished at third hands from the proceeds of the confiscated estates of the most zealous patriots of our unhappy country.

In behalf of the Poles.

ADALBERT KONARZEWSKI
Reed street No. 34.'

Adalbert Konarzewski's name does appear -- as Wojciech (Polish for Adalbert) Konarzewski -- being number 102 of the 234 numbered Polish exiles on the above-referenced "List of the Names of Polish Immigrants that Remain in the United States of America" (Lista Polskich Emigrantów Zostających w Stanach Zjednoczonych Ameryki, rkps, 5313, k. 335-338) of 1835. As such, Konarzewski's letter to Austria's Consul General in New York City is an important source of information insofar as it identifies Konarzewski as having been fluent in English.

'*The Poles in Switzerland.* The French papers contain some further particulars of the fate of the unfortunate Poles in Switzerland, which show their position to be truly deplorable. It appears that they are carted from one canton to the other without receiving admission or shelter in any. The canton of Vaud sent them to that of Berne, where they were not received. Friburg refused to let them pass through its territories, and throughout the federation the troops have been posted at the frontiers to repel these hapless and pestilent intruders. It appears that, in trying to remove them from the castle of Rolie, it had been found necessary to give orders to a body of *gens d'armes* to charge the 115 refugees in the mass with bayonet, but some humane persons interposed and saved them from this wholesale butchery. It is not known what is to become of them'."

Article 204. (May 17, 1834, page 190)

This news-brief attests to the fact that Poles who arrived in Philadelphia did so at a time when sectionalism, abolitionists and anti-Jacksonist "Whigs" dominated the discourse in the American political arena, yet despite that fact the *Niles' Register* reported that:

Some individuals at Philadelphia are making considerable exertions for the present relief of the Polish exiles arrived at New York. Few that are both able and willing to assist the distressed, have not a sufficiency of calls or demands on both; but, a trifle from many to these few strangers would render good service to them, and evince a national feeling that we might have a just pride in.

Article 205. (May 17, 1834, pages 196 and 197)

An unlikely friend of Polish exiles, had been, in fact, United States Senator George Pointdexter (1779-1853) of Mississippi who served in that capacity from 1830 to 1835, had been President Tempore of the Senate from June 1834 to November 1834, and during which he had also had served as Chair of the Senate Committee on Private Land Claims beginning in 1831. As such, his Committee took up the cause and petition of Polish exile Lewis (Ludwik) Bańczakiewicz et al in 1834 for a grant of land for a township, to be possibly located either in the state of Illinois or in the territory of Michigan, to be provided by the United States government for their settlement.

In the United States, the name of Ludwik Bańczakiewicz, leader and spokesman of the 300 Polish exiles from Austria, who worked for approval of the petition with Senator Pointdexter in Washington, DC, is confirmed by Kraków's Czartoryski Library (Biblioteka Czartoryskich w Krakowie), in its "List of the Names of Polish Immigrants that Remain in the United States of America...," of 1835, initially referenced inferentially in *Article 198*. However, in this *Article 205*, Bańczakiewicz is overtly listed as being number 13, with the total numbered individuals amounting to 234, Bańczakiewicz included, but not the 235, including him, that Senator Pointdexter's legislation referenced.

That list appeared importantly as an integral component of an article in 1969 written in Poland by Florian Stasik titled: "Activities of Charles Kraitsir During the November Uprising and in Exile (1830-1842)" -- *Działalność Karola Kraitsira w czasie powstania listopadowego i na emigracji (1831-1842)* -- that was published in Poland, in the Polish language, for the journal, "Historical Review" (*Przegląd Historyczny*; 60/1), pages 114-129.

As Hezekiah Niles reported in this issue, sympathy for Poland generally, and for the plight of the Polish exiles who had been sent "humanely" to the United States by order of the Emperor of Austria in particular, earlier had reached, and precipitated discussion and reaction to the referenced committee report in the United States Senate on Tuesday, April 29, 1834. On that day, Senator Pointdexter reported eloquently on the floor of the Senate his committee's findings and recommendations related to the petition from

Bańczakiewicz and his other "fellow" Polish exiles, the full consideration of which served as remarkable evidence of the impact of a free press in fostering an informed American citizenry about Poland, that reflected the highest benefits of a compassionate democracy, the results of which were articulated by Pointdexter, who strongly supported granting the petition of Bańczakiewicz *et al.* Whereas Pointdexter introduced legislation in the Senate designed to benefit the Poles exiled from Austria, other related legislation likely had also been introduced in the House of Representatives by Congressman Churchill C. Cambreleng (1786-1862) of New York. However, *Niles' Weekly Register* only provided news coverage on the Senate side of the proposed legislative equation that I could identify, which had been reported as follows:

THE POLISH EXILES. IN SENATE -- Tuesday, April 29, 1834. *Mr. Pointdexter made the following report,* (accompanied by a bill to carry into effect the object recommended.) 'The committee on public lands, to which was referred the petition of Lewis Banczakiewicz and others, acting as a committee for and in behalf of two hundred and thirty five Poles, transported to the United States by the orders of the emperor of Austria, have had said petition under consideration and submit the following report:

'The committee do not admit the justice or policy of granting any petition of the public domain to emigrants of foreign countries who voluntarily seek an asylum on our shores from arbitrary governments of Europe.

Neither the usages of civilized nations, or the principles of our free institutions require of this government more than is due to the rites of hospitality and the protection of the laws, to the inhabitants of the old world who come among us to enjoy the blessings of liberty, and partake of the general prosperity and happiness of this highly favored country. These have been uniformly extended, and in no instance denied, to foreigners of every nation, besides the privilege of becoming naturalized citizens according to the liberal system established by law for that purpose.

To justify a departure from this general rule, in any particular case, facts and circumstances, appealing forcibly to the benevolence of the nation, ought to be clearly demonstrated as the basis on which the exception is founded. The committee have attentively considered the peculiar condition of these unfortunate exiles from their native land, in connection with the strong claims which they seem to present for relief, and who have unanimously agreed to recommend their case to the favor of the senate. *The history of the recent revolution in Poland is so well known and understood, that any attempt to recapitulate the events of that glorious and arduous struggle in the great cause of human liberty may be deemed superfluous and unnecessary.* These petitioners constitute a small remnant of that gallant army who engaged in the desperate and unequal conflict with the overwhelming power of the Russian empire, and who firmly resolved that Poland should be free or blotted forever from the map of nations. They bravely fought for the independence of their country, to which they were bound by every feeling of patriotism and affection; they won many battles by prodigies of valor never surpassed in any age or country; they stood undismayed by the powerful enemy against whom they had to contend, and confidently appealed to the sympathies of the civilized nations of Europe to sustain them in a cause so just; but their appeals were made in vain, and their hopes were destined to end in cruel disappointment.

This short and bloody war was terminated in the overthrow of a persecuted, brave, and generous people, contending for their liberty, and the restoration of their ancient rights, as one of the great family of independent nations. Overpowered by numbers, and driven by repeated defeats to the verge of despair, the noble chivalry of Poland retired from the contest, and bade farewell to freedom, country and every thing dear to the heart of civilized man. These petitioners, it appears, sought refuge and protection in the provinces of Austria and Prussia, asking only a passage into France, which they allege, was promised them by the Austrian government. They assembled at the city of Brunn, in Moravia, to receive their passports according to previous assurances given them, when they were suddenly arrested, thrown into close confinement, and, after an imprisonment of three months, the alternative was presented to them of returning to Russia, or of embarking on board an Austrian vessel for transportation to the United States of America. They accepted the latter proposal, and were removed to Trieste; again imprisoned for three months, and finally embarked on board of two Austrian frigates prepared for the purpose; and, at the expiration of

U. S. Senator George Pointdexter of Mississippi.

four months and three days, *were landed in the city of New York, at which their petition is dated.* These facts are set forth by the petitioners, and the committee have no reason to doubt their accuracy. *The question then arises whether this government ought to extend its beneficence to these petitioners, and grant to each of them a few acres of land for actual cultivation, on which they may find a new home, where, by honest industry, they may earn a comfortable subsistence for themselves and their families, free from the persecutions of their inexorable oppressors?*

The committee believe that both principle and precedent combine to recommend the adoption of such a measure, under suitable modifications and restrictions. The emigrants from France, in the year 1817, who were expelled from their country soon after the downfall of the emperor Napoleon, received a grant of four contiguous townships of land in Alabama on the most favorable terms, amounting nearly to a donation. Many similar grants are to be found on our statute book, made to individuals and associations for useful or benevolent purposes. Again, in the year 1812, congress actuated by like feelings and considerations, appropriated the sum of $50,000 to the sufferers by an earthquake at Venezuela. But, without regard to these cases, in which the general principles of legislation were departed from, the committee perceive in the circumstances, under which these emigrants ask of congress a grant of land, enough to warrant the conclusion at which they have arrived in favor of the prayer of the petitioners.

Poland, so often the theatre of sanguinary wars, originating in violations of solemn compacts on the part of those powers by whose combined arms that ill-fated country was conquered and partitioned, made a last desperate and expiring effort to regain her freedom and independence. The surrounding nations looked with cold indifference on the struggle, evidently prepared, if necessary, to render their aid to the emperor of Russia in the subjugation of the Polish army. The result, though for some time suspended by the valor of that small and inadequate force, was at no period of the conflict doubtful. The army was dispersed, the country desolated, the fugitives who escaped the general slaughter were denied the hospitality of neutral states, and could find no resting place on the territories of the crowned heads, whose despotic rule they had resisted in asserting the natural and inherent right, as free men, to govern themselves. Expelled from their own country, imprisoned in Austria and Prussia, refused permission to enter France, they were left to choose between despotism, and perhaps the gibbet, by returning to Russia, and involuntary transportation to those states, where they now enjoy, for the first time, the protection of the laws, and the rights and immunities which belong to the human race, wheresoever they may be cast by the dispensations of Divine Providence.

Humbled by misfortunes; deprived of a country and a home; destitute of the ordinary means of subsistence; in a strange land, whose language they do not speak or understand, and with whose customs they are wholly unacquainted; these petitioners throw themselves on the liberality and clemency of a magnanimous people, and a free government, for a habitation where they may repose in peace and safety, and where, by the labor of their own hands, they may be enabled to rescue themselves from their present wretched condition of want and dependence. *The committee thinks that, in granting the prayer of the petitioners, this government will manifest a proper regard for sufferings of the unfortunates of all countries who may be cast on our shores; a comity due from one portion of the human family to another, which ought to be acknowledged and felt by all; and thereby exhibit to the civilized world a glowing contrast between the arbitrary rulers who oppress and persecute these exiled patriots and defenders of liberty, and the chivalry of a free people who receive them with a friendly welcome and provide for their immediate necessities. The noble example may not be lost in its effects on the great cause of free principles.* The history of our own glorious struggle for liberty and independence, and of the distinguished foreigners who mingled in the conflict, is well calculated to urge the claim of the petitioners to the relief which they ask at our hands. Shall the countrymen of Pulaski, De Kalb, and of Kosciusko supplicate in vain the descendants of the patriots of the revolution for succor and support, when the tyrants of Europe refuse them a resting place, because they are the soldiers of liberty? The committee think not, and, in this opinion, they confidently rely on the cordial co-operation of the senate, and of the great body of the American people. *The committee, therefore, without entering into the question of pecuniary assistance which they respectfully leave to the sound discretion of the senate, unanimously concur in recommending that a donation of one entire township of land, to be located under the direction of the president of the United States, in the state of Illinois, or territory of Michigan, be granted to the two hundred and thirty-five Poles, and divided among them in equal proportions, for actual habitation and cultivation, for which purpose they report a bill.*

Some two months to the day that Senator Pointdexter delivered his Committee's report to the Senate on April 29, 1834, and spoke convincingly at length in support of granting the petition of Ludwik Bańczakiewicz *et al* for a grant of land -- either in the state of Illinois or in the territory of Michigan -- to settle on for the 235 Poles exiled from Austria, and here please note that the number of the involved Polish exiles was referenced at the time as having been 235, by way of Pointdexter's actual proposed bill, (or it may have possibly been 234, by way of the above-referenced related "List" of 1835 in the Czartoryski Library in Kraków), the United States Senate approved, under Chapter CCXLVII on June 30, 1834, "An act granting land to certain exiles of Poland," and President Andrew Jackson went on to complete the remarkable event in the history of American Polonia by adding his signature of official approval to the Act.

All but one of the said Polish exiles from Austria had been men, the exception having been Marcela Kwiatkowska, who accompanied her freedom-fighter husband, Andrzej Kwiatkowski, who are identified as numbers 105 and 106 respectively, next to which the Polish word for marriage (*małżeństwo*) appears for both of them, in the above-referenced "List of the Names of Polish Immigrants that Remain in the United States of America" (Lista Imienna Polskich Emigrantów Zostających w Stanach Zjednoczonych Ameryki, rkps, 5313, k. 335-338) of 1835, as described in the 1969 "Historical Review" (*Przegląd Historiczny*) article written in Poland by Florian Stasik (See again *Article 198*).

Consequently, by their action, the Senators, along with House members, of the Twenty-Third United States Congress, responding to Senator Pointdexter's impassioned speech, which President Andrew Jackson supported and approved, all of which inferentially gave the earliest statutory recognition of what in effect had been extant America's earliest Polonia, which initially had been concentrated in New York City.

What occurred, therefore, in the United States Senate on June 30, 1834 stands in sharp contrast with the more than two centuries earlier history of the Poles of Jamestown colony, albeit of great historical importance in itself, but at a time when the United States hadn't existed.

So that the aforementioned Polish exiles from Austria of 1833 are remembered and studied in Polish American history as much as the Poles of Jamestown colony are remembered and studied, readers of this book who may be their descendants, and some of whom may still reside in the states of Illinois, Michigan, Wisconsin and New York, (or other states as well) will constitute the basis for any future project in identifying what occurred to said Polish exiles who began their quest on American soil in New York City, and who were to have been the founding settlers of townships in the United States government-approved (President Jackson included) "Polish colony" project, but which sadly failed to materialize, for reasons that will be addressed in Article 245.

In seeking to identify their course of action subsequent to the failure of the project, we already know, by way of this book, that at least one of them, Władysław Sokalski, the future father of the first Polish American to graduate from West Point in 1861, returned to the New York City area.

Thus, I now provide below all the names of the aforementioned list of Polish exiles from Austria. For those unfamiliar with Polish given (i.e., baptismal) names for men, please note that *Karol* (from the Latin, *Carolus*), which in English is Charles, *Jan* in Polish for John, and *Marian* are but a few examples. Today in the United States, Karol, Jan and Marian are likely used as given names for non-Polish women as well. The exiles' order of inclusion on the original list that is maintained in the collection of the Czartoryski Library in Kraków represents an age when, I estimate, there had been considerably less than a thousand Poles not only in the United States but also in all of North America. That's precisely why the names of this cadre of Poles exiled from Austria, all of whom had been *freedom fighters* for Poland's right to exist as a free and independent nation, are precious relics of the origin of Polonia in the United States.

Included among them, and entered on the List as number 95, had been Salomon Kimel, a Polish Jew who had been a Polish *freedom fighter* and had chosen to remain with his fellow Polish freedom fighters as an exile in the United States. Over the centuries, people of other ethnic origins (e.g., Italians and Romanians) also selected to emigrate to Poland on a permanent basis and become Poles; thus, in the case of Italians, number 7 on the list, Edward Bono de Mara's original Italian surname very likely may have been Buono di Mare; and number 161, in the case of Romanians, the surname of Joachim Romani literally means "Romanian" in the Romanian language. In the United States, they had been those Polish *freedom fighters* who will be remembered for having initially sought to establish the first permanent "colony" of American Polonia, in either Illinois or Michigan, and came relatively, and agonizingly, close to realizing their objective, but as fate, and local American public opinion in Illinois would have it, that objective was not to be realized.

The fact of the matter remains, that despite their inability to achieve their Polish "colony" objective in Illinois, they remained in the United States, although scattered about, thus making them *America's first large permanent Polonia of 1834,* and thus distinct from *America's first permanent Polish settlement in Panna Maria, Texas of 1854*, those Poles of Panna Maria having augmented the number of Poles that constituted Polonia in the United States, the total number of whom, I speculate, had not been in excess of 2,000 to 3,000 nationally at the time.

The names of the Polish exiles from Austria had been:

1. Abramowicz, Dominik	50. Gliński, Stanisław
2. Bernacki, Karol	51. Głowacki, Ignacy
3. Bogusławski, Aleksander	52. Gąsiorowski, Stefan
4. Bieliński, Aleksander	53. Gzowski, Kazimierz

5. Boczkiewicz, Feliks	54. Grylski, Jan
6. Bystrzanowski, Ferdynand	55. Grabowski, Sylwester
7. Bono de Mara, Edward	56. Gura, Zenon
8. Brzeziński, Franc[iszek], Józef	57. Górski, Antoni
9. Białogłowski, Roman	58. Garbaczuk, Mikołaj
10. Benich, Karol	59. Grabowski, Adolf
11. Berens, Karol	60. Henrykowski, Ludwik
12. Barszcz, Stefan	61. Hołowiński, Józef
13. Bańczakiewicz, Ludwik	62. Hyż, Jan
14. Barczewski, Henryk	63. Horodyski, Ludwik
15. Beter, Teofil	64. Jaszowski, Maksymilian
16. Benit, Roman	65. Janowski, Walery
17. Bienias, Jan	66. Jakubowski, August
18. Bełżecki, Feliks	67. Jakubowski, Franciszek
19. Batowski, Michał	68. Jabłoński, Józef
20. Białkowski, Michał	69. Jaworski, Tomasz
21. Borkowski, Wojciech	70. Jaworski, Mikołaj
22. Browiński, Mikołaj	71. Jełtuchowski, Mikołaj
23. Borzek, Ksawery	72. Juźwikiewicz, Julian
24. Bartkowski, Aleksander	73. Jański, Antoni
25. Cwierdziński, Wiktor	74. Jaroszewski, Ignacy
26. Czerwiński, Józef	75. Jagiełło, Hieromin
27. Chłopicki, Ludwik	76. Iliński, Kwasery
28. Ciechanowski, Józef	77. Iwanowski, Aleksander
29. Czernicki, Józef	78. Jerzykiewicz, Ludwik
30. Czechowski, Ignacy	79. Jakutowicz, Antoni
31. Czechowski, Tytus	80. Jasiński, Kazimierz
32. Dembicki, Napoleon	81. Jasiński, Jan
33. Dymowski, Jan	82. Kuryłowicz, Franciszek
34. Dłuski, Tomasz	83. Kosyłowski, Napoleon
35. Dąbrowski, Jan	84. Kowalski, Konstanty
36. Dobiecki, Władysław	85. Komorowski, Władysław
37. Dobiecki, Fortunat	86. Komar, Karol
38. Dobiecki, Józef	87. Kossowski, Józef
39. Dąbski, Teodor	88. Kunicki, Alfons
40. Dziwanowski, Klemens	89. Krawczyński, Mateusz
41. Dryniewicz, Józef	90. Kułasiewicz, Jan
42. Eysmont, Lucjan	91. Kotowski, Franciszek
43. Filipowski, Kacper	92. Kisielewski, Paweł
44. Faliński, Kazimierz	93. Kotowicz (wyjechał)
45. Gwinczewski, Feliks	94. Kwiatkowski, Józef
46. Gajkowski, Antoni	95. Kimel, Salomon

47. Górski, Michał	96. Kwiatkowski, Józef
48. Głuszecki, Konstanty	97. Korczyński, Franciszek
49. Gutowski, Rudolf	98. Kręgliński, Jan

At this point on the original list, the next number appeared, for some reason, in the left column. Please note as well that the given name of the entry for number 156 was provided as Taodor Pietrowicz rather than Teodor Pietrowicz, likely had been recorded in error. Note as well that the Polish word -- wyjechał -- meant that the person surnamed Kotowicz, number 93 in the group, either decided to leave the group for some reason.

99. Kwieciński, Franciszek	152. Praniewski, Aleksander
100. Kadmus, Jan	153. Pędziński, Jan
101. Kamiński, Jan	154. Piotrowski, Kwasery
102. Konarzewski, Wojciech	155. Poniatowski, Antoni
103. Kwiatkowski, Jan	156. Pietrowicz, Taodor
104. Kwiatkowski, Karol	157. Pawłowski, Dominik
105. Kwiatkowski, Andrzej (małżeństwo)	158. Piekarski, Aleksander
106. Kwiatkowska, Marcela(małżeństwo)	159. Rostkowski, Wojciech
107. Kuczmiński, Mateusz	160. Rutkowski, Teofil
108. Krzyżanowski, Piotr	161. Romani, Joachim
109. Krajewski, Roman	162. Romer, Kacper
110. Krysiński, Tomasz	163. Rrążewski, Ludwik
111. Łepkowski, Numa	164. Rojecki, Tomasz
112. Liskowacki, Florian	165. Rychlicki, Jan
113. Łebedowicz, Antoni	166. Rosienkiewicz, Marcin
114. Ludwikowski, Daniel	167. Rodziewicz (Werner)
115. Lemański, Stanisław	168. Rosenfeld, Ludwik
116. Lange, Władysław	169. Rutkowski, Józef
117. Lepin, Jan	170. Radzimiński, v. Lust – Karol
118. Lewkowicz, Marian	171. Rosnowski, Kazimierz
119. Łuszczyński, Paweł	172. Szablicki, Antoni
120. Molisan, Mikołaj	173. Sobolewski, Paweł
121. Markiewicz, Fabian	174. Sumowski, Antoni
122. Mniszek, Stanisław	175. Szymański, Antoni
123. Młodzianowski, Edward	176. Sienicki, Franciszek
124. Mostowski, Wiktor	177. Szemetyło, Teodor
125. Marski, Dyonizy	178. Szczurowski, Bonawentura
126. Miliński, Edward	179. Sokalski, Władysław

I use the opportunity to again point out that the List's entry number 179 (Władysław Sokalski), who had served as a Lieutenant in the Polish

Army, eventually settled down in the greater New York City area where, after marrying his wife, who later gave birth to their son, George Oscar Sokalski (1839-1867). After graduating from high school, George Oscar Sokalski went on to become the first Polish American to graduate from the United States Military Academy at West Point, with the Class of 1861, and had fought as an officer of our nation's Union Army (i.e., the United States Army) against the Army of the Confederate States of America, rising to the rank of Lieutenant Colonel during the Civil War.

127. Morawski, Sebastian
128. Maszewski, ---
129. Mierzwiński, Cyprian
130. Materski, Franciszek
131. Morozowski, Józef
132. Niedźwiedzki, Karol
133. Nowakowski, Michał
134. Nowomiejski, Michał
135. Nietupski, Feliks
136. Naruszewicz, Hipolit
137. Oladowski, Hipolit
138. Ostapowski, Julian
139. Olszański, Honory
140. Olszewski, Teodor
141. Pieńkowski, Tadeusz
142. Plinta, Karol
143. Polkowski, Edward
144. Paustecki, Józef
145. Plewiński, Karol
146. Puchalski, Eugeniusz
147. Pawliński, Stanisław
148. Porczyński, Eugeniusz
149. Piechowski, Aleksander
150. Podosowski, Grzegorz
151. Petranowski, Franciszek

180. Snitowski, Adolf
181. Stachurski, Daniel
182. Stachowski, Aleksander
183. Sikorski, Apolinary
184. Skrzyński, Aleksander
185. Stefański, Michał
186. Swierdziński, Teofil
187. Szeleszczyński, Andrzej
188. Sulkowski, Jan
189. Sularzycki, Jan
190. Sanicki, Józef
191. Sosiński, Antoni
192. Sadowski, Michał
193. Sadowski, Aleksander
194. Skibiński, Józef
195. Sulmierski, Wincenty
196. Skorupski, Jan
197. Stasiewicz, Grzegorz
198. Strzelecki, Konstanty
199. Słoma, Jan
200. Samiec, Mikołaj
201. Swak, Józef
202. Szumlański, Jan
203. Sawicki, Albert
204. Turowski, Ludwik

At this point on the original list, the next number (205) and those up to 219 appeared in the left column, after which numbers 220 to 234 appeared in the right column, all of which follow below:

205. Turzański, Karol
206. Teliga, Ignacy
207. Trzaskowski, Bolesław

220. Wnorowski, Józef
221. Wierciński, Bertold
222. Węgierski, August

208. Tołoczka, Karol	223. Żukowski, Tomasz
209. Wierzbicki, Szczęsny	224. Żółkiewski, Józef
210. Wyszyński, Karol	225. Zygadło, Józef
211. Wyszyński, Eustachy	226. Zajączkowski, Wincenty
212. Wesołowski, Ludwik	227. Zelazowski, Józef
213. Wierzbicki, Aleksander	228. Zaręba, Franciszek
214. Wardzyński, Andrzej	229. Żywicki, Mikołaj
215. Wojciechowski, Antoni	230. Zacharzewski, Mikołaj
216. Włodecki, Franciszek	231. Zakusiło, Jan
217. Wyszomirski, Paweł	232. Zalewski, Tomasz
218. Wolnicki, Tomasz	233. Zalewski, Jan
219. Wodzyński, Józef	234. Zakrzewski, Mikołaj

At this point as well, the official list of the 234 (rather than 235) exiles from Austria ends. However, following that list, also included had been the unnumbered names of other Polish exiles in the United States who arrived later, each of whom I have identified in quotation marks, and after all of which, I have provided an English translation in italics, and parenthetically enclosed, where necessary as reflected in what follows next:

"Paryż 16 stycznia 1835 r." (Paris, January 16, in the year 1835 .) 30 Apr. wyjechali z Triestu, a 30 lipca przybili do Nowego Yorku na korwecie 'Lipsja':" (30 approved [NOTE: the Apr. above seems to have been abbreviated from the Polish word, aprobacja] and embarked from Trieste, [and] 30 arrived in New York in July on the corvette, 'Lipsja':")

Bohuszewicz	Skarzyński
Czarnecki	Sadowski
Dolański	Targowski
Gorecki	Jaroszyński

Znalezieni w Ameryce (Found in America):

Kopecki	Pral, Jan
Kruszewski	Krajcer, Karol
Kocowski	Szymański
Lewandowski	Mycielski
Magnuski	Izdebski -- odpłynął do Gibraltaru
Nyko	Kotowski -- odpłynął do Gibraltaru
Putrament	Wierciński – do Londynu
Straszewski	Nyko -- do Londynu

In closing this immediate section above, I offer several observations with the text beginning with, "Paryż 16 stycznia 1835 r.": (1) Among transatlantic vessels under sail, corvettes tended to be smaller but faster than the average; however, speed may not have been a consideration for the Lipsja, the corvette identified above, since it may have made several other ports-of-call between Trieste and New York City, perhaps as a tactic to avoid drawing attention to its passengers and itself; (2) Whereas 30 Poles had been approved for passage, only 16 officially boarded the corvette; if in fact the other 14 boarded, they must have been equivalent of paid and thus approved "stowaways" who likely had been forced to do so anonymously by virtue of being sought by Russian and/or local police authorities; (3) Of those in the right-hand column titled, "Znalezieni w Ameryce" (*Found in America*), both Izdebski and Kotowski had the notation meaning, *set sail for Gibraltar* ("odpłynął do Gibraltaru"), which to me, at least, substantiates that they found that remaining in one place, for too long a time, to have been dangerous. The exile Nyko's travel gambit *from Paris-to-New York City-to-London* appears to have been an example of the proverbial "man on the run" or, if that hadn't been the case, someone who simply couldn't make up his mind.

Notably, Karol Krajcer went on to author the work, "The Poles in the United States of America, Preceded by the Earlier History of the Slavonians and by the History of Poland" that was published in Philadelphia, in 1837, as I have referenced in the *Introduction*. In the United States, his surname at the time of publication had been identified as Kraitsir.

Article 206. (June 7, 1834, page 256)

Niles' Register reported in this issue that:

...according to a document drawn up with immense labor by the French government, it appears, that in Russia, one child is educated out of every 387 inhabitants; in Portugal, 1 in 88; in Poland, 1 in 78; in France, 1 in 20; in Austria, 1 in 13; in England, 1 in 11; in Bavaria, 1 in 10; in Prussia, 1 in 6; and in the United States, 1 in 4.

It also reported that Roman Catholic Bishop Dubois presented $900 to the committee established to help the Polish exiles in New York City as a gesture of:

"a praiseworthy example of liberality".

Article 207. (July 5, 1834, page 317)

> The value of wheat in Stettin (Szczecin) versus Amsterdam, Antwerp, Hamburg and London was reported as well.

The following prices will show the difference between the value of wheat in London and cities on the continent. The prices affixed are for eight bushels of wheat, imperial measurement.

London red wheat	52s.	white do. 58s.
Hamburg	do. 27s. 1d.	do. 29s. 8d.
Amsterdam	do.	do. 30s. 8d.
Antwerp	do. 23s. 8d.	
Stettin	do. 23s. 10d.	

Article 208. (July 5, 1834, page 325

> An order in memory of the Marquis de Lafayette (1757-1834), friend of the United States, and Poland:

IN MEMORY OF LAFAYETTE: Order number 46, Headquarters of the Army, Adjutant General's Office, Washington, June 21, 1834

The major general commanding the army, has received through the war department, the following 'general orders' from the president of the United States:

GENERAL ORDERS

Information having been received of the death of general Lafayette, the president considers it due to his own feelings, as well as in the character and services of that lamented man, to announce the event to the army and navy. Lafayette was a citizen of France, but he was distinguished friend of the United States. In early life he embarked in that contest which secured freedom and independence to our country. His services and sacrifices constituted a part of our revolutionary history, and his memory will be second only to that of Washington in the hearts of the American people. In his own country, and in ours, he was the zealous and uniform friend and advocate of rational liberty. Consistent in his principles and conduct, he never, during a long life, committed an act, which exposed him to just accusation, or which will expose his memory to reproach. Living at a period of great excitement and of moral and political revolutions, engaged in many of the important events which fixed the attention of the world, and invited to guide the destinies of France at two of the most momentous eras of her history, his political integrity and personal disinterestedness have not been called in question. Happy in such a life, he has been happy in his death. He has been taken from the theatre of action, with faculties unimpaired, with a reputation unquestioned, and an object of veneration wherever civilization and the rights of man have extended; and mourning as we may and must his departure, let us rejoice that this associate of Washington, has gone as we humbly hope, to rejoin his illustrious commander, in the fullness of days and in honor. He came in his youth to defend our country. He came in the maturity of his age to witness her growth in all the elements of prosperity. And while witnessing these, he received those testimonials of national gratitude, which proved how strong was his hold upon the affections of the American people.

One melancholy duty remains to be performed. The last major general of the revolutionary army has died. Himself a young and humble participator in the struggles of that period, the president feels called on as well by personal as public considerations, to direct that appropriate honors be paid to the memory of this distinguished patriot and soldier. He therefore orders that the same honors be rendered on this occasion at the different military and naval stations as were observed upon the decease of Washington, the father of his country and his contemporary in arms. In ordering this homage to be paid to the memory of one so eminent, so wise in council, so endeared in private life, and so well and favorably known to both hemispheres, the president feels assured, that he is anticipating the sentiments, not of the army and navy only, but of the whole American people.

ANDREW JACKSON

In obedience to the commands of the president, the following funeral honors will be paid at the several stations of the army. At day break, twenty-four guns will be fired in quick succession, and one gun at the interval of every half hour thereafter till sunset. The flags of the several stations will, during the day, be at half mast. The officers of the army will wear crape on their left arm for the period of six months. This order will be carried into effect under the direction of the commanding officer of east post and station, the day after its reception.

By command of maj. general Macomb, commanding in chief.

R. JONES, adjutant general.

> Seventeen years earlier, Lafayette had delivered a eulogy in honor of Kościuszko, his old frère d'armes, at a memorial Mass held in Paris at the Roman Catholic Church of Saint Roch on October 30, 1817, some two weeks following Kościuszko's death in Switzerland, during which Lafayette stated in part, that:
>
> "To speak of Kościuszko is to recall a man who was greatly respected by his enemies, even the very monarchy against whom he had fought. His name belongs to the entire civilized world and his virtues belong to all mankind. America ranks him among her most illustrious defenders. Poland mourns him as the best of patriots whose entire life was sacrificed for her liberty and sovereignty. France and Switzerland stand in awe over his ashes, honoring them as the relic of a superior man, a Christian, and a friend of mankind. Russia respects in him the undaunted champion whom even misfortune could not vanquish."

Article 209. (July 19, 1834, page 343)

> Whereas most, if not exclusively, donations in New York City for the support of Polish exiles had been collected in Roman Catholic churches, yet to the credit of the compassionate Americans *in one Protestant church during one Sunday collection* in Boston, Massachusetts in 1834, a truly remarkable large sum of money had been collected, and most likely the largest amount collected "for the benefit of the Poles" anywhere in the United States on one day, along with a memorable check, and which had been reported by Hezekiah Niles as follows:

A collection was taken up in Dr. Channing's church, in Boston, on Sunday week, for the benefit of the Poles, and $2,432 was collected. In the contribution plate of Dr. Channing's church in Boston, on Sunday, was found a bank check, in the following words:

'Pay to Count Pulaski, my commander at the battle of Brandywine, his brethren, or bearer, one hundred dollars.' The individual who gave the above sum is col. Henry Purkett, who was a sergeant in Pulaski's troop, and shared the confidence of his great commander. He is now eighty years old.

Article 210. (September 13, 1834, page 24)

> In Europe, however, even some Swiss were turning their backs on the Polish exiles as *Niles' Weekly Register* reported very briefly, that in Switzerland:

...a majority of the diet had approved of the conduct of the *vorat* in its *expulsion* of the Poles.

Article 211. (September 27, 1834, pages 52 and 53)

> Alas for Poland! Once free and independent, Poland remained blotted from the map of free and independent nations of Europe, and had become a province of Russia, in which sadistic Russian authorities and their Polish lackeys ordered the mutilation of prisoners (who had been the original young Cadet leaders in Warsaw of the Uprising that began on November 29, 1830), prior to beheading them, so that the condemned Polish heroes, one may speculate, after suffering the initial act(s) of mutilation, would beg the Russian or Polish executioner, to behead them, rather than suffer added inhuman mutilation of their bodies performed by disgusting barbaric sadists, as readily visualized by any imaginative person who reads this particular original article below:

We have the following from an English paper:

'The tribunal at Warsaw, consisting of Russian generals and Polish magistrates instated for the purpose of trying the actors in the late Polish revolution, concluded their labors, condemning to death the government of the five, together with gen. Skrzynecki.

Of all the members of the government affected by this judgment, the venerable Vincent Niemojowski is the only one remaining in Poland, the others having taken refuge in foreign countries. After the publication of the judgment, lieutenant general of the kingdom, prince Paskewitsch, had Niemojowski brought before him loaded with chains, and recommended him to implore the clemency of the emperor, but the noble-minded old man rejected the counsel. The lieutenant general, however, had demanded his pardon of the emperor, attributing the obstinacy of Niemojowski to mental alienation in consequence of the sufferings he had undergone during his confinement in his dungeon.

The same judgment also condemns to death all who filled public offices before the revolution, and afterwards took part in the regency of Zakioczym. This class is very numerous, as they have included in it all the deputies as public functionaries. This mode of execution varies according to the degree of culpability. Some of them are to be decapitated, and others to be gibbetted, and judges have carried their barbarity so far as to order that the execution of young men who gave the first signal of the revolution by attacking the place of Belvidera, shall be *preceded by mutilation*.

Prince Czartorysky, Messrs. Morausky and Barsikowsky are condemned to death, as well as Niemojowski, as members of the government of five. The same penalty is to be inflicted on Lelewel, as a conspirator, and on Sczarnisky, Bienazhy, B. Niemojowski, and P. Wysczki; Vincent Niemojowski and P. Wysorzky, are alone reprieved.'

Article 212. (November 1, 1834, page 135)

Hezekiah Niles had clearly been responding to some of his subscribers and others who must have expressed their disbelief that Imperial Russia actually had acted with such heinous barbarity against the Poles, children included, in what in effect can best be characterized as an agonizingly prolonged, consistently brutal act of atrocity characteristic of the *ethnic cleansing* (as we equate that modern day terminology with Russia's actions in those years) of Poles from Poland, that never seemed to end, in which Cossack brutes participated, and in this report that appears below, raping a 15 year old Polish girl.

To his credit, Niles' answer could not have been anything other than what he had stated.

Today in the 21st century, it should not be forgotten that there had been an official Imperial Russian Legation Minister in Washington City and an Imperial Russian Consul General in New York City during the times in question, both of whom likely had been attentive readers of *Niles' Weekly Register,* and of other American newspapers as well, and who submitted official objections with the U. S. Department of State against what they likely termed as being contrived, inaccurate news reports and outright "calumnies" against the good name of Russia and its allegedly-beloved and worship-worthy Emperor, Nicholas I (1825-1855).

We should not too readily credit all the reports that we hear of the outrages of the Russians on the unfortunate Poles, *but so many savage sets are so well attested*, that persons are prompt to believe almost any abomination that can be stated. We have the following from a late English paper:

'The most atrocious cruelties are still being perpetrated by the cruel autocrat of Russia against the unfortunate Poles. The nobles are compelled, within two years, to produce their titles, or be condemned to menial service in the Russian army, or to labor in the mines of Siberia. Several young students in whose possession was recently found a volume of Wiletynska, have had their heads shaved in public, and one of them, aged 12, scourged to such a degree that he died a few hours later. A beautiful Polish girl at a boarding school at Warsaw, aged only 15, who was found playing the national air, *La Pologne n'est pas encore perdue!* was seized by the governor, dragged to the guard house, and there whipped and violated by the Cossacks so shockingly, that she died of shame and grief! Many of the Poles, in consequence of their misery have committed suicide.'

Please note that the article referenced above was most likely written in Europe by a French correspondent who could not have been expected to articulate Poland's national hymn, "Poland is not yet lost" (*Jeszcze Polska nie zginęła*) and as such, used its French equivalent, *La Pologne n'est pas encore perdue*, instead.

Article 213. (November 22, 1834, page 180)

And as for the Lithuanian portion of the once great Commonwealth of Poland and Lithuania:

In unfortunate Lithuania persecution knows no bounds. Among a great number of mothers, wives, and sisters, who made heroic although vain efforts in 1833, are Madame Grondska, confined in a convent of the Bernadines at Grodno, for three years; Madame Bilgorayska, for a year; Madame Pilsudska, for six months; Madame Starzynska, for three months; and Mesdames Jurewicz and Dobrowolska, for an unlimited time. Madame Szpak was condemned to three years in prison, and her daughter to a year, for having given asylum to her son, who was afterwards beheaded. Madame Nowakowska, of Lubin, was confined to ten years in Soluian in Lithuania. In Volhynia and the Ukraine the same system of oppression is pursued.

The French print above reminded all Europeans, and Americans by extension, how Russia brought order to Warsaw in 1831 by virtue of the whip and lance of the undisciplined, murderous Cossack cavalry, lingering on for years.... Indeed, "Order reigned in Warsaw," as the well-known expression of the times proposed in French, "L'ordre règne à Varsovie."

Article 214. (January 17, 1835, page 335)

A report is sent forth that *Russia* will demand of *France*, as an indemnity due on account of *Poland*, in the sum of 150 millions of francs! Some think it is a joke, others say it is serious.

Article 215. (January 24, 1835, page 259)

> Russia's war on Polish women continued unabated. In the article below, Czar Nicholas enforced punishment against Polish women for their patriotism in the Polish cause for national freedom, and particularly, if they had been married women, for refusing to denounce their imprisoned husbands (historically, a favored method of compulsion employed by authoritarian-totalitarian regimes worldwide both present and ages-past), which caused them to be imprisoned as well, but separately from their husbands.

Poland. The emperor Nicholas traversed Poland without leaving a trace of his presence. The mitigation of the condition of the political prisoners, which was promised, has not taken place. *The women who were arrested for not having denounced their husbands, remain in prison.*

A few days before the arrival of the emperor a revolting sentence was placed upon the sister of the unfortunate Szpeck, who was shot at Warsaw for some political offence. This young girl has been sent to the military colonies, where she is to be forced to marry a Russian soldier. Her mother has at the same time been sentenced to ten years' hard labor at Wilna. Mademoiselle Karska, an inhabitant of the Palatinate of Kelicz, has been torn from her family and sent no one knows where. The motive for her arrest is said to have been the discovery of a ring which had a motto displeasing to the Russian police. The presence of the emperor did not lead to any change in these arbitrary and atrocious sentences. Prayers and supplications were made in vain.

Article 216. (February 7, 1835, page 406)

> Here reported under the title, "The Poles," are two remarkable letters, one written by exiled Prince Adam Czartoryski, who at one time had been a personal friend of Czar Alexander I, and by whom he had been ap-

pointed to serve both as Minister of Foreign Affairs and as Chairman of the Council of Ministers of the Russian Empire from 1804 to 1806; and the other, by Julian Ursyn Niemcewicz (1758-1841), who at one time had been the aide-de-camp of Tadeusz Kościuszko in 1794, both letters of which had been addressed to Polish exiles in the United States. Though sympathetic to Poland's existential struggles and the plight of its exiles in the New World, the original American commentary, most likely written by Hezekiah Niles himself, to Czartotyski's letter to the Polish exiles in the United States, strenuously proposed that there should only be one nationality, as it applied to any exiles in the United States, that being the American nationality. Worthy of special note had been the fact that Czartoryski's letter, written by him in France, of course included the correct spelling of Kościuszko's surname, and thus Hezekiah Niles spelled it correctly as well, but without the appropriate diacritic. Replication of the operative Polish, or for that matter, any or all, European diacritics in the American press, however, would have been impossible in North America at the time, in terms of state-of-the-art in printing. Nevertheless, it had been a major step in the right direction for the correct spelling of Kościuszko's surname.

The following extracts from two letters written to the Poles in the United States, have recently been published. They are excellent, we think, *except in this*, the advice that they should dwell together, and preserve their own language: the rightfulness of which appears to depend on the fact, whether they should become *Americans*, they and their descendants, or remain *Poles*. In giving up their own native land, it is their *duty* to study and make themselves acquainted with the language and laws of that to which they have been driven, affording them liberty and safety, with peace. There should be only one 'NATIONALITY' in the United States, with which *politics* has nothing to do, whether of foreign or domestic origin. It is of a character far beyond the precedents of the times.

'Countrymen: Though the scarcity of our funds and our urgent necessities allow no more, we send you a thousand francs. Receive this trifling offer only as a token of our remembrance and solicitude for you and the measure of our sentiments and sorrow for your fate. I feel happy to annex a letter of the hon. J. U. Niemcewicz, the venerable veteran in the misfortunes of our unhappy country. Keep his paternal advice in your mind, and act in yonder far country, to which you have been carried by fate, and where the Polish name is not unknown, so that it may not become disregarded. America received you undoubtedly as

RUSSIAN POLICY TOWARD POLAND DISPLAYED IN ACTION DURING THE 1830s.
Kidnapping of Polish children by Russian soldiers in Warsaw's Castle Square ("Porwanie dzieci polskich przez żołnierzy rosyjskich na placu Zamkowym w Warszawie"). Being an example of the Russian policy of the "ethnic cleansing" of Poland.

countrymen of Casimir Pulaski, and of Thaddeus Kosciuszko. Pulaski, the first hero of our still enduring struggle, fell fighting for the independence of America. There rest his bones. Several districts of the new world bear his name. Kosciuszko, more fortunate, returned from the remote war to his fatherland. Here he fought gloriously, and yielding but to overwhelming power, bequeathed his name to posterity as an incentive to new struggles, which can end only with our success. Soldiers of the same cause and the same struggle! Remember these two glorious Polish names.

I suppose that you will dwell together, or you will mutually know of each other. Inform us especially what has been done for you by government, and by private persons. What kind of occupation did you choose? What are your prospects for the future?

We take interest in every thing concerning you. Take this my first communication, with my brotherly greeting, and with my most sincere regards for you.

PRINCE ADAM CZARTORYSKI
Paris, 15th August, 1834'.

As Reported in the "Niles' Register"

The leaders of the Polish National Committee in Paris met for social and cultural events in the Hôtel Lambert which had been purchased by Prince Adam Czartoryski, depicted here promi-nently standing alone on the left, to serve as his residence, located in the 4ᵗʰ Arrondissement on the Quai Anjou. This painting by Teofil Kwiatkowski, also depicted Princess Izabela Czartorys-ka on the left, Poland's and Europe's great Romantic national poet, Adam Mickiewicz, possibly reciting excerpts of a poem on the right, and sitting at the piano, Poland's and Europe's great Romantic pianist and composer, Fryderyk Chopin, fittingly performing the début of his latest Polonaise. Scattered among those gathered for the occasion had been several men attired as the near-legendary Winged Hussars of old, whose eagle wings never failed to attract patriotic attention.

'From senator Niemcewicz.

We received the news of your fortunate arrival in the Unit-ed States of America with great joy. The deepest felt wishes of your countermen are directed towards you in yonder hemisphere: we trans-fer ourselves in mind to the fertile lands granted to you there by con-gress, where you will see over your heads but the canopy of heaven, the dwelling of the Almighty, where there is nothing around you but the silence of space interrupted by the rustling of primeval forests, or by the voices of unknown animals. The inscrutable sentence of Prov-idence commanded you to seek a new home. Permit me to give some counsel, as coming from an old man, who knows the country, and who is taught by experience. Begin every thing with God. Before you can build a church, pray in the shadow of a tree, for the deliverance of your country from under her yoke, for your brethren remaining therein, and for those who also are scattered abroad, on the whole earth, that they may be purified in this fire of adversity, and some day return to the country of their birth. Be industrious, and behave so as to procure you the esteem and love of the citizens, and secure independence. No community can exist without organization. Choose from among you such men as deserve and are qualified to be the trustees of your settlement. Brotherly harmony, and unity of purpose are most required in the beginning, which will be hard. Success will crown your united efforts. Droop not before difficulties. Beware of inconsistent schemes, of planless undertakings. Remember that we are all amongst foreigners, who are ignorant alike of our deeds and of our present true condition. *They will judge the whole Polish nation by your actions. How sacred is our duty to keep the honor of Poland, our good name, from being darkened by the least spot.* Preserve the language of your forefathers, as the palladium of our nationality, so, if our too powerful and cruel foes should succeed in suppressing it in Europe, its relics may remain in America, where oppression and slavery are unknown. Why does my age and my strength, broken by so many misfortunes, not permit me, to see again America, that country which gave me an hospitable asylum during ten years, whose citizen I have the consolation and honor to be: with which I am united by the dearest ties and consanguinity! How happy would I be, to end my miserable life amongst you. A field stone over my grave in your free country, would be more glorious to me, than the most gorgeous mausoleum in the country of slaves.'

Please note again Niemcewicz's prophetic words, written twenty years prior to what was to occur in Panna Maria, Texas: "Begin everything with God. Before you can build a church, pray in the shadow of a tree...," which had been precisely what the Reverend Father Leopold Moczygęba and his fellow-immigrant Polish parishioners from Silesia (Śląsk in Polish) had done in Texas twenty years later in 1854. Had Moczygęba been familiar with Niemczewicz's advice? Perhaps. But that's a task to be pursued and researched by other historians.

Of itself, that task alone characterizes the historian's inclination to search for the who, what, when, where and why of the human experience, which equates with the search for truth, as opposed to reliance on mindless speculation or pure fabrication. In ancient Greece, as I recall, perpetration of lies had been a crime punishable by death. In short and to the point, "liars and perjurers beware" had simply been the message to those members of the polis whose propensity to lie had been viewed as a supreme danger that disrupted the tranquility, order and welfare of the typical Greek community of classical times.

Pana Maria, Texas by Arthur Szyk

Article 217. (February 28, 1835, page 442)

In the following news-brief, Czar Nicholas invoked precedent for a claim going back to the Grand Duchy of Warsaw, that had been creation of Napoleon Bonaparte, by linking it to contemporary international affairs in his days, one example being my earlier-referenced settlement of American claims on France, as the justification for the attempt of Russia to have liberal France pay the bill for the Polish revolution of 1830-1833 which, he argued, the French allegedly conspired with the Poles to ignite. By so doing, the Czar had yet again spread the seeds of chaos and division in diplomatic circles and among the nations they had represented, a tactic that always proved helpful to Russia, and still does today.

It is now gravely stated as a fact, that the emperor of *Russia*, on account of the acknowledgement of the American claims, has made a serious one on *France* on behalf of the kingdom of *Poland!* That admitted, will *Prussia, Austria, Holland, Spain, Portugal*, and the kingdoms and states of *Germany, Italy*, etc., etc., not present theirs?

Article 218. (February 28, 1835, page 446)

A tragic story for Polish exiles who had fought for Poland's freedom and independence, only to find themselves -- a world apart in a strange land -- being forced to defend themselves somewhere in the Texas badlands against an attack by native American Indians.

It appears from a letter received this week from a respectable Polish immigrant, at New Orleans, that about 20 of his countrymen, not meeting with any means of support, and totally without funds, departed from New Orleans for Mexico, by land, through the Texas country. Having no guide, nor knowledge of the wilderness route, they became utterly lost, when they were fiercely attacked by the Indians.

The Poles had but few guns, but maintained a long and bloody conflict, until they had killed a large number of their enemy. They, however, suffered severely, having two of their number slain, and the remainder wounded. Only one Pole was able to reach New Orleans.

{*Louisville Journal*}

Article 219. (March 7, 1835, page 5)

Czar Nicholas continued to pursue the matter of indemnification from France because of French support, at least in spirit rather than substance, for Poland's revolution. A major complication, however, existed because of the American claim, as this issue of March 7, 1835 referenced in considerable detail, but particularly as it related to the Grand Duchy of Warsaw that Napoleon Bonaparte had created, when Alexander I had been Czar of Russia (1801-1825).

The *London Times* of the 26th publishes a letter from the Paris correspondent of the 24th, of which the following is an extract:

'The claim advanced by the emperor of Russia, as king of Poland, in the name of the grand duchy of Warsaw, against the present government of France, in virtue of a convention for the reciprocal adjustment of claims and counter claims between the two countries, concluded on the 27th of September 1816, to likely to become a stumbling block in the way of the settlement of the American question, from the fear that is entertained lest the recognition of the one debt should be regarded as a precedent for the acknowledgement of the other.

300

M. Dupin, the president of the chamber of deputies, has been heard within these few days to express himself very strongly against the ratification of the Washington treaty by the chamber; and the idea seems to gain ground among members generally that a second refusal may be hazarded without any serious risk of a rupture with the government of the United States. However erroneous this view of the matter may be, after the attitude assumed by the American President in the late message to congress, the fact of its being so generally entertained may possibly lead to very inconvenient results....'

Article 220. (March 21, 1835, pages 44 and 45)

Russia's continued Poland-related demands for financial indemnity from France were rejected by France, which itself owed Poland a much greater debt than that of a purely monetary consideration, in the opinion of some in France, as reported in this issue of *Niles' Weekly Register*.

POLAND. M. Isambert, a distinguished deputy of the opposition, held in the French chamber on January 26th, the following bold and eloquent language with reference to the recent Polish claim put forward by Russia.

After referring to the present situation of Poland, he observed that if Russia made a claim in her own name, the treaty of 1818 might be brought forward in proof that France owes nothing. But if the claim was made in behalf of Poland, France denies the right of Russia to put forward such a demand, inasmuch as the latter had not fulfilled the treaties of 1815 with regard to Poland. *There was, however, one debt which France owed to Poland, her glorious companion in arms, but it was a debt of blood, which could be paid only on the field of battle. To the payment of that obligation the nation would consent.* All France would say, we owe it, and but give the word, and the eager youth of all France would rush forward to discharge it (hear, hear)! Let ministers demand from the chamber the means of defraying it, and they should be granted, but the chamber would never vote money only for the benefit of Poland's oppressor [cries of 'bravo'] and let it go forth to Russia and the world, that that debt, and THAT DEBT ONLY, WILL YET BE PAID.

The Czar's attempt to parallel Russia's claim to the one being demanded of France by the United States didn't work as what appeared on the same page of Niles' Weekly Register immediately following this March 21 article on Poland illustrated, that having been, that the United States had been sensitive to avoiding anything in its related negotiations with France, that would hurt the pride of the French, something that Russia, of course, would not do.

Private letters as well as newspaper information, state that the report made in the senate by Mr. Clay, as chairman of the committee on foreign relations, on the subject of our difficulties with France, was received in Paris, by way of England, and the unanimous vote of the senate on the resolution appended to it, reached there by the packet Francis....

The bill was to have been examined in committee on the 12th ult. And the general opinion was that it will pass.

The Paris correspondents of the English papers affirm that there cannot be the least doubt now that the bill for payment of the American indemnities will pass in the chambers, as the commission appointed to report on the question was unanimously in its favor. The vote of the United States senate, *had removed most of the objections raised by the hurt pride of the French against the payment of the claim*; and hence it is probable that it will pass without any paragraph throwing blame on the ministry, as was proposed by M. Passy.

On the division in the bureau in the choice of the commission, the vote stood 240 favorable to the indemnities and 161 against them.

Article 221. (July 5, 1835, page 312)

In this issue, Hezekiah Niles included an account of the release from imprisonment in 1796 of Tadeusz Kościuszko by Czar Paul I (1796-1801) of Russia. When asked by the Czar where he would go following his release, Kościuszko allegedly replied, "To America, where I shall find brothers in arms and glorious recollections." The entire news-brief follows:

When, on the death of empress Catherine, Paul ascended the Russian throne, he went, accompanied only by his two eldest sons, the grand dukes Alexander and Constantine, to the castle in which state prisoners were confined, released Kosciusco and in the following words did homage to his virtues: 'I restore to you your sword, general, asking you to pledge your word never more to use it against the Russians.' Kosciusco is said to have declined the sword, saying: 'I need none, having no mother-land,' but pledged his word as to the price of his liberty. The Czar inquired whither the released prisoner would go! To which Kosciusco firmly replied, 'To America, where I shall find brothers in arms and glorious recollections.'

Article 222. (August 8, 1835, page 399)

The Washington Monument Society" article originally appeared in the National Intelligencer newspaper of Washington City. Niles' Weekly Register reprinted it and drew added attention to the progress being made to raise a national monument to the memory of George Washington by appealing to an even wider-reading public, given that the article compared, in a highly compelling manner, the ostensibly slow progress to build the Washington Monument in our nation's capital, with in contrast, the success in Poland to honor Tadeusz Kościuszko with the "noblest monument," forever known as the Kościuszko Mound (Kopiec Kościuszki) in Kraków, that was completed in 1823. This is indeed a very informative article as well, for more than the obvious reason, insofar as it sustained the idea of Poland's existential struggle for freedom and independence, among informed Americans at the same time.

The presidency of the *Washington National Monument society* having become vacant by the lamented decease of chief justice Marshall, ex-president Madison was unanimously elected to fill the vacant office. The following is his beautiful and appropriate reply to the letter of judge Cranch (first vice president of the society), announcing his election.

'Montpelier, July 25, 1835.

Dear Sir: I have received your letter of the 20th, informing me that I have been unanimously elected president of the Washington National Monument Society in the place of the late lamented president, chief justice Marshall.

I am very sensible of the distinction by the relations to which the society has placed me; and feeling, like my illustrious predecessor, a deep interest in the object of the association, I cannot withhold, as an evidence of it, the acceptance of the appointment; though aware that in my actual condition it cannot be more than honorary, and that, under no circumstance, it could supply the loss which the society has sustained.

A monument worthy of the memory of Washington, reared by the means proposed, will commemorate, at the same time, a virtue, a patriotism and a gratitude truly national, with which the friends of liberty, every where, will sympathise, and of which our country may always be proud.

I tender to the society the acknowledgements due from me, and to yourself the assurance of my high and cordial esteem.

JAMES MADISON.'

William Cranch, esq. 1st vice president of the Washington National Monument society.

The *National Intelligencer* adds:

'The noblest monument that has been erected in modern times was to the memory of one of the greatest patriots that ever lived, Kosciusko. He was buried at Cracow, in his native land, and the Polish nation, who appreciated his worth, and his glorious struggles against tyranny, resolved to erect a monument to his memory, which should withstand the assaults of the elements, and even of time itself.

This monument was in the shape of a mound, raised on an eminence, which commands a view of the Vistula. At this work, the aged and the young, the rich and the poor, the nobleman and the serf, even ladies, reared in the halls of wealth and luxury, labored with their own hands. Every one was anxious to pay this tribute of their respect to the memory of the 'great Naczelnic.' It was commenced in October 1820, and finished in three years. It was known by the name of *Mogila Kosciuskio*, (Kosciusko's Mount), and measures 276 feet in diameter at the base, and 300 feet in height, and is the most stupendous work ever performed by human hands.'

Worthy of note here is that the editor of the National Intelligenser who wrote the original article had depended on someone else who provided in almost, but not quite, correctly-worded Polish, Mogila Kościuskio, that was to have meant Kościuszko's Grave or Tomb which fully-correct with diacritics should have been written as Mogiła Kościuszki. As such, there was no need to add an 'o' to the properly-applied Polish word, Kościuszki. Moreover, the Kościuszko Mount or Mound, from its inception as a concept and an objective in 1820 through its final realization as a man-made structure in 1823, had always been known in Poland as the Kopiec Kościuszki.

The reference to Kościuszko as having been Poland's "great Naczelnic" was fairly close to being accurate with regard to the Polish word, Naczelnik.

Honorable indeed to the spirit of the people of Poland was this tribute of respect of the noble defender of their liberties, and the more so from the manner by which it was rendered. The people of the United States are invited to pay a similar homage to the defender of their liberties. Was a deeper debt due by them to Kosciusko, than us to *Washington*? Or shall Polish gratitude outstrip that of America?'

The Kościuszko Mound (Kopiec Kościuszki) completed in 1823 as it appears today.

Article 223. (September 26, 1835, page 54)

The following from Silesia, in the *Augsburg Gazette*, is dated July 30: 'The police have received a description of 54 emissaries of the Paris propaganda. They are Frenchmen, Poles, and Piedmontese, who design nothing less than the assassination of the emperor Nicholas during the reviews at Kalish! Uneasiness prevails on every side, and even those who had a tendency to liberal opinion open their eyes and contemplate with horror the career of crime through which those men would lead the people to a new order to things.'

Kalish in west-central Poland was known, and still is, as Kalisz by Poles.

Article 224. (January 16, 1836, page 341)

In 1835, Czar Nicholas personally delivered a stern speech to the municipal authorities of Warsaw, wherein he stated that: "if you persist in your dreams of a distinct nationality, of the independence of Poland, and all of these chimeras, you will only draw down upon yourselves still greater misfortunes. I have raised this citadel, and I declare that, on the slightest insurrection, I will cause its cannon to thunder upon the city, Warsaw shall be destroyed and certainly shall never be rebuilt in my time." His full speech follows:

Paris, November 11. Mention has been several times made by the German papers of a speech addressed by the emperor Nicholas to the deputation of the municipal body of Warsaw, upon his late visit to that city, which was only remarkable for its extreme severity and irritating character. Although these papers have not published this document, the following is said to be an authentic copy, which, from its tone and spirit, we are led to wish may be spurious.

'Gentlemen! I know that you have wished to address me, and am acquainted with the contents of your intended address; but, to spare you from delivering falsehood, I desire that it may not be pronounced. Yes, gentlemen, it is to save you from falsehood; for I know that your sentiments are not such as you wish to make me believe them to be. How can I put faith in them, when you held the same language to me on the eve of the revolution? Are you not the same persons who talked to me five and eight years ago of fidelity and devotedness, and made me the finest protestations of attachment, and yet, in a very few days after, you violated your oaths, and committed the most violent actions. The emperor Alexander, who did more for you than an emperor of Russia ought to have done; who heaped benefits upon you; who favored you more than his own subjects, and who rendered your nation the most flourishing and happy; the emperor Alexander was treated with the blackest ingratitude.

You never could make yourselves contented with your most advantageous position, and, in the end, became the destroyers of your own happiness. I thus tell you the truth in order to throw a true light upon our relative positions, and that you may know upon what you have to depend, for I am now seeing and speaking to you for the first time since the disturbances. Gentlemen, we require actions and not mere words; repentance should come from the heart. I speak to you without anger and you must perceive that I am perfectly calm; I have no rancor, and I will do you good in spite of yourselves. The marshal who stands before you fulfills my intentions, seconds all my views, and also watches for your welfare.' At these words the members of the deputation bowed to the marshal. 'Well, gentlemen, but what signifies these salutations? *The first duty is to perform one's duty and conduct ourselves like honest men. You have, gentlemen, to choose between two alternatives: either persist in your allusions as to an independent kingdom of Poland, or to live tranquilly as faithful subjects under my government. If you persist in your dreams of a distinct nationality, of the independence of Poland, and of all these chimeras, you will only draw upon yourselves still greater misfortunes. I have raised this citadel, and I declare that, on the slightest insurrection, I will cause its cannon to thunder upon the city. Warsaw shall be destroyed, and certainly shall never be rebuilt in my time.*

It is painful to me to speak thus to you, it is always painful to a sovereign to treat his subjects thus, but I do it for your own good. It is for you, gentlemen, to deserve an oblivion of the past; it is only for your obedience to my government that you can obtain this. I know that there is a correspondence abroad, and that mischievous writings are sent here for this purpose of perverting the minds of the people. The best police in the world, with a frontier such as yours, cannot prevent clandestine relations. It is for you to exercise your own police, and to keep *evil* away. It is by bringing up your children properly, by instilling them into the principles of religion and fidelity to the sovereign that you can keep in the right path. *Among the disturbances that agitate Europe, and those doctrines that shake the social edifice, Russia alone has remained strong and intact. Believe me, gentlemen, that it is a real blessing to belong to this country, and to enjoy its protection.* If you conduct yourselves well, if you perform all your duties, my paternal solicitude will be extended over you, and, notwithstanding what has passed, my government will always watch over your welfare. Remember well all that I have now said to you.'

Article 225. (March 5, 1836, page 5)

Poland, the balance of power in Europe, support for preserving the Polish nationality, and peace in Europe had been discussed in the French

Chamber of Deputies on January 8, 1836 and reported in this issue of Niles' Weekly Register.

CHAMBER OF DEPUTIES. Sitting of Jan. 8. At 8 o'clock last evening, the grand deputation of the chamber of peers was received by the king, and presented to his majesty the address from the chamber in answer to the speech from the throne, already published....
The following is his majesty's reply:

'Gentlemen, I am affected by the sentiment that you have expressed towards my children and myself, and, both as a father and a king, I feel joy from those which you manifest towards my eldest son. The increasing prosperity of France, the testimonies of confidence and attachment with which I am more and more surrounded by the nation, are additional motives for my receiving happiness from the congratulations you present to me. I participate in your hopes that all our wishes will be accomplished, and that our efforts, crowned with success, will continue to preserve to France that repose, that liberty, that grandeur, which I am happy in having contributed to her.'

'*Sire*, The chamber of deputies, faithfully interpreting the desires and the wants of the country, congratulates itself on having to lay before your majesty words of satisfaction and of hope. Profound peace reigns in this state, and France has faith in its duration. This security, by cementing our union at home, augments the assurance of our power abroad. Happy the country which feels so high a degree the consciousness of its strength, when all wishes are for peace....

Peace, sire, can only serve to augment the prosperity of our finances; their satisfactory condition, as your majesty informs us, will permit us at length to obtain, in all its reality, that equilibrium which is so desirable between the revenues and expenditures of the state. To obtain and preserve this important result, we are aware of the maturity that is required in the regulation of the credits, of all the steadiness that is necessary in the maintenance of their limits, and of all the prudence that must be observed in the valuation of the receipts which are to provide for that object. In this spirit we shall examine the financial laws that may be presented to us. A well-advised economy is a sacred duty to the government, and also for a chamber: which is the guardian of the public fortune....

This happy harmony affords us a hope that, in concert with Great Britain, and the powers whose interests are connected with ours, *you may be able, sire, to restore, the European balance, so necessary to the maintenance of peace, and that the first pledge of it may be the preservation of the ancient nationality of Poland, which has been consecrated by treaties.*'

The adoption of this amendment was received with loud and prolonged cheers of the deputies of the opposition.

The *Journal des Debats* says the paragraph on which the amendment was moved, evidently related to Poland, and was so understood by every body; it was therefore incumbent upon the chamber to make it explicit, or to withdraw it altogether. As for the ground work of the matter, every body was agreed; the government had protested against the union of Poland with Russia, and expressed its determination to maintain their protestations in face of the chamber, that is to say, of all Europe; there was, therefore, every reason why the address should embody those opinions. This would, perhaps, not have but for the speech of Warsaw, which made the chamber refuse to pass over in silence a usurpation upon which Russia had effected no reserve; the address of the chamber is, therefore, a just satisfaction given to the public indignation. Although there was a difference of opinion as to the suitableness of the protestation, there was none as to the foundation of the matter.

Article 226. (March 5, 1836, page 6)

Russian troops massed on the border with Austria's province of Galicja, and Russia refused tò recognize the independence of the Republic of Kraków, making "exorbitant pretensions and pecuniary demands," as reported in this issue of *Niles' Weekly Register*:

A letter from Lemberg, in Gallicia, dated Dec. 31, says: 'Russian troops are concentrating between Plock and Lublin; and three regiments of cavalry have taken up their quarters on the other side of the Vistula, which is attributed to the arrival of a new and strong division from the government of Wilna. The Austrian commanders appear to be carefully watching these movements. The republic of Cracow is urging the three courts to acknowledge its independence, to which Russia opposes exorbitant pretensions and pecuniary demands, which it is impossible for Cracow to satisfy. They are waiting for answers from Vienna.

Poles knew Lemberg, Plock and Wilna as Lwów, Płock and Wilno.

Article 227. (May 7, 1836, front-page)

> On this occasion, the Niles' Weekly Register devoted front-page mention of the fact that:

...the French Chamber of Deputies have voted a supplementary grant of 500,000 francs ($100,000) in favor of Polish and Italian refugees residing in France. The sum previously voted to them, and which was turned out short of their wants, was 5,500,000 francs ($500,000).

> It had become clear prior to that point, that liberal France, by welcoming those seeking to escape Russian oppression in Poland, had created a financial burden for French taxpayers, in actual, as well as in future terms.
>
> With the inclusion of Italian exiles as well, for example, it was feared that other nationalities in Europe might also look to France as exiles in search of succor. As a final consideration, with the death of Lafayette, Polish exiles in France particularly, as well as in Europe generally, had lost their greatest and most influential champion in Europe.

Article 228. (August 20, 1836, page 410)

> All relationships are not solely political in nature. International commerce between nations has always been and will continue to be important as well. In this article, Niles' Weekly Register reported on "Trade of Russia" (Poland included) wherein 75% of Russian hemp exports and more than 75% of Russian tallow exports were destined for England. As such, Russia had to maintain good diplomatic relations with England, a major consumer of Russian hemp and tallow at least, and England had to maintain good diplomatic relations with Russia, despite their strained opposing relationship over Poland's unrelenting struggle to exist as a free and independent nation.

TRADE OF RUSSIA: The following particulars relating to the foreign and domestic trade of Russia, are extracted from a late number of the Petersburgh Gazette, in which it is admitted that one-half of the exports of the empire are sent to England, although not more than a twentieth part of the exports for Russia are sent to Russia. In the year

1834 the total value of the exports amounted in roubles to 230,419,880, including 10,656 sent to Poland, and 2,440,995 to Finland. In the same year the imports from foreign countries amounted to 214,524,630 roubles, from Poland 2,798,804, and from Finland 969,919. The following is a comparative statement of some of the leading articles of raw produce imported into Russia in the years 1832, 1833 and 1834, respectively. The figures represent poods, a pood being equal to rather more than 36 lbs. *avoirdupois*.

Cotton wool	127,124	139,032	152,110
Cotton twist	544,255	517,693	525,296
Indigo	33,318	22,950	25,284
Madders	69,565	46,613	79,440
Oil	200,079	251,958	305,529
Raw sugar	1,357,723	1,537,673	1,574,157

Of manufactured articles the following is a statement showing the progress of importation during the same three years:

	1832.	1833.	1834.
Cottons	10,583,165	10,586,723	8,786,072
Linens	946,694	779,284	905,634
Silks	10,317,676	8,289,817	9,442,567
Woolens	10,982,916	8,412, 957	7,699,198
Lace, blonde, etc.	2,259,288	1,693,463	1,267,744

From the tables it is to be inferred that even in Russia manufactories are making considerable progress, from the increase in the amount of importations of raw produce coinciding with the decrease of manufactured articles. Three-fourths of the whole exports of Russian hemp, and more than three-fourths of the exports of tallow, are sent to England, without counting the shipments for Elsinore, which, in the end, have the same destination.

The city of Helsingør in Denmark was also known as Elsinore among English people.

Article 229. (September 1, 1836, page 16)

A decree of the Russian government in Warsaw establishing greater censorship, was reported in this issue of *Niles' Weekly Register*.

The Poles. We have already announced that a decree has been promulgated by the Russian government at Warsaw, subjecting all medals, prints, drawings, and objects of art, to censorship. The *Swabian Mercury* contains a letter from the frontiers of Poland, in which the cause of this decree is explained. It appears that since the regulations of the government have become so severe that no secret correspondence can be carried on between any of the Polish refugees and their friends in the country, a method has been devised of forming a kind of symbolical correspondence. Many houses in the engraving line, and dealers in hardware had received, almost simultaneously, from Paris, considerable quantities of works in bronze and marble sculpture, executed with much taste and with a moderate price. The police, however, found out the mystery, and the decree above alluded to was issued in consequence.

{*Galignani's Messenger*}

On the condition of Jews in Poland, *Niles' Weekly Register* reported in this issue under the caption, "Jewish Disabilities," that:

Article 230. (October 8, 1836, page 96)

...a decree has been promulgated at Warsaw, forbidding the Jews to use the baptismal names of Christians as their first names. The ground allegedly is, that the police may have better means of surveillance over them.

Better surveillance indeed. Control as well. By Imperial Russian regulations, Jews were restricted in virtually all aspects of life. Following the Partitions of Poland by Russia, Prussia and Austria in 1772, 1793 and 1795 they had been forced to live in the so-called "Pale of Settlement" or "Purple Pale" that had been created by Czarina Catherine II of Russia, the Empire that absorbed the greatest portion of Poland's territorial extent, including Lithuania, thereby absorbing as well, the vast majority of former Polish and Lithuanian Jewry. The referenced decree of 1836 further enabled Russia to better control -- for purposes of police surveillance -- the remaining Jews in the Kingdom of Poland as well, which also had been an integral part of the Russian Empire.

Article 231. (October 22, 1836, page 128)

> In this issue, *Niles' Weekly Register* reported that Czar Nicholas had issued oppressive ordinances against Poland in the matter of military service, and the forced placement of Roman Catholic Polish peasants in the Russian Orthodox (i.e., Greek) Church, as follows:

POLAND. The emperor of Russia has aimed another blow to Polish liberty. An ordinance has been issued by him, which declared that the autumnal recruitment in Poland and the Polish provinces shall be to the extent of two in five hundred, and in the empire, one in five hundred. The peasantry of several villages of the Palatinate of Lublin have been induced, either by the promises or threats of the government, to renounce the Latin for the Greek church, and Russian priests have taken the places of the Roman Catholic clergy. In Russia, the sovereign is not only the head of the empire politically, but the head of the church.

Article 232. (January 7, 1837, page 304)

> Beginning in 1837 and into the final year of its existence in 1849, Hezekiah Niles' newsmagazine that was launched by him as *The Weekly Register* in 1811, became *Niles' Weekly Register* in 1814, and then in 1837 became *Niles' National Register*, one of our Early American Republic's most highly-esteemed sources of world as well as American news, in the pages of which, following his death in 1839, all three of his successors as Editor, went on to sustain coverage of events in Poland that documented its unrelenting struggle for national freedom and independence, against all odds. Thus, they honored Hezekiah Niles' original commitment to relate that exceptionally worthy story as well as many others, never deviating from his original promise that: *"we shall hold it our duty to preserve a history of the feelings of the times on men and things."*

The oppressed Poles. The Russian government has published a list of one hundred and forty-two noblemen, of the government of Vilna, whose property is confiscated, for having taken part in the revolution of Poland.

Article 233. (April 29, 1837, page 132)

The dismal condition of Polish peasants, those elsewhere in northern Europe, and in Russia, was reported by Niles' National Register in this issue.

In *Sweden*, the dress of the peasantry is prescribed. Their food consists of hard bread, dried fish, and gruel without meat.

In *Denmark*, the peasantry are still held in bondage, and are bought and sold with the land on which they labor.

In Russia, the bondage is even more complete than it is in Denmark. The nobles own all the land in the empire, and the peasantry who reside on it are transferred with the estate. A great majority have only cottages, one portion of which is for the family, while the other is appropriated for domestic animals. Few, if any, have beds, or upon parts of the immense stoves by which their houses are warmed. Their food consists of black bread, and other vegetables, without the addition of any butter.

In *Poland*, the nobles are the proprietors of the land, and the peasants are slaves. A recent traveller says: 'I have travelled in every direction and never saw a wheaten loaf to the eastward of the Rhine, in any part of northern Germany, Poland or Denmark.' The common food of the peasantry of Poland, 'the working men,' is cabbage and potatoes, sometimes, but not generally, peak black bread and soup, or rather gruel, without the addition of butter or meat."

Article 234. (April 29, 1837, page 133)

And in the same issue on the following page, *Niles' National Register* reported that Poles of the upper classes seeking employment by the Empire would be subject to two major mandatory considerations, or prerequisites, if you will, those being prior service in the Russian military or civil administration, and adherence to the Russian Orthodox faith, as follows:

Poland. A letter of the 20th Feb. from Warsaw states that an ukase has been published in the month of January last, by the terms of which no subject could enter the ministry, or occupy any high employment in the empire, unless he had previously served five years in Russia. Those Poles alone who are of the Russian Greek religion enjoy the advantages granted to Russian subjects.

Article 235. (July 29, 1837, page 339)

Letters received in Paris mention the failure of the great (Hebrew) house of Daneker and Co. of Warsaw. It was said they had large connexions with Dantzic and Berlin.

Article 236. (May 12, 1838, page 162)

Russia's sordid treatment of abducting young Polish women was attested by no less than a Russian nobleman, as described in this particular issue of *Niles' National Register*:

The horrid story is reiterated by the Paris correspondent of the *London Times*, viz: 'Count Anatole Demidoff has again written to the *Journal des Debats*, alluding to the transportation of 600 young Polish women to the camp at Woesnesenk, and repeating his surprise that any one should continue to disbelieve that statement. 'Now, on the very highest authority, I reiterate that the wholesale abduction in question did take place, and with your permission I shall re-state that a great number of those unfortunate young persons were carried off from the confiscated estates of prince Czartoryski; that the victims to whom the horrible preference was given were married women, that they were habited in the Russian costume, not as Tyrolese (as mentioned in the French paper). None of them have since returned to their homes'.

The women in question had likely been rounded up by Russian authorities and sent to the Russian military camp principally for the carnal amusement of Russian and Cossack forces, and subsequently transported to Russian military "colonies" in the interior of the Empire, where they likely were to be used, largely if not exclusively against their will, to give birth to more Russians. That would explain why the women reportedly never returned home.

Article 237. (October 27, 1838, page 132)

Poland's wheat crop was referred to as its having been the principal integral part of "the great granary of Europe," as was reported by Niles'

National Register in this issue, along with other news as well, that recalled the long-lasting effects to starve Great Britain into submission by Napoleon Bonaparte's imposition of a naval blockade.

London, Sept. 27. The following is an extract from a letter dated Dantzig, 17th Sept. instant, from a first rate house in the city, in direct communication with Poland in all her provinces. The letter was received here on the 24th. 'Since our last reports nothing has been done here in wheat, except a parcel ordinary stuff, hardly better than screenings (30 lasts) has changed hands at 85s. The weather remains remarkably fine. From the reports that we have received from Poland, it appears harvesters have not been lazy in carrying wheat crops during favorable weather. Their work appears to be finished at Cracow, in Sandomir, and in Lublin, and upon the left bank of the Bug river. The wheat has been completely dried by the sunny weather, and is housed in excellent condition. It is estimated to yield less than one-fourth of an average crop in Cracow and Sandomir, and half an average in Lublin and Volhynia. The fine weather has, however, not had every where the effect to repair old injury. The crop of rye is satisfactory in quantity, it being uncommonly light. On the right bank of the Bug river, (Russian side), both rye and wheat are reported to be short in quantity. Some ships that came in chartered remain without employment. No grain freight can be got for them. They have been obliged to cut ports into these new vessels in order to make a poor freight by taking in timber at 23s per load.

Our readers will be able to estimate from the above extract what prospect there is of any supply being derived during the next year *from the great granary of Europe.* The fact is that all the stocks in the Baltic ports are swept out. Our corn laws have produced their effect; for it is an undoubted fact that the breadth of wheat is diminished to a great extent on the continent, our custom being so very uncertain that people are ruined for waiting for it. Our land owners have now brought things to the pass. If we are independent of foreign countries with respect to food, they are equally independent of us, so that they may have the satisfaction during a scarcity of knowing that we cannot escape the destruction which they have intended for us.

We regret to say the domestic accounts hold out but little hopes to the poor for the coming year.

{*Morning Chronicle.*}

The "corn laws" had been imposed by London during the period of Napoleon Bonaparte's naval blockade of Great Britain that prevented importation of foodstuffs, mainly wheat, from the European continent. Whereas the blockade had been intended to starve Britain into submission, it actually had forced British landowners to adopt modern agricultural methods for considerably increasing productivity, the reward for which had been the government's approval for its wheat-growing landowners to charge high prices for their products during the blockade. However, those high prices were never reduced, and remained in effect long after the Napoleonic era ended, even though post-war unemployment prevailed and the price of food remained high. Nevertheless, the Corn Laws were not repealed until 1846.

Article 238. (August 3, 1839, page 354)

Examples of national debts in the world, with debt per head in pounds sterling (£), shillings (s) and pence (d), were first reported for the year 1829 (see *Article 116*) by *Niles' Weekly Register* on April 30, 1831, and now again for a second time in *Niles' National Register* on August 3, 1839, some four months to the day after Hezekiah Niles died on April 2, 1839. Whereas Poland ran up a bill for its rightful Revolution against Russia, its creditors expected it to honor its financial obligations despite its ostensibly having "lost" its valiant struggle. Note as well that England's national debt in the year 1839 was 800 million in pounds sterling, which had been a truly incredible amount of money for those days. Also recall, as noted earlier in this book, that the sign for pence (meaning penny) had been a d because its origin was the denarius of Roman Britain. Of special interest, Poland's national debt at the level of five million seven hundred forty thousand (5,740,000) pounds sterling should be kept in mind because of what was to occur in subsequent reports included in *Niles' National Register* on the extent of national debts among European countries, Poland included.

National Debts. It will be seen by the following table, copied from a recent speech in the English house of commons, that Sweden, Switzerland and the United States, are the only nations which are free from national debt:

	£	Debt per head, Proportion of		
		£	s.	d.
England,	800,000,000	32	0	6
France,	194,400,000	5	19	7
Russia,	35,550,000	0	11	7
Austria,	77,100,000	2	7	6
Prussia,	29,701,000	2	7	7
Netherlands,	148,500,000	23	5	5
Spain,	70,000,000	5	0	8
United States,				
Sicilies,	18,974,000	1	18	4
Bavaria,	11,311,000	2	16	0
Sardinia,	4,584,000	1	1	2
Turkey,	3,667,000	0	7	8
Sweden,				
Portugal,	5,619,000	1	2	6
Denmark,	3,790,000	1	18	4
Rome,	17,142,000	7	9	0
Poland,	5,740,000	1	3	3
Saxony,	3,300,000	2	9	1
Hanover,	2,234,000	1	10	0
Baden,	1,570,000	1	9	2
Wirtenberg,	2,506,000	1	12	7
Tuscany,	1,384,000	1	4	11
Hesse, (Darmstadt),	1,184,000	1	3	11
Hesse, (Electorate)	220,000	1	1	1
Switzerland,				
Norway,	252,000	0	3	1
East India Company's territories	47,609,000	0	9	0

Article 239. (August 3, 1839, page 358)

As it related to the subject, "Review of the Corn Trade," matters concerning Poland's commercial export status had been incorporated more so than inferentially, and from all appearances Poland appeared to have been holding its own competitively as best it could in an activity that, fortunately or unfortunately, depended on the vicissitudes of weather.

The Green Gate (Brama Zielona) in Gdańsk.

London, July 9, 1839. At most of the upper Baltic ports the value of grain has been pretty steadily maintained, and in some instances a slight advance has even been obtained on former prices; this was the case of *Stettin* on the 25th June, the English mail having brought orders for the purchase of wheat, but subsequently the markets became dull again, and on the 29th ult. the enquiry had again subsided.

From *Danzig* we have letters on the 28th June; the holders of wheat had for some days previous insisted on higher process for wheat, and one or two small parcels had been disposed of at an improvement of 1s. per quarter; the business, had, however, been checked in consequence of the rise, and the London letters of the 21st holding out no encouragement to expect a renewed demand, sellers had consented to take previous rates, at which several [illegible word] changed hands, 50 lasts of very fine high mixed new wheat brought 47s. 6d. and 50 lasts of do. do. old at 48s., good old high mixed had been sold at 43s. 6d. to 44s. the best runs of high mixed *Volthynia*, of crop of 1838, at 42s. 6d. mixed *Volthynia* of indifferent color at 40s. 6d.; good red *Galicia* at 41s. to 41s. 6d. and inferior mixed at 38s. per qr. free on board, the weight of the best parcels averaged about 61 to 62 lbs. and of the inferior kinds 60 to 61 lbs. per bushel. Rye had further declined in price, 16s. 6d. to 17s.

6d. being the top quotations. In other articles nothing of importance had taken place. The weather was wet, which interfered with the working of grain. There were plenty of vessels seeking freights, and one had been fixed for Leith at 4s. 6d. per quarter for wheat, a further reduction.

When Hezekiah Niles died in 1839, his lifetime's massive labor of love that he had dedicated to the Niles' National Register, had ended, and his son, William Ogden Niles (1804-1858), who succeeded him as Editor and owner, sadly hadn't been inclined to equally dedicate his own life to it, and thus had offered, for the first time, to sell *Niles' National Register* on September 7, 1839, and eventually sold it.

Article 240. (September 7, 1839, page 19)

The matter of Poland's salt mining industry at Wieliczka (here incorrectly identified as Wieleska) had been in the process of negotiation "at different times" by the appropriate Russian commissioner in Paris. Note that Warsaw (Warszawa in Polish) was referenced in French as Varsovie, suggesting that the news-brief likely had been written by a French Parisian correspondent.

Poland. In relation to the duchy of Varsovie and the mines of Wieleska, a great question is pending. The negotiations on this subject have been resumed at different times. An imperial Russian commissioner was sent to Paris some years ago for this object. There has yet been no result of these negotiations, but they will soon be renewed.

Part Four: 1840 - 1849

Article 241. (March 28, 1840, front-page)

At Dantzic, there has been a great inundation. The Vistula, being dammed up by the ice, the floods, about four miles from the city, broke through the land and made a short cut of about ten miles in the river.

> In the Polish language, Dantzic (or Danzig) has always been known as Gdańsk.

Article 242. (July 11, 1840, front-page)

> Whether it was a one-sentence news bulletin or a fully-developed article several pages long, the matter of Poland, in this case, the Free City of Kraków, *Niles' National Register* had continued in its own final decade of existence, the long-standing tradition established by Hezekiah Niles of documenting the sad story of Poland's largely-endless suffering at the hands of its Russian, Prussian and Austrian tormentors, as this front-page news bulletin of July 11, 1840, under "FOREIGN ARTICLES") attests.

The *Times* is severe on Lord Palmerston, for deferring the address of the Poles at Cracow, who call on the British parliament to protect them in their liberties as guaranteed by the congress of Vienna.

> Recall that the Congress of Vienna occurred in November 1814 until June 1815.

Article 243. (June 19, 1841, page 242)

The Emperor Nicholas, on the occasion of the marriage of his son, has conferred some favors on the inhabitants of Poland, of the kingdom of Poland. All persons under the sentence of death have their punishment commuted to punishment.

Article 244. (July 19, 1841, page 289)

Prussia to be aggrandized by the acquisition of Saxony, a part of Poland, and Hanover...

> In terms of Europe's language of diplomacy -- French -- it often seemed that the sole *raison d'être* (reason for existence) of its divine-right monarchies had been characterized by one word, "aggrandizement."

Article 245. (August 28, 1841, page 416)

Warsaw, Judaism and the Jews. By late returns the number of Jews, throughout all of Russia, is found to be 1,654,349. In Poland, there are 111,307. In the city of Warsaw, they form one-fourth of the whole population.

Titles. The emperor of Russia has assumed the title of 'defender of the Christians of the east.' The Christians of the west will have to get on as best they can without his protection.

Article 246. (October 9, 1841, page 82)

Poland. Advices from the frontiers of Poland, contradict the reports of changes of institutions of that country. The emperor, it was thought, would not visit Warsaw this year. The Russian troops in Poland have been reduced to the peace footing.

Article 247. (March 26, 1842, page 60)

> In this issue, under the section titled, "TWENTY-SEVENTH CONGRESS, Second Session," Niles' National Register reported that on March 18, among bills that:

...were then severally read a third time and passed"

> ...and that notably included among them had been

...a bill relative to the act entitled 'an act granting land to certain exiles from Poland,' approved June 30, 1834.

323

Please note that the succinct news report of March 26, 1842 refers back to this book's *Article 205* of May 17, 1834, that described Mississippi's United States Senator George Pointdexter's proposed legislation on behalf of Lewis (Ludwik in Polish) Bańczakiewicz *et al* in Congress to grant land to Polish exiles, on which they could settle, and had been approved by Congress on June 30, 1834, and subsequently by President Andrew Jackson as well. The fact that the Act of 1834 had been read, according to *Niles' National Register*, for a third time, some eight years later in 1842, was ostensibly puzzling if viewed solely as a stand-alone item of news. It hadn't been a stand-alone news item, however. It had in fact been preceded by the following item of news that had been included in the same *Niles' National Register* article, "TWENTY-SEVENTH CONGRESS, Second Session," of March 26, 1842, page 60:

March 18. The president of the senate submitted a communication from the legislative assembly of Wiskonsan, in relation to the boundary line between that territory and the state of Michigan. This paper says the only true line is the middle of lake Michigan, and protests against any other.

Had the matter of establishing the border between Wisconsin (referenced as Wiskonsan by the original author of the news article at the time) and Michigan anything to do with what had occurred in the United States Senate on June 30, 1834? Perhaps, at first glance to some extent, but not primarily, if at all.

In those days, the Wiskonsan territory had been what we know today as being Wisconsin. However, most importantly, the matter of "a bill relative to the 'act granting land to certain exiles from Poland, approved June 30, 1834'," had not been tied either to Wisconsin and Michigan in combination, but rather to Illinois and Michigan *in combination*, an important difference, specifically on June 30, 1834 in the United States Senate, about which I quote verbatim, not from *Niles' National Register*, but rather, from page 743 of the "ACTS OF THE TWENTY-THIRD CONGRESS of the UNITED STATES" as follows:

'Passed at the first session, which was begun and held at the City of Washington, in the District of Columbia, on Monday, the second day of December, 1833, and added on the thirtieth of June, 1834.

ANDREW JACKSON, President; M. VAN BUREN, Vice President of the United States and President of the Senate; ANDREW STEVENSON, Speaker of the House of Representatives, until Monday, the second day of June, one thousand eight hundred and thirty-four, and JOHN BELL for the remainder of the session.

****

TWENTY-THIRD CONGRESS. Sess. I, Ch. 247, Res. 1, 1834, Page 743

Chap. CCXLVII. – An Act granting land to certain exiles of Poland

Be it enacted by the Senate and House of the United States of America, in Congress assembled, That there be, and is hereby, granted to Lewis Banezakiewitz and his associates, being two hundred and thirty-five exiles from Poland, transported to the United States by the orders of the Emperor of Austria, thirty-six sections of land, to be selected by them, under the direction of the Secretary of the Treasury, in any three adjacent townships of the public lands which have been, or may hereafter be surveyed, situated within the limits of the state of Illinois or the territory of Michigan.

Sec. 2. And be in further enacted, That it shall be the duty of the Secretary of the Treasury to obtain an alphabetical list of the names of the aforesaid two hundred and thirty-five Polish exiles, and cause the same to be filed and recorded in the office of the commissioner of the general land office.

Sec. 3. And be it further enacted, That immediately after the said thirty-six sections of land shall be surveyed and located in the manner prescribed in the first section of this act, under such regulations as the said Secretary may prescribe.

Sec. 4. And be it further enacted, That it shall be lawful for each and every of the grantees to enter upon and take possession of the respective lots of land assigned to them and each of them; and, after the expiration of ten years, the said grantees, respectively, shall be entitled to a patent for the lot of land assigned to them as aforesaid: PROVIDED, that the said grantees shall, during the said term of ten years, without intermission, actually inhabit and cultivate the said township of land in the ratio of one settlement for every five hundred acres thereof; and, on due proof of such habitation and cultivation to the Secretary of the Treasury, and of the payment into the proper land office of the minimum price per acre, at the time of such pay-

ment, within the said term of ten years, patents, shall be granted as aforesaid, and not otherwise.
APPROVED, June 30, 1834'

****

Note that the third reading occurred with some two years' time remaining, of the required ten year waiting period, for the grant of land that had been provided by the United States Senate in 1834 to the 235 Polish exile grantees from Austria during which the exiles had to prove that they not only had taken possession of the land, but also had inhabited and cultivated it, as stipulated by Section 4 of Chapter CCXLVII of the Act. That's what the brief *Niles' National Register* report of March 26, 1842 was all about.

In 1834 Senator Pointdexter correctly spelled the Bańczakiewicz surname, but without the diacritic, but he anglicized Bańczakiewicz's given name from Ludwik to Lewis. Shortly thereafter, the Clerk, acting as custodian of the rolls (custos rotulorum) for the Senate incorrectly referenced the Bańczakiewicz surname that Pointdexter had assiduously spelled correctly, but without the diacritic, forever incorrectly proclaiming on Capitol Hill the Bańczakiewicz surname to have been Banezakiewitz.

However, although what the United States Senate and the President of the United States enacted had been unprecedented in the evolving history of Polonia in the United States, subject to the provisions of the above-mentioned Act, the "thirty-six sections of land" on the soil of the United States, somewhere either in the state of Illinois or in the territory of Michigan, had actually been granted as a "preemption pact to purchase" the land once Bańczakiewicz et al made the decision where to locate their settlement. Unfortunately, their selection of the land in Illinois had already been occupied and cultivated by American squatters.

Despite that propitious and momentous opening chapter of Polonia in the United States (and here, the Poles of Jamestown centuries earlier, comparably had not been part of an entity of the United States *per se*, for the reason that our nation hadn't existed at the time), the final chapter of the story of the 235 Poles exiled to New York City by the Austrian Emperor, had ended in failure.

The major problem had been that the area of land in Illinois, in the present-day area of Rockton and Rockford, selected by the Poles, had found that its occupants -- American squatters -- had simply and adamantly refused to defer to the Poles. Apparently, neither side expressed interest in a compromise, or even in the case of the Poles, of selecting an uncontested alternative site for colonization elsewhere, possibly in Michigan, which -- in the case of the latter alternative-site option -- had been a serious and regrettable miscalculation on the part of the Poles and their fellow-exile agent, Ludwik Chłopicki, who had fluency in English and whose name appears as number 27 (see Article 203) in Kraków's Czartoryski Library (Biblioteka Czartoryskich w Krakowie), in its earlier-referenced "List of the Names of Polish Immigrants that Remain in the United States of America" (Lista Imienna Polskich Emigrantów Zostających w Stanach Zjednoczonych Ameryki, rkps, 5313, k. 335-338) of that contemporary period of time. Discouraged and dejected, the cohesion of the Poles dissolved, and they went their separate ways, assimilating into American society as best they could, with some perhaps making their way to Chicago, while others returned to New York on foot, just as they had traveled from New York to Illinois to begin with, to save money for food and shelter during their journeys, with several still wearing their original November 1830 Polish Army uniforms, or at least remnants of what was left of their uniforms.

In retrospect, one may speculate, to no avail, whether Michigan would have been a better choice.

The best modern analysis of the failed "Polish colony" -- as it was termed to be at the time -- was published by Eric Willey, in a faculty and staff publication of the Millner Library of Illinois State University, under the title, "The Squatters and the Polish Exiles: Frontier and Whig Definitions of Republicanism in Jacksonian Illinois," in the Journal of Illinois History, 13, no. 2 (Summer 2010), pages 129-150.

Accordingly, Willey concluded that Congress changed its outlook about the Polish exiles for whom it "had initially looked east across the Atlantic Ocean to import virtuous republicans and thought that they found them in a group of Polish revolutionaries. Eventually, however, their view changed, and Congress began to look west, finding a commercial definition of republican virtue in the native-born Americans who were already living on and improving the frontier lands," and thus sadly for the Poles, "the fire of republican liberty had passed from the sword of the revolutionaries to the plows of the settlers, from the East to the West." (And here readers should note that a "republican" with a lower-case 'r' had been, and continues to be, defined as a person who does not support a system of government headed by a monarch).

All told, had the "Polish colony" project ended with success, it would have been America's first and thus oldest, permanent Polish settlement in an extant United States. Despite its sad ending, its story should not be forgotten, and accorded at least as much attention as that of the Poles in Jamestown during a time when the United States of America did not exist.

That fact should be contemporary American Polonia's on-going obligation, not only that the story of the first "Polish colony" project -- and importantly, the related lessons learned -- of the actual documented 234 Polish exiles should never to be forgotten, but should also be presented to successive generations of Polish Americans with as much attention as is currently devoted to the story of the Poles in Jamestown, and of Panna Maria in Texas.

In closing, despite the fact that the Poles had secured approval of the United States Congress and President Jackson to begin the lengthy process of legally establishing our nation's first Polish colony, the fact of the matter had been that in Illinois apparently, local people simply viewed the matter as American land being taken away from Americans by foreigners. Thus, in terms of public opinion, as I see it, the entire matter among "other" uninvolved Americans in the region favored the hard-working squatters (*whom they knew*) over that of the Poles (*whom they didn't know*). To which the final thought, both spoken and unspoken in those days, sadly may well have been articulated among some Americans as: "to blazes with Congress and the White House" or something else to that effect. However, that is simply my opinion.

Nevertheless, all of the above began with great promise in 1834 with Senator George Pointdexter of Mississippi (another American amicus poloniae), acting on behalf of said Polish exiles from Austria, some twenty years prior to the day when the first Mass in Latin and homily in the Polish language had been celebrated under an oak tree by the Reverend Father Leopold Moczygęba on behalf of his Polish fellow-immigrant parishioners from Silesia (Śląsk) on December 24, 1854 in what would become known as Panna Maria, Texas, America's first, and thus oldest, permanent settlement of Polish immigrants.

The rest of the story of the fate of the 235 Polish exiles from Austria remains yet to be written. History is replete with stories within stories, and as one example already identified by me (see *Article 198*).

In closing the story of the unsuccessful effort of Senator Pointdexter's 235 Polish exiles to establish the proposed Polish "colony" in Illinois, I utilized the "List" of the names of the 234 Polish exiles maintained in the collection of the Czartoryski Library in Kraków rather than the one on file in the archives of the Secretary of the Treasury in Washington, DC. What prompted me to choose the former list over the latter for inclusion in this story had been the fact that Ludwik (Lewis) Bańczakiewicz's surname, as leader of the documented 235 Polish exile petitioners, underwent an insensitive and insulting transformation to Banezakiewitz at the hands of a thoughtless federal bureaucrat. Imagine what would have occurred as such with the balance of the other 233 beautiful ancient Polish, and other Poland-related, surnames of each of Bańczakiewicz's compatriots with whom he shared inclusion on the Czartoryski Library's list. I could imagine it, and thus selected, given the sad failure of the Polish "colony" project, to honor the memory -- for purposes of this book -- the above-listed (see *Article 205*) largely Polish-surnamed, and other, Polish Army freedom-fighters-exile petitioners' given names and surnames, as had been passed on to them by their parents, and ancestors over the ages, in Poland, and not in the typical and prevalent misspellings rendered by Americans at that time in history, (and sadly even to this day as a matter of fact).

Andrew Jackson (1767 - 1845), the seventh President of the United States (Thomas Sully)

Article 248. (November 3, 1842, pages 210 and 211)

The passage of Resolutions about the struggles for the national freedom and independence of Poland adopted by the Vermont legislature were reported in this issue of *Niles' National Register.*

VERMONT.
The legislature has closed its session.
BEHALF OF POLAND.

It seems that Col. Tochman, a Pole, and a well-known lecturer on the wrongs of his native country, so effectively wrought upon the sympathies of the Vermont assembly, that a series of resolutions was introduced into that body denouncing the oppression and cruelty of Russia towards ill-fated Poland, and concluding thus: *'We, therefore, on the behalf and in the name of the inhabitants of the state of Vermont, do say to all the world, that we hope and trust in Divine Providence, that Poland will continue her aspirations and her struggles for liberty, till the autocrat of all the Russias will know and feel, that it is the unalterable decree of the Ruler of the Universe that the principle of freedom once developed in the hearts of a people, can never be extinguished by any course of expression, however severe, or long continued.'*

Col. Tochman was, by special vote, admitted to the floor, when, in an eloquent speech, he enforced these resolutions, which were then unanimously passed.

Whereas I made reference to the Polish soldier, veteran of the November 1830 Uprising against Russia, and Polish exile, Gaspar Tochman (1797-1880) in this book's Introduction, and I here include, as I already have done in the case of Dr. Samuel Gridley Howe, founder of the Perkins School for the Blind in Watertown, Massachusetts (see *Article 159*), for what I deem to be a quality-control validation of Tochman's pro-Poland role in the United States as spokesman, indeed its exemplar, of Poland's struggle for the right to exist as a free and independent nation. While his spoken and written words aroused sympathy and support among Americans for the Polish cause, he labored to confront and dispel the idea of some ill-informed Americans who fell prey to deceptively "evil" Russian propaganda of the era which had proposed that: (1) "Russia is the only real and natural ally of these United States in Europe"; (2) that "the absolute administration, whether of Russia, Austria, and Prussia, is studiously beneficial to the mass of the people"; and (3) that "to expect the resuscitation of Poland, is to expect the use of human affairs to flow backward."

Representing the Polish National Committee in Paris, and its affiliate members in London, as its tirelessly unrelenting spokesman in the United States, Tochman had been a relative of General Skrzynecki on his mother's side of the family. In America, Tochman had become a naturalized citizen of the United States in 1841. He had also studied American law and had been admitted to the bar in Washington City (now D.C.) where he practiced law. A University of Warsaw alumnus and freedom fighter for Poland in November 1830 and thereafter, before emigrating to the United States, and following some two decades later as an American citizen, on the eve of our American Civil War, Tochman disappointed the likes of former Polish comrade and leader Joachim Lelewel (1786-1861), by not only announcing his support for the Confederate States of America but also being commissioned as a Colonel in the Confederate Army for which he recruited members for the Polish Brigade of the 14th and 15th Louisiana Regiments.

His support for the Confederate States of America, however, did not preclude his importance, some twenty years earlier, in bringing his first-hand knowledge to the attention of Americans, of Poland's struggle for the right to exist as a free and independent nation, along with his warnings to Americans not to fall victim to Russian propaganda.

Confederate States of America Colonel Gaspar Tochman

What appears below, for which I thank Mariessa Dobrick and Bethany Fair of the Vermont State Archives and Records Administration in Montpelier, who brought the following letter written by Tochman to the Editor of the *Commercial Advertiser* in New York, to my attention upon my inquiry, in a newspaper article printed in Vermont that illustrates the nature and substance of Tochman's many speeches about Poland and Russia, that speaks for itself:

"For the *Vermont Watchman & State Journal*
VERMONT -- POLAND

To Colonel Stone, Editor of the *Commercial Advertiser*, New York

Sir, I read yesterday in the Commercial Advertiser of the 24th of November, your sportive remarks as to the proceedings of the Legislature of Vermont, expressive of their sympathy in behalf of Poland, and of their indignation for the wrongs done to her once free people.

I do not want to be told, that you are as good a friend in my country as "the Green Mountain Boys"; but your "hearty laugh" at their proceedings can be used by the enemies of Poland to counteract the exertions of her exiled sons, designed, as they are, to show the friends of liberty in Europe the real public opinion of the great mass of the people of this happy Republic, as to the affairs of Poland.

I have not been traveling and lecturing in these United States, as you believe and announce to your readers, *to gain a living.* True it is, that 'the grand master Nicholas' having confiscated my estates, I often charge for admission to the lectures, to raise a fund to pay the rent of the lecture rooms, the advertisement, and the other expenses concerned with my mission; but, as out of eight villages and towns, I am obliged to give free lectures in five, and never make any charge for admission when I address the members of the Legislatures, I should not be able *to gain my living* by lecturing, without the assistance on the part of my own countrymen, residing in France and England as exiles, who, to promote my mission to this country, lay on its altar a part of the produce of their daily labor.

You may have observed, sir, that in the last ten years that many a writer has propagated in your country the doctrines, that 'Russia is the only real and natural ally of these United States in Europe'; that 'the absolute administration, whether of Russia, Austria, and Prussia, is studiously beneficial to the mass of the people'; that 'to expect the resuscitation of Poland, is to expect the use of human affairs to flow backward.'

Such doctrines and arguments, circulated in these United States, have been enumerated in Europe as emanating from the political opinions of the mass of the people of this Republic, and this misrepresentation naturally has very injurious influence on the future destiny of Poland, and the cause of liberty in general. It is therefore to counteract this evil, that Poland appeals to the American people, and asks that they should tell the world whether they are friends of the people and of free governments in Europe, or of the despots endeavoring to extend their iron sway over the earth, and already attempting to undermine the free institutions of this great republic.

The members of ten State Legislatures, and more than a hundred public meetings, held by the citizens of the Western States and New England, have answered this appeal by passing resolutions similar to those of the Vermonters. These meetings were conducted by the most prominent and leading men of the country, of both political parties: Gov. Kent, in 1841; Gov. Hubbard, last summer; Ex. Gov.'s Fairfield, of Maine, Marcus Morton, of Massachusetts, and Wallace, of Indiana; many members of Congress, Senators, Speakers and Members of the House of Representatives, in the Whig and Democratic Legislatures, acted as chairmen, committees, and secretaries of these meetings. And I hope that you yourself will permit Poland to place your name with theirs, on the long list of her friends.

The National Intelligencer, criticizing these same proceedings of the Legislature of Vermont, closes its remarks by saying that 'the Legislature of Vermont might as well have proclaimed a crusade from Vermont against Russia, and appoint Colonel Tochman to lead it forth.'

I was only a major in the Polish army, and as I gained this rank in the field of battle, against Russia, I could not accept the appointment of Colonel from the National Intelligencer; but I would willingly accept the appointment of a leader of the crusade against Russia. And should the Vermonters comply with the suggestion of the National Intelligencer, and honor me with this appointment, I promise you, sir, to take under consideration the plan of marching the 'Green Mountain Boys' through the way of Behring's Straits into Asia. I believe this to be an excellent plan. The first men being created in Asia, the aborigines, must have come to this continent across Behring's Straits, and why should we not lead the brave Green Mountain Boys through the same way, to assist Poland, and to repel the fiend, laying his grasp on the western territory of these United States?

I am only sorry, that Poland does not ask for a crusade from these United States against Russia, and that I am not authorized to support the proposition of the *National Intelligencer*.

I dare hope, sir, that, as an act of justice to the cause of my country and to myself, you will open your columns to this communication, and will please accept the assurance of the highest consideration from

> Yours respectfully,
> G. Tochman, *A Polish Exile*
> Providence, R. I., Dec. 14, 1842"

FINAL NOTE: Tochman's undying love for and loyalty to Poland had driven him to discuss its prospects for freedom and independence wherever he could seek out audiences across the United States and for working with State legislatures, Vermont being one example, to pass Resolutions in support of Poland's freedom fighters against Russia, Prussia and Austria in the despotic Old World. On behalf of the Polish cause in Europe, he had addressed some hundred or more audiences in the states of Connecticut, Indiana, Kentucky, Maine, Maryland, Massachusetts, New Hampshire, New Jersey, New York, Ohio, Pennsylvania, Rhode Island, Vermont and Virginia that represented 54% of the 26 states constituting the United States at the time.

Of great importance, he prevailed successfully upon the State Legislatures of Ohio (1841), Massachusetts (1842), New Hampshire (1842), New York (1842), Vermont (1842), Connecticut (1843), Virginia (1843), and New Jersey (1844) to pass Resolutions supporting Poland's righteous cause. Insofar as state Resolutions also memorialized their Congressional delegations on Capitol Hill in Washington City, Tochman became Poland's best-known spokesman in the first half of the 19th century.

As the author of this book, I take great pride in the fact that both Massachusetts (where I and my wife were born and lived in for most of our lives) and New Hampshire (where my wife and I now reside in retirement) were among the States whose legislatures passed resolutions in support of Poland's right to exist as a free and independent nation, largely as the result of Tochman's truly remarkable Polish patriotism, physical energy, mastery of oratory, and written English as well, and resourcefulness in pursuit of accomplishing his mission.

Article 249. (February 4, 1843, page 356)

"So Poland Still Lives." Quoted from this issue of Niles' National Register as it pertained, among other matters, to Servia which is known today as Serbia, relating to Russia's expansionist policy against the Circassian people of the north Caucasus region on the eastern shore of the Black Sea, where unsurprisingly some Polish regiments of the Russian Army went over to the side of the Circassians, and also that the affairs of the Circassians were reportedly being managed by Polish exiles! Of other related interest, the use of the word "porte" had been a synonymous term meaning the government of the Ottoman Turkish Empire. As a matter of fact, the August 3, 1839 issue, page 354, of *Niles' National Register*, ever the educator as a newsmagazine, reported that:

"Many are confused by the various terms which they find in the papers; they read of the Ottoman porte -- the sublime port, etc., without gaining any distinct ideas, and either they omit the oriental news as unintelligible, or content themselves with a very superficial acquaintance with it.... We therefore turn hastily to several works of reference, and give the following:

Ottoman, the appellation given to the Turkish empire, is derived from the name of its founder, Othman, Ottoman or Osman.

Ottoman porte, or *sublime porte*, is the name of the Turkish government. The word, (Latin, porta, a gate) was applied because this was the name given to the gate of the Sultan's palace.

Sultan, is the title of the Turkish despot. It is a word of Arabic origin signifying *mighty*. The power of the sultan is hereditary, and knows no limit, except the precepts of the Koran...."

And of course, included below as well had been the latest progress report of the Russian-Prussian-Austrian "wheeler-dealers" who continued to manipulate the fate of Europe in the area of the Danube River basin as they alone saw fit, in keeping with their common view that all of their related expansionist activities had been appropriate to rule by Divine Right, and despite the strenuous objections of the Sultan.

A serious misunderstanding has arisen between Russia and the porte respecting Servia. An angry correspondence had passed between the Russian ambassador and the porte on the subject. The final answer of the latter has been transmitted to St. Petersburgh, and there the matter rests for the present.

The *Leipsic Gazette* repeats the report, as prevalent amongst the Danubian countries, that the emperor of Russia had chosen the duke of Leuchtenburg, his son-in-law, as chief of a new Byzantine empire, of which he mediated the foundation. Prussia and Austria, it was added, had given their consent to the plan, upon the condition that Austria should have Moldavia and Wallachia; and Prussia, Russian Poland, as far as the river Bug; while Greece would receive Thessaly, to consolidate it better; and the commercial league have the liberty of commerce as well as Austria on the banks of the Danube.

Circassia. Accounts from St. Petersburgh state that several Polish regiments, engaged in the war against the Circassians, passed over with their arms and baggage to the enemy, and fought against the Russians. It is said that they committed dreadful havoc on the latter, and that their vengeance was terrible. *So Poland still lives.* The affairs of the Circassians are regulated by Polish exiles. Five large steam frigates, it is said, are now building at Blackwell, London, for the emperor of Russia, to be used in the Black Sea for the prosecution of the war against the Circassians. One of the steam frigates is now completed.

Article 250. (May 6, 1843, page 146)

A letter from St. Petersburg of the 16th ultimo, published by the *Gazette des Tribunaux*, states that the emperor of Russia had granted a full amnesty to a number of Poles exiled to Siberia, or the interior of Russia, for the part that they had taken in the revolutions of November, 1830.

Article 251. (October 12, 1843, page 96)

Riches. On demolishing an ancient Roman Catholic chapel at Warsaw, recently, two barrels filled with gold, valued at $600,000 were discovered in the foundation. They are to be used now in constructing a bridge to connect Warsaw and Praga.

Article 252. (October 21, 1843, page 114)

A London letter writer remarks that 'the state of Poland, however apparently helpless and hopeless, has of late called forth an additional feeling of sympathy. Her *nationality* appears to slumber only; for a well organized conspiracy has been discovered at Warsaw, consisting of 3,000 persons, whose object was to effect a revolution. About 300 have been arrested. God preserve them!

Article 253. (December 30, 1843, front-page)

In this issue, *Niles' National Register* included a front-page article: "Europe, Her Debts" that it re-printed from the *Buffalo Commercial Advertiser*, describing the progress in the extent of national debts among the nations of Europe, which included for this occasion the combined debt of Russia and Poland. Note that whereas Imperial Russia's debt is combined with that of Poland and is listed at 545 million dollars (U.S.), the impact of that average debt to each inhabitant of the Russia-Poland combination is the lowest among 16 European entities (i.e., "countries") included, but just as importantly, the *combined national* debt of Russia and Poland placed it 4th from the top under England, France and Holland.

There may have been something more here than meets the eye. Furthermore, in the matter of England's national debt, please note that it had risen from *800 million in pounds sterling* in 1839 (see Article 238) to *5 billion, 556 million in pounds sterling* in 1843, which had been an incredibly spectacular amount of money, anywhere in the world, at the time. Whereas virtually no one in the West had anything good to say about Czar Nicholas I of Russia, his observation (see *Article 162*) that England (i.e., Albion) was "loaded with debt," however, had been appropriate, and worthy of consideration, particularly so as it related to the burden of the "average of debt to each inhabitant."

Please note as well that whereas the figures reported in this article of December 30, 1843 had been for all of Europe's 39 "sovereignties" that amounted to 10,499,719,000 (I say again, ten billion, four hundred ninety-nine million, seven hundred nineteen thousand "German" dollars), that the debts of the 16 Europe's "larger powers" had amounted to 10,315,000,000 (ten billion, three hundred fifteen million "German" dollars; representing 98% of the total) are included here. Indeed, the matter of being "loaded with debt" had been a clearly-sobering characteristic of Europe's divine right monarchies, particularly from the perspective of the tax-paying general public, if in fact the proverbial "man on the street" had been fully aware.

The debts of Europe, is the subject of an interesting article in the late number of *Hunt's Magazine*. From this it appears that every nation in Europe, without exception, is heavily in debt. Each of the petty German states pays a large amount of interest. The aggregate of the debts of the thirty nine sovereignties is 10,499,719,000 *German dollars, equal*

336

to 82 cents of our currency. The English debt swallows up in interest, more than one half of the revenue out of which it is to be supported. Debt about £800,000,000, interest £28,000,000 a year. It would require ten millions a year for eighty years to pay the principal of this immense debt. We extract from the full table the following estimates of the debts of the larger powers.

Country.	Debt.	Average of debt to each inhabitant.
Holland,	$ 800,000,000	$266
England,	5,556,000,000	222
Frankfurt on the Main,	5,000,000	90
France,	1,800,000,000	54
Bremen,	3,000,000	54
Hamburg,	7,000,030	45
Denmark,	93,000,000	44
Greece,	44,000,000	44
Portugal,	142,000,000	38
Spain,	467,000,000	35
Austria,	380,000,000	31
Belgium,	120,000,000	30
Papal States,	67,000,000	26
Naples,	120,000,000	16
Prussia,	150,000,000	11
Russia and Poland,	545,000,000	9

How is it possible for the governments of Europe with such a mass of debts upon their shoulders, to accept a system of free trade? In addition to the payment of the annual interest on the above ten and a half millions of dollars, the current expenses for the support of royalty and the armies and navies by which it is everywhere upheld, call for a much larger revenue than can be raised by any system of direct taxation alone. How absurd then to suppose that they will admit the productions of American industry to be consumed on the payment of a less tax than is imposed upon the products of their own home industry. Will they love foreigners better than themselves?

{*Buffalo Com. Adv.*}

Article 254. (March 23, 1844, front-page)

Letters from St. Petersburg confirm the account of the Russian victory achieved by Can Fregtag, at which 6,000 Circassians were slain or taken prisoners. The Prince Tschesscheng had written to the Emperor Nicholas that, if the least violence was offered to the Prince's son, who was among the Circassian prisoners, he would visit the most terrible vengeance upon the Russian officers in his power.

> Please note, that "Can Fregtag" was likely Khan Fregtag whose title the journalist rendered phonetically. And below, a report that French *communists* were in Poland.

The *Augsburg Gazette* states that the doctrines of the French communists were spreading in Poland, and that several persons, convicted of entertaining them, had been banished to Siberia.

> Highly interesting is the fact that "French communists" reportedly had been spreading their doctrines in Poland some four years *before* the "Manifesto of the Communist Party," written by Karl Marx and Friedrich Engels, was published in London in 1848.

Accounts from St. Petersburg state that on the 27th of January the question of establishing trials by jury was carried by a majority of seven votes in the second chamber of state.

Article 255. (April 20, 1844, front-page)

> Included two news-briefs, the first mentioned that Czar Nicholas intended to visit England in the fall of the year, and the second one was titled, "Expulsion of the Poles from Posen" (Poznań in Polish) which identified German mistreatment of *Russo-Polish refugees*:

The emperor of Russia it is stated intends to visit England next September.

The *Augsburg Gazette* gives the following from Posen, under the date 25th ult.: The fate of the Russo-Polish refugees is decided. This morning about two-thirds of them were sent under escort to Magdeburg. The remainder of them will follow in a few days, with the exception of a few, who have received permission to stay until the end of March. Amongst the persons affected, by the measure are the Count de Plater, who has always resided here in a very retired manner and who recently purchased an estate in the Grand Duchy; the rich Count de Potocki, son-in-law of Count Edward de Razzinski, Count Eugene Breza, and M. de Luszewski, who is the owner of two houses in Posen.

As Reported in the "Niles' Register"

Castle Square in Old City Warsaw in the 19th century

Article 256. (June 15, 1844, page 245)

In this issue, yet another article on national debts in *Niles' National Register* combined Prussia and Poland as a single unit of measure in the matter of national debt, and the *Register's* final Editor, George Beatty, offered a related comment. What appeared in this report, was similar to what had been reported in *Article 253*, except that, in this report, the national debt of Prussia and Poland at $545,000,000 ranks fourth from the top behind England, France and Holland, *thus matching to the dollar tied in 4th place, the same $545,000,000 unit of measure for Russia and Poland,* about which I will offer comment after readers examine this *Niles' National Register* article of June 15, 1844. Please note that what may appear redundant in the matter of the debts of Poland, Russia, and Prussia had not been, for the period that ended in 1849, specifically at times when both Russia and Prussia combined their debts with Poland on one hand and then didn't on the other hand. In contrast, for the period of the reports of 1829, 1839, 1843, 1844 and 1849, Poland's debt was reported twice, Russia four times, Prussia four times, Russia combined with Poland twice, and Prussia combined with Poland twice. The coincidences are striking and, one might conclude, suspect. In contrast, whereas Austria had reported its own national debts for the period, it never reported a combined Austria – Poland debt.

National Debts. The following is an estimate of the *several nations of Europe* reduced to our currency:

Country.	Debt.	Average of debt to each inhabitant.
England,	$5,556,000,000	$222
France,	1,800,000,000	54
Holland,	800,000,000	265
Frankfurt on Main,	5,000,000	90
Bremen,	3,000,000	54
Hamburg,	7,000,000	45
Denmark,	93,000,000	44
Greece,	44,000,000	44
Portugal,	142,000,000	38
Spain,	467,000,000	35
Austria,	380,000,000	31
Belgium,	120,000,000	30
Papal States,	67,000,000	26
Naples,	126,000,000	16
Russia,	150,000,000	11
Prussia and Poland,	545,000,000	9

With the annual interests of these enormous debts, to be paid, besides supporting the large armies, navies, invalids, half pay officers, civil lists, foreign ministers, all on the expensive scale of monarchical governments, how is it possible for the great maritime nations of Europe to abolish import duties, and adopt a system of universal free trade? Evidently, the proposition is entirely impracticable....

Having reviewed the particulars of four reports (1829, 1839, 1843 and 1844) of the Niles' National Register applicable to the reported units of measure utilized for the separate national debts of Poland, Russia, Prussia and Austria beginning in 1829, followed in 1839, 1843 and 1844 with Russia and Poland *combined*, and Prussia and Poland *combined* respectively, I coalesce, from my purely non-financier's perspective, with a final consideration of what I have arranged based on the separate and combined units of measure, the following:

ELEMENTS OF THE COMBINED DEBT REPORTS, IN (£) AND ($), OF 1829, 1839, 1843 AND 1844:

Country:	Debt (£) in 1829:	Debt ($) in 1839:	Debt ($) in 1843:	Debt ($) in 1844
England	819,600,000	800,000,000	5,556,000,000	5,556,000,000
France	194,400,000	194,000,000	1,800,000,000	1,800,000,000
Holland/Neth.	148,500,000	148,500,000	800,000,000	800,000,000
Russia/Poland	not incl.	not incl.	545,000,000	not incl.
Prussia/Poland	not incl.	not incl.	545,000,000	545,000,000
Austria	78,100,000	77,100,000	380,000,000	380,000,000
Russia	35,550,000	35,550,000	150,000,000	150,000,000
Prussia	29,701,000	29,701,000	150,000,000	not incl.
Poland	5,729,000	5,740,000	not incl.	not incl.

To the question, what might have been the national debt of Poland alone, as *structured by Russia and Prussia*, I propose that it may have been as high as $790,000,000 if one subtracts the $150,000,000, that both Russia and Prussia reported as their own national debts, from the $545,000,000 that they each owed in combination with Poland, and then multiply the balance ($395,000,000) by the factor of 2 which amounts to $790,000,000. Whether "Poland" actually incurred and repaid its indebtedness at that level, or defaulted on that debt, or that both Russia and Prussia "cooked the books" on solely their own indebtedness at that combined level, by writing it off as having been created by the *fiscal irresponsibility* of "Poland" -- we likely may never know (as we will likely never know the total value of the confiscated estates of Polish nobles such as that of Adam Czartoryski throughout the period of this book), unless, of course, someone chooses to do so by way of a doctoral dissertation, if, in fact, today's Russian Federation would ever allow access by someone from the West to Imperial Russia's financial archives for the first half of the 19th century. On the other hand, I am only a standard-issue historian, not a financial analyst as well. All of which, however, leads to another question, that being: WHO HELD THESE EUROPEAN NATIONAL DEBTS, AND WHY, OTHER THAN FOR THE OBVIOUS REASON (I. E., TO INFLUENCE SAID GOVERNMENTS IN MATTERS POLITICAL AND/OR PERSONAL RATHER THAN SIMPLY FINANCIAL) HAD THE HOLDER(S) OF SAID DEBTS ALLOWED THE HIGH-END NATIONS TO INCREASE TO THE LEVELS ILLUSTRATED HERE? Could government bonds have been involved? Perhaps, but that requires research above and beyond my capability.

Article 257. (July 13, 1844, front-page)

The emperor of Russia, whilst in England, sent for a ticket to the Polish ball, and paid £500 for it. He might well afford a display of liberality in regard to Poland. The Poles returned back to him his £500.

341

Article 258. (November 16, 1844, front-page)

The *Silesian Gazette* says, from Poland, Oct. 1, that about twenty students had recently been arrested at Warsaw, on the charge of belonging to a secret society. The youngest of them, who were *only 12 to 14 years old*, were, it is added, sent into the interior of Russia, but the others were sent to the army of Circassia, as common soldiers.

Article 259. (December 14, 1844, front-page)

> You have read the above correctly. Twelve to fourteen year old children, to the everlasting shame and characteristic cruelty of brutish Imperial Russia, as added evidence of its relentless Russification to eliminate the Polish national identity forever.

Poland. A conspiracy was detected, or rather *suspected*. Arrests were made, and several persons were ordered to the mines of Siberia.

News Article 260. (December 28, 1844, front-page)

The Russian government, in the kingdom of Poland, has issued an order, by which all males, without distinction, are henceforth prohibited from contracting marriages until they have completed the thirtieth year of their age. The cause of temperance societies has received a severe blow in the kingdom of Poland. They had been particularly successful in the parts of the kingdom which bordered on the republic of Cracow, and in Upper Silesia, where the country people following the example of the clergy, renounced in a body the use of brandy. But the government has lately interfered to check the temperance societies, and has published a circular prohibiting them, and forbidding the clergy to promote by addresses from the pulpit an object which is so beneficial to the country people.

> In yet another front-page news-brief, this issue of *Niles' National Register* reported that males in Poland, by order of *the Russian government, in the kingdom of Poland*, had to have reached 31 years of age before being able to marry, that was used as a means by which to reduce the number of Poles born in successive generations, that, from any perspective, would reduce and eliminate, over successive generations and centuries, the Polish

nationality if carried out an *ad infinitum basis*. In addition, the Czar had decreed that temperance organizations in Poland were to be outlawed (apparently so as to sustain Polish men readily controlled in a drunken stupor and, as well, to sustain the profitable production of spirits), both measures being designed to enforce the yet to be defined, albeit authentic, flagrant *ethnic attack* of Poland, in concert with condemnation to Siberia, for the reduction of ethnic Poles, all being crude and disgusting forms of Russia's intent to remove the Polish nationality forever from among the nationalities of Europe and the world.

Article 261. (October 16, 1845, page 98)

In this issue, it was reported that Czar Nicholas, upon visiting Warsaw, personally had spoken to two Polish students who either ignored him as he passed by in a horse-drawn, open landau or fiacre carriage, or simply hadn't realized who he was, for which he subsequently ordered all students and their governors and faculties to appear the following day grouped by their respective schools in military-like formations, for his personal review and inspection in Castle Square (plac Zamkowy), during which time, he mouthed an obscenity (róża morda) and warning, addressed to one particular student, and by extension, to all male Polish students and their families.

A recent letter from Warsaw gives an account of the visit of the Emperor Nicholas to that city. The letter says that all the emperor's time at Warsaw was engrossed in military pomp and parade. He repeatedly visited the citadel, as if to convince himself with his own eyes that it is in a good posture of defence; and he betrayed in this respect some of the anxiety usual with one who examines his weapon on the eve of using the same. He also made several trips to Georgiesk, situated a few miles from Warsaw, and destined to check the country all round. The rest of his time the emperor spent in reviews, military exercises, and ceremonial levees.

He also paid a visit to the students of Warsaw, on the following occasion. One day, the emperor, perambulating the streets of Warsaw in his carriage, fell in with two students, who neglected to uncover their heads in his presence. He immediately ordered his coachman to overtake them, and he himself asked them if they did not know who he was. One of them having answered, 'No, my general,' he abruptly retorted, 'What then, not know your sovereign!' This apostrophe struck the two young men with terror, while his majesty added, 'Look at me well, that another time you may not forget the person of your emperor; but I shall take care besides, to make myself known to all of my students.'

Next morning all the schools received an order to appear before his majesty, with due solemnity, their governors and professors at their head. The emperor walked slowly through their ranks, inquiring of Marshal Paskewicz whether he was satisfied with the students of Warsaw. The marshal, always on his guard, and knowing well his master, cautiously replied, 'that he was not altogether quite satisfied.' The emperor then cast a frowning look over the poor students, and fixed his eye upon one of them, unfortunately a plain-looking youth, whom he pointed out with his fingers to his suite, saying, 'Mark, what mouth, what snout (*roza morda*, literally a vulgar and contemptuous expression applicable to a pig). I will wager that he is a wretch, capable of any crimes.'

The unhappy student thus described happened precisely to be remarkable for his good conduct and proficiency; and as the professor ventured to whisper the fact to the counsellor of state, Muchanow, who is at the head of the public instruction in Poland, Muchanow thought it his duty to repeat it to the emperor, but his majesty rebuked him in no gentle terms, and told him to hold his tongue, while he himself gave vent to his angry feelings, in a lecture to the students, in a tone and spirit very similar to his celebrated speech, bestowed on the municipality of Warsaw. On this occasion he closed his personal admonition to the students with the exhortation that they were henceforward to behave in such a manner as to deserve the good opinion of the marshal, as otherwise he would close their school and distribute the students without distinction among his different regiments, where they would be obliged to serve as common soldiers and recruits. It is not difficult to imagine the consternation which this imperial speech has spread in every Polish family.

Article 262. (April 25, 1846, pages 122 to 126)

On these five pages of this issue, *Niles' National Register* had reported on a major address given to the appropriate committee chairman of the United States House of Representatives on February 26, 1846 by one of its members, concerning tariffs and the price of wheat and grain from the Baltic region of Europe versus wheat exported to Great Britain from the United States, a matter that accentuated a mutual problem both for farmers in the United States and for peasants in Poland. In that remarkable speech, Congressman Charles Hudson (1795-1881) of Massachusetts, speaking on the matter of the greater exportation of American wheat to Great Britain, on one hand, nonetheless expressed, in the next to the last paragraph of his report, a concern for the competitive exportation of wheat from the Baltic region to England *by down-trodden Polish, and Russian, for that matter, farm laborers of that era*, on the other hand.

The present, Mr. Chairman, is an important era in the history of our country. The president, at the opening of the session, recommended the abandonment of that policy which is coeval with our government, a policy under which the nation has grown and prospered. We have also been told by the secretary of the treasury that we must abandon all protection of domestic industry, in order to procure the repeal of the English *corn laws*. The British ministry approve of the policy recommended, endorse the doctrines of the American secretary, and order his report to be published and laid upon the desks of the members of parliament as a valuable document to promote British interests. An effort has been made on both sides of the Atlantic to change fundamentally the policy of this country, by the introduction of a system which would check the prosperity of the people, paralyze every interest, and so greatly impair that very commerce which these improvements are calculated to promote. We see Sir Robert Peel and Sir Robert Walker in what the gentleman from S. Carolina (Mr. Rhett) calls 'a disastrous conjunction,' to bring about this result, a result truly disastrous to our beloved country, but to Great Britain a consummation devoutly to be wished.

The subject of the corn trade of the United States has of late attracted the attention of our people; and, although, it is one of importance, I am confident that its importance has been greatly overrated. From the language that is sometimes employed we might naturally infer that wheat and flour constituted a great portion of the exports of the country. But a recurrence to official documents will show that for a series of years our export of wheat and flour does not exceed one-twentieth of our whole export.

I propose, Mr. Chairman, to take a brief view of the wheat trade of the United States. And here I will state, once for all, that I shall use the term wheat to include *flour*; and, in all my estimates, I make a barrel of flour to be equal to five bushels of wheat. The wheat crop of the

United States in 1840, according to the census returns, amounted to 84,823,000 bushels, and in 1844, according to the report of the commissioner of patents, to 95,607,000 bushels. Of this 96,000,000 bushels, which is about the average for the last five years, we have exported about one-thirteenth, or 7,400,000 bushels. Nearly one-tenth of the whole crop will be required for seed. In Great Britain the estimate has been about three bushels of wheat to the acre, but with us two bushels to the acre would be a fair average, for all parts of the country. Now, if we should take from the whole crop the amount required for seed and the amount exported, it would leave for home consumption 79,000,000 of bushels. This amount divided among our population, 19,600,000, would give 3 and 9-10ths bushels to every man, woman and child in the country.

I have no disposition to disparage the wheat trade of the country; it is an important trade, and one which should be cherished with the greatest care. But devotion to any cause should never lead us to overlook an important fact. I am able to rejoice that we are able to wheat at an average rate of six million dollars a year. I am in favor of the corn trade of the country; and for that very reason I wish to inform the wheat growers that the proposed change in the British corn laws will probably operate against them, and may prove highly detrimental to their interests.

I am confident, Mr. Chairman, that there is a great apprehension on the subject of trade. Some gentlemen seem to take it for granted that Great Britain is the principal, and almost the only market for our breadstuff. But nothing can be more false. I have data, drawn from the official documents of the government, which confute any such hypothesis:

Table of exports of Wheat and Flour in bushels, to some of the principal markets, and also the total amount of exports, to all foreign countries, for fourteen consecutive years: 1831-1844.

Year	G. Britain.	British N. A. colonies	Cuba.	Brazil.	All foreign countries.
Average	944,536	1,166,048	386,155	896,711	5,505,162

But suppose that her demand increases, where will she obtain her supply? Where has she obtained it in years past? In 1841, 1842, and 1843, when she made her largest importations, averaging 18,300,000 bushels, or about 54,000,000 for three years, her supply was obtained from the following nations in the proportion:

346

As Reported in the "Niles' Register"

Importation of wheat into Great Britain from the principal wheat countries for 1841, 1842, and 1843, in bushels, together with the sum total from each country:

Countries.	1841.	1842.	1843.	Total.
Russia,	498,205	1,1824,688	269,368	2,592,261
Denmark,	1,915,019	617,636	565,248	3,098,183
Prussia,	7,134,400	5,938,065	5,311,000	18,383,465
Germany,	5,215,674	1,626,172	1,027,224	7,949,070
Holland,	815,964	73,990	6,864	896,502
France,	1,643,932	4,216,400	29,248	5,889,280
Italy & Isl.,	901,600	4,878,597	24,810	5,805,037
N. America colonies,	2,333,354	3,729,402	2,790,504	4,853,548
United States,	3,227,540	1,195,873	749,601	3,053,278
All other countries,	866,859	1,816,340	272,407	2,955,606

Reading the original copy of a newspaper article some 174 years old is a reminder of what occurred -- best described by the expression, "ravages of time" -- to the clarity of the print during that period of time. As such, sorry to say, that the aggregated numbers appearing in the three-year table above had been so distorted by age, fading and blotting, so that, at best, the totals per country can only be held to approximate (on a "ballpark estimate" basis, as yet another expression goes) the original figures.

Here, sir, we have a view of the demand and supply of the English market for three successive years. And does it appear that that market is ours? And is the United States the only country on which Great Britain is to depend on their breadstuff? A glance at this table will show at once that our supply, when compared with that of the continent, dwindles almost to insignificance. *Russia supplies nearly as much as the United States....* To show the relative importance of our trade to G. Britain, it is barely necessary to that of every hundred bushels sent to the English market, we supply only five....

In 1840, the British government called upon their consuls, at some of the principal marts of the corn trade, to inform them what amount of grain could be sent to the English market in case the English duty were reduced to a nominal sum. The substance of their replies will be seen in the following table, submitted with their support, to the parliament in 1841:

St. Petersburgh	1,540,000 bushels
Liebau	240,000 "
Warsaw	2,400,000 "
Odessa	1,200,000 "
Stockholm	8,000 "
Dantzic	2,520,000 "
Konigsburg	520,000 "
Stettsic	2,000,000 "
Memel	47,712 "
Hamburg	4,324,000 "
Elsinore	1,400,000 "
Palermo	1,600,000 "
	17,779,000

> The same occurred with the numbers associated with the export ports reported above. At this point in my book, I also remind readers that once-Polish cities of Dantzic, Konigburg and Stettsic had been known to Poles as Gdańsk, Królowiec and Szczecin.

From Riga the consul writes: 'When the foreign demand is very urgent, the distant provinces of Smolensk, Kaluga, and Orel send supplies to Riga.... From Warsaw the answer is, 'that the quantity of wheat grown in Poland has increased considerably for the last six years, and the production might no doubt be further gradually increased if there were a steady demand for foreign corn in England.'

The questions which now present themselves for our consideration are these: Why have we sent so little to England direct? And why so much to England through Canada? The answer to each of these questions is obvious. *In our direct trade we come in competition with the north of Europe, and the low prices of labor enables them to undersell us in the English market.* This is the reason, and the only satisfactory reason, why our direct trade with England has been so small. And the reason why we have sent so much to England through Canada is equally obvious. Our wheat which goes into Canada is, after being manufactured into flour, admitted into Great Britain on the colonial duty, which is much less than her duty on the flour from this country. I have examined the English tables of actual duties paid during each week of 1843, and I find the mean differences between the duty actually paid on colonial and foreign wheat to be fourteen shillings per quarter, or thirty-three cents per bushel. All the wheat, therefore, which we send through Canada, is admitted into the English market on terms more favorable by thirty-three cents a bushel, than the wheat which we send direct. From this, however, we must take the Canadian duty of the average of eight cents per bushel which reduces the sum to twenty-five cents.

Now this advantage of twenty-five cents per bushel, this monopoly of the colonial trade which we enjoy, and of which the north of Europe is deprived of is what enables us to send more than two-thirds of our export of wheat to Great Britain. *But repeal the corn laws of England, and we are deprived of this monopoly, and are brought directly into competition with the great wheat growing countries on the Baltic, where the agricultural laborers can be obtained for from eight pence to a shilling per day, and board themselves.* Are the independent yeomanry of the west prepared to yield all the benefits of the Canada trade, and thus lose two-thirds of the market which they now enjoy? *Are they willing to be brought into competition with the down trodden Poles and serfs of Russia, and to be compelled to labor* for *fifteen of twenty cents per day?* Would devotion to party, or the satisfaction of following out the delusive theory of free trade, reconcile them to a condition so degraded? If they possess the independent spirit of freemen, if they are Americans, they will spurn such an idea....

The great mass of our people are born to other inheritance than the privilege which our country holds out to every industrious man of obtaining a comfortable living by the fruit of his own toil; and he is a free man, indeed, who is born to such a patrimony. The consciousness that he can sustain himself by his own hands, and that well directed industry will enable him to provide for the maintenance of his family and the education of his family, and the education of his children, more than any thing else, gives character to all Americans, and makes what he was designed to be by his Creator – a man.

Article 263. (April 25, 1846, page 128)

This issue reported the end of Poland's latest struggle to reclaim the right to exist as a free and independent nation by way of the miniscule Republic of Kraków, on one hand, and Imperial Russia's determination to eliminate even that tiny remaining vestige of the once-extensive Commonwealth of Poland and Lithuania. Finally, an accusation that Russia abused and martyred Catholic nuns had been disproved by an inquiry conducted in the Vatican.

{CHRONICLE.} POLAND. We had, in a German paper the manifesto of the revolutionists of the Free City of Cracow, which presents their movement in a more imposing aspect than we had attributed to the movement. The Polish committee at Paris, too, we perceive, countenanced the affair, though they say it had been prematurely developed. Prince Czartorisky had been called upon, and responds favorably; his estates in Gallicia {sic} are now therefore confiscated.

POLAND. Unhappy Poland! The revolution has been suppressed. The Austrian forces again occupy Cracow.

Sentence of the Polish prisoners. The *Courier de Varsovie* contains the following: 'The undermentioned is the result of the investigation set on foot owing to the events at Siedlec, and the arrests of various persons: 1. That a conspiracy took place, with ramifications in the Polish provinces; 2. That the head of the conspiracy, Bronislas Dombrowski, sent from Posen, was chosen leader of the conspiracy on the right bank of the Vistula; 3. That the principal abettors were Pantaldon Potoski, Stanislaus Koeischewski, Ladislas Zarski, Jean Lytinski, Michel Mireski, and Antony Deskur. The agents and accomplices of Dombrowski were Stephen Dobritch and Charles Ruprecht. All these individuals brought before a counsel of war, have been found guilty of rebellion and sedition. According to the powers entrusted by his majesty the emperor, the prince-governor, after sentence of death was pronounced, has ordered Potoski, Koeischewski, and Zarski to be hung; the first at Siedlec, the other at Warsaw. As regard Dobrich and Ruprecht, their sentence is to be commuted on the scaffold to banishment to Siberia, with a loss of all their rights. Mireski and Deskur are deprived of all their rights, and share the same fate as Dobritch and Ruprecht. Lytinski, who showed a true repentance, is equally banished to Siberia, with the loss of all his rights, after receiving 500 stripes. The law to enter into full force, as regards the confiscation of their property, according to Art. 171, book 1st, of the military criminal code. As regards any property falling to them by inheritance, it will be adjudged according to Polish law. This sentence was fulfilled the following day at 10 o'clock, a.m., in front of the citadel, with the exception of Potoski.

RUSSIA: *The tale of the Catholic nuns*, having been subjected to ill treatment and martyrdom by Russian authority, has, by enquiry conducted by the Catholic authorities of Rome, been entirely disproved. The authors of the slander have not yet been detected.

Article 264. (May 2, 1846, page front-page)

In this issue, *Niles' National Register* reported two additional news-briefs about the Republic of Kraków, which was all that was left of the once-great Commonwealth of Poland and Lithuania.

FRANCE: "M. Guizot, it is said, has applied to Lord Aberdeen proposing to have a consul for each nation at Cracow, in order to watch the proceedings of the three continental powers, in regard to any encroachment on the liberties of that republic.... In a discussion on Polish affairs, M. Thiers has assailed vigorously the policy of the Louis Philippe Guizot policy."

POLAND: "The insurrection is crushed. The leaders were being imprisoned in all quarters. Potocki, one of the leaders of the late revolt has been condemned to death, and executed at Siedlec."

Article 265. (October 3, 1846, Page 69)

Despite Poland's struggles for the right to exist as a unified, free and independent nation and nationality in all its aspects, her people continued to sustain the fact of Poland's having been considered to be Europe's bread-basket, as the statistics supporting the news-article titled, "The Grain Crop of 1846," and its sub-set table titled, "Prices of Grain," readily illustrated in *American dollars*, nearly throughout the period of the aftermath of the November Uprising of 1830 through 1849. Of special note had been the fact that as the November Uprising continued, Poland's grain production suffered, so much so that its landowners apparently had been forced to lower their costs per bushel so as to remain competitive in price with the other European marts of trade, but as the years moved on, the high quality of Poland's grain enabled its landowners to recover at higher prices per bushel remarkably during the years 1840 to 1842. Whereas the 1830 price per bushel of $1.07 at Dantzic (Gdańsk), for example, never recovered until 1840, when it reached the same per bushel price it had enjoyed a decade earlier, the inescapable fact of the matter had been that the costs per bushel at Hamburg, Amsterdam, Antwerp and Odessa had also been influenced by Russia's having created, along with Prussia and Austria, the political and social turmoil in Poland and elsewhere that disrupted other European marts of trade as well.

The year 1843 ominously anticipated the coming "Spring of Nations" upheavals and disruptions not only in central and eastern Europe, but also, for other reasons, in western Europe as well, with France being the key example of having precipitated yet another domestic revolution leading to the governance, beginning in 1848, of the Second Republic of France, by Charles-Louis Napoleon Bonaparte (1808-1873), who had won election by the people of France to be its President. He had been the nephew of the earlier Emperor Napoleon Bonaparte (1804-1814). In 1852, President Charles-Louis Napoleon Bonaparte, having been unable constitutionally to run for re-election as President, seized power and declared himself to be Napoleon III, "emperor of the French."

Prices of Grain. The following table taken from 'parliamentary reports,' will show the prices of wheat, per bushel, in the principal marts of trade on the continent of Europe, from 1830 to 1843, inclusive:

	Dantzic	Hamburg	Amsterdam	Antwerp	Odessa
1830	1.07	93	1.13	95	68
1831	1.18	1.19	1.15	1.07	71
1832	93	90	1.10	90	62
1833	83	70	89	55	61
1834	70	67	66	50	77
1835	60	65	76	68	57
1836	70	79	76	70	52
1837	73	76	81	99	50
1838	94	79	1.20	1.48	65
1839	96	1.15	1.33	1.37	79
1840	1.07	1.30	1.11	1.48	71
1841	1.23	99	1.09	1.45	74
1842	1.10	1.11	1.11	95	66
1843	76	82	78	76	48
Avg.	91	90	99	98	64

Please note for those readers who might be inclined to corroborate the averages (i.e., of the "Pieces of Grain") displayed in this particular *Niles' National Register* issue of October 3, 1846, one must first consider all prices that included a decimal to be (for obtaining the average for a column, for example, such as that for Gdańsk) a single unit of measure without the decimal where 1.07 should be entered as 107 in the tabulation, thereby producing 91 as the average. By so doing, here finally, the numbers work precisely.

Article 266. (October 28, 1846, page 128)

As an example of its capacity for vengeance, Imperial Russia, with great audacity, sought to extradite Major Gaspar Tochman -- a Pole by birth, who before he became a naturalized American citizen, had participated in the Polish Uprising against Russia in 1830, some 14 years earlier! He is the same Tochman (see *Article 248*) who lobbied for the passage of the Vermont Resolutions and others cited earlier in my study. He had been a well-known publicist in the United States about the massive Russian cruelties perpetrated against Polish civilians and military prisoners of war. That had been the precise reason -- to end his campaign for informing Americans about the true nature of Imperial Russia -- why Russia sought to extradite him. *Niles' National Register* credited the source of the following story as having been the *N. Y. Herald* newspaper.

A Russian Movement. A Washington letter in the *N.Y. Herald* says: -- 'Major G. Tochman, a Polish exile, but now a citizen of the U.S., and a regular practicing attorney at this city, is at present involved in some little international difficulty, about which, however, we need have no sort of apprehension. The Autocrat of All the Russias has his minister here, the Baron Bodisco, to have major Tochman surrendered over to the Russian government and its tender mercies, as a criminal against her laws. The mildest fate of the major, if given up, would be his transfer to the mines of Siberia. His crime is a participation in the Polish revolutionary war of 32. We have only to say, that as the major has since become a citizen of the United States, we can't spare him. The information of this movement we received this morning, unofficially, at the State Department. We shall be able to lay before you the details in the case in a day or two, most likely.

The referenced "Baron Bodisco" had been Alexander Bodisko, Russia's "Minister" (i.e., Ambassador) to the United States at the time, whose dates of service in that capacity had been 1837-1854. During his long tenure as Russia's ambassador to the United States, one of his objectives had been to soften Russia's image, and that of Czar Nicholas I, as it had been portrayed in the American press, particularly as it related to Poland, but generally as well. When he had been an urbane 54 year-old widower and diplomat, Bodisko -- fatefully, as far as his personal life had been concerned, and as well professionally, as far as discharging his duty to Russia had been concerned -- fell in love with a Washington-born 16 year-old American beauty, Harriet Williams, whom he married. With her, he staged lavish receptions, dinners, recitals and soirées in their home that reportedly had been the "talk of the town" among the city's socialites, the ambassadorial corps, and our nation's lawmakers on Capitol Hill, among others. An affable, highly-skilled and popular diplomat throughout his service, on the day of his funeral, the United States Congress had been placed in recess so that its members could pay their final respects when he was buried in the city's Georgetown section.

On July 15, 2020, via the front-page of the website of the *Russkiy Mir* (Russian World) Foundation that Vladimir Putin created in 2007, included prominently was the article titled, "Alexander Bodisko, the Wisest and Most Popular Diplomat," with its related statement that: "As the ambassador, Alexander Bodisko urged the imperial government to maintain ties with the United States as Russia's 'traditional ally' and 'the only one real and reliable political friend' (a definition by Alexander Bodisko). He also persistently suggested Nicholas I to join efforts with the United States and divide the territory of Upper California and San Francisco Bay between Russia and the US. However, Karl Nesselrode, then Chancellor and Minister of Foreign Affairs of the Russian Empire, did not support such position."

Incredibly, therefore, the related *Russkiy Mir* (Russian World) website expressions quoted above of the February 19, 2019 posting date on its website, of the story of Alexander Bodisko, *nearly matched verbatim* those of Gaspar (Kacper in Polish) Tochman some 176 years earlier, when he warned Americans, in that instance, by way of writing to the Editor of the New York Advertiser newspaper, not to be hoodwinked by Russian propaganda, stating: "*that in the last ten years that many a writer has propagated in your country the doctrines, that 'Russia is the only real and natural ally of these United States in Europe....*" Furthermore, Tochman also warned Americans that Russia had been "attempting to undermine the free institutions of this great republic...." Sounds familiar, doesn't it, as we reflect on the period beginning in 2016 and thereafter in the United States. Refer back to *Article 248* once again for the full recounting of the substance of Tochman's warning of some 176 years ago.

That's precisely why Bodisko sought to extradite Tochman, a naturalized American citizen, to Russia, so as to permanently silence his voice of opposition to a U. S. - Russia détente (in which Russia would aspire to enjoy for itself being on a "most favored nation basis" with the United States), and of course, to punish Tochman for having been a Polish freedom fighter against Russia in the November Uprising of 1830 and thereafter.

Article 267. (December 26, 1846, front-page)

The expression -- "too little, too late" -- best describes Western European attempts to prevent the demise and extinction of the Republic of Kraków. These two front-page articles about Austria's annexation of the once-independent Republic of Kraków reported that the final small free vestige of the once-powerful and geographically extensive Commonwealth of Poland and Lithuania, no longer existed.

The Republic of Cracow. The diplomatic world seems to have been surprised and shocked by the annexation of the republic of Cracow to the Austrian dominions, with the consent of Prussia and Russia. The English and French papers consider this a violation of the compacts of the treaty of Vienna. The London Times says: 'The sensation produced by this event in France and throughout Germany has been deep and strong. Such acts of power are not wrought with impunity; such calamities are not endured in vain. The imperious violence of Russia, the timid craft of Austria, have combined to strike off one of the branches of the treaty of Vienna; and the weak and vacillating court of Berlin, disapproving of the harshness of one of its accomplices and the lesser practices of the other, has lent itself to sanction the work of encroachment and oppression. The protest against such deeds is one of opinion even more than of political influence and authority; and we venture to affirm that the protest will be universal throughout the world, and must again bring the governance of England and France to co-operate in a common cause.

Protest of England against the occupation of Cracow. Lord Palmerston had despatched the protest of the British government against the occupation of Cracow, to Lord Posonby, at Vienna. In this document Lord Palmerston argues on the assumption that the occupation of Cracow is as yet but a project, and he exerts himself to demonstrate the mischief (inconvenience) of such a measure. He subsequently discusses the two questions of 'right' and of 'necessity.' On the question of right he establishes, by reference to treaties, that the articles agreed to solemnly by eight powers could not be modified or annulled by three of them. Upon the question of necessity, Lord Palmerston does not admit the solution which the northern courts wished should be adopted.

Article 268. (December 26, 1846, front-page)

Throughout my work on this book, and impossible for me to ignore, had been the persistent deadly undercurrent of the spread of cholera, not only on the blood-soaked battlefields of what had once been part and parcel the Commonwealth of Poland and Lithuania, but also in Europe generally, usually progressing out of central Asia from the East to the West, in the manner of a virus even though cholera is a bacterial disease rather than a viral disease. Accordingly, I have noted that *Niles' National Register* had reported on this health-related scourge of European and Eurasian nations as best it could, based on reports from Europe. To his credit, Jeremiah Hughes, the third in the line of the four Editors of *Niles' National Register*, corrected related mistakes reported on cholera or anything else that impacted the lives of embattled and suffering Poles and others as well, either of his own doing, or that of his European correspondents, on whom the *Register* depended for European and world news, as the following added front-page news article illustrates:

Cholera. The telegraph, from which the abstract of intelligence in our last, brought by the *Cambria*, was communicated from Boston, *was misunderstood as to twelve of the Royal family of France having died of cholera*. It should have read, twelve of the Royal Family of *Persia*, in which kingdom the disease was raging with terrible violence. The number of deaths already ascertained in the principal cities are given as follows: Teheran, 14,000 to 17,000; Kermanshah, 9,000; Ispahan, 7,000; Reschid, 3,000; Hamadan, 3,700; Meshed, 2,000; Shiras, 750. A letter on the 14th from Tabriz, mentions the breaking out of the cholera; two hundred victims fell the first day of which we have any record.

The accounts received in England from Asia Minor, of the 15th ultimo, left its cities in a state of complete consternation. Some estimated the number of deaths as high as 40 or 50,000 but this is regarded as an exaggeration. The latest intelligence mentions the presence of that malady at Mossoul, Orfa, Diarbekir, Aleppo, Damascus, etc. From a letter of recent date from Teheran, it appears that from the 1st to the 7th ultimo, the mortality was so great that there was no time for the decent burial of the dead; they were brought out of the city in loads, to be thrown into large pits dug for that purpose. In Kermanshah the ovens and shops were closed, the butchers and bakers refusing to supply the

356

city with provisions, and most families were by this reduced to such a state of famine that there were considerable apprehensions of a general revolt against the government. In other parts of the country, the population had fled to the mountains, often abandoning their families, goods and property, and happy is the family, indeed, that has not lost one of its members.

Article 269. (December 26, 1846, page 268)

Niles' National Register reported about commerce and trade, on the supplies of grain stored in major European entrepots, including Gdańsk (Dantzic), referenced under "Breadstuff Statistics." The report's reference to *New Russia* bears special attention. One of the aspirations of Czarina Catherine II (1762-1796) had been to match Western Europe's colonization of the New World in the Western Hemisphere where in North America there had been proclaimed a New Amsterdam, New England and New France, along with sub-sets of states in the united States, known as New Hampshire, New Jersey and New York; and in Canada with the province of Nova Scotia (New Scotland); and in American cities such as New Ashford, New Bedford, New Britain, New Brunswick, New Chester, New Gloucester, New Ipswich, New Kent, New Orleans, New Oxford, New Suffolk, New York and New Windsor.

With the creation, if accomplished, of an equivalent New Russia region by eliminating and replacing the Ottoman Empire's control of the Balkan lands and others, including Ukraine, along the entire littoral of the Black Sea, the plan might have included moving the capital of Imperial Russia from, or at least create a warm-water co-capital apart from St. Petersburgh (or perhaps, on a similar version of the much later 20th century-like "summer White House" in the United States) to a new location, likely to be termed *Czarigrad*, which was to replace what originally had been the great ancient Greco-Christian city, Constantinople (Konstantinopolis), the seat of one of ancient Christianity's Patriarchs, that after its fall to the Turks in 1453, became known in Turkic as Istanbul.

With the fall of Constantinople by the sword of Islam in 1453, Russian Orthodoxy held Moscow concomitantly to have become the "Third Rome" (after Rome itself, the original seat of a Patriarch of Christianity and of the burial site of Saint Peter, the first "Vicar of Christ" on Earth), following Constantinople which had been Christianity's "Second Rome" in the opinion of the Russian Orthodox Church, from which the worldwide leadership of purely untainted Christianity had passed allegedly -- both the-oretically and permanently -- per God's divine will, thereby making Russia the world's paramount Christian nation, that included Moscow's succession as Christianity's "Third Rome."

The harvest has been magnificent in the ancient Polish provinc-es and in New Russia which supply Odessa, in the Black Sea, Taganrog, Rostow, and the other ports on the Sea of Azof. The enormous expor-tations in the years 1844 and 1845, give, in those countries, a great im-pulse to the cultivation of white crops; the extraordinary temperature of the present year has been favorable to their development. As to the quantity, the people of Poland and Russia, living on rye, and the peo-ple of Bessarabia, living on maize, nearly the whole of the wheat may be considered as surplus and for exportation. In 1845, nearly 4,000,000 hectolitres of grain were exported from Odessa; and the quantity dis-posable in 1846 and 1847 will not be less than 6,000,000 independent of the produce of Poland. The countries of the Sea of Azof may supply above 1,500,000 hectolitres....

The table of the stores of grain the principal entrepots of Europe in the last fortnight in October:

Nice	qrs.	20,793
Genoa		22,083
Leghorn		25,290
Amsterdam		431,021
Rotterdam		46,224
Hamburg		18,300
Danzic		90,000
London		149,700
Liverpool		134,040
Glasgow		53,727
Leith		40,077
TOTAL		998,274

Whereas the numbers displayed here had been crystal clear upon my inspection of the original on-line copy of *Niles' National Register*, the actual total comes to 1,031,255.

Article 270. (October 2, 1847, pages 69 and 70)

In this issue, a comprehensive account of the origin and history of the Republic of Kraków's insurrection was provided to American readers of *Niles' National Register*. Before engaging the referenced article, I believe that the importance of Hezekiah Niles' publication vis-à-vis embattled Poland from 1811 to 1849 cannot be overstated.

Despite the fact that Hezekiah Niles passed away in 1839, his steady unwavering support for the cause of Poland, influenced his three successors as Editors of the *Niles' National Register* to sustain his tradition of portraying Poland, based on the publication of news reports as they developed, as the unyielding, principled, and always-courageous victim of a barbarous, unprincipled and inhumane Russia under Czar Nicholas I.

For the purposes of this book, the original *Niles' Register* tradition of standing up for Poland had its clearly purposeful origin, I propose for your consideration, in Hezekiah Niles' decision to publish his editorial -- "The Russians and the Cossacks" -- in the April 30, 1814 issue of the *Niles' Weekly Register* as his innovative newsmagazine had been termed at that time. Indeed, in *Article 6* of this book, Hezekiah Niles introduced an example, as I consider it to have been, of the concept of a yet-to-be-defined ethnic cleansing in extremis, perpetrated by Russia under Czarina Catherine II as it pertained to the fate of some 70,000 Armenians who had been removed during the winter of 1778 from the Crimea for re-settlement in the lands taken from the Nogai Tartars by Russia on the western shore of the Sea of Azov. Moving that many people on foot during the winter, at the cost of the loss of some 63,000 of the 70,000 Armenians who basically froze to death, their only shelter having been to dig holes in the ground and covering themselves by whatever could be used as protection against the frigid elements, and writing off their deaths as "owing to the bad management of those who were commissioned to provide for them," the managers having been Imperial Russian administrators, most likely on the military side of the equation, reflects a well-known characteristic of Russian national heartlessness and disregard for human rights and human suffering, for the ages.

Had the fate of the 70,000 Armenians of Crimea been more than *ethnic cleansing*, or could it be held to have been an early attribute, along with the example of Poland, of yet another Russian prototype of an as yet-to-be-articulated genocide of sorts, in this case, "accidental" because of what had been reported as "bad management," versus having been a cleverly-planned "purposeful" genocide since Russia had been adept at staging both disgusting options?

Along with his having addressed the late 18th century's yet-to-be-articulated *ethnic cleansing* of the Armenians of Crimea by Russia that involved attributes of annihilation that led to what in the 20th century might have been deemed to be a *genocide* (but as I have agreed earlier that during the 19thcentury's first half in European history, the word annihilation is more aptly applied, given the absence of the word genocide in those days), no better example of the continued dedication of Hezekiah Niles' successors' determination to engender sympathy and support for Poland, in its struggles against Russia, can be demonstrated than by this much later example, being the fully-transcribed text titled "EUROPEAN POLITICS," next presented below, taken from the October 2, 1847 issue of the *Niles' National Register*.

Our readers are aware that the Russian government recently ordered two of the Polish patriots that had partaken in the Cracow insurrection, to be executed. That government has found no little difficulty since their execution, to suppress the sympathetic demonstrations of their suffering countrymen. Their graves immediately became a shrine, and the dormant devotion to Poland was everywhere discernable amongst the millions of that once glorious republic now galled by the yoke of despots.

Please remember that the entire article had been written by Americans, successors of Hezekiah Niles, who taught them well, to be on the right side of history in their support of Poland's relentlessly gallant, battle-proven aspiration to restore its right to exist as a free and independent nation among the nations of the world. As this article proceeds, it is appropriate that it includes reference to Ludwik Mierosławski (1814–1878), the Polish general who took part in the November Uprising of 1830 in Poland, the Great Poland Uprising of 1846, the uprisings of 1848 in Poland and Germany, the Italian Revolutionary Army, and in the January Uprising of 1863 in Poland. Thus, his life had served, and will continue to serve forever, as a classic example of a 19th century Polish freedom fighter in the struggle for freedom in Europe, beginning in Poland.

As Reported in the "Niles' Register"

EUROPEAN POLITICS: The remarkable and probably eventful revolution now taking place in Italy, to which we devoted a considerable portion of our last week's *Register*, is but one of many portentous movements which at this time threaten the existing peace of Europe. The south of Europe, Spain and Portugal, seem to be effectually split into petty factions, that there is little difficulty in their royal neighbors keeping them as mere incidental appendages to their own objects, so long as peace can be maintained. The same appears to be the unhappy fate of Switzerland and Greece. But Prussia presents at present a more imposing front in the political field. We have looked with deep anxiety to the course which her hesitating King, her new diet, and her more enlightened people shall take in the army that is about being made in behalf of liberal principles. Seeds have not only been widely sown, but are rapidly germinating in that direction, which portend a coming harvest. May it be allowed time and fair opportunity to mature into peaceful blessings upon mankind.

POLAND: The revolution of Cracow. Our readers are aware that the Russian government recently ordered two of the patriots that had partaken in the Cracow insurrection, to be executed. That government has found no little difficulty since their execution, to suppress the sympathetic demonstration of their suffering countrymen. Their graves immediately became a shrine, and the dormant devotion to Poland was every where discernable amongst the millions of that once glorious republic now galled by the yoke of despots.

The authorities of Prussia have between two and three hundred of the Polanders, implicated in the revolution of Cracow, now on trial for the alleged offence. *The eyes of all Europe, of all intelligent mankind, indeed, are directed towards Prussia, now standing as she has done on the verge of revolution herself, to see how these will be disposed of. Popular feeling is alive upon the spot, and whoever has deplored the fate of Poland, will be as anxious for the fate of these additional victims.*

Ludwik Mierosławski. freedom fighter

That our readers may be in possession of a more accurate history of the revolution of Cracow, and of the nature of the impending trials, we subjoin a fuller statement that has heretofore been inserted, the facts derived principally from the *Schnellpost*.

The Polish Prisoners at Berlin. The trial of the Polish prisoners apprehended at Posen in February last, part of them fugitives of Cracow, has been in progress at Berlin during the few weeks of latter arrivals from Europe. The state advocate Wenzel drew up the act of accusation. We learn from the *Schnellpost* that it forms a folio of 450 pages besides an appendix of 25, and it is subdivided into special accusations against each one of the 254 accused and exhibits some idea of the organization principles and aims of the 'Polish Democratic Union' which is organized in Europe. The fate of the prisoners it is feared will be condemnation to death, but in fear of Polish sympathies, may be softened as far as respect for its allies Russia and Austria will allow, into perpetual imprisonment to some and temporary to others.

The Cracow insurrection was started from the partial machinations of the 'Polish Democratic Union' whose seat exists in France. The 'aristocratic' Polish exiles have no concern with this union. *The democratic union is based upon the impression that Poland cannot rely upon the efforts of her nobility and gentry alone, that they are not sensible of what is needed in order to arouse the true popular feeling of the masses of the oppressed nation, and that it must be based in equality, liberty and fraternity if the desire of again raising Poland is to be effectively carried out.*

'The Polish Democratic Union' as organized in France consists of a central administration committee with its ramifying sections named according to their geographic seat. The former had its seat in Paris, but in 1837 was transferred to Poitiers, and in 1840 to Versailles.

In 1838 discussions were commenced throughout their bodies as to the questions, what are the internal resources of Poland socially and politically; how must the supreme power be organized at the crisis of insurrection; what rights must be suspended during its progress; what political maxims are to be held forth in the organization and struggle of their military powers; what civil rights to be guaranteed to the masses to secure their sympathy or secure their adhesion; what system of warfare is the most appropriate for their objects; lastly what shall be the nature of their government during the insurrection.

In 1843 the union formed a military school. The number of its members is now estimated at 3,600. Next a finance chamber was organized in Posen. Another influence in this quarter infused itself into its body, bearing the same relation to it that the terrorists bore to the Girondists. The democratic union made use of the ready pen of Mieroslawski, (first named and reputed head of the late revolt) to combat this tendency. In Posen, it found supporters, and they formed themselves into detached unions. Mieroslawski went thither in order to compose the differences and obtain funds; but after ineffectual efforts and the partial detection of the conspiracy, he discovered that to procrastinate would lead to a wider discovery and the consequence was, that the whole plot in its immatured state necessarily exploded, with but a shadow of its original plan realized in Cracow.

On December 4th, 1833, the central body at Poitiers put forth a manifesto, in which they set forth to bring to their fellow countrymen among other things, the grounds of the failure of former struggles in Poland, and what is more important, the requisitions to be brought to their support in any future effort.

'The crime committed against Poland has not destroyed the political existence of the nation; its life is not annihilated. Our ceaseless struggle for independence since the confederation of Bar, the streams of blood we have poured forth in so many centuries, our present exile, the ruthless animosity of the dividers of Poland, and the universal sympathy of other people gives incontrovertible testimony, that the Polish nation still lives, and that she is secure of her future. Poland feels in herself her exhaustless resources. People are accustomed to demand new points of starting. Their oppressors then tremble. What can be so universal cannot be a falsehood. The voice of humanity was ever the voice of God. The great mission of Poland is not yet completed.'

The manifesto then went on to show the futility of any attempt which would be made by the mere nobility, etc. of Poland, without enlisting the masses by some amelioration of their condition in their social requirements.

> To their credit, the patriotic Polish freedom-fighters always understood what the stakes had been -- as established by Imperial Russia -- from the outset, that objective clearly having been the full "annihilation" of Poland's free and independent *political existence, Poland's history*, the Polish nationality and language, and the *Roman Catholic Church of Poland*. Being familiar with all aspects of their existential challenge enabled them to fight, resist and survive.

The design of the democratic union was to re-unite the divided parts of Poland into an independent dominion, a kingdom filled with democratic institutions. When in 1845, Mieroslawski went for the second time to Posen, he found the most extensive preliminaries, already prepared by other bodies, which were opposed to what they deemed the tardy movement of the central committee. Hence matters were immaturely precipitated. By his conferences with the Posen agitators, Mieroslawski became satisfied that an outbreak could no longer be deferred. He therefore came to understanding with them. At the desire of those implicated in Austrian and Russian Poland, Cracow was chosen as their centre. There agents might more readily gain access. At the house of Thaddeus Luciejewsky in Posen, they met and chose a member for Posen; Dr. Liebelt was selected. Mieroslawski next went in haste accompanied by Kosinski to Cracow to meet delegates from Little Russia and Galicia, it having been promised, that all proper measures should be taken during his absence. At Cracow he met with the agent from the kingdom of Poland, Liebowski, who informed him that the inception must not be made in Russian Poland but in some one of the neighboring provinces, and that on its full future development, the former would at once rise. After discussing, it was at last determined that it should commence in Galicia. Tyssowski, (afterwards dictator of Cracow and now in the United States, exiled by Austria) who was the head agent and of the democratic union for the district of Tarnow, Louis Gorzkowski, revolutionary organizer and chief for Cracow and upper Silesia, Count Francis Wiesiolowski, organizer of Galicia, also Count Ad. Bobrowski, Miecyslaus Skarzinski, each preferred commencing with Galicia.

On the 18th January, they proceeded to the choice of a national government, and elected Aleyato on the apart of all exiles, Dr. Liebelt for Prussian Poland, Count Wiesiolowski for Galicia, and Gorzkowski for Cracow; Victor Heltman, of the emigrants, was chosen secretary. This government it was determined should constitute itself at Cracow, and from the instant of revolt should exercise the dictatorship. The evening of 21st February, 1846, before the last of the carnival feast was fixed as the day.

In their second meeting, Mieroslawski made a report on the plan of campaign. Tyssowski and Kosinski dictated the proper instructions to the subordinate organs. On the 24th of January, some changes were adopted. Tyssowski was substituted in the place of Wiesiolowski, and later placed over Russian Poland. Mieroslawski next made return to the central body at Paris that they might now consider their eleventh year as finished, and that every member be ordered to betake himself to his post. Alevato, Wysocki and Heltman immediately started for Cracow. Mieroslawski put himself into extraordinary activity, was at Swiniary on the 5th of February, and gave directions for operations at Pletsch on the 13th, and at Rogowo on the 18th. On the 12th February he was arrested, and two days later, other confederates also.

The undertaking by this lost its leaders. In Posen it never came to a fair development. The news spread to Cracow, and in Galicia numerous arrests took place. The places of the arrested were supplied in Posen by others.

On the 18th February, an Austrian army approached Cracow, and on the following day commenced the siege. Aleyato who had arrived a few days previously fled. Liebelt was not to be found. Of the members of the national government, only Tyssowski and Gorzkowski were to be found.

On the night of the 20th and 21st of February, a body of insurgents in rear of the Austrian army made a serious attack upon them but were repelled, yet the army was forced by this attack to retreat to Podgorze. The government of Cracow was immediately organized and a manifesto issued proclaiming the Polish republic. Tyssowski and Gorzkowski have appointed Alexander Erzegorzewski as their colleague for the kingdom of Poland and Charles Rogowski as secretary. On the 23rd, Erzegorzewski and Gorzkowski withdrew from their offices. On the 24th it was proclaimed that Tyssowski was proclaimed as dictator. He made rapid exertions, but on the 1st of March, an overwhelming Austrian army forced him to fly into Prussia. On the 4th of March the allies retook Cracow. Tyssowski was delivered up from Prussia to Austria, and by the latter deprived of his estates and property and banished to America.

The principal names implicated by the present trials are Mieroslawski, Kosinsky, Dabrowski, Sadowsky, Ogrodowicz, and Tulodzesky. Their defence is based upon the plea that no high treason was meditated against Prussia, but that their efforts were against Russia.

The foregoing details enables us to account for the unhappy dissensions which took place between the Polish people and the Polish noblemen, after the surrender of Cracow, and *which resulted in the massacre of too many of the latter, dissensions and massacres which the French papers have never ceased accusing Austria of fomenting and occasioning. They give plausible reasons for the charge.*

Plausible reasons indeed. In the final paragraph above, benign reference is made to the "unhappy dissensions" between "the Polish people and the Polish noblemen" that in fact resulted in "the massacre of too many of the latter," which had been yet another tragedy, and more so a calamity as well, that befell Poland. Insofar as the Austrian government, in its effort to put down the uprising in Kraków, reputedly encouraged Galicja's peasants to rise up against and murder landed aristocrats and their families and for so doing, receiving cash payments from Austria as bounty for the severed heads of Polish noblemen, noblewomen and their children. This black episode of Austria's having precipitated the lethal outburst of class warfare in Polish history is known by way of a related hymn, the work of Kornel Ujejski (1823-1897), titled: Z dymem pożarów ("Through fiery smoke"), and in an original painting titled, "Massacre in Galicja" (Rzeź Galiczyjska) by Jan Lewicki (1795-1871).

Massacre in Galicja by Jan Lewicki

Article 271. (May 1, 1847, page 130)

Included in this issue, listed among a wide variety of topics, not the least of which had been that males outnumbered females in St. Petersburg by a ratio of 66% to 33%; another reflected the absolute degree of Russia's supremacy over Poland; a third, being the penalty for declarations of bankruptcy in the Russian Empire; a fourth, being the reference to Russia's "American colonies" which, at the time, meant Alaska that the United States went on to purchase from Russia twenty years later in 1867; and finally, abolishment of the knout in favor of the whip as an instrument of corporal punishment in Russia.

Russia. The *Warsaw Courier* states that, by order of the authorities, a *Te Deum* was chanted in the Cathedral at Warsaw in that city, 'as was a thanksgiving to God for permitting the Poles *to retain the happiness of living under the Russian dominion.'*

Reform -- the *knout*, is to be abolished in Russia and the whip to be substituted.

Bankruptcy -- By a recent ukase of the emperor, bankrupts are to be condemned to a perpetual banishment in Siberia. *The population of Russia* amounts at the present time to sixty millions, of which 52,092,000 are in European Russia, 4,850,000 in Poland, 1,520,000 in Finland. Siberia, the Caucasian provinces, and the American colonies have not been included in the census.

The population of St. Petersburg, what is now composed of 440,000 souls, presents singular circumstances, which is certainly unique in Europe, that it contains twice as many men as women, 292,000.

Article 272. (July 10, 1847, page 304)

A Polish Leader. The bark *Marcellus*, which arrived at this port from Palermo, brought passengers, John Tysosowski, his wife and three children. This gentleman took a prominent part in the last unfortunate Polish revolution, and was the supreme Dictator when it was brought to a close. He resided in Cracow, where he was an advocate of some distinction, having completed his legal studies at Vienna. When his hopes of freeing his country failed, he fled to Dresden, the capital of Saxony. He was demanded by the Austrian government, but was not surrendered until after long negotiations, and when given up it was stipulated that he should not be kept a prisoner. He was accordingly banished to the United States, and in consideration of his written agreement not to return, the government of Austria undertook to pay his passage over and to supply him with a certain sum of money on his arrival. He has now gone to Washington to receive this from the Austrian Ambassador. [*N.Y. Trib.*]

In Poland, Tysosowski's actual given name and surname had been Jan Tyssowski (1811-1857).

Article 273. (September 11, 1847, pages 27 to 29)

Great Britain's continuing official view on the matter of Poland is again illustrated here. Considerations of *realpolitik* by the government in London negated popular sympathy among the British people for Poland's struggle for a free and independent national existence by way of the remaining miniscule Republic of Kraków, and reveal Lord Palmerston's well-documented rationale for Great Britain's reluctance to go to war over the matter of the Republic of Kraków's freedom and independence, are worthy of a review and a better understanding.

ENGLISH ELECTIONEERING. The following address of Lord Palmerston to the electors of the borough of Tiverton, on the occasion of the last election to the new parliament, besides being very amusing, and withal a very favorable specimen of English electioneering speeches, is deserving of perusal for the information it affords on European politics, and the exposition which it gives of the views of a leading member of the British government. It is only necessary to explain that the Mr. Harvey who is repeatedly referred to in the speech, was an opposing candidate, who preceded Lord Palmerston in a long address, in which he had impugned the whole policy of the administration, for which he held the noble lord responsible, as the secretary of foreign affairs, both under the present, and under the late Whig administration. After the speeches were ended, Mr. Harvey withdrew from the canvass, and Lord Palmerston and Mr. Heathcoat were declared chosen without a poll.

The above had been written by the Editor of *Niles' National Register,* after which he included the original story from London, beginning with the actual remarks of Lord Palmerston.

I think that I have now touched upon nearly every topic to which my opponent referred, except the subject of Poland. I am far from under-valuing the great services, which, in former times, the Polish nation rendered to the Christian nations of Europe. By the partition of Poland, I consider that a heinous crime, a great political offence, was committed, but it was consummated many years ago, and long before I had anything to do with public affairs. The practical question that was recently discussed in the house of commons, to which Mr. Harvey referred, related to Cracow, a small republic, placed between three military despotisms. The position was certainly one of great danger; because when the lamp of freedom was placed in the midst of despotism it was hardly to be supposed that despotism would not, sooner or later, extinguish the sacred flame. So it happened. We protested against the proceeding. Mr. Harvey complains that our protest was couched in too civil terms, that we did not threaten more, that we did not show ourselves more angry. I must say that in the case of nations and governments as well as of individuals there is no dignity or wisdom in threatening to do what you are not prepared and may not be able to accomplish. (Hear, hear.) Much as we deplored the extinction of the free state of Cracow, and much as we condemned the act as a violation of the treaty of Vienna, I put it to you, what do you think would have been the verdict of the House of Commons, or of the country, if we had proposed to go to war with Austria, Russia, or Prussia, *for the hopeless purposes of re-establishing the republic of Cracow.* (Hear, hear.) The only way by which we could have compelled the restoration of the independence of Cracow would have been making war against these three great Powers, with such success that, in order to purchase peace, they would be ready re-establish the republic. I would like to know how many millions of money must have been expended, how many thousands of lives must have been sacrificed, and what torrents of blood must have been shed before we could have brought those three Powers on their knees before us, prepared to sue for peace on terms of our own dictation. Why, it is childish to talk about it; and if it was out of the question to go to war with three great powers for re-establishment of the republic of Cracow, it would not have been dignified, wise, or becoming the honor of this country to threaten what it was not prepared to execute. (Hear, hear.).

Lord Henry John Temple (1784-1865) had been the 3rd Viscount Palmerston who began his lengthy speech by stating that his "view of government is that there are two objects of which it should aim, those objects are truth and justice. He held that the object of all science is truth; and the science of government is the investigation of truth...," an example of which he applied to the Republic of Kraków, the final remnant of the once free and independent Commonwealth of Poland and Lithuania, in an era when Poles looked to France and Great Britain for support, but sorry to say, to no practical avail, other than in the semi-clandestine, occasional shipment from London of arms to Poland's freedom fighters. In the matter of sending British armed forces to assist Poland's patriots against Imperial Russia, Lord Palmerston's position, as evidenced in this *Article 273* about related matters in London in the year 1847, was exactly the same as it had been in 1833, fourteen years earlier, that has been referenced in *Article 191* of this book. Most sobering of all of Palmerston's considerations, however, certainly had been the memory of Britain's allies in 1814, having been Russian and Cossack forces, in alliance with the forces of Prussia and Austria, all of which had been led by Czar Alexander I, and having pursued a defeated Emperor Napoleon Bonaparte and French forces into France and Paris, where, in 1814, Bonaparte abdicated, while Russia and its allies occupied the city and France.

Article 274. (September 25, 1847, page 536)

The population of Prussia's principal cities, among them being the once-Polish cities of Breslau (Wrocław) with 112,941, Danzig (Gdańsk) with 66,287, Posen (Poznań) with 43,058, and Stettin (Szczecin) with 45,807 at the end of 1846, as computed by a census carried out in Berlin, reported in this issue *Niles' National Register*, and extrapolated for inclusion in this book. Of great interest had been Berlin's reported *annual growth* of 17,000 persons.

Berlin. The result of the census made at the end of 1846 of the Prussian population has recently been published and is as follows: Prussia, the superfices of which is 5,080 square miles counts 16,181,195 inhabitants, that is to say 641,863 more than there was at the close of 1843. Of the whole population, 11,682,228 individuals inhabit the flat country, and 4,508,967 the cities, the number of which is 980. The following is the population of the twelve principal cities of Prussia: Berlin, 408,502; Breslau, 112,941; Cologne, including Deutz, 95,202; Konigsberg, 74,234; Dantzic, 66,827; Magdeburgh, 56,816; Aix la Chapelle, 48,557; Stettin, 45,807; Posen, 43,058; Potsdam, 39,551; Eberfeld, 38,249; and Bremen, 34,932, forming a total of 1,639,929 individuals. The number of inhabitants of Berlin increases about 17,000 a year, of which only 3 to 4,000 arises from the excess of births over deaths; the rest is made up of persons who come from other places to establish themselves in this capital.

Article 275. (October 8, 1847, page 96)

In this issue, *Niles' National Register* reported the article, "Martyrs of Poland." Of interest here, the original European correspondent identified the two renowned martyrs as being surnamed Wisniowski and Kapus-czinski, without diacritics. For all intents and purposes, with the appropriate diacritics, the names would have appeared to be accurately rendered as Wiśniowski and Kapuscziński. In 2021, websites in Poland refer to the latter martyr as Kapuściński. I cannot offer an explanation other than *phonetically* Kapuscziński and Kapuściński virtually sound alike, but allowing for the local Polish patois associated with each pronunciation, there is a slight difference in pronunciation.

On the 1st of January next Poland will officially be incorporated with Russia.

Martyrs of Poland. We have the sad particulars of the double execution at Lemberg, of the two Poles, Theophilus Wisniowski and Joseph Kapusczinski. The sentence which condemned them to be strangled was read to them three days before, in front of the criminal court house, in presence of the whole population. They were accused of high treason, and they were told that they would be executed by the cord. Their execution took place on the 31st of June, and the crowd made of it an ovation, in testimony of their sympathy. Every one uncovered himself and stood bareheaded as they passed. They greeted them every where with shouts of acclamation; the men waved their hats, and the women their handkerchiefs, and on all sides garlands of flowers were showered on their heads to such profusion that to procure them, for some time previous, everything of the kind had been exhausted and more could not be procured at any price. The armed force in attendance was very numerous, but nothing could affright the multitude, neither the number of bayonets, nor the presence of the agents of the police. No one looked upon the condemned as criminals, but as martyrs of Poland, who were sacrificed for their country -- Kapuszcinski, as he stood on the scaffold, exclaimed -- 'May God bless poor Poland!'; Wisniowski added, 'Be none of you frightened by our death, but persevere!'

Teofil Wiśniowski (1806-1847) Martyr for Polish Freedom: "Be none of you frightened by our death, but persevere." (In Polish: Nie bójcie się żadnej z was przez naszą śmierć, ale wytrwajcie.)

> Lemberg, prior to the Partitions of Poland in 1772, 1793 and 1795 had been a Polish city known as Lwów. Today, it is a city known as Lviv in the Republic of Ukraine.

Article 276. (October 23, 1847, page 116)

The *Asiatic cholera*, is making fearful ravages in Russia, and in consequence of its appearance in Warsaw, the emperor has deferred his visit to Poland, a circumstance not regretted by the people of that country.

Article 277. (October 23, 1847, page 128)

The Cholera. That scourge of nations, *the Asiatic cholera*, is again on its way from the plains of central Asia (where it first springs into its noxious existence) to the borders of western Europe. Its course is about in the same direction, and at the same rate of movement, as in 1830-1831. It has already full possession of the European towns and district adjoining the sea of Azof, and at the last advices was rapidly making its way toward Poland, so that authorities at Warsaw were preparing hospitals.

> Was the Asiatic cholera identified in 1847 by way of the article of news above, something other than cholera as it related to its typical geographical progression?

Article 278. (November 6, 1847, page 150)

> Vindictive, malicious and essentially stupid Russian hostility to universities in Poland deprived the Empire of two of its greatest scientists, after which, appropriately, Niles' National Register in its news-brief titled, "Science in Russia," had been reported in this issue.

An uncommon effort is now working in Russia to produce a knowledge of the natural sciences. This is more extraordinary, when it is recollected that the imperial government has executed an unparalleled hostility toward the only two universities of distinction in poor, degraded, miserable Poland. Two professors of geology, whose high attainments would confer honor on any country, have been dismissed, and the cabinet of the former sold in Russia, in order to prevent the possibility of having the higher departments of useful knowledge taught in territorial Poland.

Please note that the article above only included universities in the Imperial Russian-controlled Kingdom of Poland. As such, ancient Poland's oldest and indeed, greater Europe's, venerable Jagiellonian University in Kraków wasn't included simply because it was located in the Imperial Austrian-controlled part of Poland known as Galicja (rather than Galicia) in the Polish language.

Article 279. (November 27, 1847, page 197)

The Cholera. In our paper of October 5th, was announced that the cholera had reached Europe. It has committed fearful ravages on both sides of the Black Sea, and for some days has raged at Odessa. In southern Russia the population of whole villages have been nearly swept away. Cases have been observed at Orel, Toula, and in the village of Pensa, which is situated only 50 leagues from Moscow, and where four peasants have been attacked. In the province of Astracan, which contains 31,300 inhabitants, there have been 5,915 cases, and 3,131 deaths. The epidemic reigns with great intensity at Techarno Jarsk and its environs. At Saratow, capital of the province of the same name, 2,500 persons have been attacked, and 1,991 have died. In the country of the Don Cossacks, there have been 13,651 cases, of which 7,017 have proved fatal. At Charkow, 53 persons have died of the disease; at Karak there were, on the 4th of September, 580 sick, and since there have been 20 cases per day, and 150 deaths.

On the 16th there were in the hospital 1,019 cholera patients, of whom 418 had been attacked the same day; the number of deaths on that day had been 152. Without counting Georgia, Caucasus, and the country of the Cossacks of the Black Sea, it already reigns in sixteen governments. On the 17th October it broke out at Warsaw, and on the 30th at Moscow. Only one case has occurred in Austria, and one in Prussia. Up to the 29th it had not visited Constantinople. The *Allemeine Zeitung* on the 27th October says: 'The cholera is advancing from the east to the west, but as yet has not reached a more westerly point than Keriach, on the sea of Azoff. The winter will impede its progress, but not change the direction it has taken.'

[*Wilmer & Smith's European Times*]

Descriptions of the east-to-west advance of cholera in Russia, Poland and Europe during the first half of the 19th century made it appear to have been viral, somewhat akin to ordinary, but deadly, influenza of the 20th century, and the very deadly coronavirus known as Covid-19 in the 21st century. If the undefined 19th century viral-like scourge wasn't bacterial cholera, could it have been influenza? Could it have been an incorrectly-identified plague in its own right?

Article 280. (January 22, 1848, front-page)

Here a variety of reports including confirming the method by which news from Europe arrived in the United States; cholera subsided in Russia, but appeared in Prussia, while famine was in Austrian Gallicia (Galicja in Polish); the debate in Great Britain's Parliament on the status of Jews in England, including eligibility for Parliament; and the matter of large nations threatening small nations, appeared on the front-page of this issue of *Niles' National Register*, beginning with what had been placed at the top of the left-hand column of three columns, under the caption, *FOREIGN*; and ending in the middle column with news of the death of Napoleon Bonaparte's wife and the political implications for her successor, and finally, the reported harassment of the Pope's Swiss Guards.

The arrival of the American mail steamer *Washington*, the French mail steamer *Missouri*, and finally, the British steamer *Cambria*, which latter left Liverpool on the 1st instant has furnished us during the present week with European intelligence of some interest. For the state of trade and the markets, see our 'business' items. The president's message was published in London on the 30th ult. The *cholera* is subsiding in Russia and Turkey. A few cases have occurred in Prussia, none as yet in France or England. The health of London has improved. Mr. Bancroft, the American minister, has gone to Paris.

GREAT BRITAIN: Parliament adjourned for the holidays, to re-assemble on the 3rd of February. *The Jew bill.* A debate occurred upon the resolution for a committee to report a bill to place the Jews upon the same footing as the Roman Catholics. The resolution was passed by a vote of 253 to 186, and lord John Russell is at the time the head of the committee. Earl Winchester calls upon his countrymen in the most strenuous manner to oppose admitting a Jew to a seat in Parliament.

Whereas It hadn't been possible for me to ascertain whether the crudely-worded reference titled, *The Jew bill*, had been written as such in London or in the United States to best represent the antisemitism of the Earl of Winchester, it is worthy of note that, a generation later, the first Earl of Beaconsfield, Benjamin Disraeli (1804-1881), of Italian-Jewish descent, who became an Anglican at age 12, and as an adult, went on to become Prime Minister of the United Kingdom on two occasions, first in 1868 and again in 1874-1880.

AUSTRIA, appears determined to interfere in the affairs of Switzerland. Metternich has become infirm and feeble. The emperor is a man of weak mind, but a zealous Catholic, and is, as well as the empress controlled by a few talented Jesuits. An official article in the *Austrian Observer*, of the 17th amounts almost to a declaration of war against the diet.

At the Congress of Vienna (1814-1815), Prince Klemens von Metternich (1773-1859), Imperial Austria's Foreign Minister (1809-1848), had been authorized principally by Czar Alexander of Imperial Russia, with the task of restoring to power all the "legitimate" monarchs that had been removed from their thrones by Napoleon Bonaparte. During the years of his service as Foreign Minister, Austria secured its place among the big powers of Europe, both East and West, as witnessed by the all-important post-Napoleonic Congress of Vienna, being held in Imperial Austria's capital when, in fact, Czar Alexander rightfully could have insisted on holding the Congress in St. Petersburg, Imperial Russia's capital. While the Congress of Vienna created two alliances, the first being the *Quadruple Alliance* of Great Britain, Russia, Austria and Prussia that had defeated Napoleon and subsequently focused as well on preventing the military resurgence of France; the second alliance -- known as the *Holy Alliance* -- only involved Russia, Austria and Prussia because its objective had been to prevent the rise of "systems of representative government" anywhere in Europe, which, among other reasons, the British refused to engage in. As a measure of his mastery of diplomacy, Metternich adroitly managed both alliances to the extent that he utilized Russia "as a hedge against France" -- as noted by Henry Kissinger in his 1994 opus, "Diplomacy" -- to promote the interests of Austria (which historically had viewed France as its principal competitor for European leadership). Indeed, Metternich masterfully conducted the so-called "Concert of Europe" which reflected post-Napoleonic *realpolitik* with such finesse that his system of orchestrating European affairs as befitting a maestro had been known in some quarters as the "system of Metternich," or simply, *metter-nichmus*.

Famine and disease are committing such awful ravages among the peasantry of Austrian Gallicia, that in almost every village, a third, and in some places even the half, of the people have died.

ITALY is quieter, with the exception of Tuscany and Naples, and Sicily, all of which are disaffected. Austrian troops continue to advance to the frontiers of Italy. Field Marshal Radetzky, commander of the Austrian forces in Lombardy, has received additional powers. His army is to be increased to 60,000 men. Six batteries of artillery are on their way; twelve battalions of infantry are ordered to march at a moment's notice. A rumor was current at Paris that the French government had received telegraphic despatches, announcing that the Austrian troops had entered Parma, Placentia and Modena. So says the London *Times* of 1st January.

MARIA LUISA, Archduchess of Parma and Placentia, widow of Napoleon, died on the evening of 17th December. There are intricate difficulties arising from this circumstance. Which Austria desires to have settlement of, as Tuscany is interested. The duke of Lucca succeeds to the sovereignty. Letters from Bologna to the 21st ultimo, announce that the Swiss troops in the service of the pope had arrived at Ferrara on the 19th ult., and after having been detained several hours outside the gates were at length admitted.

Article 281. (July 5, 1848, pages 13 and 14)

RUSSIA: "The cholera us again making sad havoc in Russia. According to the *Berlinishe Nachrichter*, there were in one week, 155 cases in Moscow, 57 of which terminated fatally."

RUSSIA AND POLAND: "The *Augsburg Gazette* states, from Vienna, under the date of 6th ult. that the Russians have crossed the Pruth, on the frontier of Bessarabia, and that baron Sturmer, the Austrian minister at Constantinople, has protested warmly against this movement.

According to seemingly trustworthy advices from Poland, it is asserted that the Russian forces concentrated in the kingdom of Poland, amount, at the present time, to nearly 400,000 men, with an immense force of artillery. The inhabitants along the Prussian and Austrian frontier, have been latterly kept on the *qui vive* because of the constant reports of artillery. Some of the more credulous supposed that a serious insurrection had broken out in Russian Poland, but the more probable account of these continued discharges seemed to be that the Russian Generals were employed in exercising the forces under their command in the use of their guns."

> The expression above, "kept on the qui vive," simply meant "kept on the alert."

Article 282. (July 12, 1848, page 23)

> The Czar's anxiety over Poland continued while Russia's frontier with western Europe bristled with bayonets, and the Czar Nicholas, seated beside his personal telegraph installation watching for news from Poland, also pondered ending personal servitude of the Empire's peasants, as reported by Niles' National Register.

RUSSIA. Advices from the Danube announce that a Russian army of 30,000 men had entered Wallachia. It is asserted that the Emperor Nicholas contemplates enfranchising all the peasants in his dominions from personal servitude. Poland, *although invested with two hundred thousand troops*, is a cause of much uneasiness to the Emperor, who is said to spend whole days and nights in watching the telegraphs now established as far west at Warsaw and the frontiers of Prussia.

There can be no doubt that three large Russian armies are assembling at different points between Tilsit and Cracow; and these, in conjunction with the appearance of the Russian fleet in the Baltic, show that the Czar is inclined, in certain cases, to act with decided hostility against Germany.

In the Breslau journals, of the 16th inst., it is stated that the whole Baltic Sea is covered with Russian men-of-war. The whole western frontier of the Russian Empire bristles with bayonets. The troops advance forward from Lithuania and Volhynia by forced marches. The chief force of the Emperor Nicholas stands already on the river Pruth ready at any moment to march into Moldavia, and of course into Wallachia.

> To Poles, Breslau had been known as Wrocław and remains known as such today, a Polish city.

Article 283. (July 12, 1848, page 26)

> It had been reported that Austria's Army was on the march destined for Poland.

AUSTRIA. We learn that Vicensea has been returned to the Italians; that Padua has capitulated to the Austrians; that Trieste has been placed in a state of blockade; and that the Lombard army has been defeated in an engagement near Verona. It is rumored that the Austrian army has been ordered to invade Prussia. There is little doubt that an immense force is on the march for Poland. There is a prospect for the speedy termination of the Germanic war, and the establishment of peace. The draft of a new constitution has been proposed and is likely to be approved of.

Article 284. (September 6, 1848, page 156)

> This issue had reported that large elements of the Russian Army were deployed near the Prussian frontier in Poland.

An imperial ukase, under the date of 31st July, orders the recruiting of seven men per 1000 inhabitants in the governments of the eastern moiety of the empire.

The first detachments of the Russian army are to be seen about two German miles from the Prussian frontier. The Cossacks and the light cavalry form the vanguard, next comes the infantry, then the artillery, and the heavy cavalry in the rear. A camp of 40,000 men is established near Warsaw; and another under Gen. Radziwill, is in the direction of Gallicia. The army in Poland consists of two corps, amounting to about 30,000 men; a part only of a third corps has entered the kingdom, the rest remaining in the camp near Luck, on account of the presence of the cholera in the ranks.

The emperor was expected at Warsaw, but the journey has been postponed, probably in consequence of the ravages of the cholera in St. Petersburg.

The *St. Petersburg Journal* of the 1st ult. publishes a long *expose* by the emperor on his motives for intervention in the principalities of Wallachia and Moldavia. It states, in the most positive terms, that the intervention is with the consent and concurrence of the Ottoman Porte, and that the Russian troops will act only in accord, if action should become necessary, with those of the Sultan.

Article 285. (September 6, 1848, page 158)

Notwithstanding the threat of war, the other scourge of nations, deadly cholera, still haunted Poland's population as well, insofar as it had been an integral part of the Russian Empire, for which the basis of the report had been Russia's *Military Medical Gazette*.

The Cholera. From a late number of the *Military Medical Gazette*, it appears that since the appearance of the epidemic in Russia, there were seized at St. Petersburg, from its first appearance, the 30th of June to the 31st of July, 19,772 persons, of whom 4,384 recovered, and 11,068 died. In the whole of Russia, since the first appearance of the cholera, from the 28th of October 1846, to the 5th of July, 1848, 200,318 were seized with the epidemic, and 116,658 died. On the 28th of July there were at St. Petersburg 2,396 cholera cases. In the course of the day, 137 fresh cases occurred; 211 recovered and 82 died, 45 of whom were in their own dwellings. On the 29th there were 2,240 sick, 132 new cases; 188 recovered and 63 died. On the 30th there remained 2,116 cases under treatment.... A letter from Tarnopolis, in Austrian Gallicia, dated the 26th July, states that the cholera had declared itself with great intensity at Okapa, a Russian town, thirty leagues distant from Tarnopolis, whence it had spread with extreme rapidity over the entire western frontier of Gallicia. It is asserted that the cholera is not only raging at Stockholm, but that it has penetrated into the interior of the country, into Finland and Lapland, and that it is of a most malignant character.

In the Polish language, the city of Tarnopolis had been, and still is, known as Tarnów, a Polish city.

Article 286. (October 4, 1848, page 220)

Queen Victoria of Great Britain, whose reign began in June 1837 and ended in January 1901, delivered her annual address to Parliament at its "prorogation" in 1848, during which she offered a statement about the loss of tranquility in Europe.

Events of deep importance have disturbed the internal tranquility of many of the States of Europe, both in the north and south. These events have led to hostilities between neighboring countries. I am employing my good offices, in concert with other friendly powers to bring to an amicable settlement of these differences, and I trust that our efforts may be successful. I am rejoiced to think that an increasing sense of the value of peace encourages the hope that the nations of Europe may continue in the enjoyment of its blessings.

The major problem "in the north" had been between imperial Russia and its endless victimization of the reluctant dependent kingdom of Poland at the time, but Poland and Russia were not identified per se by the Queen. Whereas she extended her government's "good offices" to mediate or at least reduce the malicious level of suffering imposed on the Poles by Russia principally, the fact that her subjects had been generally sympathetic for Poland, but also had been highly influenced by Lord Palmerston's non-interventionist policy in the 1830s and 1840s, left her unable to lessen Poland's suffering, and given that Czar Nicholas rejected all such efforts outright, no nation in western Europe had been willing to challenge his persistent obstinacy and cruelty, as well as his enormous army, except in well-chosen words, diplomatically conveyed, for the official record in the matter, at the least.

Article 287. (November 11, 1848, page 315)

Russia's-combined-with-Poland's national debt, revenue, and expenditures had again been reported by *Niles' National Register* in this particular issue. Although *Articles 116, 238, 253* and *256* addressed the matter of national debts for the years 1829, 1839, 1843 and 1844 respectively, the matter of revenues and expenditures apparently hadn't been sufficiently addressed by the "divine right" regimes, witness the number of reports on the matter having been publicized. As data had been reviewed in this particular issue published on November 11, 1848, Prussia as one unit of measure, which nearly-perfectly balanced the books on its revenues and expenditures, was closely matched by Belgium, Portugal and Spain in that regard; and whereas Russia and Poland combined as yet another unit of measure, that *perfectly balanced* the books on revenues and expenditures, had achieved yet another prodigious feat indeed (if in fact it had occurred). In contrast, France reported a huge national debt, but with an amazingly modest burden on French tax-payers. Of the total 19 nations included in this report, 11 (58%) failed to submit anything about their revenues and expenditures, possibly being that their rulers by Divine Right had likely rationalized being accountable solely to their Heavenly Father, rather than to "systems of representative governments" as discussed earlier in this book. For the year 1848, the total European debt of ten billion dollars was noteworthy, to say the least, even viewed from the perspective of the year 2021.

DEBTS OF EUROPEAN NATIONS – INCOMES AND EXPENDITURES

Country.	*Debt.*	*Revenues.*	*Expenditures.*
Great Britain	$4,000,000,000	$293,801,700	$276,363,850
France	1,200,000,000	271,469,265	291,744,651
Holland	800,000,000		
Frankfurt-Marne	5,000,000		
Bremen	3,000,000		
Hamburg	7,000,000		
Denmark	93,000,000		
Greece	44,000,000		
Portugal	142,000,000	10,890,033	10,797,302
Spain	467,000,000	141,908,185	125,923,187
Austria	380,000,000	64,240,000	76,379,903
Belgium	120,000,000	22,602,814	22,548,448
Papal States	67,000,000		
Naples	126,000,000		
Prussia	150,000,000	79,984,231	79,319,475
Russia & Poland	545,000,000	41,366,948	41,366,948
Bavaria	15,000,000		
Sicily	79,000,000		
Belgium	200,000,000		
	8,634,000,000		
Others not			
Enumerated	1,366,000,000		
Total	10,000,000,000		

	Population.	Average of debt to each inhabitant.
Great Britain	27,000,000	$222
France	25,000,000	30
Holland	3,000,000	260
Frankfurt on Marne	1,000,000	100
Denmark	2,200,000	45
Greece	1,000,000	44
Portugal	3,800,000	38
Spain	13,000,000	38
Austria	37,000,000	35
Belgium	4,600,000	30
Papal States	3,000,000	23
Prussia	15,000,000	10
Russia and Poland	60,000,000	9
Sicily	8,000,000	9
Total population	214,000,000	
Population not enumerated	36,000,000	
Total	250,000,000.	

For the purpose of placing in a proper position the financial affairs of European nations, compared with those of this country, we annex the following table:

PUBLIC INDEBTEDNESS OF EUROPE AND THE UNITED STATES

	Aggregate Debt.	Population.	Aver. per head.
Principal Countries of Europe	$10,000,000,000	250,000,000	$40.00
United States of America	$80,000,000	23,000,000	$3.50

The vast difference in the aggregate amount of indebtedness, and the average indebtedness, per head, is the best commentary upon the condition of Europe, and the favorable condition we occupy in the scale of nations.

Indeed, this entire book might be reduced to documented evidence of the fact that rule by Divine Right, the antithesis of governance by "systems of representative government," as referenced earlier in *Article 132* concerning the "secret" Treaty of Verona, wherein Europe's rulers, for the most part, had not been answerable or accountable to anyone but God, in the manner and disposition of their autocratic governance that enabled them alone to define their Creator's divine will that always, in practical terms, favored them largely, rather than the masses of common people over whom they ruled.

Apart from the topic of Great Britain itself, which had a better-than-adequate parliamentary system of governance in place, it nonetheless sustained the world's largest financial indebtedness, and as far as Russia and Poland's combined indebtedness in particular, and that of Prussia by itself, was concerned, it appears that someone may have "cooked the books" once again, as the expression goes, in the matter of their perfectly-balanced revenues and expenditures reported in this particular news article.

Article 288. (December 13, 1848, page 375)

In Poland, cabbage and potatoes supply the food of the ordinary workmen. Poverty among them is universal. Sometimes, though by no means commonly, they partake of black bread and soup, or butter, or meat. One who had travelled extensively in this country, and was a close observer of things, remarks: 'I have journeyed in every direction and have never seen a wheaten loaf to the eastward of the Rhine, in any part of northern Germany, Poland or Denmark'.

Article 289. (January 8, 1849, page 289)

In this front-page issue, *Niles' National Register* printed its final news-brief about Gaspar (Kacper in Polish) Tochman, the exiled Polish military officer of the 1830 Uprising, whom I have referenced earlier (see *Introduction* and *Articles 248* and *266*) with regard to his exemplary work as spokesman and activist in the United States for the Polish National Committee in Paris, and in the matter of Vermont, and other, state Resolutions.

INDICTMENTS FOR SENDING A CHALLENGE, ETC. – The grand jury of Washington, D.C. have, within the last few days, found true bills to the following effect: United States vs. G. Tochman, for sending a challenge to fight a duel; United States vs. same, for libel upon J. H. Bradley, Esq.; United States vs. same, for posting and publishing J. H. Bradley, Esq., as a coward, etc.; and United States vs. Capt. Schaumburg, for bearing a challenge. [*Alex. Gaz.*]

Article 290. (February 21, 1849, page 128)

Russian America" had been the focus *Niles' National Register*'s report in this issue of February 1849, included under "Various Items." Although the subject of Russia in the western hemisphere has been referenced earlier in my study for this book, it is worthwhile to remember that the United States went on to purchase Alaska from Russia on October 18, 1867 for the total sum of $7,200,000, truly a bargain for the United States. On its part, Imperial Russia had been running up a national debt of unclear and questionable proportions, as the national debt data that I have included in five separate *Articles* in this book illustrate. Living beyond its means, Russia had no other choice concerning Alaska in 1867. In the 21st century, as a consequence, Vladimir Putin likely bemoans, as do many of his contemporary hard-right nationalists, the great loss of Russian America in the second half of the 19th century, almost as much as Putin and they do about the fall and demise of the Soviet Union in the final decade of the 20th century.

Our Pacific Settlements: *Russian America*, the only part of our continent held by the Sclavonic race has to our Republic been almost an unknown land. Still an American is there, Mr. Moore, whose employment is to instruct the natives born of Russian parents, how to build steam engines, and steam vessels for that distant coast. This steam voyaging will connect them with Oregon, and California, and thence by our new line, with Panama, and thence again by the present existing line with Valparaiso and Chili. The western coast of America, both North and South, will have a continuous line of steamers from near Behring's Straits down to near Cape Horn! Though the eastern coast of our continent has no such continuous line by steam. Westward the star of Empire takes its way; and the West coast of America is destined to witness mighty things, overlooking the virgin Pacific to China, Japan, Siberia and the Australian shores beyond. A voyager entering the port of Archangel found there the following mercantile fleet. It speaks of life, of energy, and the speed of civilization:

Helen	350 tons	Promyale	80 tons
Alexander	300 tons	Morisehold	80 tons
Sitka	300 tons	Qua-pak	80 tons
Biehal	200 tons	Nicholas	steamer, 60 horse power
Constantine	200 tons	Moore	steamer, 7 horse do.
Ochotsk	150 tons	Small steamer	
Chiechakoff	150 tons	Small steamer	
Polypheme	150 tons		

This would do credit to many a proud port in Europe or the United States. We must learn more about that land. Her fleet is occupied almost exclusively on those northern shores, above the famous *54*

40, running to the Aleutian Isles, to the Kurile Isles which reach to Japan, to Kamschatka, and to Ochotsk in Siberia, except for an occasional trip to Oregon for flour, or to the Sandwich Islands for sugar and other supplies.

Sir George Simpson, Governor of the great northern British portion of our continent, speaks of the establishment of Mr. Moore, the American in the employ of Russia, in terms of high commendation; the entire work of an engine, the casting, forging and finishing being finely done. 'He is a man of superior ingenuity, and has taught five or six natives to do the work almost as well as himself.'

New Archangel, the capital of Russian America, is situated on the island of Sitka, which is separated from the main land by a narrow arm of the sea. The population is about 1,500, besides two Indian suburban villages. Smaller posts are situated at many points along the coast all the way to the peninsula of Alaska, and thence even along the chain of Aleutian Islands, which form the natural stepping stones to Siberia. Recently some posts have been formed on Behring's Straits! To protect the fur trade on the east side of the Schukichi. These are the dwellers on the western side, and once a year at the great fair at Ostroynoye in Siberia, they purchase tobacco and other articles, and with these they are powerful competitors, every summer, with the Russian company, among the extreme north-western Indians of our continent.

The climate of Russian America is mild for its latitude, like Western Europe, in both cases the prevailing westerly winds from the ocean temper the land. No part of the coast north of Oregon grows wheat, but potatoes and other garden vegetables are abundant, even to Cook's Sound and Aieshka. Cattle thrive well. The forests are filled with game, and the waters swarm with fish, especially the salmon. The extremity of our continent is destined to support a considerable population, though their flour must come from Oregon.

Our northern neighbors there are [illegible word] people. 'New Archangel,' says Sir George, 'notwithstanding its isolated position,' is a very gay place. Much of the time of its inhabitants is devoted to festivity: balls and dinners run a perpetual round, and managed in a style which in this part of the world may be deemed extravagant.' Their Easter Holidays are especially full of life, and the ancient fashion of sporting colored eggs, delights the children of Sitka, though the custom has travelled the other way around the globe.

The names of the days of their week have marched eastwardly around the world, and hence their Sunday is the Saturday of the Oregonians. It is curious how the same day is called, and with propriety too, both Saturday and Sunday, from America westward to China.

385

Through the *center* of the Pacific, civilization has travelled westward, and hence at the Sandwich Islands, the Ladrome Islands, and the Phillipine Islands, the day is Saturday; while both through the *Southern* Pacific, from the Society Islands to Australia, and through the *Northern* Pacific from Russian America from the Aleutian and Kurile Islands to China, civilization has travelled eastward and the day is Sunday. These facts will always stand as eloquent historical monuments; they show that the eastern and western streams of civilization have overlapped each other more than 6,600 miles! Their explanation to centuries yet unknown will make lucid the history of the past, that great point in past history when Christianity first belted the globe!

To return to North America. The oldest settlement on the western coast of America, *North* of California, is the village of Kodiak, containing 400 inhabitants, and situated on an island at the extreme North. It was founded in 1783, just at the close of our Revolution, and as we began to settle the valley of the Mississippi. What a coincidence! The great West entered upon simultaneously by the Spaniards in California on the South, by ourselves on the East, and by the Russians on the Northwest. Those extensive movements by the masses of mankind 'to replenish the earth, and subdue it,' have ever been plainly under the direction of Providence, as when the Israelites migrated from Egypt, under the guidance of the pillar of cloud by day and the pillar of fire by night. At the present date, the Russian American Company, who have the entire government of the country, do not encourage emigration, as it tends to destroy their monopoly of fur. But a change must come with the general increase of population, and that boreal region will be filled with human life, and enjoyment. Mr. Moore, the ingenious American there, will have many companions speaking his own language.

Article 291. (March 21, 1849, page 192, center column)

> Even In its final days of existence, *Niles' National Register* never failed to overlook the opportunity to identify the existence of Poland apart from Russia, Austria and Prussia, on any topic, so as to keep the "Polish question" on the table by simply mentioning Poland as an entity, as this article in this issue about the extent of railways in Europe and the world demonstrates.

RAILROADS: The *American Railroad Journal* gives the following interesting statement of the length, cost per mile and total cost of the Rail Roads in the United States, Canada, Cuba and Europe. According to this account it will be seen that the cost of the Railroads in the United

States are less per mile than in any other country in the world, with the exception of Holland and the Island of Cuba.

Country.	Miles.	Average per mile.	Total.
United States	6,421	$30,000	$192,630,000
Canada	54	30,000	1,620,000
Cuba	250	28,000	7,000,000
Total in America	6,725		200,250,000
United Kingdom	4,420	145,000	640,900,000
France	1,250	110,000	137,500,000
Germany	3,370	50,000	168,500,000
Belgium	459½	80,000	39,640,000
Holland	162½	25,000	4,062,500
Denmark & Holstein	282	40,000	11,280,000
Switzerland	78	50,000	3,600,000
Italy	162½	90,000	14,625,000
Russia	113	60,000	6,780,000
Poland	187½	50,000	9,375,000
Hungary	157	50,000	7,850,000
Total in Europe	10,678		$1,044,402,509
Total	17,403		$1,244,852,500

The above embraces all the railways in operation, except a short line of 15 miles recently opened in Spain, from Barcelona to Malaro, from which no returns are obtained.

The vast sums stated above have all been expended for railways within the last twenty years. It may be safely asserted that the roads now in progress, including all those which will be completed within the next *five* years, will represent an additional amount of capital equal to the sum expended upon those already finished. The speculative feelings of 1845, in England, pushed forward many schemes that have since been discarded; and the stringent law which required a deposit of 20 per cent of the capital before the effect of the grant of authority to build, had the effect to reduce the number of speculative schemes at once. In no other country in Europe has the railway spirit exceeded the limits of legitimate speculation.

Article 292. (March 21, 1849, page 192)

Also appearing on the same page that contained the article on the extent of railway development in Europe and essentially North America as well, had been an article of an aspect of the United States Census of 1840 that reported on the expansion of public libraries in the world's greatest democracy, the United States in America. Public libraries had been both anathema and virtually non-existent in the world's greatest autocracy, Imperial Russia, where suppression of knowledge and news of the day was unquestioned, except for the high aristocracy, and clearly designed to control Russia's slave-like society in ignorance among ordinary people by the factor of the absence of fact-based information.

In the American public libraries section of the 1840 United Stated Census illustrated below in this March 1849 issue of *Niles' National Register*, there had been two tables reporting on each State of the Union. Those states with italic print in each table reflected what I found for the number of volumes of books in one table that didn't match the number of volumes of books in the other table for a particular state. Whether that had been the fault of the Census Bureau or the type-setter in the employ of the *Niles' National Register* is open to question. Nonetheless, the portion of the article displayed here illuminates the difference between an open and free society which, although far from being perfect (e.g., the persistence of slave-holding states in the United States of America), valued the importance of educating its general population via public schools, public libraries and newspapers in a democracy, versus its antithesis, in this case having been, autocratic and totalitarian Imperial Russia, which preferred to maintain all of its subjects in slave-like darkness and ignorance.

Imperial Russia's national libraries had largely been augmented as the product of war-booty (e.g., Poland's Załuski Library collection, having been an example, one of Europe's finest and largest collections. It had been removed from Warsaw for relocation to St. Petersburg in 1795 by order of Czarina Catherine II). In Russia, the Załuski collection's availability was designed to be enjoyed by a very small trusted fraction of the Empire's population, ranging from accommodating principally some trustworthy members of the nobility eager for genuine useful knowledge, on one hand, to providing a mere visual display for superficially impressing viewers, on a "big books at the bottom, small books at the top" basis, that had been so colorfully described by one of Czarina Catherine's "male-prostitute" lovers, who happened to be an illiterate man, but who admired that particular aspect of a simpleton's arrangement of books on shelves, (apart from the majority *standard librarian's universal shelf arrangement*), of Catherine's private book collection, in her intimate living quarters. (See *Article 6.*)

As for the growth of public libraries in the United States, what appears below speaks for itself.

As Reported in the "Niles' Register"

The Załuski Library under construction (Zygmunt Vogel, 1801)

Public Libraries – The following compiled by Dr. Ludwig, of New York, shows the number of public libraries, and the volumes, in the United States:

State.	Number.	Volumes.
Maine,	4	4,300
New Hampshire,	5	26,800
Vermont,	2	16,000
Rhode Island,	5	43,400
Massachusetts,	30	203,000
Connecticut,	4	71,000
New York,	33	174,900
Pennsylvania,	32	176,100
New Jersey,	2	28,500
Ohio,	23	68,800
Michigan,	5	9,500
Indiana,	5	6,800
Illinois,	3	3,700
Delaware,	1	3,600
Maryland,	11	54,500
Virginia,	9	58,300
North Carolina,	3	16,000
South Carolina,	5	38,400
Georgia,	4	22,000
Alabama,	2	12,200
Louisiana,	5	13,300
Mississippi,	2	5,000
Tennessee,	6	26,700
Kentucky,	9	44,600
Missouri,	5	20,500
District of Columbia	9	75,000
	235	1,209,800

The sub-joined table gives the population of each State according to the census of 1840, the number of volumes in the public libraries of each State, and the proportion which the number of volumes in the public libraries bear to the population:

389

State.	Population.	Vols.	Proportion.
Rhode Island	168,830	43,000	1 to 2½
Massachusetts	737,697	203,000	1 to 4
Connecticut	309,979	71,000	1 to 4
Pennsylvania	1,724,033	176,100	1 to 10
New Hampshire	284,564	26,800	1 to 11
New Jersey	373,386	28,500	1 to 13
New York	2,428,921	174,909	1 to 14
South Carolina	594,398	38,400	1 to 17
Kentucky	779,823	43,600	1 to 17
Missouri	383,702	20,500	1 to 18
Vermont	291,948	16,000	1 to 19
Virginia	1,239,797	58,300	1 to 21
Michigan	212,267	8,500	1 to 21
Ohio	1,519,467	68,800	1 to 22
Louisiana	352,411	13,300	1 to 27
Tennessee	729,210	26,700	1 to 30
North Carolina	753,419	16,000	1 to 47
Delaware	78,875	3,600	1 to 50
Alabama	590,756	12,200	1 to 50
Georgia	691,392	22,000	1 to 61
Mississippi	375,416	5,000	1 to 75
Maryland	470,019	54,500	1 to 86
Indiana	685,866	6,800	1 to 98
Illinois	476,183	3,700	1 to 119
Maine	501,793	4,300	1 to 125

> The article included a contrast of European public libraries where in London, for example, there reportedly:

...were four public libraries, containing, in the aggregate, 397,000 volumes," and in Paris which "possessed five public libraries, in which the people have free access, that contain 1,300,000 volumes..., the European libraries have been centuries collecting, while those of the United States have been collected principally within the half century's decades; *the libraries of Europe are patronized chiefly by comparatively few persons*, whose pride is to make a *learned display*. In the United States, the collection of books and the founding of libraries is the work of the whole people, and they are established on a scale combining the greatest economy as well as the greatest benefit. They are here diffused among the people, and benefit thousands where hundreds are benefited by the libraries of Europe.

Whereas the first two tables of three on page 192 of Niles' National Register contained the report on the growth of public libraries in the United States, the third table contained a very brief report titled, "The Production of Iron in Europe" -- wherein it implied correctly -- that production of iron equated with the full-range capability of industrially-powerful nations, of which the production of weapons had been a major consideration, a point that must have been a source of great pride for the administration of Czar Nicholas in St. Petersburg.

Countries.	Cwt.	Proportion per head of population.
Great Britain	6,000,000	12 - 5
Belgium	3,000,000	3 - 4
Sweden	1,000,000	1 - 2
Prussia	3,000,000	1 - 5
France	5,000,000	1 - 7
Russia	6,000,000	1 - 9

Article 293. (April 25, 1849, page 270)

In this issue, *Niles' National Register* included an article, "Russia in 1847," that identified the surface area of Russian Poland and the number of its inhabitants.

Russia in 1847. – *The Almanac of the Imperial Academy of Science of St. Petersburg contains the following details*:

Russia in Europe, upon a surface of 90,117 square miles, counts 54,490,000 inhabitants; the Duchy of Finland upon a surface of 6,814 square miles, 1,549,700; the Kingdom of Poland upon a surface of 2,930 square miles, 4,589,000....

Article 294. (April 30, 1849, page 145):

This article was apparently selected by George Beatty, the final Editor of Niles' National Register, because of the reputation of the near-legendary, often-barbaric Don Cossacks as well as potential interest for some American scientists who might have been attracted by Russian coal from the land of the Cossacks as having "great heating power." The Don Cossacks were known as such because their population was concentrated in the basin of the Don River in Russia.

RUSSIAN COAL. -- Before the National Institute, Prof. Walter R. Johnson, the Corresponding Secretary of the Institute, exhibited a specimen of anthracite from the town of Gruschofka, in the country of the Don Cossacks, Southern European Russia, and instituted a comparison between it and the anthracite of our own and other countries. He observed that it was usual for anthracite to break with as much facility across the surface of deposition as in directions parallel to those surfaces, and that, when surfaces of deposition were exposed by the fracture, they exhibited less brilliancy than the surfaces of fracture in other directions. The reverse of this was true of the Russian specimen exhibited, and the lustre of its surface was owing to the presence of innumerable very minute organic remains resembling scales. In this particular, it resembles several bituminous coals examined by Prof. J., and especially that found near Greenupsburg, in Kentucky, save that in the latter the scales are without lustre. The specific gravity of the Russian anthracite is 166, in which property it is surpassed by few of the anthracites of Pennsylvania. The amount of its volatile matter is 7.17 per cent.; the proportion of ash left after burning 1.6 per cent, and consequently the amount of its fixed carbon 91.23 per cent. A coal with these properties must possess great heating power; and will rank as equal to some of the best varieties of Pennsylvania anthracite.

Article 295. (May 16, 1849, page 316)

...it was reported at Vienna on the 19th, that an insurrection had broken out at Cracow.

Polish soldiers joined Hungarian armed forces in the cause of Hungarian independence, while a Prussian Army of "Observation" was deployed to watch Poles in Posen (Poznań in Polish), as reported by *Niles' National Register* in this issue.

Article 296. (May 23, 1849, page 334)

News from the Continent. This is in most particulars of a very interesting character. The war in Hungary may involve Prussia as well as Russia yet in the conflict. It is daily assuming a more serious aspect. The Austrians defeated and driven to the borders of Hungary, if not from the country entirely, have become dispirited and has caused dismay to the seat of empire; Vienna dreads their triumphant approach. The Hungarian army is made up of Magyars chiefly, joined by a body of Poles, and patriot volunteers from Italy and other States. It consists of about 100,000 men, entered to great hardships, of a warlike character and education, and entertaining towards Austria and Russia a desperate hatred. So far, they have been signally victorious, driving the Austrians from their strongholds, and making numbers of them prisoners.

Austria, acknowledging her inability to suppress the rebellion, calls on Russia for aid, and it is stated that official notice of the intervention of Russia has been received at Paris. The Autocrat, *partly under the pretence of preventing a revolution of the Poles on his own borders*, has placed an army, consisting of 80 to 150 thousand men, commanded by Russian Generals, and sustained wholly by Russia, at the disposal of the Austrians. *Prussia is also about to send an army of observation to the Silesian frontier to watch the Poles in Posen.*

So much for the Russian effort to eradicate the very use of the words, "Poland" and "Polish" after 1795, from the memory of European, and indeed, world civilization.

Of Poles who volunteered to fight either as individual soldiers and officers, or as members of voluntary Polish military units of the Hungarian army, and as general officers, General Józef Bem having been one major example, but not the only one, with the other major example having been General Henryk Dembiński (who at one point had been appointed and had served as commander-in-chief of the Hungarian army), continued to be referenced in intelligence reports about the related battles in Europe during the "Spring of Nations," one of which had involved Hungarians fighting for their own national independence from Austria which was aided by Russia to defeat the Hungarians, as this additional article appearing in the same issue of Niles' National Register illustrates. Please note that Russia, Prussia and Austria had been this news-article's referenced "Imperialists."

Polish General Józef Bem (1794-1850.)

393

Article 297. (May 23, 1849, page 334)

Austria and Hungary. Letters from Pesth to the 29th ult. confirm the news of the evacuation of the city by the Imperialists. The same letters assert that at Pesth the people were displaying, it may be said in sight of the Imperialists, the Hungarian cockade and colors. The Austrians were hurrying away to Vienna.... Bem has not gone in the direction of Wallachia, but has marched to Temeswar.

Thus, one of the best-known Polish military leaders who volunteered to serve alongside the Hungarians in their war of independence against Austria, therefore, had been General Józef Bem (1794-1850). In this issue a related news-brief titled "Russia," the *Niles' National Register* noted that:

Article 298. (June 6, 1849, page 366)

The emperor reached St. Petersburg on the 15th inst. There had already marched into Gallicia, en route to Hungary, to the assistance of the Austrians, 120,000 Russians, with 350 cannon and 27,000 cavalry. Gen. Bem is prepared to give them a warm reception...

The June 13, 1849 issue of Niles' National Register, page 372, carried an exceptionally praiseworthy article about Polish general Józef Bem, an iconic Polish freedom-fighter of that era, along with other Poles, for Hungary and the Ottomans as well as for Poland.

Article 299. (June 13, 1849, page 372)

General Joseph Bem. Is a native of Tarnow in Gallicia. He was born in 1795, descended from an ancient and noble family, of four hundred years standing, and though originally of foreign origin, like the Geraldines in Ireland, they have by nobleness and virtue, become true and patriotic Poles. He was educated at the University of Cracow; he attended the Military School at Warsaw, conducted by the French General, Pelletier. At the termination of his studies, he entered the army as a subaltern in the Mounted Artillery. He was with Davoust and McDonald in the disastrous Russian campaign of 1812, and finally became a prisoner of war by the capitulation of Dantzig, and was sent back to Poland. He subsequently entered the Polish army under the command of the Grand Duke Constantine, and attained the rank of Captain and the position of Professor of the newly organized Military School. His patriotic feelings involved him in difficulties with the government, and he was confined for a long time as loathsome, as a refined Russian barbarity could invent. When, however, he obtained a trial, he was declared innocent; at the instigation of the Grand Duke he was tried a second time for the same offence and was sentenced to three months' imprisonment. He soon after retired from the Russian service, and employed his leisure in literary pursuits, and wrote his great work upon the 'Steam Engine, as applied to Mechanics.' On the rising of his countrymen in 1830, he hastened to Poland, and was made Major and Commander of Flying Artillery. He took part in the battle of Iganie, where 8,000 Poles were successful over 20,000 Russians, and Bem's sixteen guns silenced forty of the enemies. For his gallant conduct on this occasion he was made Lieutenant Colonel on the field. Before the defence of Warsaw he was Major General. After the suppression of the Revolution, he escaped to France; in 1832, we find him in Portugal, supporting the cause of Don Pedro. After the last French Revolution, he went to Vienna where he organized the militia (*Wahrmannschall*) and became their commander. After the bombardment, a price was set upon his head, but he was fortunately enabled to escape in disguise to Hungary, where he was placed at the head of affairs. The subsequent success of the Hungarian arms justify their high opinion of the military talents of General Bem. *It is somewhat singular that the three leading men of the Magyars, at the present time, are Poles, viz; Bem, Dembynski and Chrzanowski, all highly distinguished in the Polish Revolution. They are fighting today as nobly for foreign nationality as they did for their own on the bloody fields of Poland."*

Article 300. (June 13, 1849, page 381)

Informed 21st century Americans have become familiar with the expression, "follow the money," as it involves criminal and other investigations. All told, the chronicle of the struggles for Poland during the precedent-setting legacy of Hezekiah Niles' journalistic endeavors -- that he had sustained from 1811 until his death in 1839, and then sustained by his successors until 1849 -- had to have identified a concomitant economic liability (i.e., Poland's national debt) incurred during Poland's struggles to regain its once free and independent government. Thus, whereas *Poland* may have despised being an integral part of Imperial Russia, Russia and Poland were bound to one another when it came to displays of the national

debt. The same was true of the combined national debt of Prussia and Poland. The fact that both Russia and Prussia each reported their national debts
in combination with Poland, each of which combinations at times had been
$545,000,000 conveniently rounded off to the exact dollar, it appears that
Russia and Prussia may have colluded, or at least collaborated, in the matter
of each arriving at that amount, and despite having separately wished not
only to remove Poland from the maps of Europe but also to eliminate the
very word Poland and the memory of its existence historically, and substituting their own-named designations in its place. They may have been grateful
to have Poland, as their scapegoat, to blame for their own excessive national
expenditures versus imbalanced revenues.

Consequently, the more Russia persisted in its attempts to eliminate
the memory of the once free and independent Poland, the more Poles had
been determined to succeed in the task of restoring Poland's freedom and
independence, on one hand, and the more the process of seeking annihilation
of Poland and the Poles raised the total cost involved in achieving that objective on the part of Russia and Prussia. *Austria, to its credit, did not create
its own combined 'Austria and Poland' measure of unit.*

Clearly, European economists, as well as the other European governments of the times, had been able to reflect the concept of an extant Poland
as an integral part of the Russian Empire in all of its aspects, save for national freedom and independence, as this June 13, 1849 "Debts of Foreign
Countries" article included in the *Niles' National Register*, illustrates.

As such, *Niles' National Register* published yet another report on
the national debts of European nations, wherein Russia and Poland were
grouped together as a single entity. *Russia likely rationalized and insisted
that this was appropriate because of the massive funds it had to expend from
the imperial treasury, or had borrowed, in its protracted efforts to subjugate
Poland which, in theory and in practice, meant that the victim of the crime
(Poland) was compelled to remunerate the criminals committing the crime
(Russia largely, and Prussia; with Austria to a lesser extent) for the cost
of having been victimized. Moreover, while adding to its imposition of an
ever-greater economic burden on the Kingdom of Poland, Russia never acknowledged the vast wealth it conveniently had amassed from the arbitrary
confiscation of very significant properties of the Polish rebellion's leaders
and followers during the period, 1831-1849, and earlier (1772, 1793 and
1795) as well.*

Please note that whereas the table below for Great Britain began with
the dollar ($) sign, the table's grand totals ended with the pound (£) sign.
Niles' National Register offered no explanation, and thus, neither can I. Finally, note as well that the Russia and Poland combined debt reported here
differed in extent than it did in previous reports. Although the Russia and Po-

land combined debt was sufficient to keep the Russia and Poland combined debt's in fourth place behind the very same three other European nations of earlier reports, Russia and Poland's combined debt of $110,000,000 was considerably lower than the $545,000,000 of earlier reports. How that happened and why, is anyone's guess insofar as I had been unable to identify anything else reported about the matter by *Niles' National Register*. After what appears next, I will offer a final perspective on the national debts as reported in this book by Hezekiah Niles et al for the years 1829, 1839, 1843, 1844 and 1849:

DEBTS OF FOREIGN COUNTRIES. The debts of the various countries of Europe may be thus classed in round numbers:

Great Britain	$860,000,000
France	320,000,000
Holland	160,000,000
Russia and Poland	110,000,000
Spain	93,000,000
Austria	84,000,000
Prussia	30,000,000
Portugal	28,000,000
Naples	26,000,000
Belgium	25,000,000
Denmark	18,000,000
Sicily	14,000,000
Papal Dominions	13,000,000
Greece	8,000,000
Bavaria	3,000,000
Bremen	600,000
Frankfurt	1,000,000
Hamburg	1,400,000

	£1,785,000,000
Debts not enumerated	£215,000,000
	£2,000,000,000

Requiring an annual provision to the extent of £100,000,000 for interest, in addition to at least 20 to 25 million pounds for expenses of collection, administration, etc.

Please note that the original figures reported in the table above had been printed clearly and thus, readily transcribed. Consequently, the initial sub-total of £1,785,000,000 should actually have been £1,795,000,000 which, with the addition of the £215,000,000 "debts not enumerated," should have increased the grand total to £2,010,000,000.

Finally, I have combined the *National Debt* articles for 1929, 1839, 1843, 1844 and 1849 into a single table below. Insofar as England's (i.e., Great Britain's) financial excesses had been the largest in Europe, it is placed at the top of the list and all others under England appear in descending order:

ELEMENTS OF COMBINED NATIONAL DEBT REPORTS, IN (£) AND ($): 1829, 1839, 1843, 1844, and 1849

Nation:	1829 Debt (£):	1839 Debt (£):	1843 Debt ($):	1844 Debt ($)	1849 Debt ($):
England / Gr. Brit.	819,600,000	800,000,000	5,556,000,000	5,556,000,000	860,000,000
France	194,400,000	194,000,000	1,800,000,000	1,800,000,000	320,000,000
Holland / Nether.	148,500,000	148,500,000	800,000,000	800,000,000	160,000,000
Russia / Poland	not included	not included	545,000,000	not included	110,000,000
Prussia / Poland	not included	not included	545,000,000	545,000,000	not included
Austria	78,100,000	77,100,000	380,000,000	380,000,000	84,000,000
Russia	35,550,000	35,550,000	150,000,000	150,000,000	not included
Prussia	29,701,000	29,701,000	150,000,000	not included	30,000,000
Poland	5,729,000	5,740,000	not included	not included	not included

As it relates to the "National Debts" reports published by Niles' National Register, the monetary units of the British pound sterling (£) and the dollar ($) had not been applied uniformly by the final editor who succeeded Hezekiah Niles. Therefore, this book's *Articles 116, 238, 253, 256* and *300* reflect the following monetary characteristics:

Article 116 = Begins and ends in Pounds Sterling.
Article 238 = Begins and ends in Pounds Sterling.
Article 253 = Begins and ends in German dollars.
Article 256 = Begins and ends in American dollars.
Article 300 = Begins in American dollars and ends in Pounds Sterling.

Closing thoughts:

(1) Who held the debts, one again may ask, for all the countries included in these reports? Especially so in the matter of England and France on whom Poland's *freedom fighters* had hoped for military intervention against Russia.

(2) Using the example of England as it related to accountability on the part of the realm to its subjects, how did its national debt of eight hundred million in Pounds Sterling for the year 1839 rise to an astronomical *five billion, five hundred fifty-six million* for the year 1843?

(3) The same to be said for France whose national debt in 1839 had

been one hundred ninety-four million, but had risen to *one billion, eight-hundred million* for the year 1839 as well?

(4) What had been Poland's true national debt for the entire period 1829-1849?

(5) How did Prussia reduce its 150,000,000 debt in 1843 to 30,000,000 in 1849?

(6) If Russia's debt without Poland had been 150,000,000, but when *combined with Poland as a separate measure of debt* -- it became 545,000,000 -- what proportion had been Russia's and what had been Poland's?

(7) In contrast, Prussia's individual debt had been reduced from its highest of 150,000,000 in 1843 to 30,000,000 in 1849, whereas Prussia's combined debt with Poland remained constant at 545,000,000 both in 1843 and 1844, but ended with nothing being reported in 1849.

(8) All of the foregoing of which suggests that something of significantly large (indeed of epic dimensions) financial implications had transpired in Poland's victimization by Russia and Prussia which likely will never be known.

(9) Apart from, but symbiotically related to items 5 through 8 of the foregoing, what, in the final analysis, had been the true number of Polish souls forever lost in seemingly-unrelenting battles, both large and small, and via deportations of Polish children to Russia's interior as well as to the Caucasus, mass deportations of adult Poles to Siberia, Poles lost to disease and hunger during war-time and/or war-like conditions for the period 1831 to 1849, and by way of other forms of *punishment* for having had the audacity to precipitate the November Uprising of 1830?

Moreover, why had all of the foregoing of which apparently had been justified by Russia for the relentless application, without remorse or accountability, of its policy for the *ethnic cleansing and annihilation of Poland and the Polish nationality* on the soil of the former territorially extensive and culturally diverse Commonwealth of Poland and Lithuania -- with large numbers of said population thereof, it relocated forcibly, not on locomotives or horse-drawn wagons, but largely as Russia preferred, on foot and at times in chains as well, extensively to the Caucasus and Siberia, and God only knows elsewhere as well -- with virtually no substantially-compelling threats of economic sanctions having been elicited from Great Britain and France against Russia in 1849 whose weak financial situation caused it to sell Alaska to the United States less than two decades later?

Article 301. (June 20, 1849, page 386)

In this issue of the *Niles' National Register*, its article titled, "Ukase of the Emperor of Russia," demonstrated that Czar Nicholas I referenced the "Polish traitors of 1831" as having been responsible for the "Spring of Nations" nationalist-based revolutionary turmoil throughout Europe in 1848-1849, so much did he hate Poles, Poland and the Polish Uprising of 1830.

In his thirty year reign (1825-1855), the vindictive Czar Nicholas stood for the essence of Russian *samobytnost* or the fact of being Russian, that importantly included the denial of what Russian Orthodox Christians termed to be "Roman-Germanic falsehood" in matters of religion, and in its place acceptance of so-called "Greek-Slavic truth" that supported his brutal dictatorship, an aspect of which, as it related to the religious duties and obligations that Poles owed to their imperial master, had been presented earlier in *Article 196* of this book.

In what follows below, the *Niles' National Register* article of June 20, 1849 illustrated that in Russia there was no place for any ethnicity other than Russian. In his ukase, Nicholas included particularly precise reference to the "Polish traitors of 1831," whom he blamed for inciting the revolutionary turmoil of 1848-1849 in Europe among Czechs, Italians, and Hungarians as well as others. Poles and Poland had been and remained a core hatred for the Czar, nearly 19 years after the November Uprising of 1830 began. His ukase of April 25, 1849 illustrated the point.

By the Grace of God, We, Nicholas I, Emperor and Autocrat of All the Russias, etc., declare to the nation, having by our manifesto of the 14th of March 1848, informed our subjects of the miseries which inflicted Western Europe, we are at the same time made known how we were ready to meet our enemies wherever they might show themselves, and that we should, without sparing ourselves, in conjunction indissoluble with our sacred Russia, defend the honor of the Russian name, and the inviolability of our frontiers.

The commotions and rebellions of the West have not since then ceased. Guilty delusion, enticing the thoughtless crowd with visionary dreams of that prosperity which can never be the fruit of willfulness and obstinacy, has entered the East and the dominions contiguous to us, and subjects of the Turkish Empire, viz: Moldavia and Wallachia. Only by the presence of our troops, together with those of Turkey, has order been restored and maintained; but in Hungary and Transylvania the efforts of the Austrian Government, distracted already by another war with foreign and domestic enemies in Italy, have not been able to triumph over rebellion. *On the contrary, strengthening itself by hordes of our Polish traitors of 1831, and by other foreigners, outcasts, runaways, and vagrants, the rebellion has developed itself to a most threatening degree.*

In the midst of these unfortunate events the Emperor of Austria has addressed himself to us with the wish for our assistance against our common enemies. We shall not refuse him.

Having called to the assistance of this righteous enterprise, the Almighty Leader and Lord of Victories, we have commanded our armies to move forward for the extinction of rebellion, and the destruction of audacious and evil-intentioned men, who endeavor to disturb the peace of our dominions also.

Let God be with us, and who shall be against us?

So, we are convinced of it, so feels, so hopes, so aspires our God preserved Nation, every Russian, every true subject of ours, and Russia will fulfill her mission.

Given at St. Petersburg, this 25th day of April, in the year from the birth of Christ, 1849, and the 24th of our reign.

signed, Nicholas I

Article 302. (June 27, 1849, page 394)

A week later, in its final-ever issue of June 27, 1849 on page 394, Niles' National Register included succinct mention that:

...rumor prevailed that the Russians had been defeated by Dembinski, at Jordenow.

...and that Polish general Bem who also had volunteered to fight alongside Hungarians for the independence of Hungary, commanded one corps of the eleven Hungarian army corps that combined amounted to 446,000 men. Fitting, indeed, that this final news report kept the idea of Poland and its fighters for freedom and independence in the hearts and minds of American readers of the *Niles' National Register*, as its days as an independent newsmagazine ended forever, by way of referencing the service in the cause of liberty of the two Polish military commanders, Henryk Dembiński (1791-1864) and Józef Bem (1794-1850), who had fought for Poland's cause in the November Uprising of 1830 and thereafter, and later for the Hungarian cause in 1848-1849, as freedom fighters for two nations in the well-known altruistic Polish spirit of za wolność naszą i waszą ("for our freedom and yours"), each of which struggles for national independence had involved Russia sending its considerable forces in support of an oppressive status quo, beginning with late 18th century Poland, and in Hungary as well, during mid-19th century.

All the foregoing of which, beginning with *Article 1,* is what American subscribers of *Niles' Register* had read about Poland's existential struggles for national freedom and independence -- for the God-given right to remain Poles -- throughout the period from 1811 to 1849.

Indeed, whereas the life of *Niles' Register*, struggling Poland's *amicus poloniae*-worthy entity in the United States during the first half of the 19th century, ended in the year 1849, the struggles of Poland for the right to exist as a free and independent nation continued relentlessly, and in many respects continue today, as it relates to the Russian Federation in the 21st century. And thanks to Hezekiah Niles, Americans from 1811 to 1849 saw Russia for what it was. While as for Russia's behavioral characteristics in 2021, "the more things change, the more they remain the same," continues as a truism in the 21st century. "Eternal Russia" indeed. Dangerous Russia in a reality far-exceeding its 19th and 20th century capabilities because of mastery of cyber warfare against a divided and vulnerable West and transatlantic unity of purpose as we enter the third decade of the 21st century, progressing relentlessly toward the November Uprising's bicentennial and its painful lingering aftermath in the long history of Poland, among many of its other subsequent painful episodes as well, when *polskość* was continually forged as it had been through the ages. All never to be forgotten, and if so, at our own peril.

As the result of the January Uprising of 1863, yet another wave of generations of Poles, both young and old, suffered their own "modern" painful loss and punishment for daring to struggle and fight for their national freedom and independence, for the end of being an nine century old European nationality without a free and independent nation of their own since 1795. Exile to Siberia, being Imperial Russia's favored slow-death punishment for such Poles, went on to continue into the 20th century.

Despite it all, the dream of a free and independent Poland persisted as well.

The Prisoners (Więźniowie) depicted by Jacek Malczewski in 1883. Although this image is from the era of January 1863 revolt, it is in keeping with the image of adult Polish prisoners being transported to Siberia. Yet a not inconsiderable number of Polish children were exiled as well, as follows in the next illustration:

"Students' Exile" (Zesłanie Studentów) by Jacek Malczewski in 1891 corroborated the fact that Imperial Russia's readily recognizable, albeit yet to be identified as such, policy of the ethnic-cleansing of Poland's male children continued.

APPENDIX

THE WEEKLY REGISTER (1811) – NILES' WEEKLY REGISTER (1814) – NILES' NATIONAL REGISTER (1837)

(1) Hezekiah Niles (Founding Editor in Baltimore, Maryland): Volumes 1 through 50;
(2) William Ogden Niles (Editor in Baltimore, Maryland): Volumes 51 through 56*
(3) Jeremiah Hughes (Editor in Baltimore, Maryland): Volumes 57 through 73
(4) George Beatty (Editor in Philadelphia, Pennsylvania): Volumes 74 and 75
Volume 1 = September 1811 to March 1812
Volume 2 = March 1812 to September 1812
Volume 3 = September 1812 to March 1813
Volume 4 = March 1813 to September 1813
Volume 5 = September 1813 to March 1814
Volume 6 = March 1814 to September 1814
Volume 7 = September 1814 to March 1815
Volume 8 = March 1815 to September 1815
Volume 9 = September 1815 to March 1816
Volume 10 = March 1816 to September 1816
Volume 11 = September 1816 to March 1817
Volume 12 = March 1817 to September 1817
Volume 13 = September 1817 to March 1818, or Volume I, New Series
Volume 14 = March 1818 to September 1818, or Volume II, New Series
Volume 15 = September 1818 to March 1819, or Volume III, New Series
Volume 16 = March 1819 to September 1819, or Volume IV, New Series
Volume 17 = September 1819 to March 1820, or Volume V, New Series
Volume 18 = March 1820 to September 1820, or Volume VI, New Series
Volume 19 = September 1820 to March 1821, or Volume VII, New Series
Volume 20 = March 1821 to September 1821, or Volume VIII, New Series
Volume 21 = September 1821 to March 1822, or Volume IX, New Series
Volume 22 = March 1822 to September 1822, or Volume X, New Series
Volume 23 = September 1822 to March 1823, or Volume XI, New Series
Volume 24 = March 1823 to September 1823, or Volume XII, New Series
Volume 25 = September 1823 to March 1824, or Volume I, 3rd Series
Volume 26 = March 1824 to September 1824, or Volume II, 3rd Series
Volume 27 = September 1824 to March 1825, or Volume III, 3rd Series
Volume 28 = March 1825 to September 1825, or Volume IV, 3rd Series
Volume 29 = September 1825 to March 1826, or Volume V, 3rd Series
Volume 30 = March 1826 to September 1826, or Volume VI, 3rd Series
Volume 31 = September 1826 to March 1827, or Volume VIII, 3rd Series
Volume 32 = March 1827 to September 1827, or Volume VIII, 3rd Series
Volume 33 = September 1827 to March 1828, or Volume IX, 3rd Series
Volume 34 = March 1828 to September 1828, or Volume X, 3rd Series
Volume 35 = September 1828 to March 1829, or Volume XI, 3rd Series
Volume 36 = March 1829 to September 1829, or Volume XII, 3rd Series
Volume 37 = September 1829 to March 1830, or Volume I, 4th Series
Volume 38 = March 1830 to September 1830, or Volume II, 4th Series
Volume 39 = September 1830 to March 1831, or Volume III. 4th Series
Volume 40 = March 1831 to September 1831, or Volume IV, 4th Series
Volume 41 = September 1831 to March 1832, or Volume V, 4th Series
Volume 42 = March 1832 to September 1832, or Volume VI, 4th Series
Volume 43 = September 1832 to March 1833, or Volume VII, 4th Series
Volume 44 = March 1833 to September 1833, or Volume VIII, 4th Series

Volume 45 = September 1833 to March 1834, or Volume IX, 4th Series
Volume 46 = March 1834 to September 1834, or Volume X, 4th Series
Volume 47 = September 1834 to March 1835, to Volume XLVII, or Volume XI, 4th Series
Volume 48 = March 1835 to September 1835, to Volume XLVIII, or Volume XII, 4th Series
Volume 49 = September 1835 to March 1836, to Volume XLIX, or Volume XIII, 4th Series
Volume 50 = March 1836 to September 1836, to Volume L, or Volume XIV, 4th Series
Volume 51 = September 1836 to March 1837, to Volume LI, or Volume XV, 4th Series
Volume 52 = March 1837 to September 1837, to Volume LII, or Volume XVI, 4th Series
Volume 53 = September 1837 to March 1838, to Volume LIII, or Volume XVII, 4th Series*
Volume 54 = March 1838 to September 1838, to Volume LV, or Volume LIV, 5th Series*
Volume 55 = September 1838 to March 1839, to Volume V, or Volume LV, 5th Series*
Volume 56 = March 1839 to September 1839, to Volume VI, or Volume LVI, 5th Series
Volume 57 = September 1839 to March 1840, to Volume VII, or Volume LVII, 5th Series
Volume 58 = March 1840 to September 1840, to Volume LVIII, or Volume VIII, 5th Series
Volume 59 = September 1840 to March 1841, to Volume LIX, or Volume IX, 5th Series
Volume 60 = March 1841 to September 1841, to Volume LX, or Volume X, 5th Series
Volume 61 = September 1841 to March 1842, to Volume LXI, or Volume XI, 5th Series
Volume 62 = March 1842 to September 1842, to Volume LXII, or Volume XII, 5th Series
Volume 63 = September 1842 to March 1843, to Volume LXIII, or Volume XIII, 5th Series
Volume 64 =March 1843 to September 1843, to Volume LXIV, or Vol. XIV, 5th Series
Volume 65 = September 1843 to March 1844, to Volume LXV, or Volume XV, 5th Series
Volume 66 = March 1844 to September 1844, to Volume LXVI, or Volume XVI, 5th Series
Volume 67 = September 1844 to March 1845, to Volume LXVII, or Volume XVII, 5th Series
Volume 68 = March 1845 to September 1845, to Volume LXVIII, or Volume XVII, 5th Series
Volume 69 = September 1845 to March 1846, to Volume LXIX, or Volume XVIII, 5th Series
Volume 70 = March 1846 to September 1846, to Volume LXX, or Volume XX, 5th Series
Volume 71 = September 1846 to March 1847, to Volume LXXI, or Volume XXI, 5th Series
Volume 72 = March 1847 to September 1847, to Volume LXXII, or Volume XXII, 5th Series
Volume 73 = September 1847 to March 1848, to Volume LXXIII, or Volume XXIII, 5th Series
Volume 74 = July 1848 to January 1849, to Volume LXXIV
Volume 75 = January 1849 to July 1849, to Volume LXXV

* Produced in Washington City

INDEX

BY WAY OF AN INTRODUCTION, pages 4 – 16

Whereas the 302 Articles appearing below and constituting this book have a brief description of their content, in the actual associated texts the vast majority contain many more subjects in addition to the ones presented here. Please note that multiple-numbered Articles appearing under one date reflect the fact of separate stories on different pages in a particular issue of Niles' Register. Of the three columns represented here, the first designates the Article number in this book, the second designates the date of publication in Niles' Register and the third represents the subject (or at least one of the subjects contained in the particular entry):

40	Jul. 4, 1818	Viceroy Constantine elected to Poland's Diet by Praga's citizens in 103 to 3 vote
41	Nov. 7, 1818	Since 1814, the small-pox has not been seen at Stettin (Szczecin)
42	Apr. 3, 1819	A statistical survey of Poland has been published at Warsaw
43	Apr. 17, 1819	Suicide rates in Prussian cities, including Breslau (Wrocław)
44	Jun. 19, 1819	On the "Mitigation of Slavery" and Czarina Catherine II of Russia
45	Sep. 4, 1819	Freedom of the press in Warsaw (Warszawa in Polish) is an illusion
46	Nov. 13, 1819	Alexander I of Russia to be crowned in Warsaw as King of Poland
47	Nov. 27, 1819	Alexander has abolished the "liberty of the press" in Poland
48	Dec. 11, 1819	In absence of a Monroe Doctrine, Spain cedes California to Russia
49	Jun. 17, 1820	A monument in memory of Kościuszko raised in Janów, Poland
50	Oct. 28, 1820	Rumor implying a free and independent Poland will be restored
51	Nov. 4, 1820	Sources cannot place faith that Russia will re-establish a free Poland
52	Nov. 11, 1820	Alexander addresses Sejm in Warsaw on September 13, 1820
53	Nov. 11, 1820	Hezekiah Niles comments on Alexander's pledge to protect Poland
54	Dec. 23, 1820	"Examine your own consciences," Alexander states to Poland's Sejm
55	Jan. 13, 1821	The Russian yoke cannot sit easy on the neck of Poland
56	Apr. 14, 1821	Report on the progress to erect the Kościuszko Mound in Kraków
57	May 5, 1821	A rising of the Poles against the crusade of the kings is spoken of
58	May 12, 1821	Reportedly a Polish Legion was to be formed in the Kingdom of Naples
59	Jul. 28, 1821	A force of 100,000 Russians cross the Dwina, with 80,000 sent to Minsk
60	Aug. 11, 1821	Grand duke Constantine suspected of having imbued liberalism
61	Mar. 16, 1822	Russia's army exceeds 1,000,000 with 5 corps of 75,000 to 80,000 each
62	May 4, 1822	Plot for an insurrection in Poland is discovered by arrests at Paris
63	Jun. 8, 1822	Large numbers of 1812-era Poles freed from Siberian captivity by Czar
64	Oct. 12, 1822	Alexander orders punishment for anyone sheltering Army deserters
65	Oct. 12, 1822	French papers rumor that Poland might be restored under Pole as king
66	Nov. 2, 1822	5,500,000 Catholics in Russian Empire, all being Poles and Lithuanians
67	Apr. 12, 1823	Hezekiah Niles accuses Alexander of moral parricide in Czar Paul death
68	Aug. 2, 1823	Hezekiah Niles decries Catherine II, the Czar's wanton grandmother
69	Sep. 6, 1823	Opposition to Alexander's project to ameliorate condition of peasants
70	Mar. 13, 1824	Jewish Rabbis and Elders decide to celebrate Sabbath on Sunday
71	Nov. 18,1824	Manifesto on military recruiting issued by the Czar Alexander I Russia
72	Nov. 18, 1824	USMA Cadets announce design competition for Kościuszko monument
73	Jan, 22, 1825	Northwest USA border with Russia set at 54 degrees, 40 minutes north
74	Apr. 12, 1825	Alexander the 'deliverer' is just as ambitious as Napoleon was
75	May 7, 1825	Alexander warns Polish Sejm not to spend time in useless debates
76	Jun. 25, 1825	Comparative price of wheat in Europe, Dantzic (Gdańsk) Included
77	Jul. 23, 1825	Alexander promises tax relief to major landowners in Poland
78	Jul. 30, 1825	Salt mining and the truly hidden beauty of the Wieliczka salt mine
79	Aug. 6, 1825	Russia's official justification for not educating the lower classes
80	Aug. 20, 1825	Administration of justice in the Russian-controlled Polish kingdom
81	Oct. 15, 1825	In Poland, Alexander decrees a "fixed order" to regulate the Jews
82	Oct. 22, 1825	Editor Niles republishes aspect of his 1814 op-ed of Cossack Platoff
83	Feb. 11, 1826	Stanislaus Stalzic, minister of state, died, left fortune for civic welfare
84	Feb. 11, 1826	Alexander dies at "Taganrock after a few days' indisposition"
85	Feb. 26, 1826	Hezekiah Niles critical of Le Roy, NY Gazette editor who admired Czar
86	Nov. 11, 1826	250,000 German manufacturers said to have relocated to Poland
87	Nov. 18, 1826	Alexander's last decree created monetary basis for all titles of nobility
88	Dec. 2, 1826	Hezekiah Niles reprints the story of 1794 Russian Massacre of Praga
89	Jun. 2, 1827	During Warsaw coronation, Nicholas inducted in British Order of Garter
90	Jun. 2, 1827	To Imperial Russia, the Kingdom of Poland is a hate-admire conundrum
91	Sep. 22, 1827	4,000 inhabitants of Silesia lose all their property to great floods
92	Sep. 29, 1827	In Imperial Russia, 20 million Poles served by only 15 Polish newspapers
93	Nov. 1, 1828	Trial of Patriotic Society of Poland members draws to a close
94	May 30, 1829	Vistula River floods preclude bountiful harvest in Prussian Poland
95	Jun. 13, 1829	More deplorable accounts of the floods in west and east Prussia
96	Jul. 11, 1829	Czar Nicholas I arrives in Warsaw for his coronation as King of Poland

97	Sep. 13, 1829	VIVAT REX IN ETERNUM: a report on coronation of Nicholas in Warsaw
98	Aug. 21, 1830	Manufactories in Poland, in 1815, was at 100, is now at 4,000
99	Nov. 20, 1830	Russian canals, and one which will unite the Niemen and Vistula rivers
100	Nov. 27, 1830	Great fermentation in Prussian Poland, west Russian provinces
101	Dec. 25, 1830	Ferment prevails in Poland and Warsaw. Russia masses troops on border
102	Jan. 1, 1831	Cholera mordus in Russia, revolution in Poland, fears of general war
103	Feb. 5, 1831	The "ball of revolution is still in motion" in Poland
104	Feb. 12, 1831	Field Marshal von Diebitsch versus General Grzegorz Chłopicki
105	Feb. 12, 1831	The modern history and present state of this ill-fated country, Poland
106	Feb. 12, 1831	Lafayette addresses French Chamber of Deputies on Poland
107	Feb. 26, 1831	Russia prepares for a "war of extermination" against Poland
108	Feb. 26, 1831	Poles field 150,000 fully equipped men, and 200,000 with pikes and pistols
109	Mar. 5, 1831	Nicholas addresses two Russian manifestos against Poland
110	Mar. 19, 1831	Kingdom of Poland is heart and center of its ancient sovereignty
111	Apr. 9, 1831	Deibitsch resolved to execute severest punishment against the Poles
112	Apr. 23, 1831	Report on Poland's gallant resistance against Russian forces
113	Apr. 23, 1831	Russian forces act in accord with reputation as brutish barbarians
114	Apr. 30, 1831	Strike in the name of liberty, kill the invader, let Poland be free
115	Apr. 30, 1831	General Dwernicki is reported pursuing Russians with great fury
116	Apr. 30, 1831	Report reveals that Europe's monarchs live well beyond their means
117	May 14, 1831	A battlefield report, and another about the "Polish spirit"
118	May 21, 1831	Russian cruelty in Poland must ultimately prove fatal to Russia
119	May 21, 1831	Jan Zygmunt Skrzynecki and victory of Poles over the Russians
120	May 28, 1831	Report that Russia's 95th Regiment deserted and joined Poles
121	May 28, 1831	Report that in their holy cause, the Poles had fought like lions
122	Jun. 4, 1831	Lithuania makes a common cause with Poland for freedom
123	Jun. 11, 1831	Poland's location, and Russia's limitless forces, are a sobering reality
124	Jun. 18, 1831	A needed primer for pronouncing Polish names, but not successfully
125	Jun. 18, 1831	Report that on the whole, the accounts from Poland are cheering
126	Jun. 25, 1831	Report that Polish general Dwernicki capitulates his army to Austria
127	Jul. 2, 1831	Poles confess having faint hopes of success against the Russians
128	Jul. 9, 1831	Kościuszko's thinking about the benefits of liberty is re-published
129	Jul. 9, 1831	With 8,000 men, General Skrzynecki cuts through 24,000 Russians
130	Jul. 9, 1831	French National Guard of 750,000 men, fully armed and equipped
131	Jul. 9, 1831	Highly comprehensive "Statistics of Poland" published in London
132	Jul. 16, 1831	The "Secret Treaty of Verona of 1822" is revealed and published
133	Jul. 23, 1831	Czar willing to lose 200,000 Russian soldiers killed to defeat Poland
134	Jul. 30, 1831	Hungarians criticize Austria for siding with Russia against Poland
135	Aug. 6, 1831	On June 6 at Ostrołęka and Mariampol Polish forces battle Russians
136	Aug. 20, 1831	Russia and Austria have 400,000 men, ready to take the field
137	Aug. 27, 1831	Ships leave England with 25,000 rifles and 48 cannon, for the Poles
138	Sep. 3, 1831	Grand Duke Constantine dies, a fortunate event for the Poles
139	Sep. 3, 1831	France and Lafayette declare support of the Polish cause
140	Sep. 10, 1831	In Paris, Americans work to raise funds in USA to help Polish cause
141	Sep. 10, 1831	At military review 120,000 French soldiers shout "Long live Poland"
142	Sep. 10, 1831	Ratio of soldiers to inhabitants of Poland, Russia, Prussia and Austria
143	Sep. 10, 1831	American claims on France are a model for Russian claims on France
144	Sep. 17, 1831	Skrzynecki writes to Prussian King; Czartoryski addresses Polish nation
145	Sep. 17, 1831	"A Polish General-ess," being the story of combat leader Emilia Plater (1806-1831)
146	Sep. 24, 1831	Cholera spreads to Gdańsk; Warsaw prepares for the Russian assault
147	Oct. 15, 1831	Russians within 5 miles of Warsaw; Cholera rages in Russia and Poland
148	Oct. 29, 1831	With Russians massing for assault, terror and anarchy rises in Warsaw
149	Nov. 5, 1831	Warsaw capitulates to the Russians on the 7th at 6 o'clock, p.m.
150	Nov. 12, 1831	At Warsaw 20,000 Russians killed. Roziski has a Polish army at Kunow
151	Nov. 12, 1831	60 Russian generals in Warsaw, Wilt governs city, Korff is commandant
152	Nov. 19, 1831	Roziski (Różycki) says all is not lost, Poland is more than Warsaw alone
153	Nov. 26, 1831	1,500 of Warsaw's distinguished leaders arrested and imprisoned
154	Dec. 10, 1831	Czartoryski, Skrzynecki and Małachowski retire into Austria

155 Jan. 14, 1832 Poland news filled with gloom, destruction, wretched depression
156 Jan. 14, 1832 Warsaw reduced in 1831 by 25,000 (15,000 men; 10,000 women)
157 Jan. 14, 1832 Let us leave Europe, a heartless spectator of our struggle
158 Jan. 14, 1832 Memory of Russia's erratic/sadistic Grand Duke Constantine in Poland
159 Jan. 21, 1832 Samuel G. Howe, MD of Boston works to raise money for Poland
160 Feb. 11, 1832 Russia loses 30,649 k.i.a. for defeat of Warsaw; 180,000 for all Poland
161 Mar. 10, 1832 In Poland, Russians offer aid to families of Poles who died loyal to Czar
162 Mar. 17, 1832 Czar Nicholas threatens to teach the British a lesson for helping Poland
163 Apr. 7, 1832 Russian dominion over Poland, is perfect, all sorts of tyranny practiced
164 Jun. 2, 1832 Nicholas proclaims "The End of Poland" as of February 26, 1832
165 Jun. 23, 1832 German statistics of cholera deaths in Europe, and in some Polish cities
166 Jul. 21, 1832 The Polish exiles are yet relentlessly pursued with the vengeance of Russia
167 Aug. 11, 1832 A black and bloody despotism prevails over Poland
168 Aug. 18, 1832 48,000 Poles of all ages, sexes, chained, seen marched into Russia
169 Aug. 25, 1832 In all of Poland children particularly taken and carried away into Russia
170 Sep. 1, 1832 In Nicholas, the soul of the infanticide Herod is metamorphosed
171 Sep. 22, 1832 Many Poles are in arms in the forests of Lithuania, ready to kill or be killed
172 Oct. 6, 1832 So dies for Poland the brave Polish general, Józef Sowiński
173 Oct. 20, 1832 Baden dissolves all committees for the relief of Polish immigrants
174 Nov. 3, 1832 Pope declares that Catholic Poles must obey ukases of their legal king
175 Nov. 17, 1832 Russia's persistent ethnic cleansing of Poland's children and nationality
176 Dec. 1, 1832 Lord Durham's mission to mitigate Russia's treatment of Poland fails
177 Dec. 1, 1832 Niles' Register agrees with calls to help Polish freedom fighters in USA
178 Dec. 1, 1832 England and France hamper trade with the "Holy Alliance" over Poland
179 Apr. 13, 1833 Church with its holy icon, Our Lady of Częstochowa, defiled by Russia
180 Apr. 13, 1833 Lafayette to inhabitants of Bogotá, Columbia, remember Poland
181 Apr. 20, 1833 Russian Legation in Washington practices surveillance of Poles in USA
182 Jun. 8, 1833 Czar claims an "assiduous care and paternal solicitude" for Poles
183 Jun. 15, 1833 Podolian nobility grovels to Czar to spare their children from Siberian exile
184 Jun. 17, 1833 From Paris, Czar Nicholas learns of yet another conspiracy against him
185 Jun. 22, 1833 Polish male prisoners fettered with a 7 pound leg iron, women 6 pounds
186 Jun 29, 1833 Despite Russia's financial deficit, Czar purchases two ancient sphynxes
187 Jul. 6, 1833 Death sentence for Poles (children included) deserting from Russian army
188 Aug. 3, 1833 Paskiewicz orders whipping of Polish mothers who write to rebel sons
189 Aug. 3, 1833 Wherever beats a Polish heart, the Polish nationality still exists
190 Aug. 17, 1833 Russia degrades Polish women by rape, whipping, execution, etc
191 Aug. 24, 1833 Wodzyński's letter thanking citizens of the United States
192 Aug. 31, 1833 Russia's supreme criminal court sentences 286 Poles incontumaciam
193 Sep. 7, 1833 In Poland and Germany order reigns under influence of the bayonet
194 Sep. 14, 1833 Being an informative summary report on the Republic of Kraków
195 Sep. 29, 1833 Russian censors allow only 15 Polish newspapers to serve 20,000,000 Poles
196 Oct. 19, 1833 "State Catechism" for converting Catholic Poles to Russian Orthodoxy
197 Nov. 16, 1833 As in war, peace exists by the weight of military establishments
198 Nov. 16, 1833 300 Polish soldiers (one a woman) exiled from Austria, arrive in NYC
199 Jan. 25, 1834 Russia, Prussia, Austria each pledge 35,000 men to end Polish revolt
200 Feb. 15, 1834 Russia allows whipping a Polish woman 200 to 300 times per infraction
201 Apr. 5, 1834 Poles arrive in the USA during a period of high American unemployment
202 Apr. 12, 1834 Considerable donations made in New York City for relief of the Polish exiles
203 May 8, 1834 "Gerard, ancient Polish officer" claims Austrian Consul in NYC to be a liar
204 May 17, 1834 Some Philadelphians working for relief of Polish exiles in New York City
205 May 17, 1834 Senator George Pointdexter of Mississippi adopts Polish exiles' cause
206 Jun. 7, 1834 1 Russian child educated out of 387 Russians; in Poland, 1 of 78 Poles
207 Jul. 5, 1834 Wheat value in Stettin, Amsterdam, Antwerp, Hamburg, London
208 Jul. 5, 1834 General Orders from U. S. President Jackson in memory of Lafayette
209 Jul. 19, 1834 On a Sunday in one Protestant church in Boston, $2,432 donated for Poles
210 Sep. 13, 1834 In Switzerland, conduct of vorat in its expulsion of Poles was approved
211 Sep. 27, 1834 Leaders of 1830 Uprising punished by beheading after being mutilated first

As Reported in the "Niles' Register"

212	Nov. 1, 1834	La Pologne N'est Pas Perdue: Cossacks fatally rape a 15 year old Polish girl
213	Nov. 22, 1834	In unfortunate Lithuania persecution by Russia knows no bounds
214	Jan. 17, 1835	Russia to demand indemnity of France because of uprising of Poland
215	Jan. 24, 1835	Polish women imprisoned for not denouncing their husbands to Russians
216	Feb. 7, 1835	Adam Czartoryski and Julian Ursyn Niemcewicz write to Polish exiles in USA
217	Feb. 28, 1835	Czar makes financial claim on France on behalf of kingdom of Poland
218	Feb. 28, 1835	Polish exiles on way across Texas to Mexico forced to fight American Indians
219	Mar. 7, 1835	Russian claim on France because of Poland threatens U.S. claim on France
220	Mar. 21, 1835	What France owes Poland was a debt of blood in battle against Russia
221	Jul. 5, 1835	Kościuszko to Czar Paul in 1796: "I go to America…to find brothers in arms"
222	Aug. 8, 1835	Kościuszko Mound extant in PL in 1823, yet no Washington Monument in USA
223	Sep. 26, 1835	French, Polish and Piedmontese agents allegedly plan to assassinate Czar
224	Jan. 16, 1836	Czar warns Poles of consequence of persisting in dreams of a Polish nationality
225	Mar. 5, 1836	European balance of power and support for preserving Polish nationality
226	Mar. 5, 1836	Russia refuses to recognize the independence of the Republic of Kraków
227	May 7, 1836	France adds 500,000 francs to 5,500,000 francs in support of Poles and others
228	Aug. 20, 1836	International relationships are not solely political in nature (e.g., commerce)
229	Sep. 1, 1836	Russia subjects all medals, prints, objects of art in Poland, to censorship
230	Oct. 8, 1836	In Poland, Russia forbids Jews to use of Christian first names as their own
231	Oct. 22, 1836	The emperor of Russia has aimed another blow to Polish liberty
232	Jan. 7, 1837	Russia at Vilna issues list of 142 nobles to lose property for being rebels
233	Apr. 29, 1837	In Poland, nobles are proprietors of the land, and peasants are slaves
234	Apr. 29, 1837	For Poles, employment depends on Orthodoxy and serving in Russian army
235	Jul. 29, 1837	The failure of the great (Hebrew) house of Daneker and Co. of Warsaw
236	May 12, 1838	Russia's sordid treatment of abducting young Polish women is attested
237	Oct. 27, 1838	Poland's wheat crop considered to be a part of the great granary of Europe
238	Aug. 3, 1839	National debts of European nations, Russia, Prussia, Austria, Poland included
239	Aug. 3, 1839	In upper Baltic ports value of grain has been pretty steadily maintained
240	Sep. 7, 1839	Poland's salt mining industry negotiated by the Russian commissioner in Paris
241	Mar. 28, 1840	At Dantzic (Gdańsk), a great flooding of the Vistula (Wisła) reported
242	Jul. 11, 1840	The Times is severe on Lord Palmerston, for deferring appeals of Kraków
243	Jun. 19, 1841	On marriage of his son, Czar commutes Polish death sentences to punishment
244	Jul. 19, 1841	Prussia aggrandized by acquisition of Saxony, a part of Poland, and Hanover
245	Aug. 28, 1841	Jews, throughout Russia, found to be 1,654,349; in Poland, they are 111,307
246	Oct. 9, 1841	Report that Russian troops in Poland have been reduced to the peace footing
247	Mar. 26, 1842	USA bill related to an act granting land to certain exiles from Poland approved
248	Nov. 3, 1842	Resolution for Poland's struggle to be free adopted by the Vermont legislature
249	Feb. 4, 1843	Some Polish regiments of Russian army go over to the Circassian enemy's side
250	May 6, 1843	Czar grants full amnesty to some Poles exiled to Siberia for 1830 Revolt roles
251	Oct. 12, 1843	Demolition of old Catholic chapel in Warsaw reveals gold valued at $600,000
252	Oct. 21, 1843	A large conspiracy for revolution detected in Warsaw, 300 arrested
253	Dec. 30, 1843	The subject - "Europe, Her Debts" - including Poland and its three neighbors
254	Mar. 23, 1844	Circassian khan warns Czar if Russians harm his son, he will kill Russian officers
255	Apr. 20, 1844	Augsburg Gazette reports: "The fate of the Russo-Polish refugees is decided"
256	Jun. 15, 1844	In this issue, yet another article on national debts of European nations
257	Jul. 13, 1844	Czar receives refund on ticket he purchased for a Polish Ball in London
258	Nov. 16, 1844	Secret society of Polish students 12 to 14 years old arrested, forced to be soldiers
259	Dec. 14, 1844	Suspected Polish conspirators arrested and sent to the mines of Siberia
260	Dec. 28, 1844	Russian government forbids Polish males to marry until they reach age of 31
261	Oct. 16, 1845	In Warsaw, Czar publicly mouths an obscenity, warns all male Polish students
262	Apr. 25, 1846	Congressman Hudson of Massachusetts references down-trodden Poles
263	Apr. 25, 1846	Unhappy Poland! The revolution in Cracow (Kraków) is suppressed
264	May 2, 1846	Leaders of the revolt in Kraków being imprisoned in all quarters
265	Oct. 3, 1846	Despite decades of existential struggle, Poland's production of wheat survives
266	Oct. 28, 1846	16 years after Polish Uprising, Russia works to extradite naturalized American
267	Dec. 26, 1846	Too little, too late. England and France work to prevent Cracow Republic end
268	Dec. 26, 1846	Poland's tragedy concomitantly influenced by cholera in Europe and Russia

When Victimization of Poland Was Never in Doubt

269 Dec. 26, 1846 "Breadstuff Statistics"; Czarina Catherine II's "New Russia" aspiration
270 Oct. 2, 1847 Comprehensive account of origin and history of the Republic of Kraków
271 May 1, 1847 A thanksgiving held for permitting Poles to live under Russian dominion
272 Jul. 10, 1847 Exiled Cracovian Jan Tysosowski, his wife and children arrive in New York City
273 Sep. 11, 1847 Lord Palmerston's rationale for Britain's not going to war over Kraków
274 Sep. 25, 1847 Populations of once-Polish cities: Breslau, Danzig, Posen, and Stettin
275 Oct, 8, 1847 Martyrs of Poland: Teofil Wiśniowski and Józef Kapuszciński
276 Oct. 23, 1847 Asiatic cholera in Warsaw causes Czar to defer visiting that city
277 Oct. 23, 1847 Cholera in Poland reflects same route and rate of 1830-1831 movement
278 Nov. 6, 1847 Russian hostility to Polish universities deprives Empire of 2 great scientists
279 Nov. 27, 1847 Another report on advance of cholera into Russia, Poland and Europe
280 Jan. 22, 1848 Great Britain's Parliament debates whether Jews can be members
281 Jul. 5, 1848 Russian forces in Poland amount to 400,000 men and a huge force of artillery
282 Jul. 12, 1848 Czar sits by his personal telegraph day and night for intelligence from Poland
283 Jul. 12, 1848 Rumor that Austria will invade Prussia through Poland with an immense force
284 Sep. 6, 1848 Russian army detachments (Cossacks and light cavalry) nearing Prussia
285 Sep. 6, 1848 From Tarnów in Galicja, report that intense cholera rages in western Russia
286 Oct. 4, 1848 Queen addresses Parliament, lauds Britain for promoting peace in East Europe
287 Nov. 11, 1848 Yet another report on the national debts of European nations, Poland included
288 Dec. 13, 1848 Ordinary Polish workmen eat cabbage and potatoes. Their poverty universal
289 Jan. 1, 1849 United States vs. Gaspar Tochman, indicted for sending a challenge to a duel
290 Feb. 21, 1849 A report on the territorial and economic extent of "Russian America"
291 Mar. 21, 1849 Extent of railroads in Canada, USA and Cuba, and in Europe, Poland included
292 Mar. 21, 1849 Extent of collections in public libraries of the USA versus Europe and Russia
293 Apr. 25, 1849 Russia's population (54,490,000) versus Poland's (4,589,000) is reported
294 Apr. 30, 1849 Comparison of heating power of Don River basin Cossack coal with USA coal
295 May 16, 1849 Reported in Vienna that an insurrection had broken out at Kraków
296 May 23, 1849 Prussian Army of "Observation" deployed to watch Poles in Poznań
297 May 23, 1849 Polish General Józef Bem serves in the Hungarian Army in war against Austria
298 Jun. 6, 1849 120,000 man Russian Army deployed to Hungary in support of Austrian Army
299 Jun. 13, 1849 More on Polish general Józef Bem, an iconic freedom-fighter of that era
300 Jun. 13, 1849 FOLLOW THE MONEY: National Debts of European Nations, e.g., Russia-Poland
301 Jun. 20, 1849 Czar Nicholas I blames Russia's "Polish traitors of 1831" for all of Europe's illls
302 Jun. 27, 1849 Rumor prevails that Russians were defeated by Dembiński at Jordenow

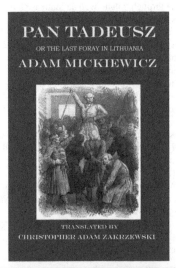

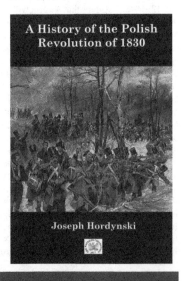

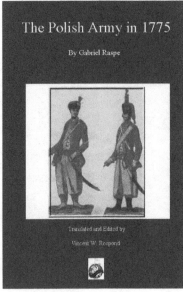

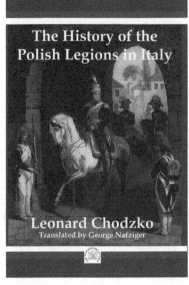

413